DESIGNING AND WRITING ONLINE DOCUMENTATION

Hypermedia for Self-Supporting Products

Second Edition

William Horton

John Wiley & Sons, Inc.
New York • Chichester • Brisbane • Toronto • Singapore

Publisher: Katherine Schowalter

Editor: Theresa Hudson

Managing Editor: Mark Hayden

Book Design and Composition: William Horton Consulting

Trademarks

Apple® and Macintosh® are registered trademarks of Apple Computer, Inc. HyperCard™ is a trademark of Apple Computer, Inc. Hyperties™ is a trademark of Cognetics Corporation. HyperWriter!™ is a trademark of Ntergaid, Inc. NoteCards® is a registered trademark of Xerox Corporation. Microsoft®, Microsoft® Word for the Macintosh®, and Microsoft® Word for Windows™ are registered trademarks of Microsoft Corporation. SmarText™ is a trademark of Lotus Development Corporation. ToolBook® is a registered trademark of Asymetrix Corporation. Many other words in this publication in which the Author and Publisher believe trademark or other proprietary rights may exist have been designated as such by use of Initial Capital Letters. However, in so designating or failing to designate such words, neither the Author nor the Publisher intends to express any judgment on the validity or legal status of any proprietary right that may be claimed in the words.

This publication is designed to provide accurate and authoritative information in regard to the subject matter covered. It is sold with the understanding that the publisher is not engaged in rendering legal, accounting, or other professional service. If legal advice or other expert assistance is required, the services of a competent professional person should be sought. FROM A DECLARATION OF PRINCIPLES JOINTLY ADOPTED BY A COMMITTEE OF THE AMERICAN BAR ASSOCIATION AND A COMMITTEE OF PUBLISHERS.

Library of Congress Cataloging-in-Publication Data:

Horton, William K. (William Kendall)

    Designing and writing online documentation: hypermedia for self-supporting products / William Horton. — 2nd ed.

        p.   cm. — (Wiley technical communication library)

    Includes index.
    ISBN 0-471-30635-5 (paper)
1. Electronic data processing documentation. — 2. Online data processing. 3. Hypertext systems. I. Title. II. Series.
QA76.9.D6H675 1994
808′.066005—dc20   94–25398
                                                          CIP

Printed in the United States of America
10 9 8 7 6 5

PREFACE

What is online documentation?

Online documentation uses the computer as a communications medium. It is the use of the computer to present information that might otherwise appear on printed pages or videotape, and it is the use of the computer to present information about the computer. It includes simple read-me files as well as vast bibliographic databases and collaborative hypertexts. It includes help facilities and computer-based training.

Online documentation is more than word-processing files. Online documentation requires more than text and graphics stored electronically. It requires a rapid and convenient way of retrieving and displaying that information. This book explains how to design and write such documents.

Use this book as a style guide

This book is a style guide. It tells what to do, but does not present system-specific details of how to do it. It won't tell you how to automatically create bidirectional links with WinHelp or how to do animation in HyperCard or how to bind LISP functions to Xerox NoteCards. It will help you decide whether you want to do any of those things at all.

This book will lead you through all the major design decisions required to create effective online documentation systems. Its practical approach draws on actual experience and is backed by academic research. Going beyond any particular program or system, it sets forth the design principles that underlie effective human-computer interaction and shows, with hundreds of examples, how to apply them to messages, menus, help files, computer tutorials, hypertext, hypermedia, and more.

Who should use it?

This book is for those who design, build, and write online documentation. It assumes they understand the basics of communication and are comfortable around computers. It does not require computer programming wizardry or a PhD in English composition or cognitive psychology.

- **Technical writers**. Many technical writers now preparing user's manuals for computer systems anxiously await the transition to writing online versions of these documents. Aware of the trend toward online documentation and away from paper documentation, many seek the special skills and techniques required for writing online documents.

- **Programmers and product developers**. Developers of application programs pursue online documentation for two reasons. Many see it as a way to reduce the costs of training and supporting their customers. They also see online documentation as a way of avoiding the expense and delays of producing paper documents.

- **Teachers and students**. Another group to benefit from this book are teachers and their students in technical writing and computer science graduate programs. This book supplements standard texts by providing information not available elsewhere.

- **Researchers in human factors and user-interface design**. Those conducting research on human-computer interaction will find a practical summary of much of the relevant research applied to online documentation systems. Researchers will, I hope, feel challenged to verify and perfect the guidelines proposed here.

What this book contains and how it is organized

This book is designed so that you can read it in whole or in part. Chapters and sections are somewhat self-contained, so feel free to skim and skip. Here is the overall organization:

Segment	Question it answers	Chapters
Overview	Why should I put my document online? Or should I?	1. Going online
Managing	How do I plan and manage an online documentation project?	2. Planning
Access	How do I make information accessible?	3. Access
Architecture	How do I structure my document? How do I divide it into modular units and link them electronically?	4. Topics 5. Links 6. Organization
User-interface	What should the document look and feel like to the user? How do I make the experience productive and fun?	7. Dialog 8. Display

Media	What media should I include in my on-line document? How do I design and integrate them?	9. Words
		10. Pictures
		11. New media
Specific forms	How do I design documents to help users at work and to train users?	12. Help
		13. Computer-based training
Conclusion	How will online documentation change my job? How can I prepare?	14. Future

How this book is written

Before delving deeply into this book, you should be aware of how it is designed.

Notes and references

First a note on end notes. I have used notes moderately, not to prove erudite scholarship or to bolster my opinions with the names of others. The opinions are mine. References supply additional opinions and possibly research on the issue under discussion. Do not be surprised if a reference does not say exactly what the text does. Much of the research is preliminary and contradictory, and I have tried to point you to all reasonable sources of information. In citing research, I have tried, where possible, to avoid the annoying practice of citing proprietary research or unavailable reports. In some cases, this required citing a secondary source, a summarizer, or a reviewer of the original.

Technical terms and jargon

This book contains many of the technical terms of online documentation. You may find many of these terms new, for they come from different fields. I have avoided the writer's urge to stamp out jargon by minting new words of my own. Where several fields each offer a term for a concept, I have ruthlessly picked the one that seemed most natural and used it.

Product names

Throughout this book I have mentioned several commercial and academic online documentation systems. Please don't take these as an endorsement or condemnation of such systems. Mentioning specific products seems worthwhile, since many of the features of online documents originated or exist only in particular products.

What's new and different in this edition?

How is the second edition better than the first? What's new? What did I get wrong in the first edition?

- **Online is a new medium**. The only outright error in the first edition was the first sentence. It said, "A book is a book, whether on paper or online." The differences between paper and online documents are profound, so much so that online documentation is a different medium, as different from books as television is from radio or movies from novels. This edition treats online documentation as the new electronic medium it is.

- **More experience, less theory**. The advice from the first edition has held up remarkably well—considering it was based on a small number of systems, many of them simplistic laboratory prototypes. Since then we have seen a burgeoning of online documents. This edition relies more on extensive experience of many real-world systems used to solve practical problems. Published product reviews now outnumber academic papers. Online documentation is clearly in the mainstream.

- **Tips on production**. This edition includes a chapter detailing how to plan and manage online documentation projects. It leads you from analyzing the needs of your users to automating production of the final document.

- **More media**. This edition reflects the progress toward multimedia computing. More examples of graphics, animation, sound, video, and interactivity are included.

About the author

William Horton applies ergonomics and human factors to guide users of computer systems. A registered professional engineer and graduate of MIT, he specializes in engineering effective electronic media.

As founder of William Horton Consulting in Boulder, Colorado, he works with corporations and other business and educational organizations in designing more effective communications. He conducts public and in-house seminars on subjects ranging from online documentation to visual literacy.

William Horton is also author of *The Icon Book, Secrets of User-Seductive Documents*, and *Illustrating Computer Documentation*.

Dedication

This book is dedicated to the authors in this new medium called *online documentation*—those whose courage and insight are creating not just effective documents but shaping this new medium itself. It offers thanks to those who have not waited till all the research was done and all the questions were answered but who forged ahead discovering, inventing, creating new ways to communicate information. It is for those who did not just theorize and pontificate but who designed and led. Thanks to you all.

CONTENTS

7   DIALOG   197

8   DISPLAY   219

9   WORDS   261

11   NEW MEDIA   303

GOING ONLINE

1

The computer as communication medium

Questions float, unanswered, upon an ocean of information. Human beings have never before faced such a deluge of information.

THE DELUGE . . . AND THE TRICKLE

Consider: The 545 miles of shelves of the U.S. Library of Congress hold over 100 million pieces of literature, including 27 million books and pamphlets, 1,200 news-papers, 100,000 films, 80,000 TV and 500,000 radio broadcasts, and a million other sound recordings.

Documentation for military equipment has grown exponentially. World War II fighter aircraft got by with 1,000 pages of manuals and drawings. By the early 1950s, fighter aircraft required 10,000 pages. This had grown to 100,000 pages by the end of the 1960s. Today, the B2 stealth bomber requires about 1 million pages of documentation to get airborne. Navy ships typically carry 10 to 40 tons of paper manuals and forms. Most of that paper is above deck, where it raises the ship's center of gravity, thus reducing its speed, maneuverability, and fuel economy [268].

The information deluge is especially critical in scientific and technical fields such as medicine, where articles are published at the rate of 5,500 per day—over 2 million a year. One $2 billion contract for Space Station Freedom included $1 billion for documentation.

Technology, instead of solving the problem, exacerbates it. Every day computers in the U.S. print out another 600 million pages. Copying machines add another 234 million pages [268]. Russell Borland of Microsoft has described the plight of the user who experiences a "mushroom cloud of manuals spewing out of the box and falling like radiation." Even supposed masters of automation, computer programmers, are victims too. One study by IBM found that it took 45 feet of shelf space to hold the documentation used by a single system programmer. New technologies, instead of reducing the amount of information, increase it.

Managing this deluge of information will require more than technology. Managing information will require careful design and deployment of that technology. This book offers a plan by which to accomplish this.

WHAT IS ONLINE DOCUMENTATION?

Online documentation is simply the use of the computer as a communication medium. This term embraces a rich diversity, from one-word messages to the proposed docuverse of project Xanadu, which would make accessible all documents ever written. Uniting all these systems is the essential goal of using the computer to get information. Do not let the word *document* mislead you. By *document* we mean any organized body of information, not just one on paper or even one suited for paper. Online documents can include animation, voice, music and other sounds, and video.

Information and access to it

Online documentation systems have two essential parts. The first is electronically stored information—words, pictures, and other media. The second essential component is a means of accessing that information. Electronically stored information is not online documentation. Online documentation requires a way for users to quickly and conveniently find and display the information they need.

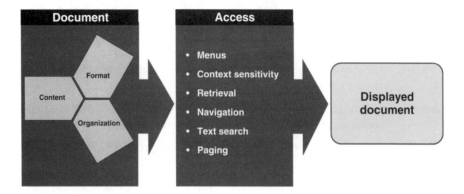

Question-answering machines

When you have a question, what do you do? Do you reach for a manual or a book? Chances are you ask another human being. Why? Because that is the fastest and simplest way to get a practical, carefully focused, and qualified answer. Although no machine will have the sympathy and sensitivity of a human being, machines can, through their enormous storage and electronic speed, help us answer our questions.

Imagine instant answers to your questions. Think of an electronic equivalent of the Delphic oracle—a device that can supply any fact, prescribe any procedure, untangle any confusion. That is the goal of online documentation.

What is not quite online documentation?

Online documentation is often confused with other media or methods of presenting computerized information. A few of the most common ones are:

CD-ROM Storage medium for digital data. These shiny 120-mm disks can hold 650 megabytes of any kind of digital data, one of which is online documentation. Merely storing information on CD-ROM does not make it online documentation any more than printed words on paper makes them a novel.

Hypertext	Modules of text and simple graphics stored electronically and accessed by electronic links between modules. For online documentation you usually must supplement the hypertext links with other methods of access.
Hypermedia	Like hypertext, except that the modules can contain animation, sound, video, and other media as well as text and graphics. Think of hypermedia as multimedia modules connected with hypertext links.
Multimedia	Mixture of text, graphics, animation, video, sound, music, and perhaps other media, usually in a linear sequence.
Help facility	Online documents designed to provide quick answers to questions that occur while using a product.
CBT	Computer-based training: online documents used to teach somebody something.
Electronic books	Existing books meant to be read from the computer screen.
Softcopy	Electronically provided information in a book format. Softcopy may be searched and read from the computer but more often is searched on the computer, printed out, and read from paper.
Electronic reference documents	Online documents that serve the same purpose as paper reference manuals and books.
EPSS	Electronic performance support systems: online documents integrated with the product they support. EPSS melds good user-interface design, computer tutorials, help facilities, and online reference manuals in a seamless environment to make products obvious.

SHOULD YOUR DOCUMENT GO ONLINE?

There are no absolute rules for what should and should not go online. The capabilities of systems and the needs of users vary so widely that such rules are of little use. You can, however, make an intelligent judgment of whether today, in your circumstances, with the computer system you have available, a particular document should go online. The formula for making this decision is simple.

> Put a document online only if the benefits of having the document online exceed the cost incurred in putting it online—for you and for the user.

Weigh costs and benefits

To decide whether online documentation will really save money, you must weigh the short- and long-term costs and savings of putting documents online. For any online documentation project you have in mind, draw up a table such as the one that follows, which lists the costs and benefits of online documentation for the producer and for the user.

	Costs	Benefits
Producer	Researching, writing, editing Creating or converting graphics Formatting text	Less paper documentation to print Less rush to print Less customer support required Revenue from sale of online documents Better product acceptance
User	Training required to learn to use online documents More disk space required Fee charged for online document Upgraded display monitor Local printing Screen space required	Less time spent searching for information Less paper documentation to store Less paper documentation to update Fewer errors due to out-of-date information

This cost/benefit formula is simple common sense. A more precise financial analysis is possible, yet in practice, this simple rule suffices.

Uses of online documentation

Online documentation, by integrating information with the computer and electronically distributing and accessing information, gives people up-to-date information when they need it.

Provide instant access to information

Online documentation offers immediate informational gratification. Many documents are not so much read as they are searched for a single piece of information. If the search strategy is systematic, the computer can perform the search. Online documents give the user a demoniacal research assistant, scurrying off to the electronic library, rooting through the card catalogs, racing along the shelves, finding the volume, bringing it to the desk, opening it to the right page, and pointing to the paragraph or picture needed—in a fraction of the time that it would have taken the user to find the information.

Good online documentation systems overcome one of the most common objections to paper books, namely, that it takes too long to find information. It is a poor online documentation system that does not answer questions at least twice as fast as the paper documentation. Some good examples:

- Replacing microfiche with CD-ROM–based online documents aboard the U.S.S. *Halsey* reduced typical search times from 4 hours to 1.5 minutes. Deployment of the system resulted in a 60 to 70 percent reduction in retrieval times [268].

- With microfiche, locating back articles from the *Los Angeles Times* took 6 to 8 minutes; with CD-ROM, less than a minute [140].

- The U.S. Food and Drug Administration typically approves Computer-Aided New Drug Applications (CANDAs) six months sooner than applications filed on paper [97].

Support products better

For many computer users, anything is better than the conventional paper manual. An IBM study found that business users rated the conventional reference manual as the next-to-worst method out of 12 for learning about a computer system [195].

Online documentation, by integrating instructions and reference information into the product itself, makes the product whole. Such a product can explain itself. In some future museum a child will come across the display of a technical manual inside its glass display case. The child will ask the curator about this strange antiquity. The curator will shrug and suggest asking the display case.

The strongest benefit of online documentation, however, is successful communication. Although difficult to measure accurately, this benefit often exceeds savings in production costs: One online documentation project at Chevron projected savings of less than $1,000 in printing and updating costs but over $44,000 in time required for training, looking up information, and correcting errors [283]. A online consultation system at IBM's Endicot Laboratory helped users answer 35 percent more of users' questions [257].

The U.S. military's Personal Electronic Aid for Maintenance (PEAM) reduced troubleshooting errors by two-thirds for the Army and by five-sixths for the Navy. It reduced the time it took tank mechanics to learn to use paper manuals from several days to minutes. It elevated the performance levels of inexperienced technicians to near that of experienced technicians [222].

Publish rapidly

Online documents can get urgent information to those who need it. With paper documents, information is often not available when the product is ready for release. Users may not know how to order the right documents or documents may take too long to arrive. Unless all changes are marked and dated, users cannot distinguish between up-to-date and out-of-date information.

- **Bypass printing**. Online documents speed distribution of information by omitting the trip through the print shop. Printing and binding paper manuals involves dozens of complex operations, many performed by hand. Online documents, in contrast, do not have to wait for printing and binding, and electronic transmission is nearly instantaneous. In one case, putting procedures online cut the time for updates to reach users from over 2 months to less than 2 days [264].

- **Distribute electronically**. Online documents can be distributed electronically and updated almost instantaneously over data-communications networks. Users can download a new online document to the product in the field from a central computer. Seconds after you load a new document on the central computer, users can read it. An example of a system that electronically updates documents is the GM-CAMS system, which overnight can update service bulletins, specifications, recall notices, instructions, and diagnostic procedures stored on technicians' terminals located in General Motors dealerships across the U.S. At the same time, the system uploads repair information from the dealerships to GM headquarters, where statistics are gathered to spot trends in repairs performed [280].

- **Update electronically**. Ink is permanent. Once printed, pages cannot be changed to communicate new discoveries, late-breaking news, or corrections of errors. Paper manuals are also difficult to update, especially when copies are widely distributed. There is no way to ensure that all copies in the field are up to date and that all users have the same information. Paper manuals, especially those in loose-leaf notebooks, frequently lose pages.

Reduce publication costs

Most large corporations spend 5 to 15 percent of their revenues creating and distributing paper documents. These organizations see online documentation as a way of reducing such costs. According to the Office of Technology Assessment, the

Congressional Record costs $624 per year for each copy distributed on paper but only $10 per copy on CD-ROM.

To understand the lure of electronic storage media, think of them as very inexpensive paper. Let's say that ZipZap Computer must produce and distribute 5,000 copies of 1,000 pages of documentation. At a typesetting cost of about $3.00 per page and a printing cost of $0.01 per page, that trickles down to a bottom line of $53,000. By using CD-ROM, they can fit the entire document on a single disk. Mastering the disk will cost $2,500, and copies will be about $2.00 each.

	Paper	**CD-ROM**
Pages/unit	1	5,000
Number of master unit	1,000	1
Cost/master unit	$3.00	$2,500.00
Total mastering cost	$3,000.00	$2,500.00
Cost/copy	$0.01	$2.00
Reproduction cost	$50,000.00	$10,000.00
Total cost	$53,000.00	$12,500.00

The result is a savings of $40,500 (76 percent) for CD-ROM. The savings really multiply if the document must be translated and published in eight languages, especially if all eight versions would fit on one CD-ROM.

Save storage space

Since about 1983, online documents—including the computer—have been smaller and lighter than equivalent paper documents. Today, a 120-mm optical disk can hold the equivalent of 200,000 single-spaced pages of text. When managers contemplate the cost of storing and shipping massive volumes of paper documents, small is beautiful.

Online documents can save space and weight. The 300,000 pages of documentation for the F-18 fighter plane require 68 cubic feet of storage space per copy on paper—1,700 times as much as it does on CD-ROM[278]. Sony's Data Discman DD-10EX weighs just 23 ounces, yet each of its 8-cm Electronic Book discs can hold 100,000 pages of text, 32,000 images, or 5.9 hours of audio—or a combination of these media. CD-ROM storage of *Los Angeles Times* archives takes about 1 percent the storage space as did microfilm [140].

Compactness benefits users too:

> Information that is maintained online does not intimidate users with its volume When there exists a truck load of manuals, the information is buried—as far as users can see—within a huge stack of manuals. Users are intimidated before opening a book and suffer from the Where do I start? malaise. Users assume it will take

too much time to sort through all the manuals. With online information, there is only one place to start, and that is at the computer [205, pp. 58-59].

Link related facts

In complex business and technical documents, footnotes and commentary may be more important than the base text, and may comprise the largest amount of text. Savvy investors know the importance of reading the footnotes in a prospectus or annual report. Articles in law journals may devote more text to footnotes than to body text. Programmers know to read the fine print listing bugs, abnormalities, and undocumented features.

Documents that send the user hither and yon with cross-references can replace manual page turning with automated links. Rather than turning to page 437 or searching for Figure 12-2, the user lets the computer find and display the referenced item. Electronic cross-references provide easy and quick access to secondary or optional information, relieving the reader of the burden of tracking it down and the writer of the need to repeat.

Some online documents, for example, highlight technical terms in the text. Users who do not understand a term simply select the term (perhaps by pointing to it with a mouse and pressing a button) and up pops a definition of the term. You can apply this technique for footnotes, cross-references, and other supplementary information not needed by all users but essential for an important few.

Unify sets of related documents

Complex systems often require more than a single document. The system may include both hardware and software, each with multiple manuals. The system may also require different manuals for different purposes and audiences. IBM's RISC System/6000 required 45 reference manuals. Maintaining consistency among such a bookshelf of documents is a Herculean chore. Putting such interdependent documents online offers significant advantages:

- Duplicate material is maintained in one place. Changes made once are reflected in the entire suite of documents.

- Changes can be made to the entire set almost simultaneously.

- Different documents can be displayed simultaneously. The user can read from two documents at once to compare alternative approaches or to gather related facts.

- The reader can effortlessly jump from document to document.

Information that is shared among multiple documents or repeated within a single document is more conveniently and economically handled online. Problems arise when information gets out of sync. To keep documents in sync, have them all refer to and display the same source documents. When the source document is changed, this change is automatically reflected in every document that refers to that document.

A single copy of the information is maintained. Changes to this single copy are immediately reflected in all the other online documents that refer to this information.

Integrate documentation and development

In a subtle way online documentation changes how technical writers are perceived and deployed within the organizations they serve. Because online documents are part of the product, they are developed as part of the same effort. This requires a closer collaboration between the writer and the developer. To the programmer or engineer, online documentation is much more a part of the product than paper documentation, which is often viewed as of secondary importance—a necessary evil, but not a high priority. Writers of online documents are more readily accepted as fellow product developers and not treated as clerical support.

Archive precious documents securely

Books printed on high-acid paper may not last another hundred years. In libraries throughout the world, priceless books, manuscripts, maps, and other documents are disintegrating. Films are yellowing. Video and audio tapes are cracking. Archivists in many countries are turning to electronic media to preserve these treasures. The New York Public Library is using CD-ROM to archive and, hence, preserve journals of Russian architecture. The Archivo General de Indias in Seville is putting online over 90 million written documents, pictures, and maps concerning Christopher Columbus and the exploration of the New World [151].

CD-ROM disks, their manufacturers claim, will last one hundred years or more, and their contents can be copied to fresh media without loss when the original disks near the end of their storage life.

Overcome disabilities

Computers can provide access to information for those with perceptual or learning disabilities. Over 20 million Americans suffer a disability that alters their daily lives. About 1.5 million Americans cannot read ordinary newsprint [2]. For these users, online documentation systems can magnify text, use speech synthesizers to read documents aloud, and shift colors to compensate for color blindness. These intelligent documents can also turn pages for those without the use of their hands and adjust the style, pace, and order of instructions for those with learning disabilities.

Special input and output devices let the disabled use online documents. Talking gloves, fingerspell devices, glove-controlled 3D positioning devices, concept keyboards, voice synthesis, dynamic Braille displays, and other techniques provide alternatives to traditional mouse-keyboard-screen systems [16].

These same techniques are useful for special environments where the reader does not have room or hands enough for paper documents—for example, in the cockpit of an aircraft, or in manufacturing environments, such as cleanrooms for manufacturing semiconductors, where paper is verboten.

Conserve resources

Online documentation can save precious natural resources. It reduces the consumption of paper and the energy required to manufacture, store, and distribute paper documents. It reduces the destruction of trees and the natural environment. Many forms of electronic storage can be reused or recycled. Let's not waste any more paper on this subject.

Drawbacks and dangers

Online documentation is not ideal for all people and purposes. Before you go online, consider some potential problems.

- **Not easy reading**. Documents that require the careful reading of long passages of text gain little value from going online. In one field study, a third of users complained that reading online documents was less convenient than paper documents [195]. Reading online text is slower and less accurate than reading from paper [249]. Also, prolonged reading has been reported to increase eyestrain [229]. Viewing information in small windows imposes tunnel vision on readers, restricting their ability to compare different pieces of information. If users must scan more than a single scrolling zone of text, paper will be faster [182].

- **Not always available**. Obviously, we can't use online documents if we are not on the computer. Some technical documents are needed away from the computer or when the computer is not available. Other documents are needed when the user is facing away from the computer.

- **New and possibly alien**. Books are solid and tangible and familiar. A screen is flat and cold, and its riches are locked behind glass. If we know anything about human behavior, it is that people prefer the familiar to the unfamiliar, concrete objects to abstract concepts, and tangible products to promised benefits. People resist things that require them to abandon comfortable habits—such as their ways of finding information. Acceptance of online documentation will not be instantaneous or unanimous.

Not paper vs. online

In deciding between paper and online documents, remember that you really have five alternatives, not two: paper, online, both, neither, and hybrid.

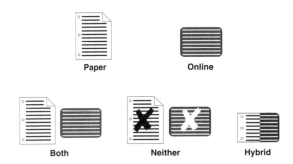

Both may be necessary for users who do not always have access to the computer or when some users refuse to use online documentation. Neither is the correct choice for information that no one really needs. Are you sure users really need all the information you want to publish? Hybrid systems combine features of paper and electronic documents. Typically, they let users search electronically and then print out and read what they find from paper. By using online resources for only those documents best suited for the online environment, you conserve scarce system resources while providing the best mix and overlap of paper and online documents.

MYTHS ABOUT ONLINE DOCUMENTATION

Like most emerging technologies, online documentation has attracted its share of superstition, bunk, and balderdash passing for truth and handed down from generation to generation of designers. Let us clear it away before proceeding.

Online documentation is science fiction

Online documentation is here and now. The resources are available. More than 120 million computers are in service around the world. Over 30 percent of American homes have computers. By the end of the 1990s, that figure could climb to 70 percent. About half of all new business computers contain CD-ROM drives.

Online documentation has escaped the university laboratories and is doing useful work.

- **Much computer documentation is online**. Hewlett-Packard has put more than 250,000 pages of text and graphics online. For its RISC System/6000, IBM put 45 reference manuals on CD-ROM in a system called *InfoExplorer*.

- **Online documentation is turning a profit**. According to a *Business Week* article in 1993, CD-ROM sales exceeded 15 million disks and were growing at 40 percent a year [240]. An electronic brochure for Buick cars doubled sales over conventional paper brochures—12 percent of those who got the electronic brochures purchased a Buick [195]. Licensing of the online version of the *Random House Encyclopedia* generates more money than sales of the print version [155].

- **The general public is reading online documents**. The *San Jose Mercury News* now publishes an online edition on America Online that includes back issues to 1985. L.L. Bean, Lands' End, and Spiegel now publish electronic versions of their mail-order catalogs. Senator Edward Kennedy uses a computer bulletin board to keep in touch with constituents.

- **Entire libraries are going online**. Bibliotheque de France, the French national library, plans to put 100,000 works of literature online.

Online documentation is better (or worse) than paper

About once a week I get a phone call from another pour soul wanting to know the one scientific study or definitive project that proves online documentation is better than paper documentation. Some want the opposite. Here, have your pick:

Studies and experiences that suggest that paper is better than online	Studies and experiences that suggest that online is better than paper
Users of a paper book were faster than users of hypertext at answering questions and their answers were more accurate for questions that involved graphics and maps [167].	Users of the HyperHolmes hypertext were more accurate than book users at answering questions, especially when the answer was embedded in text [141, 167].
In one test, online aids increased the time required to solve problems [80].	Replacing microfiche with CD-ROM reduced search times over 60 percent aboard the U.S.S. *Halsey* [268] and over 85 percent at the *Los Angeles Times* [140].
One study found that online tutorials work only for training in simple operations [63].	Users of a hypertext prototype retrieved information more quickly than those using paper [242].
Online aids slowed the work and learning process of programmers in one test [70].	Reading interactive online documents has been shown to improve comprehension [218].
Online learning aids actually increased the time required to learn to use a word-processing system [63].	In one study of undergraduate students, use of a hypermedia system increased the students' feelings of interest, importance, and self-confidence [254].
A comparison of paper and online documentation used by novice and occasional users of a database found that users of paper documentation completed tasks sooner and were more satisfied with documentation than those with online tutorials [81].	A hypertext system outperformed an expert system in helping users maintain a computer network, primarily because users could more easily update the information it contained [195].
Tests of a technical manual and a hypertext version created from it showed that users found information much faster from the paper version [233].	Customer-support technicians using a hypertext diagnosed problems more successfully (92 percent to 88 percent) than with paper documentation [40].
Adding a Help facility to one system worsened learning and productivity of users [188].	In one text, children successfully used an online library catalog, finding 80 percent of the 6 target items in about 80 seconds each [30].
Users took longer to find information in hypertext than on paper, especially for simple information at the beginning of segments [248].	Readers of a hypertext document were better at acquiring "discriminating facts" than readers from paper [76].
	Users of a SuperBook document answered more questions correctly, recalled certain facts better, and wrote better essays than those with conventional text. They also strongly preferred SuperBook [77].

The only thing these studies really prove is this:

> Good online documentation is better than poor paper
> documentation and good paper documentation is better than poor
> online documentation.

Online documentation does not guarantee success or failure. Only good design
guarantees success.

You cannot put everything online

One common excuse for avoiding online documentation is "We can't put our information online because two paragraphs on page 369 will not work online."
Clever designers can find a way to make any information work online.

Objection	Solution
Part of the information will not work on-line.	Leave just that part on paper.
Certain steps must be performed with the computer turned off.	Let users print out instructions for those steps.
Instructions are for repairing the computer.	Let users display the instructions on a separate computer. Many notebook-size computers are smaller and lighter than repair manuals.

Online documentation is paperless documentation

One very popular myth claims that online documentation obviates the need for paper documentation. Many organizations turn to online documentation in the hope
of eliminating the problems of producing paper documents. Users may have other
priorities. Users of IBM System/38 rejected online-only documentation and IBM re-
sumed conventional paper documentation [148].

In practice, online documentation systems do not replace paper documentation
and some even increase the amount of paper documentation produced. The
DOCUMENT system, in use since 1977 at Lawrence Livermore National
Laboratory, provides an interesting case study. In this system, the user can view
documents on the screen and print them out on a local printer. During the first two
years of operation, the ratio of lines printed out to lines viewed on the screen was
117—for every page viewed on the screen, users printed out over 100 paper pages
[111]. Although this ratio has dropped steadily, reaching 17 in 1986, it shows a sus-
tained demand for paper documentation [112]. This continued demand for paper
documentation does not mean that the online documentation system has failed to

communicate information, but that it serves primarily as a tool for locating and obtaining the correct paper documents.

Online documents have not replaced paper documents and probably will not until we have online documents as efficient as this one:

> High-density, laptop information display device. Nonvolatile memory with zero power consumption. Able to display text and graphics at 1250 dots per inch resolution in monochrome or up to 32,000 colors on a 100 megapixel display. Features simple, intuitive, direct-manipulation user interface with both sequential and random access mechanisms. Functional at temperatures from -120 to +451 degrees F. Cost under $40.

This amazing new computer is, as you probably guessed, the common, ordinary . . . book. The simple truth is that online documentation is not *paperless* documentation. It may reduce reliance on paper and lessen the amount of paper required to support a product. It may allow products to ship with "paper to follow." It may even shift the burden of printing onto the user. But it will not eliminate paper totally or immediately.

You can just dump paper documents online

Many attempts at online documentation offer little more than paper documents displayed on the computer screen. Unfortunately, such documents were never designed for viewing on the small display area of the computer screen and lack effective ways to access parts of the document.

Computer systems, it is said, are subject to the GIGO principle: Garbage In, Garbage Out. This homily was coined to remind us that the quality of the results is no better than the quality of the source data. With online documentation systems, the situation is worse. Online documentation systems are subject to the GITSO principle: Garbage In, Toxic Sludge Out. Displaying paper pages in a smaller, grainier, less portable, more glaring device never makes them better and often makes them unreadable. Putting marginal paper documents online is a sure recipe for failure.

Those who advocate dumping paper documents online often admit to a problem getting users to read their paper documents. If users won't read the manuals on paper, why should they read electronic mimics? Putting a bad manual online does not improve it or increase its use.

> The original design of ML INFO closely mirrored the style and content of the paper document it was to replace. We improved the organization and appearance of the original documents and placed them on-line for easy access, but for cost reasons chose not to take the time required to break the document down into hypertext format. This proved to be a mistake. Everyone who saw our preview of the system asked the obvious question: "If our analysts don't take the time to read the paper manuals why would they read the same stuff online?" [65, p. 475]

Tests of online documents created by dumping paper documents online show they work poorly compared to the original paper versions [233].

TYPES OF ONLINE DOCUMENTATION

Although you are not limited to any one type of online document, you should understand the standard types and consider their advantages before creating new types. Authoring and delivery software is often honed to produce these specific types. A package designed expressly to produce computer-based training will be more effective for that task than one for producing context-sensitive help facilities. Also, users with experience with online documents are more likely to recognize a familiar form and to expect its conventions to be followed.

Online documents can be classified by three issues: purpose, size, and relationship to the product. Online documents exist for two main purposes: for *instruction* (read to learn) and for *reference* (read to do). Most actual documents, of course, serve a balance of these purposes. In size, they can vary from simple one-sentence messages to library-sized collections. Here's how some common types can be arranged along scales of purpose and size:

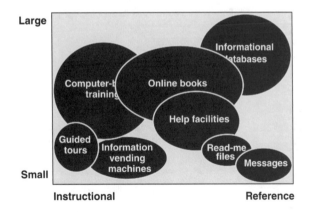

Relationship to the product concerns how the online document depends or contributes to a product. *Embedded* documents are part of a computer product and are accessed through that product. They include help facilities, guided tours, and system messages. *Standalone* documents describe a product but can exist apart from that product. Users can access these documents without accessing the product itself. These include online reference manuals and computer-based training that do not require users to run the product. The third category, *independent* documents, are not designed to support a product. They are the product. More accurately, their content is the product. These include online encyclopedias, dictionaries, and interactive fiction.

Let's look at some of the more popular types.

Help facility

Help facilities provide quick access to specific information needed while operating the product. They assist users in performing routine tasks and solving problems.

Although the help document may contain one topic or thousands, each topic is simple, providing just the information the user needs to complete the task at hand. Users routinely access the help documents in two ways. They may activate a help button or icon to trigger context-sensitive display of a topic related to their current situation. Or they may open the help document and search for a topic of interest.

A sophisticated and large help document may resemble an online book. In fact, many systems combine the two by providing context-sensitive access from the application into the online reference manual. Help, in this case, is just the subset of the online reference manual that the user can reach directly from the application.

Here is an example of a help facility.

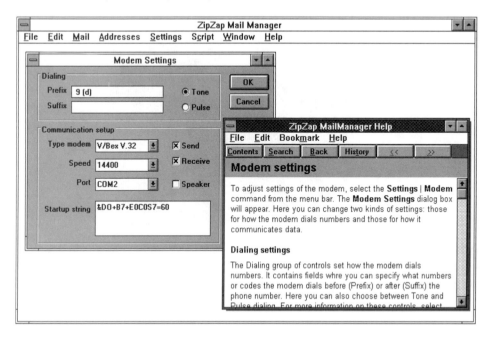

For more on help facilities, see Chapter 12.

Online book

Online books and manuals provide detailed reference information. They let users look up information but do not require users to be running the program at the time. Online books have the organization and access mechanisms (but not the physical appearance) of a well-designed book or manual.

Here is an example of a topic from a standalone online document that describes concepts of electronic mail.

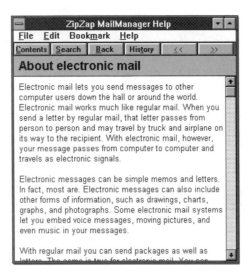

Computer-based training

Computer-based training teaches concepts and procedures. Novice users typically take a series of lessons to learn how to use a new product or feature. Here CBT teaches a concept.

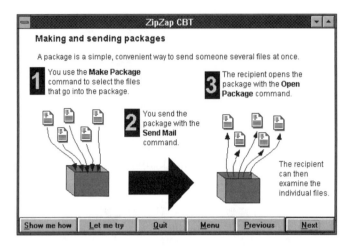

And by selecting the Let me try button, users can experiment applying the concept for themselves.

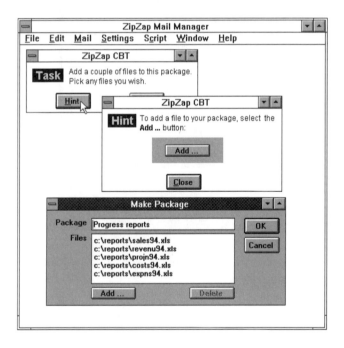

For more on computer-based training, see Chapter 13.

Read-me file

A read-me file is a simple memo to the user, typically to point out exceptions and present last-minute information. Read-me files tell about undocumented commands and uncorrected bugs. They list errors in printed documents much like a paper errata sheet. Read-me files can contain information about compatibility with other products or about converting from earlier versions of the same product, and often list the files included with the product. They are typically text files that the user can read from the screen or print out. For example, this read-me file:

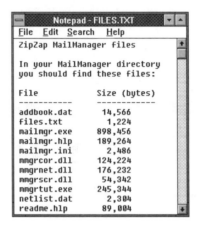

Some products format read-me files so they can be read by the online documentation delivery system used to present help and online manuals. Another example:

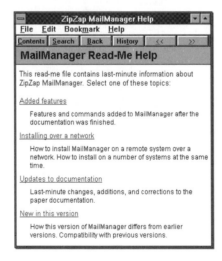

Online catalog

Online catalogs work well to make accessible information about a large number of similar items. They are simple databases with entries for each item documented. Online catalogs provide quick access to hundreds or even millions of related topics.

Online catalogs work best for collections of information about similar items, providing the same kinds of information about each item in the series. They are well suited for the types of information presented in traditional paper catalogs and computer databases. One common online catalog is the description of commands of a programming or macro language. Here, for example, are three topics from the catalog of commands:

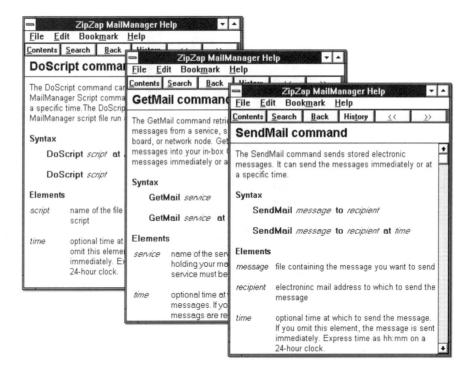

Online catalogs are too large for access by sequential reading or casual browsing. Users typically retrieve items by name or by keyword.

Guided tour

Guided tours introduce the product by leading the user through its displays and menus while pointing out how these might be used. Guided tours typically acquaint the novice with the organization of screens and menus and the terminology used in the product. Here is an example:

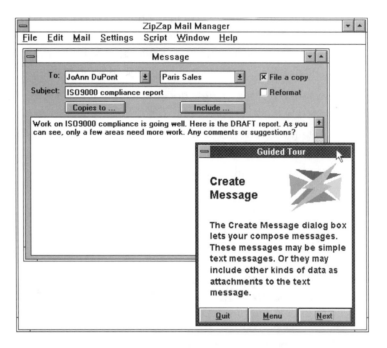

Message

Messages are small pieces of information automatically displayed to guide users of a computer program. They are an integral part of the user interface. Messages are very simple, typically a single line of text or at most a single paragraph combined with a simple picture. Messages can appear in a separate field on the screen or in a pop-up window.

PUTTING THESE IDEAS TO WORK

Essential ideas of this chapter

➡ Online documentation integrates information about a product with the product itself, making products self-sufficient, pulling writers into the mainstream of product development, and reducing the support required for these products.

➡ Online documentation is not word-processing files "dumped" online.

➡ Online documentation is not paperless documentation. It has not replaced paper documentation and will not for some time to come.

➡ Online documentation can be distributed faster and accessed more rapidly than paper documentation.

➡ Put documents online if the value of having them online exceeds the cost of putting them online.

➡ Put a document online if readers spend more time searching for information than reading it or if it needs computer media such as windows, sound, music, animation, or interactivity.

For more ideas and inspiration

Brockmann, R. John. 1990. *Writing Better Computer User Documentation: From Paper to Hypertext*. New York: John Wiley.

Gery, Gloria J. 1991. *Electronic Performance Support Systems*. Boston: Weingarten Publications.

McKnight, Cliff, Andrew Dillon, and John Richardson, eds. 1991. *Hypertext in Context*. Cambridge, England: Cambridge University Press.

Nelson, Theodor Holm. 1987. *Literary Machines*. South Bend, IN: The Distributors.

Shneiderman, Ben and Greg Kearsley. 1989. *Hypertext Hands On!: An Introduction to a New Way of Organizing and Accessing Information*. Reading, MA: Addison-Wesley.

PLANNING

2

Designing the product

Producing online documentation is complex and requires the same level of sophisticated project management as any ambitious endeavor. This chapter deals with issues unique to running online documentation projects. It is based on my own experience working on dozens of projects and from talking to leaders of teams that have made the transition from paper-based to online documentation. Note: This chapter does not repeat general advice on project management. Such advice can be found in the books listed at the end of this chapter.

DEVELOP DOCUMENTS SYSTEMATICALLY

There is no prescription for success. However, I have noticed that successful online documentation teams follow the same general pattern of decisions and actions. Many variations are possible, but the basic flow is something like this:

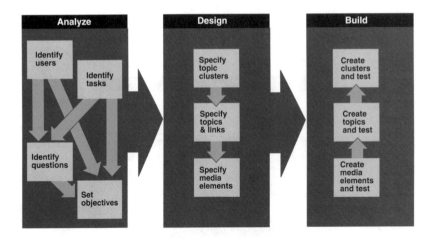

Creating online documentation requires three phases of effort: an analysis phase and a design phase, which are done top down, and a building phase, which is done bottom up. You start the analysis phase by identifying who uses the product (Identify users) and what tasks they will do with the product (Identify tasks). The next step is to learn what questions the online document must answer for users (Identify questions). With this information, you can then set clear objectives for the project (Set objectives).

In the design phase, you apply the results of your careful analysis, especially the questions your system must answer for the user. Big, general, and abstract questions lead you to design large clusters of related topics the user can read or scan conveniently (Specify topic clusters). More specific questions will require designing individual, modular topics and links between them (Specify topics). You then must specify the media elements needed for each topic: blocks of text, graphics, animation, music, and so forth (Specify media elements).

Once you have fully specified all the components of your document, begin the third phase: building the document. First you construct and test the individual media elements (Create media elements and test), then the individual topics (Create topics and test), and, finally, clusters of topics (Create clusters and test).

At any step you may encounter difficulties that require you to reconsider earlier decisions or redo earlier steps. However, with conscientious testing and persistent revision—and perhaps a little luck—your document is done.

Design top–down, build bottom–up

Allow flexibility but do not forgo the discipline of thoughtful design. Many free-form authoring tools permit or even encourage bottom–up design. In bottom–up design, the document grows by the simple addition of more and more topics. The author discovers a piece of information the user needs and then adds it as a topic. Someone mentions another fact the user might need and it becomes a topic. The author notices a relationship between the two and strings a link to connect them. A review of an early version suggests additional topics, which are dutifully grafted onto the emerging document. The document grows like ivy—with all the structural clarity of ivy. Important and unimportant facts are mixed in a jumble, and crucial relationships are obscured by less important ones.

Work out your basic ideas in storyboards and thumbnail-sized sketches. Use storyboards to test the reaction of management and potential users. Unless the ideas work with small, crude sketches, they may not work with large, expensive ones either. Alfred Hitchcock used such extensive storyboards to plan every detail of his movies that he worked through the creative process long before he began shooting. Steven Spielberg is another director who relies on storyboards. He has scenes rendered on cards, which he arranges and rearranges to plan and sequence the movie. Design before you build.

Before you start gathering media elements, make a comprehensive list of every block of text, photograph, drawing, animation, video segment, musical passage, and sound you will need. Sort them by the person responsible for creating them. Then group those that need to be created together. For example, group photographs that need to be taken at the same location or drawings of different views of the same device.

Design as a process, not an event

Developing online documentation is not a one-shot process. It is a continual process of successive refinement.

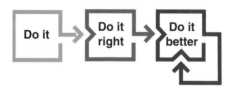

Development of online documentation is iterative, cumulative, and empirical. It is *iterative* in that several cycles of development are required, *cumulative* in that you learn and improve through each cycle, and *empirical* in that improvements are based on testing and experience with working prototypes of the system.

Remember that development is ever ongoing. The online document is never perfected but always improving. The best you can do is to make each version better than the last. Do not expect to get it right the first time. Almost no one does. Since others do not announce their failures, you seldom know about them. Do not announce yours either. Fail in private.

LEARN WHO USES THE PRODUCT AND WHY

Before you can design any product you must know who uses it and what information they need and want about it.

Categories of users

Few products are used by one stereotypical user. Most have a variety of users who change from day to day and even from minute to minute. I find it helpful to think about the needs of five potential groups of users:

- **Novices**. The novice knows little about computers and nothing about the program or online documentation. The novice is curious, but anxious about making embarrassing mistakes. Novices have trouble focusing attention, not knowing what is essential and what is trivial. Novices are reluctant to ask for assistance, as they lack a vocabulary of concepts and terms to express questions [247].

- **Occasional users**. The occasional user is one who "has mastered a system once but, because of infrequent practice, sometimes forgets an essential item" [220, p. 401]. Occasional users do not remember details of commands and procedures. They do not remember computer terms or concepts, nor do they feel they should have to. Imagine the occasional user as someone with a headache who flunked high school algebra and who uses the manual as a plant stand.

- **Transfer users**. Transfer users are those who already know how to operate one product and are trying to learn another similar one. That is, they are trying to transfer what they already know to a new environment [119]. They just want to know how the new product differs from the old.

- **Experts**. Expert or "power" users thoroughly understand how to operate the product. They know how it is organized and how it works. They hate wasting time and prefer any option that lets them do work faster. They demand short cuts and a fast response time, and resent prompts and menus as useless obstacles in the way of their goal of doing things faster.

- **Rote users**. Rote users use a product without knowing or understanding much about it. They do simple repetitive tasks exactly as instructed by a supervisor. Rote users are often stumped by unusual circumstances or exceptions that require them to depart from their securely memorized procedures. Rote users need clear, simple, low-level instructions that tell them exactly what button to press or what code to enter. The procedures they follow must be efficient to avoid wasting their time or triggering errors. Because procedures are repetitive, they must avoid awkward hand movements that can lead to repetitive strain injury.

Consider the age of users

Several surveys have found that young people are as much as 10 times more likely to use online documentation than older people [195]. The reasons for the difference in usage have to do with vision—physical vision and mental vision. Presbyopia and diminishing acuity universally afflict over-40 eyes, making difficult the task of reading small, grainy type from the screen [255]. Bifocals compound the problem, being designed to aid reading from paper, not from the screen.

Another problem concerns the user's mental vision of the computer. Those over 40 tend to view the computer as a fragile, expensive number cruncher. The computer screen looks nothing like the newspapers, books, and magazines from which they get most of their information. Younger users tend to see the computer as a rugged, ubiquitous, general-purpose tool. It physically resembles television, their main source of information and entertainment. No surprise, then, that younger users are more likely to seek answers online.

Rather than write off users of any age, we must design highly legible displays, perhaps letting users boost type sizes as necessary to ensure painless reading. And we should help them envision the computer as an accessible, rewarding communications medium.

Tasks they perform

For each group of users, analyze what they will do with the computer; that is, what work will they perform. To accomplish this work, they must perform certain tasks. Some of these tasks are work tasks that produce visible results, while others are learning or computer tasks that are necessary before the work can be performed. For each user-task combination, study when and how it is performed. How does the user know to perform the task? What helps or hinders performing the task? A table, such as the one shown in the following example, can help capture and summarize this information.

Who	Does what	Circumstances
Class of user	*Action they perform*	*Conditions under which they perform these tasks: environmental conditions, work aids, other documents available, etc.*
Occasional	Creates new job description	Shared office. No paper documents available.
Transfer	Learns to perform familiar tasks on new system	Shared office. Reference manual available on bookshelf.
Novice	Learns to fill in job descriptions	Training room. Tutors on call. Training manual beside the computer.
Expert	Creates new format for job descriptions	Private office. Reference manual available on bookshelf.
Rote	Enters job descriptions from paper forms	Shared office. Noisy, distracting environment.

Ask what do users do with the product and what information will they require to do it.

SET CLEAR OBJECTIVES

After identifying your users and their needs, the next step is to decide what you want to do and get everybody on the project to agree. The best way to do this is with clearly written objectives, approved at the start of the project. Doing so takes time but prevents disappointment and recrimination later. Clear objectives, more than any other factor, can set realistic expectations and focus the efforts of all members of the development team.

Make your objectives ambitious yet possible. Express them in enough detail that you know whether you have succeeded, but make them flexible enough to allow freedom in how they are achieved. Remember, an objective is something you want to accomplish, not something you want to create.

There are many different formats for writing objectives. All require you to specify four pieces of information: what kind of *person* must take what *action* to meet the objective, under what *conditions*, and with what *results*. Here are some typical objectives for an online documentation project.

Person	Action	Condition	Results
All users	Use of paper documentation reduced	Within 3 years	Reduced by 50%
All users	Calls to customer-support hot line for routine questions	Within 1 year	Reduced by 30%
All users	Find information they need	On the first attempt	80% of the time
Occasional users	Find information	With no more than 3 decisions or actions	60% of the time
New users	Become proficient with basic features	Using only the online tutorial	85% of users
Expert users	Learn to automate common procedures	Using online documentation about the macro facility	65% of users

To avoid disappointing your users, your management, or yourself, set realistic expectations. This may require educating others as to what you can achieve.

Unrealistic expectations	Realistic expectations
Users will immediately abandon paper documents.	Users will begin gradually to reduce reliance on paper documents.
The total costs of supporting the product will drop by 90 percent.	Costs will not increase.
Users will express total satisfaction with the first version of online documentation.	Users will applaud the concept, but ask for specific improvements.

Don't promise more than you can deliver. If you can get users to accept your first attempts as a good-faith effort, you can garner their support for proceeding toward true online documentation.

OBSERVE WHAT QUESTIONS USERS ASK

Most users do not want documentation—they want answers to their questions [217]. If the quickest way to answer their questions is online documentation, then they use it. Online documentation can answer their questions only if the author anticipates what questions users will ask and provides answers for these questions.

Paradoxically, the more that writers know about a subject, the less they can predict the questions and problems of users.

How do you learn what questions users will ask? More important, how do you learn what questions users are not likely to ask? Trying to answer every conceivable question can lead to a document so large and complex users cannot find the answers to the questions that actually occur. It can also dilute effort so that questions are not as clearly answered or the answers not tested as well as they should be. Knowing what questions users will ask is the key to effective online documentation.

Trends in asking questions

If you spend much time watching usability tests of products or just observe people trying to use any tool, you will notice some common trends in how they learn by asking questions.

- Most users ask questions or seek help only when they are stumped.

- Users prefer to ask other users. The other person helps them refine their question [217].

- If the user has a clear goal, the most likely question is how to achieve that goal. Users' questions are almost always about the task at hand or about an unexpected response from the system. Questions are seldom expressed in terms of components of the system.

- The type of question users ask depends on their situation. Novices in training tend to ask broad, orienting questions, such as "Where do I start? What do I need to know?" More experienced users in the middle of a complex task tend to ask more specific questions, such as, "How do I change the color of the third bar in this chart to light green?"

- As users advance through a procedure, they ask fewer and fewer questions and their questions tend to seek confirmation of a hypothesis they have formed on their own: "I press A then B then C, right?"

- Probably the most important question is "Huh?!?" It is the universal cry of baffled astonishment. It is the same in all languages. It means the user is stuck.

Testing for questions

The simplest and most effective way to learn what questions users ask is to observe them as they use the product to do work. What questions occur to them? What mistakes do they make for lack of information? What do they seem to figure out on their own? What words do they use to ask questions?

Here is a method that predicts ahead of time exactly what questions users of a product will ask:

> Observe what questions users ask when doing work with the product without any documentation.

To do such a tests, give a simulated *user* a realistic prototype of the *product* and a meaningful piece of *work* to do. Give them no documentation but provide an *expert* who can answer their questions. Record what questions they ask—and notice which ones they do not ask.

If you have access to actual users, get them as test subjects. You can recruit existing users from training classes for current products, from trade shows and user-group conferences, and from users of earlier versions of the product. If the product has no users yet, consider users of analogous products. Recruit users of competitors' products or of products of comparable complexity. Ask test subjects to pretend to be real users. Explain the characteristics of real users and ask them to play the role of actual users.

Study users in pairs [217]. Pair two test subjects with similar levels of knowledge and let them learn the product together. About three minutes into the test, they will forget that they are being watched and will focus their attention on accomplishing the task. They will ask questions not only of the expert but of one another. Their conversations will show how they form, test, and reject theories about how the product operates.

If the product is not ready for testing, use a prototype. A good prototype need be little more than a stack of index cards with sketches of screens, menus, and forms. It requires someone to simulate the computer's reactions to the user's inputs. This person is usually the developer of the product, the same one needed to answer the user's questions anyway.

The developer can describe displays and controls, mimic the computer's responses to inputs, and simulate sound effects.

Checklist of common questions

Make a comprehensive list of all the questions that are commonly asked by users of products like yours. Consider including answers to all of them. Here are some common questions:

How do I _____?	How do I perform an action, accomplish a goal, or achieve some result?
When do I _____?	Under what circumstances do I perform some task or take some action?
What is _____?	What does X mean? Can you show me a concrete instance of it? What does it look like? . . . sound like?
What's wrong?	Why won't X work? What must I do first? How do I fix it?
Why did _____ happen?	What caused an event to occur? What is the principle at work here?
How does _____ work?	What goes on behind the scenes? What processes take place when I take action X?
Which is better?	How do I decide between alternatives? Should I do X or do Y?
Why do _____?	What are the advantages or benefits of X? What are the reasons for doing Y? What will persuade me to do Z?
Why not do _____?	What are the disadvantages, costs, or dangers of X? What are the reasons for not doing Y?
Why believe _____?	What facts, evidence, research supports the idea X? What will convince me?
Why not believe _____?	What facts, evidence, research contradicts the idea X? What will convince me otherwise?
How else can I _____?	How can I do X better, faster, more reliably?

How are ____ and ____ related?	What is the relationship between X and Y? How are they alike? . . . different? What is like this? What is the opposite?
Why is ____?	What is the purpose or goal of X?
Where is ____?	Where is component X? How does it relate to other components? What is it a part of?
What does ____ contain?	What are the parts of X?
How is ____ organized?	What are the parts of X? How do they fit together?
What can I do with ____?	What tasks can I perform with X? What is it used for? What problems does it solve? What are its capabilities? How exactly can I apply it?
What do I do next?	What is the next step in this procedure? What do I do now?
What must I do first?	What are the prerequisites of X? Where do I start?
How do I recognize ____?	What does X look like? What does it sound like? What are its distinct characteristics?
What happens if ____?	What will be the results or consequences of X? What are the dangers?
Is ____ true?	How do I know if X is true? How do I test a hypothesis?

Users also ask metaquestions, that is, questions about the information or the online documentation system itself. These include:

What else?	What else should I know? What is another way of saying the same thing?
Do I understand?	How well did I do? Can I do it on my own?
Where am I?	How did I get here? How do I go back? How much have I read? How much more is there?
What's here?	What kind of information is here? How is it organized and presented?

Other ways to learn what questions users ask

There are other sources of information for making sure your online document answers the right questions.

- **Usability testing**. Formal usability testing will reveal much about how users react to products, including what questions they spontaneously ask, what problems they encounter, and what information they look up in paper and online manuals.

- **Training classes**. Sit in the back of a training class and listen to the questions students ask of the instructor. Notice how the type and frequency of questions changes as the class proceeds.

- **Customer-support phone lines**. Collect a list of the 100 most-asked questions. Ask phone-support veterans what questions should be answered in the documentation.

- **Competitors' documentation**. See what questions your competitors strive to answer. Pay special attention to the indexes where each entry represents one question the manual answers.

- **Using the product**. Use the product and observe what questions occur to you. Where do you get stuck and what can you figure out on your own?

- **Visiting users**. Ask how they learn to use products and how they answer their questions. If they pull out a sheet of handwritten notes, photocopy it and study it well.

USE STATE-OF-THE-ART PEOPLEWARE

Computers are necessary to convey online documentation, but only people can design, create, and evaluate online documentation. Successful online documents require a team of multitalented individuals who are well motivated and clearly managed.

Assemble a multitalented team

Online documentation projects, especially large projects or those involving multiple media, require a team effort. The makeup of the team depends on the nature of the project but will typically include:

- **Communication designer**. The overall "author" who keeps the communication objectives in mind and who integrates the pieces contributed by other team members. May be the nominal leader. The communication designer needs to know enough to specify, critique, and evaluate all the media used on a project and to fine-tune the efforts of the specialists who actually create those media.

- **Media specialists** for each medium. Each specialist creates particular media elements and ensures that they work with other elements. Some specialists may work in more than one medium, for example, illustration and animation. Other rare specialists (animators and video producers) may work on multiple teams at the same time. Common media specialists include:

  - Writer

  - Illustrator

  - Animator

  - Sound-effects specialist

  - Video producer

- **Computer whiz**. Online documentation is software and software requires programming. Although many tools for creating online documents promise "No programming required," the ability to enhance the basic product with custom scripts and macros makes programming a desirable skill on the team.

- **Ergonomics specialist**. Online documentation must be as easy to use and to learn as possible. This requires concern for the human factors of its design and extensive usability testing of prototypes and early versions.

- **File-conversion specialist**. Data comes in many formats. A large, complex project may require converting from the format recognized by one program or operating system to that recognized by another.

Recruit and develop people of the right personality. Staff the project with pragmatic optimists with good interpersonal skills. Avoid grumblers, whiners, and lemon-suckers—no matter what their academic credentials might be.

Organize as a team

A team is a group of individuals who work as one. A team is not a:

- **Committee**. A team does the work after deciding as a group what to do.

- **Horde**. A team is small enough to make decisions quickly. In general limit teams to six or seven members.

- **Legislature**. Teams decide by consensus, not by majority vote.

- **Collection**. Teams share responsibility. A team is not an assembly of self-absorbed geniuses working alone.

- **Temporary**. An effective team is too valuable to waste. Do not automatically disband the team at the end of the project. Give it another challenge.

Ride out the dip in morale

Several teams have reported a characteristic bobble in team morale as they make the trek from paper to online documents. That morale swing typically looks something like this:

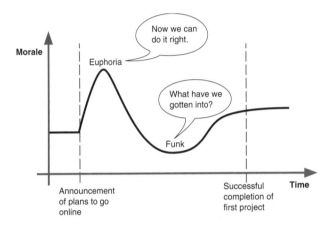

Team members soon discover that producing online documentation is hard work. Tools for producing online documents are cruder and less productive than those for producing paper documents. Often time is required to learn new tools, new techniques, and new concepts. Seldom is enough time available. As a result, team members often feel squeezed to work longer and longer hours.

There is no magic remedy other than realistic expectations and unwavering persistence. Most teams make it through the drop in morale, and many that do report that online documentation is more fun, more exciting, and more satisfying to produce.

Anticipate learning costs

Your first few online documentation projects are likely to be more expensive than you might guess. As a rule of thumb, costs, exclusive of printing and distribution, of your first online documentation project will be two to three times what they would be with paper.

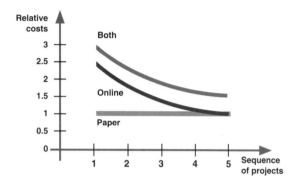

The increase is due to the need to learn new tools, develop new techniques, and correct many mistakes. With experience these costs drop so that after a few projects, you should be able to produce online documentation for the same cost as paper documentation.

Perhaps even better news is that documents that must exist in both paper and electronic forms do not cost twice as much to produce but only about 1.25 to 1.5 times as much as one or the other—provided you have used good project management.

SELECT SOFTWARE CAREFULLY

This section will help you specify or select the software you need to author and deliver your online document. It does not discuss individual programs. There are over 300 programs available, and any specific details about particular programs would be out of date by the time you read this. Instead, it shows you what you need to do to decide among them.

Types of software required

Software is needed for two processes: authoring and delivery. *Authoring* is the process of creating the online document. *Delivery* software gives the user access to that document.

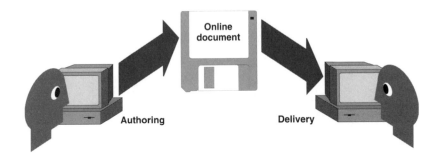

Both authoring and delivery may use the same program. Or the delivery program may be a read-only version of the authoring program. Or the delivery program may be a separate program that can read files produced by the authoring program.

Authoring systems

Authoring an online document is a complex process involving multiple activities. The whole process may be done with one program or with separate programs for each activity. The activities required to author an online document can be grouped into four phases: data capture, content preparation, database preparation, and mastering and replication.

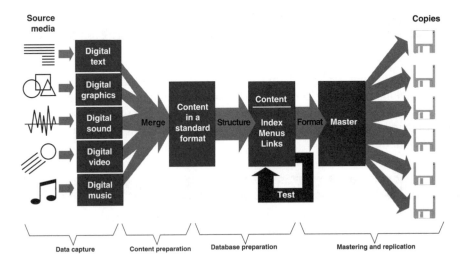

In the *data capture* phase, individual media elements are created and stored as digital data. Words, pictures, sounds, music, animation, and video segments are all created or captured electronically and stored in a digital format. In the *content preparation* phase, the different media elements are integrated into a consistent form. Individual files are imported or referenced from a file or database of topics. In the *database preparation* phase, the topics are structured and indexed so that users can access individual topics. Links are added to connect topics, keywords are added to let users retrieve topics, and menus are created to permit selecting individual topics. In the final phase, *mastering and replication,* a master copy is made and multiple floppy disks or CD-ROMs are produced from it.

Delivery systems

Delivery systems are the program or collection of programs that let users access the online document. They typically contain two parts: a search engine and a front end. The *search engine* is the internal software that finds and fetches individual topics. Its speed and efficiency are critical on large documents with thousands of topics. The *front end* is the user interface. It provides the menus, icons, and screens that the user interacts with to control the system.

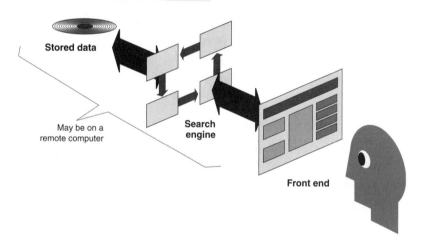

Although the search engine and front end may be parts of a single program, it is useful to consider them separately. Many products have strengths in one but not both. Some products, such as HyperCard and ToolBook, have an easy-to-use interface but lack efficient search engines. Many search engines, on the other hand, have a rudimentary user interface. Some have none at all, being intended to be embedded in a product with its own user interface. Often you may need to combine the search engine of one product with the front end of another.

Steps in selecting products

There is no algorithm, no recipe that will guarantee success in selecting software for online documentation. However, an orderly, systematic process can eliminate many of the pitfalls of a purely subjective choice made on incomplete information. Use the following procedure as a model for your own investigations.

1. **Know what you want to do**. A clearly worded statement of objectives will tell you what technical features to look for in the software. Specify clearly the kind of online document you want to create.

2. **List essential features**. With your objectives in mind, compile a complete list of required features. The other chapters of this book should suggest a complete list of essential and desirable features.

3. **Rank these features**. Assign a priority to each desired feature. Clearly distinguish essential features from merely desirable ones.

4. **Compile a list of candidates**. There are over 300 products for online documentation on the market. New products and new versions of existing products appear daily. For up-to-date information, look at the sources listed in the following section.

5. **Gather information**. The next step is to gather information about candidate products. Ask vendors and users of products.

6. **Pick the best three to seven products**. Select a handful of products for closer scrutiny. Rank the products according to your list of desired features and select the best three to seven products. **Caution: Do not prematurely eliminate products**. Before rejecting a product that lacks a few "must-have" features, consider whether you can add those features.

7. **Prepare a chapter-sized document in each**. Try a small, simple project with each product. This will give you some hands-on experience with the product. Select a chapter-sized document that is typical of the documents you plan to put online. Use your normal staff and carefully record both objective results (time required, assistance required, errors) and subjective reactions.

8. **Test the finalists with a larger document**. Select a book-sized document and put it online with each product. Before you dismiss this suggestion as an extravagant waste of resources, consider the costs of failing on your first real online documentation project. The cost of picking the second-best online documentation product may be considerable indeed.

9. **Decide**. You have four choices: buy the best product now, wait until it adds the needed features, consider other products, or cancel the project. Avoid "chasing the rainbow." The ideal product may not be available when you need it. To make any progress, you may have to adapt to an inconvenient, awkward product or to combine several products. Remember that bright people using a poor tool will outperform dull people with the best tools.

10. **Communicate your decision**. Not even a perfect product can succeed unless its benefits are visible and understandable by those who must purchase and use it.

Announce your choice and communicate the reasons for it to all those affected, especially to the authors who must use the product.

Learning about products

For information on software for online documentation, consult the feature articles, product reviews, and advertisements in magazines and newsletters such as those in the following list.

Byte
Subscription
P. O. Box 552
Hightstown, NJ 08520
(800) 232-2983

CD-ROM Professional
Pemberton Press, Inc.
462 Danbury Road
Wilton, CT 06897
(203) 761-1466

MacUser
Ziff-Davis Publishing Company
950 Tower Lane
Foster City, CA 94404
(415) 378-5600

Multimedia Review
Meckler Corporation
11 Ferry Lane West
Westport, CT 06880
(203) 226-6967

New Media
901 Mariner's Island Blvd.
Suite 365
San Mateo, CA 94404
(415) 573-5170

Publish!
Subscriber Services
P. O. Box 55400
Boulder, CO 80322
(800) 274-5116 or
(303) 447-9330

Seybold Report on Desktop Publishing
P. O. Box 644
Media, PA 19063
(800) 325-3830 or
(215) 565-6864

UNIXWorld
McGraw-Hill
1900 O'Farrell Street
Suite 200
San Matero, CA 94403

Other lists of possible software packages include these:

Guide to CBT Authoring Systems
Weingarten Publications
38 Chauncy Street
Boston, MA 02111-2303
(617) 542-0146

No Hype, Just Media: An Independent Evaluation of PC Hypermedia Software
PDR Information Services
2901 Tasman Drive, Suite 215
Santa Clara, CA 95054
(800) 869-5621

Multimedia Today
Redgate Communications Corp.
660 Beachland Blvd.
Vero Beach, FL 32963
(407) 231-6904

The World of Macintosh Multimedia
Redgate Communications Corp.
660 Beachland Blvd.
Vero Beach, FL 32963
(407) 231-6904

WEAN USERS FROM PAPER DOCUMENTS

People do not spontaneously or voluntarily change something as fundamental as the way they get information. You must give them good reasons to change and allow them time to make the change from paper to online documents.

Start with a five-year plan

How long does all this take? Typically, the transition from paper to online documentation takes five to seven years. Here's a timeline showing the composite experience of several companies making this transition:

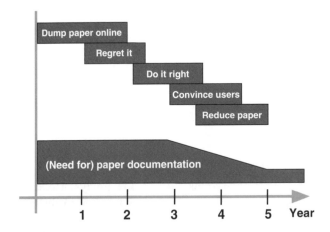

Notice that the need for paper documents, as perceived by users, does not vanish upon release of the first version of online documentation. It does not even start to diminish until you get online documentation right, and enough time elapses for users to gain confidence that they can find everything they need in the online document. Even then the decline is gradual, as some users will hold out for paper documents regardless of the advantages of online documents. Notice also that the need for paper never goes away entirely but levels off at about 10 to 20 percent of what it was before the introduction of online documentation.

Engineer the change

Do not suddenly eliminate paper documents. Instead engineer a smooth, painless transition that avoids activating the user's panic button.

1. Put documents online.

2. Improve online documents until users can quickly and reliably find information.

3. Make paper documents optional. Let users print from online documents.

4. Increase the price of paper documents.

5. As demand evaporates, cease printing paper documents.

Publicize online documentation

Before users will forgo paper documents, they must know what online documents exist and have confidence that the documents will provide all the information they need. Use every opportunity to tell users what online documentation you provide, why they should use the online documents, and how to access these documents. Tell users about online documents in these sources of information:

- Sales brochures, data sheets, advertisements of products

- Demonstrations of the product

- Training classes

- Customer-support hotlines

- Paper manuals

- Other online documents

- Notes on the box containing the product

CONVERT OR REDESIGN?

Should you convert an existing paper document to online documentation or must you redesign it from scratch? Although it is tempting to convert existing documents, that is not always wise or even possible.

Conversions are never simple, easy, or cheap

Programs for automatically converting word-processing files to online documentation are not as "automatic" as their vendors sometimes claim. Considerable clean-up and rework is needed.

Converting paper documents to online documentation typically takes 2 to 10 hours per page [182]. Converting computer-science conference papers to hypertext took two months work by two or three experts [6]. Converting the word-processing files for a 1000-page paper document may cost $20,000 to $100,000 [122].

What can be converted?

As a rule, convert modular reference works but redesign free-form, flowing tutorials.

Poorer candidates for conversion	Better candidates for conversion
General information	Specific information
Philosophy	Concrete facts
Theory	Operating instructions
Long reading passages required	Passages are skimmed or searched
Long flowing passages	Short chunks
Small documents	Large sets of documents
Unstructured material	Regularly structured information
Sequential structure	Hierarchical, tabular, or web structure
Seldom-changing documents	Continually changing information
Tutorials	Reference works
Implied cross-references	Explicit cross-references
Inconsistent use of language	Consistency, consistency, consistency
Free-form layout and format	Consistent format
No index or table of contents	Good index and table of contents
Complex graphics	Simple line art
Inaccurate, out-of-date	Accurate, up-to-date, correct information
Many wide tables	Simple tables
High-resolution photographs	Low-resolution art OK
Text mostly in paragraphs	Text mostly in lists, tables

DESIGN FOR EFFICIENT PRODUCTION

Unless you have unlimited time and budget, you must take care to produce online documents efficiently. Good management techniques help control costs and keep projects on schedule.

Build from reusable components

Automate the routine tasks of creating topics and enforcing standards by designing reusable, modular templates. Using templates of topics and clusters can improve the productivity of authors and consistency of the resulting document [103]. The use of a modular, template-based approach on one project reduced authoring time by 50 percent and assembly time by 90 percent while improving quality [209]. Such an approach also keeps creative designers from become bored and resisting what they see as arbitrary standards [156].

Create a template for common kinds of topics and clusters. A *template* is a fill-in-the-blanks model with all the required and standard elements already in place but with no content. The author adds the content and any other items that are unique to this topic or cluster. For example, teachers at one school created a generic answer-matching template that could be filled with different content to produce lessons on a variety of subjects [120].

Create a library of reusable elements: boilerplate text, pictures, animations, video clips, music, sounds, and scripts. Start with common system actions such as pressing buttons and selecting from menus. To make elements more reusable, store them in separate files and include them by reference or link.

Design each topic and media element so you can improve it independently without having to change many other topics at the same time. Keep careful records of how and where each element is used.

Where possible, use variables to refer to information that appears in multiple locations but which may change later or may vary from version to version. On one project the name of the product changed seven times in the two weeks before its release.

If producing online documentation with nonprofessional writers, use fill-in-the-blanks templates to gather information. Have editors revise and correct the filled-in forms before automatically converting them to the final format. Once in final format, perform another round of editing.

Track tasks and components

Keep track of your files. Even a simple project can require dozens of files and a complex project, thousands. If your project requires creating more than 25 to 50 separate files, set up a project-tracking database. Catalog all files and keep track of every change made. Establish standards for naming files and enforce these standards fiercely [10].

For each topic, record:
Name
ID
File name
Media elements
Author or person responsible
Date created
Date last modified
Current version
Size (including media elements)
Keywords

For each media element, record:
Name
ID
File name
File size
Copyright or licensing status
Creator
Date created
Date last revised
Running time
History (source, transformations)

Build from a document database approach

In a document database approach, a document is not defined as a file or series of files but as a collection of database modules. Each document consists of three parts:

- **Topics**. Units of content. Different topics appear in different documents. Topics may include other elements, but it is the topic as a whole that appears or does not appear in the document.

- **Organization**. How the document is organized. Different organizational schemes include different groups of topics with different patterns of links connecting them.

- **Format**. How the document looks when displayed or printed. The format specification determines layout, typography, and color of the resulting display.

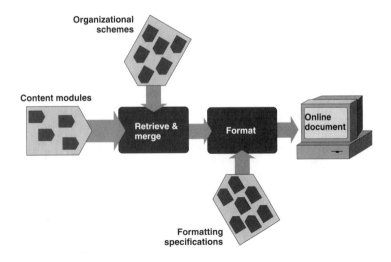

To create a document, the creator designates an organizational scheme (like a shopping list) that triggers the retrieval of the topics included in that scheme and creates links to organize them as specified in the scheme. A formatting specification is chosen automatically to match the display device of the user. This formatting specification can vary depending on the resolution, size, or number of colors available on the user's monitor or on whether the document is to be printed or viewed online.

The document database approach is complex but warranted on large projects. On these projects many documents must be produced from subsets of the same modules where online and paper formats are required for the same information. A document database in one comparison lowered publication costs from $239 to $78 over conventional methods [163].

Most implementations of document databases are custom built using generically tagged files or relational or object-oriented database managers.

Distribute development

In the distributed approach, the document is compiled from components maintained separately. Components can be in different formats, maintained by different people, on different computers throughout a network. When a new version is needed, the most up-to-date components are assembled to create the document.

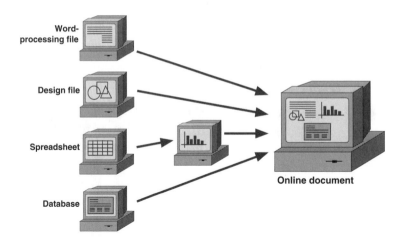

Develop for multiple platforms

Designing online documents to run on different types of computers requires fore-thought and planning, yet it is possible. Compton's has ported its *Multimedia Encyclopedia* to nine different platforms. In planning and design, carefully consider how to bridge the incompatibilities among systems.

- **Fonts**. Select fonts common to all systems or carefully select equivalent fonts. Fonts of the same name are not always the same on different systems. Windows TrueType fonts, for example, are not the same size as Macintosh TrueType fonts of the same name.

- **Names for files**. Either use compatible filenames or come up with conventions for renaming files. Watch out for restrictions on the length, format, and characters that can be included in filenames. Macintosh filenames can include spaces and be 31 characters long. DOS filenames can be only 8 characters long with a 3-character extension. They can include hyphens and dollar signs, but not if included on ISO #9660 CD-ROMs.

- **Directory structure**. Some operating systems thrive on many small files while others do best with a few large files. If delivering on CD-ROM, you should include no more than 40 files per directory, and put the most frequently accessed files near the beginning of the CD-ROM. Other media impose other restrictions.

- **Colors**. Systems differ in the number of colors in the system palette, which colors these are, and which can be redefined. Create equivalent color palettes for all platforms. For best results, custom design a palette by picking the colors you need most.

- **Features in delivery software**. Different versions of the delivery software provide different sets of features or implement the features differently. Sound that plays fine on one computer may cause another to crash. Read the fine print in the documentation—including read-me files.

- **Display monitor**. Users may have screens of different sizes, shapes, number of colors, and resolutions. Either you must design for the most common combinations or make your document dynamically adjust to whatever display is available.

PUTTING THESE IDEAS TO WORK

Essential ideas of this chapter

➡ Design top–down, build bottom–up. Design and specify the document before you begin creating it.

➡ Design is iterative, cumulative, and empirical. Try, try again until you get it right. Successively refine your design through extensive testing.

➡ Design the document to answer questions that users will ask. The best way to learn what questions to answer is to test with actual or potential users.

➡ Assemble a multitalented team including a communication designer, media specialists, computer whiz, ergonomics specialist, and file-conversion specialist.

➡ You can convert well-designed, modular reference works. Redesign others.

➡ Automate routine chores of development and maintenance. Design modules of information that can be combined for different documents and different purposes.

For more ideas and inspiration

Bouldin, Barbara M. 1989. *Agents of Change: Managing the Introduction of Automated Tools.* Englewood Cliffs, NJ: Yourdon.

Brooks, Frederick P. 1978. *The Mythical Man Month: Essays in Software Engineering.* Reading, MA: Addison-Wesley.

DeMarco, Tom and Timothy Lister. 1987. *Peopleware: Productive Projects and Teams.* New York: Dorset House.

Hackos, JoAnn. 1994. *Managing Your Documentation Project.* New York: John Wiley.

ACCESS

3

Making information available

Finding information is different in online documents and is potentially more powerful and efficient, especially for large documents. Making information accessible requires careful choices and the careful design of access methods.

ACCESS ÜBER ALLES

Access is the essential requirement for online documentation systems. Unless users can find answers to their questions quickly, they will not use the document—regardless of how enthralling the text, how luscious the graphics, and how entertaining the animation. Unless users can find what they need, all your other efforts are wasted. On the other hand, if the system answers users' questions quickly and easily, they will forgive almost any other defect. They will squint to read ungrammatical pink text on a lime-green background if doing so answers their questions. Get access right and you buy time to fix the other problems.

Making online documents accessible requires designing both document and system with access in mind. Searching for a specific nugget of information in a vast online document is akin to seeking the proverbial needle in a haystack. If it is hard to get a topic, few people will actually get there. Each additional action required to display a topic subtracts some portion of the audience. The designer must shorten and simplify the path to the topic of interest.

My rule of thumb is that users reject any online document that does not make finding information at least twice as fast as the next best method, such as reading a book, phoning the vendor, or asking a friend.

Several strategies are possible for finding a specific topic. I have divided them into three categories by whether the computer or the user decides what information is needed and then retrieves it.

Access strategy	Who decides what the user needs to know?	Who locates the information?
Automatic	Computer	Computer
Semiautomatic	User	Computer
Manual	User	User

Here, when we say the computer does something, we really mean that is how it appears to the user. The computer merely does what you, the designer, have prepared it to do.

In any practical system you will need to include several methods for each strategy. Different users will require different strategies, and users will mix and match search strategies freely.

AUTOMATIC ACCESS

With automatic access, the computer or the author of the document controls what information the user sees. Automatic techniques are useful when users are unable or unwilling to decide what information they need, or when the designer can better decide what users need to know.

Reading the entire document

In many documents the only way to find information is to start in the upper-left corner and read the entire document until we find what we are looking for. Except in very short documents, this is a very inefficient way of finding information. And, except for one- or two-page read-me files, this strategy has no place in online documentation.

Grazing passively

Grazing is a method of seeking information in which the user passively observes what is presented until the information sought appears. It is sometimes called *couch-potato* mode because it is how many people get information by watching TV. With grazing, however, the user is passive and attends to only a fraction of what is presented.

Grazing is appropriate for timid or uncommitted users and when users do not yet know the basic controls needed to take a more active role. Use grazing:

- For unattended demonstrations where the user may not know enough or be courageous enough to take control.

- For attracting attention. For kiosks and public terminals you can display a series of screens enticing the user to request more information. In CBT training these are called *attract loops*.

- For teaching basic navigation skills. Users cannot select from a menu of lessons to get to the lesson that teaches them how to select from menus. Grazing is a way to present background information needed to get started.

Autoscanning

Autoscanning displays a series of topics at a user-controlled rate. It lets the user automatically scan or page through a document. The computer picks the topics, but the user sets the pace.

Quantum Leap search software from Quantum Access, Inc., lets users scan through long listings at nine different autoscrolling speeds. *The Writer's Pocket Almanack 2.0* contains an option to flip through quotations, pausing long enough for an average reader to read each quotation. Longer quotations have longer pauses than shorter ones.

In scanning, we visually search for information of interest. We do not try to sample the writer's style or absorb details. We seek only to recognize the information we want to read. In paper documents, one of the most common ways of finding information is to flip through the pages until we spot what we are looking for. Although not practical for lengthy documents, scanning is effective for finding a specific piece of information in a short document or a single display [89]. Presenting information in the reader's field of view in a way that is easy to search visually is essential for scanning. A visual glossary is a necessity for systems that use an iconic user interface [239].

Autoscan is helpful for users who can recognize the item they seek. It is also helpful when the user wants to focus full attention on the content and leave page-turning to the computer.

Context sensitivity

Context-sensitive systems automatically select the topic to display based on conditions at the time the document is requested. Typically, a context-sensitive help facility will display the document concerning the current command or the most recent error message.

Context sensitivity has no direct parallel in paper documents. It is as if we had an intelligent robot, who, sensing our need for information, runs to the library, finds the one book we need, and brings it to us, opened to the page that provides just the piece of information we need.

Context sensitivity requires close coordination between the software and the document, usually through invisible codes embedded in the help file and used by the software to specify which topic to display. Unless these codes match perfectly, the right topic will not display. Checking this correspondence between the software and the document requires painstaking review—or automated testing.

Types of context sensitivity

Systems vary widely in the way the context is defined and the precision with which the help response matches the current conditions.

Use same menus

The simplest type of context sensitivity allows the user to access the help document from within the program itself. The user selects a topic within the help document using the same menus used for selecting commands. To access information, the user presses a Help button that turns the cursor to a ?, which is used to select from menus.

User selecting command from menu

User selecting help topic from menu

Such a strategy uses command menus as a table of contents to the help document. Users have to learn only one organization and only one selection mechanism.

Automatically select topic

More advanced forms of context sensitivity automatically select the topic that describes the user's current state in the program, for example, the most recent command, error, menu displayed, or the current location of the cursor.

Suppose the user presses the Help button while the cursor is in a particular field on a form.

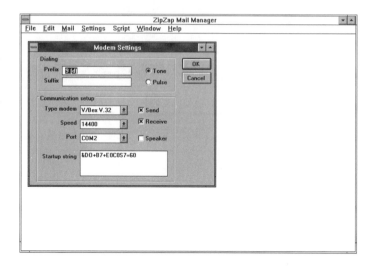

The Help
system dis-
plays infor-
mation
about that
particular
field.

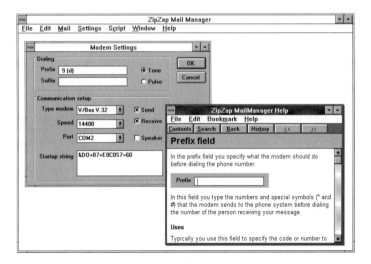

Later if the
user makes
an error fill-
ing in the
form, an er-
ror message
appears. If
the user now
requests
help . . .

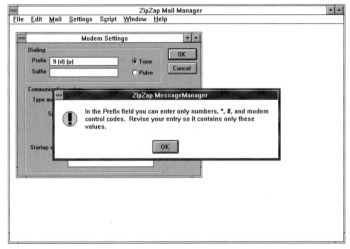

. . . the system displays more detailed information on that specific error.

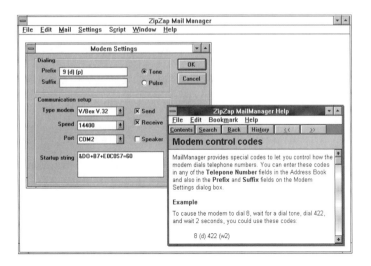

Track user's actions

In a few advanced systems, the program and help display appear at the same time. As the user performs operations in the program, the help display continually updates to show the current state of the program.

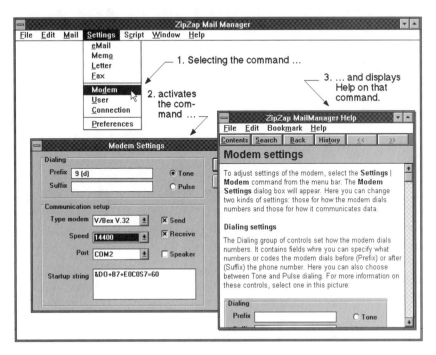

An example is the help facility for Intergraph's I/EMS, which responds to a help re-quest by displaying a quarter-screen window containing information on the current command. The user can move the window on the screen, resize it, collapse it to an icon, or slide it behind another window. As the user continues working with the program, the help window continually updates itself, so it always displays informa-tion on the command the user is currently executing.

Dangers of only context-sensitive access

Online manuals and help messages are typically accessed from within the program that the document describes. To read the document on the ZIPZAP program, the user must start up the ZIPZAP program and then access the document. If the only access to the document is through the program, users may resent the extra time and effort required to start up the program in order to read the document. Novice users may refuse to start up the program for fear they will damage data. These fears are sometimes well founded.

Context sensitivity often answers the wrong question. Unless the user's question relates to the current context, information provided by context sensitivity is usually irrelevant. Telling the user what values can be entered into a field is of no value if the user wants to do something entirely different.

Paging through the document

If presenting topics in sequence, it is important to let the user step and skip forward and backward through the topics in order. Provide commands to move forward and backward in the sequence. If the sequence is more than a few topics long, provide a command to jump back to the first topic in the sequence. If the last topic is of special interest, say, a summary, then provide a command to jump directly to it, too.

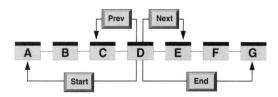

Even if the topics are not organized in an explicit sequence, you can still allow the user to skip through the document in a systematic fashion. For instance, in a hierar-chical document, after reading a topic, the reader goes to the first subtopic if there is one. Otherwise, the reader goes to the next topic at the same level, that is, to the next sibling topic. For example, if the document had the structure shown here, the user would see topics in this order: A, 1, 2, a, b, c, 3. This is same the order of top-ics as in a paper technical manual.

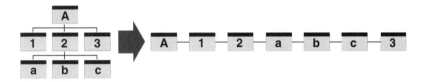

But what about free-form structures where links are not limited to a sequence or simple hierarchy of topics and subtopics? There are two approaches. In an auto-matic procedure, you start with one topic and using a simple rule pick an outbound path to any unvisited topic. You proceed this way as far as you can without repeat-ing topics. Then you back up until you find a link to an unvisited topic and follow that link. Such a policy ensures that each topic is visited once and only once al-though the order may seem arbitrary to the user.

The other approach is to have the author designate a *reading trail* or *browse se-quence* regardless of the overt organization of the document. Although more work for the author, this approach lets users see topics in a more meaningful order.

You might wonder why anyone would page through an irregularly structured online document. Have you ever noticed what people do when they get a new book? They flip through the pages. It does not matter whether the book is a novel or a dictionary. People feel a need to examine the document, to learn what it contains, how it is organized, and how it presents information.

Another reason for paging is to scan for something. Often users will use one search technique to narrow the number of topics under consideration and then switch to paging to examine the remaining topics one by one.

Paging is used in a third situation. When users are tired or absorbed in some other task, often they will page through online documents. Even expert users when fa-tigued or mentally overloaded will fall back on simpler search techniques. It is as if the monotonous rhythm of repeatedly pressing the Next button has a soothing hyp-notic effect.

Guides

Guides are animated or human characters that appear on the screen to lead the user to helpful and interesting information. Guides are more than entertainment. They include software that attempts to infer what the user needs and wants to know.

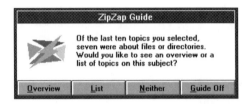

Guides can organize information to reflect a particular point of view. By selecting, organizing, and emphasizing a portion of the document, the guide expresses a view of what is important and what relationships exist among concepts. Guides are good for casual browsing but not for quickly finding the answer to a specific question [162].

Let guides suggest the next topics for the user to visit. Observe the topics the user selects and lingers over and then recommend other topics of the same nature. Record users' reading paths. Then when the user asks for a hint, recommend the links and topics selected by other users [170]. Show the user a list of suggested destinations with the default at the top of the list. Let the user learn why the guide recommends each destination.

The first time the user accesses the document, interview the user, and, based on the user's answers to simple questions, customize the online document, its access and display, to the user's needs. (Of course, explain why you are asking these questions.) Then prepare a reading syllabus for the user suggesting the topics that seem most promising and those that can be skipped because they are not critical or because the user already seems to understand the subject matter. Recommend a reading path that ensures prerequisite information comes before it is needed. Warn the user when a topic is especially important or especially difficult, point out its prerequisites, and offer to make a bookmark for it [170].

Several different types of guides may be useful [85].

- **Specialists.** Who guide the user in one particular aspect of the overall subject.

- **General librarians.** Who direct the user to resources that may answer their specific questions.

- **Reference librarians.** Who answer the user's specific questions.

- **Peers**. Who suggest areas that other users have found of interest or value.

- **Philosophers**. Who point out the broader implications of ideas and show how ideas are interconnected.

- **Computer whizzes**. Who help the user operate the system efficiently.

Recommend, but do not compel, reading paths. Avoid Gestapo documents. Always let users turn the guide off and search on their own. Also let users select the background, experience level, gender, and other characteristics of the guide [60].

SEMIAUTOMATIC ACCESS

With *semiautomatic access,* the user specifies what information is required and the computer finds it. Semiautomatic access is typically called *retrieval* or *search*. The user can request topics by describing the characteristics of the information and having the computer fetch topics that match those characteristics. Searching does not work unless users know what they want and can express it in terms of what the document contains.

Name search

Some retrieval systems require users to find topics by name. Other help systems must have the name of the command or feature specified before displaying help ("help copy"). But you can't retrieve what you don't know is there. Or, if you do know it's there, you can't retrieve it if you don't know its precise name. And if you know its name, you probably don't need it. Some systems try to solve this problem by displaying a list of available topics and then asking the user to select the topic to view.

Keyword search

Keyword retrieval systems tag topics in an online document with invisible keywords that describe the topic. To retrieve information, the user enters keywords to describe the information sought. The system then finds and displays the topic whose keywords match those entered by the user.

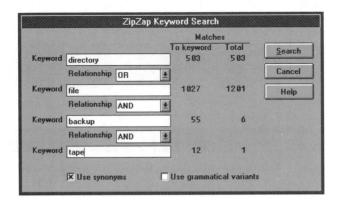

Full-text search

A *full-text* search differs from a keyword search in that the system tries to match a word or phrase in the text of the topic itself. This approach is like using the Find or Search command in most word-processing programs. For example, to locate definitions of hypertext:

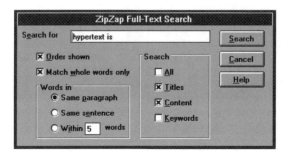

Use full-text search to find many matches. Tests of the online *Harvard Business Review* found that full-text search retrieved about 4 times as many relevant articles as searches of just abstracts and about 2.5 times as many as keyword searches [267]. In general, full-text retrieval systems do not work well with small topics (a paragraph or two) because such topics contain too few unique descriptive terms [89].

Searching for other characteristics

Many retrieval systems also let the user specify topics by other predefined tags or values, the date added, date revised, author, and so forth. For example, to see what Hanna Buscaglia has written since 1 May 1993 on the subject of geology:

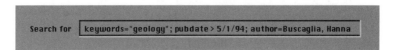

Boolean search

Many search systems let users specify the goal of search using Boolean logical constructions. *Boolean logic* uses operators of AND, OR, and NOT to combine search conditions.

Boolean expressions work like this:

If these topics . . .	Contain these keywords . . .
1	Aluminum
2	Barium
3	Aluminum, Barium
4	Aluminum, Calcium
5	Barium, Calcium
6	Zinc

Then this query . . .	Retrieves these topics . . .
Aluminum AND Barium	3
Aluminum OR Barium	1, 2, 3, 4, 5
NOT Aluminum	2, 5, 6
Aluminum AND (Barium OR Calcium)	3, 4
(Aluminum OR Barium) AND Calcium	4, 5

MANUAL ACCESS

In *manual access,* users decide what information they need and track it down on their own. The system provides pathways to the information but leaves decisions to the user.

Zooming in

In a *zooming in* technique, the user progressively narrows the field of search. This can be done graphically by selecting ever-smaller parts of a diagram, map, or picture.

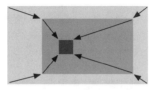

Or, users can zoom in by selecting ever-narrower categories from a hierarchical series of menus going from general to specific topics.

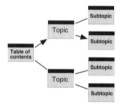

Many online documents are organized as a hierarchy of topics and subtopics. The user starts at the top of the hierarchy where the system presents the most general information or perhaps an overall table of contents. The user selects a subtopic and then a subsubtopic and so on, until reaching the specific information sought.

In *zooming in*, let the user jump directly to a subtopic for more specific information. Present subtopics as a list at the end or as references scattered throughout the text.

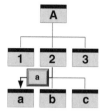

Just as you let users zoom in (or descend) a level in the hierarchy to receive more specific information, let them zoom out a level to receive more general information or to read an overview. Provide an Up command to take users to the parent of the current topic.

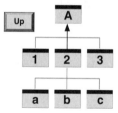

If the document has more than a few levels, provide a command to zoom all the way out. Then, if users get lost, they can return to the widest view without having to jackhammer the Up button.

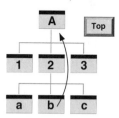

Consulting a directory

In a long document we often seek information by looking up its location in a directory.

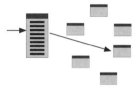

Such *directories* include alphabetical indexes, tables of contents, lists of tables, lists of figures, and so forth. In paper documents, the location listed in the directory is a page number, or sometimes a paragraph or heading number. For online documents, these references may appear as screen buttons that whisk the reader to the referenced piece of information. Such directories are popular, especially with novice users.

Online documents can provide several different kinds of directories ranging from those found in paper documents to some possible only in computer-based documents.

Table of contents

A *table of contents* is a list of topics grouped in logical categories. A table of contents shows how topics are organized and the relationships among them. It can easily establish a mental model of the document's content. One test of a hypertext help system found that users preferred a table of contents and paging to an alphabetical index for finding topics [43].

For simple documents, the table of contents consists of an indented list of topics. For online documents, the table of contents is usually the main menu. Each item in the table of contents is a link to that topic. More complex documents use a hierarchy of menus. Selections on the top-level menu call up a menu of more specific choices. Several systems present an outline of the document. The user can expand and contract headings with + and - buttons next to the headings.

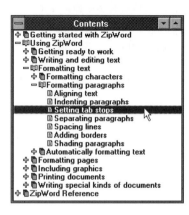

Searching through a hierarchy of menus is reliable but often inefficient. Users typically find what they are looking for 75 percent of the time, but make mistakes on about 25 percent of menus and end up using 1.5 times as many menus as necessary [67]. In large hierarchies of menus, typically 15 to 25 percent of users give up before finding what they are looking for [273].

Index

An *index* is an alphabetical lists designed to ". . . enable the reader to find topics according to the reader's way of thinking" [28, p. 6]. Each index entry is a link to the topic discussing that subject.

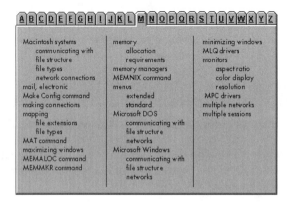

Indexes are simple and familiar. Everybody can use an index, and everyone complains when a big technical book lacks an effective index. One test of online and paper documentation found that information seekers relied more on the index than on any other access aid [212]. Users who get lost in a large document may be rescued with a good index [191]. An index alone, however, may not reveal relationships among categories of information in the document [107].

If most users are computer novices, make the index look and work like one for a paper book. Follow established practices [28], but instead of listing page numbers, make the entry a link to the topic. Avoid the practice of having multiple destinations for an entry. This may require indexing to greater detail to ensure that each entry is linked to only one topic.

✗ No	✔ Yes
(OK on paper)	**One topic per entry**

Sending messages 22, 28, 34

Sending messages
    <u>To users on your system</u>
    <u>To users elsewhere in your office</u>
    <u>To users in other offices</u>

Ensure that users can quickly find the index entry they need. When users select a letter in an index, display the entries for that letter, not just the first entry [236]. Looking up *platypus* in the alphabetical index of Webster's *Ninth New Collegiate Dictionary* CD-ROM for the Macintosh required selecting the letter P and then paging through 92 displays of entries. The index of an online book on hypertext requires 56 button presses to find the index entry for *hypertext*.

Also allow users to sort index entries in various useful ways. *The Presidents* CD-ROM lets users organize the list of presidents alphabetically or chronologically.

For guidelines on preparing online indexes, see page 277.

Map

A *map* shows users where they are and where they can go. In online documents, maps are both orienting aids and menus of possible destinations. Users can study a map to see their current location in the document. They can also select a topic in the map to jump directly to that topic.

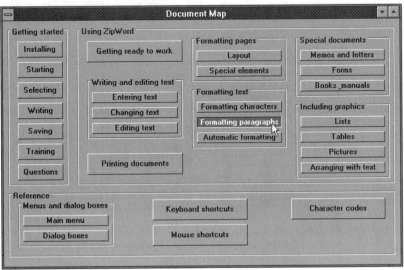

For more on using maps in online documents, see page 215.

History

Most searching is re-searching—60 to 75 percent of searches are for information the user has seen before but forgotten [67, 257]. Let users select a topic from a list of topics they consulted recently. Many systems let the user select from a simple list of recently visited topics, while others display a complete list of what, when, and how long the user read.

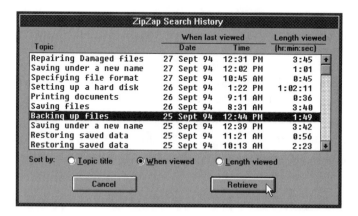

Picture gallery

Let users access visual images from a contact-sheet or picture-gallery display that presents a selection of images. Use such displays when users can select a topic by graphical characteristics. An example is HyperCard's Recent Screens display, which shows miniatures of the last 42 screen displays.

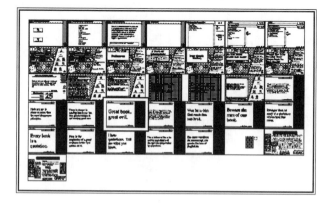

Such a display works only when topics are graphically distinct. If all screens were covered with text, the user would be picking from 42 gray postage stamps.

Bookmarked topics

Readers of paper documents dog ear pages and insert strips of paper to mark pages they want to return to. Many readers are five-fingered readers: They use all five fingers on one hand just to mark interesting topics. Online documents can provide an electronic equivalent of bookmarks. These markers let users maintain a list of topics of special interest, serving as a personal menu. To return to one of these bookmarked topics, the user simply selects it from the list. To provide bookmarks, give the user commands to mark and unmark topics, to display and put away the list, and to select topics.

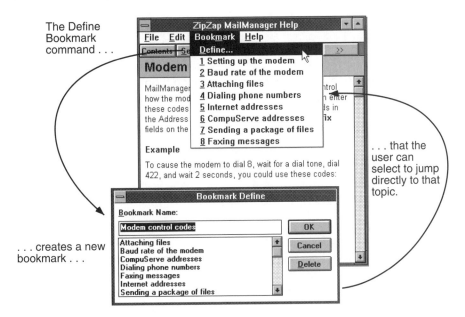

The Define Bookmark command . . .

. . . creates a new bookmark . . .

. . . that the user can select to jump directly to that topic.

Another use of bookmarks is to let the user resume reading where he or she left off. When the user quits an online document, offer the option of leaving a bookmark. Then when the user returns to the document, open it exactly where he or she left off reading.

Navigating

Navigation means jumping from topic to topic in a systematic, but free-form, quest for knowledge. Navigation is *convergent* search. The user jumps to a topic and reads it, considers what has been learned, and jumps to another topic to read some more and jump again. Each jump takes the user closer to the answer to his or her question.

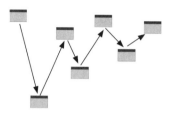

If you want the user to navigate a large document, provide a repertoire of standard commands for moving between topics.

To cross-references

Online documentation systems must let the reader flip back and forth between topics with the same ease as do paper documents. Such flipping and jumping is made possible by cross-references, which provide shortcuts between organizationally distant topics.

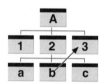

Cross-references let the user jump to another document or to another place in the current document. Cross-references differ from subtopic references in that they do not affect the structure of the document. Cross-references do not appear in the table of contents; subtopics do. Selecting a cross-reference whisks the reader to the cross-referenced topic, just as selecting a subtopic takes the reader to the subtopic.

To a home base

Define a *home base*, say the top of the menu hierarchy, and provide a simple, obvious action that whisks information seekers who have lost their way or reached a dead end back to the home base. No matter where you are in the document, the Home command returns you to a familiar location from which you can start your search again.

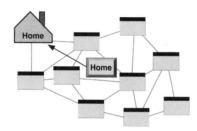

Some systems provide both a *global-home* command to take the user to an overall home topic for the whole document and a *local-home* command to take the user back to the start of the current reading sequence.

Back along a reading path

Sometimes the user may want to go back to a previously read topic. The online documentation system can simplify this backtracking by keeping a record of topics read and letting users retrace their steps along this trail. Each time the user issues the Back command, the system moves backward one topic.

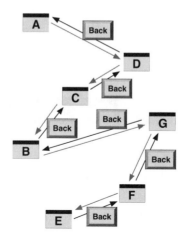

Browsing

Paper books, by their very construction, encourage browsing. They fall open at interesting places. Pictures and headings draw the eye, encouraging exploration. Pages turn easily, and flipping back and forth is natural and common. Many online documentation systems, especially hypertext systems, use the dynamic power of the computer to promote a similar fluidity of movement among topics. Such browsing systems suit the mind's tendency to jump from topic to topic. Whereas navigation is convergent search, *browsing* is *divergent* search.

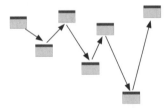

Browsing is exploring. It is information-seeking without a definite goal, jumping among linked pieces of information and encouraging serendipitous discovery [107]. Users browse to find information in a document when they do not know what the document contains or how it is organized. Along the way, users form a useful mental model of the structure of the document. Browsing motivates the reader, because exploring, finding one's own way, and learning how something is organized are intrinsically rewarding activities.

Browsing is appropriate for users who ". . . have long-term commitments to an area of research and may later benefit from extraneous information in that area" [175, p. 71]. It is also good for brainstorming and exploring new areas of information. Browsing alone is seldom adequate for rich, complex subject domains and may then require information retrieval, menus, and other techniques as well [124].

COMBINING ACCESS STRATEGIES

Provide a rich, but not overwhelming, choice of access techniques. A document with a variety of ways to find information may be better than one with artificial intelligence [47].

Since no one access technique works for all users all the time, different types of users apply different strategies. In searching for information in text files, for example, experts tend to search for words and phrases in the text while novices page through the file [79]. In the Book House project users employed a variety of strategies [195]:

Selecting by category	31%
Browsing pictures	27%
Searching by analogy	23%
Browsing randomly	20%

Users pragmatically mix and match search methods [236]. They often combine a visual scan with in-depth perusal. Users will often browse or skim an area until they spot something of interest. They will then search more systematically for other topics in this same area and examine them in more detail. Users of the online *Oxford English Dictionary* browse by first specifying a phrase to search for and then jumping manually to nearby topics [215]. A study of a Hyperties online document found that many users followed a retrieve-scan-select strategy to find information. They first entered a query to narrow the field of search, and from the list of possible topics they selected individual topics and scanned them for relevant information [175].

Some users will learn a few access techniques and use them for all searches [43]. As users gain experience, they use more and different access techniques [149]. Initially, users of the *HyperHolmes* hypertext followed a hierarchical search strategy but soon broadened their searching to more free-form navigation [167].

Remember that users expect and demand traditional paper access tools, such as tables of contents, indexes, glossaries, typographically coded headings, illustrations, page (display) numbers, and bookmarks.

The following table shows recommended access techniques for particular groups of users. Darker shades represent stronger recommendations.

Access strategy	Novice	Occa-sional	Expert	Transfer	Rote
Automatic strategies					
Grazing passively					
Autoscan					
Context sensitivity					
Paging					
Guides					
Semiautomatic strategies					
Search by name					
Full-text search					
Keyword search					
Manual strategies					
Zoom-in					
Navigating					
Directory					
Browsing					

IMPROVING CONTEXT SENSITIVITY

Context sensitivity can automate the task of finding the answer to a question. However, this technique requires the system to infer the user's question and locate the answer to that question.

Identify the correct context

If the topic chosen by the online documentation system matches the user's situation, the information presented is immediately useful. If not, the user must search further to find the information. Context-sensitive systems vary in how they determine the context that selects a particular topic. In general, the more specific the context, the more useful the information presented.

Place in the program

Many systems automatically access a different document depending on what the user is doing at the moment. Because the document pertains to the user's current activity, the user does not have to electronically root through the entire library to find the document. Systems vary widely in how they define the scope of the current context. Common contexts include:

Context	Likely question
Program as a whole	What can I do with it? How is it organized?
Command being executed	What does it do? What inputs does it require?
Menu now displayed	What does it contain? How do I decide what to select?
Option on a menu	What does it do? What inputs does it require?
Field containing the cursor	What can I enter here? What happens to the data I enter?
Prompt now displayed	What can I enter here?
Icon pointed to by the cursor	What does this do? What is it called?
Currently selected tool	How do I use this tool? What inputs does it require?

Most recent error message

Beep! Flash! Boing! The user made an error. If the user now requests help, context-sensitive systems display a detailed explanation of the error. The content of this message depends on the latest error. Some systems, such as Helix Express, provide a separate "Why?" command to request an explanation of an error message.

Pattern of usage

The user's past choices and actions also define a context. More sophisticated systems maintain models of the user and the user's goals and watch for actions by the user that clearly do not further these goals. Detecting such "suboptimal behavior," active help facilities offer information to get the user back on track [83]. For example, when the user attempts to retrieve information from a Double Helix II database by specifying values for fields that have not been indexed, the program beeps once; and if the user asks why, it explains that the user can make the search more efficient by creating an index for that field. Other suboptimal behaviors that an active help facility can detect include:

Pattern	How an intelligent system might respond
Repeating the same error	The first time, assume the cause was a typo. The third time, assume a conceptual error. The fifth time, assume the user is totally confused.
Moving up and down a menu hierarchy without selecting any commands	Assume the user is looking for a command. Help him or her find it.
Typing more than the minimal abbreviation or specifying values that are already defaults	Accept the input as is but, while processing it, point out how the user could have saved effort.
Procedures started but not completed	Assume the user is afraid of possible negative results. Explain how to undo the results of a command.
Using several commands to do what one command can do	Point out more efficient methods—gently and unobtrusively.
Repeated sequences of commands	Offer to make a macro of those commands.

Personal characteristics

Context can include the personal characteristics and interests of the user. An online encyclopedia could note that since I am a mechanical engineer, when I request information on *stress*, I am talking about forces applied to a material. When my friend the psychologist asks about *stress*, she gets information on the psychological effects of anxiety. Context can also include the user's state of mind, that is, the goals, desires, conceptions, degree of frustration, and level of experience. Such intangibles are difficult, but not impossible, to detect or infer.

Open the right part of the document

When the user requests an online document, the system opens the document at a particular topic or position in the document. The aptness of this choice often determines whether the user finds the information sought or gives up.

- **Start of sequence**. If the answer to the user's question is organized as a sequence of displays or topics, start the user off at the first display in the sequence. The reader can then read along the sequence.

- **Bottom of hierarchy**. Context-sensitive systems typically deposit the reader in the topic that corresponds to the current conditions of the program. These specific topics live at the bottom or most specific level of the document hierarchy.

- **Top of hierarchy**. If the document is organized as a hierarchy, systems that lack precise context sensitivity can start the reader at a general or overview topic. The user can then go down the hierarchy to more specific topics.

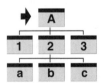

IMPROVING SEARCH SYSTEMS

In this section, we look at some of the ways to improve traditional information retrieval procedures for use in online documentation systems.

What's wrong with search systems?

Information retrieval systems seldom live up to their developers' promises or their users' expectations [25, 95]. They are hard to use and they miss many useful topics while finding many that are not useful.

Search techniques are difficult

Users familiar with the subject matter of a document but untrained in search techniques usually fail with traditional retrieval systems [67]. There is as much as a 10:1 difference in the ability of users to form queries. The variation is nearly as great for a single individual at different times [86]. Typically, if two people search for the answer to the same question on the same system, only 40 percent of the results will be common to both searches [56]. Lawyers, in two tests, retrieved only about 25 percent of the relevant document [25, 291]. Even professional researchers, experienced in performing online searches, find less than half the available information on the subject of their search [291].

Searcher and author use different words

Many search mechanisms require the user to translate concepts and ideas into words. These words must match exactly those chosen by the author or indexer of the document. However, *synonymy* (multiple words per meaning) and *polysemy* (multiple meanings per word) thwart conventional retrieval mechanisms.

Even trained indexers often use different terms for the same concept [67]. And typically only 10 to 20 percent of the search words of an untrained searcher match the words of a topic [96]. Search systems do not know what the searcher wants. A user who searches for the words *stress*, *strain*, and *tension* may receive information on human psychology when he or she wanted information on mechanical engineering.

Precision and recall are too low

Online documentation systems—and all database systems as well—are subject to the twin problems of *recall* and *precision*. *Recall* concerns how many topics the user's search uncovers. *Precision* concerns the relevance of the topics the user retrieves. An ideal system would retrieve all relevant topics but none that are irrelevant. In the real world, precision and recall are often too low. With *low recall*, the user misses many potentially useful topics. With *low precision,* the user must sort through many irrelevant topics to find those that are useful.

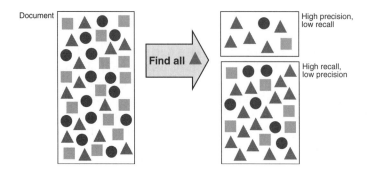

Research with hundreds of databases and online documents has found a practical limit and trade-off between recall and precision. Up to a point we can improve both, but beyond that point, any change that improves precision diminishes recall and vice versa.

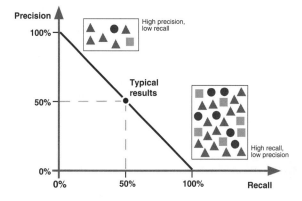

There is a direct trade-off between the two. Precision and recall typically add up to 100 percent [237]:

% of topics relevant + % of relevant ones found = 100%

Typically systems find 50 percent of the desired topics, but only 50 percent of what they find is relevant [67]. When 80 percent of the desired topics are found, only 20 percent of the topics found are relevant.

Make specifying searches easier

Search mechanisms should require no more effort or knowledge than the index of a paper book. However, search mechanisms often require users to express requests in a special query language using Boolean expressions, which require a level of detailed logical thought that is difficult for ordinary users. In library systems, for ex-ample, most users are restricted to simple searches because they can't or won't learn how to use Boolean expressions to phrase requests [20]. In one test both pro-grammers and nonprogrammers made errors 10 to 35 percent of the time with simple searching commands, and up to 90 percent with more complex functions [219]. However, other tests show that even inexperienced computer users can create rules for selecting information to meet their needs [171]. We can simplify the process of retrieving information, especially for untrained users.

Teach users to search

Teach users unfamiliar with databases or with retrieval mechanisms the concepts and procedures of effective searching. Explain to users the difference between full-text and keyword searching mechanisms. They must understand that full-text searches find specific words and phrases but that keyword searches find semantic categories [214].

Although users can learn a formal query language, few need to learn the entire lan-guage. The simplest commands and concepts may suffice for many users [219]. This suggests designing a simplified version of the language for novice and occa-sional users while providing the full language to expert users.

Simplify the language

Most users require extensive training before they can use a query language effec-tively. Poor readers and many good readers have trouble with logical connectives AND, OR, and NOT. Few can understand nested IFs ("If A then if Y . . ."). Further-more, the exact format varies from system to system. In a single library, I found some systems that used # for a single-character wild card while others used ?; however, ? was used by another system for its multiple-character wild card. Still other systems used *, $, and : for multiple-character wild cards. In some systems the OR operator was assumed; in others, the AND operator. No wonder that not even librarians could use the systems without making mistakes and continually consulting handwritten notes. The same inconsistencies show up in CD-ROM en-cyclopedias and dictionaries intended for use in the home. If searching online doc-uments is to be as easy as searching paper ones, we must simplify and standardize the query language.

As an alternative to full, formal query languages, linear keyword query languages, such as SQL, combine elements of human and computer languages. They have a restricted vocabulary and syntax but resemble English in syntax and structure [277].

```
SELECT BIOGRPH
FROM AUTHOR A, EDITOR B
WHERE A.NAME = B.NAME
```

We can go further by extending the language to let users express queries in their own words. In search systems, use phrases that users will understand. Let them say "greater than" as well as ">" when referring to numbers. When referring to text, let them say "alphabetically after" instead of requiring "greater than."

Graphical approaches are another possibility. The Queries-R-Links systems let users specify queries by marking up text. Users would draw circles around words to search for. Lines connected circles of words to be ANDed. The absence of a line indicated an OR relationship [114].

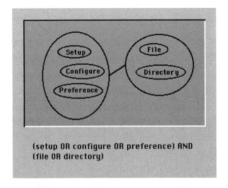

(setup OR configure OR preference) AND
(file OR directory)

Replace a language with menus

For untrained users you may want to replace a language with menus that let users spot the item they want rather than have to remember or guess what it is called [43].

Fill-in-the-blanks forms

Item-by-item prompting builds up a query by successively asking the user questions about the information sought [277].

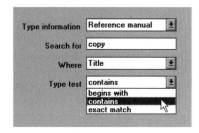

Such an approach can lead to more accurate queries. Where witnesses in police investigations were prompted feature by feature, they were more likely to correctly describe a suspect [164].

Structured retrieval

In *structured retrieval,* the user selects buttons and icons on the screen to construct a query. The interface is structured so that the user cannot request information the document does not contain and cannot make a syntax error. This example lets the user select a command from the list at the left and a category of information from a button at the top. It then displays the requested information in the large area below the buttons.

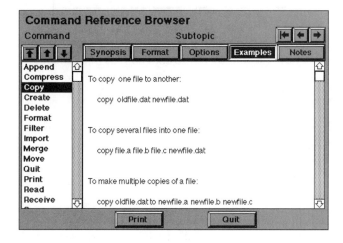

By pressing buttons, the user has generated this query Command="Copy" AND Sub="Examples" without having to type or know any query language.

Structured retrieval is limited to very simple queries for well-organized information. It is much like looking up something in a large table by row and column.

Restricted search

Restricted search lets the users search keywords or full text, but restricts them to words contained in an index. The search mechanism in Help for Microsoft Windows lets the user type a few letters to scroll the list of available search terms to ones beginning with those letters. The user then selects one of the search phrases and the system displays the titles of topics matching that phrase. The user then selects a topic to view.

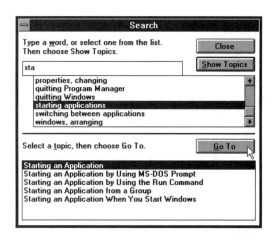

Restricted search means users can scan for rather than guess the search terms. It also removes the requirement to learn the conventions of a language.

Use natural language

Why not go all the way and have the computer understand the user's natural language? Although perfect natural-language recognition is not practical yet, many systems can use restricted natural language.

Natural-language systems are possible

Simple natural-language recognition systems have shown that users familiar with the terminology of a field can successfully find information in that field without extensive training [127]. In one test, untrained users were able to answer 59 percent of their questions with one such document and 64 percent with another [287]. Longer natural-language queries work better, but even queries with an average of only 3.5 words worked well in one test [127]. Natural language can serve as a query language, provided [277]:

- It is restricted to a well-defined subject domain.

- Users understand the structure and vocabulary of the document.

- They use it frequently enough to learn and remember its restrictions.

The success of natural-language recognition hinges on the degree to which language can be made unambiguous and still remain natural. A system can often interpret the ambiguous terms in the user's query by assuming they relate to the context of the most recently read topic or series of topics, or to the user's most recent series of questions [287].

Restricted natural-language dialogs

Restricted natural-language systems use a simplified version of a natural language, such as English, restricting syntax, vocabulary, and subject domain. Question-answer systems, for instance, accept questions in everyday language and reply in everyday language. Such systems syntactically and semantically analyze the user's natural-language question to convert it to a formal query which they then process to retrieve information. These systems translate the retrieved information back into a natural-language statement before presenting it to the user.

```
What is the density of gold?
   19.32 grams per cubic centimeter
How about lead?
   The density of lead is 11.35 grams per cubic centimeter.
What is its melting point?
   Do you mean gold or lead?
gold
   1064 degrees Centigrade
```

For better natural-language retrieval, explicitly state the subject-domain of the document. In all messages *to* the user, use the vocabulary and syntax that the system recognizes in messages *from* the user. Users will readily adopt this style in their queries of the system [287].

Menus to construct natural-language questions

One effective use of menus is to let users construct natural-language questions. Such a system can unobtrusively restrict the user to questions that are indeed answered by the document and can ensure that all questions are expressed in a form that both the user and the computer can understand.

In this system, users start by selecting a question and then filling in the blanks until they specify their question. As they fill in the blanks, the options for the remaining blanks are restricted to match the items specified so far and information that the document contains.

Why should I move file later?

The user starts by selecting the previous question.

Why should I move file later?
How do I **action object method**?
When do I **action object method**?
Why should I **action object modifier**?
What is the **characteristic** of **object**?
What does **object** do?

A list displays the types of questions the system can answer. The user selects one.

How do I **action object method**?

Words in bold type represent slots the user can fill in to further specify the question. The user selects one.

How do I **action object method**?
file
file
command

A list of possible ways to fill in the slot appears.

How do I **action** file **method**?

The user selects another slot-word.

How do I **action file method**?
create
delete
copy
move
modify

Its possible values appear for the user to select from.

How do I move file **method**?

The user selects the final slot-word

How do I move file **method**?
by mouse
by keyboard
by function key

and chooses a value for this slot.

How do I move file by keyboard?

The question is now complete.

Help users perfect their searches

Many one-shot query systems require the user to get it right the first time or start over again. This is not how human beings work best. We do most things by a process known as *successive refinement.* We make an attempt that falls short of our goals. But we do not quit. We compare what we accomplished with our goal and make adjustments and try again, eventually getting to our objective. Successive refinement in searching requires feedback on success and the ability to refine a query that did not work.

With *relevance feedback*, the system presents the results of a query for the user to critique. The user identifies relevant items. The system then adjusts the query in this direction. Relevance feedback can improve search 20 to 50 percent [237].

Let's look at some steps to incorporate successive refinement and feedback into the search process.

Allow fuzzy matches

In many systems, matching is all or nothing. More sophisticated systems calculate the degree to which the user's query matches various topics. The simplest way is to count the number of keywords in the user's query matched by each topic.

A more precise way is to assign weights to keywords to specify the relative importance of the keyword. Users can assign weights when they enter keywords for a search. Indexers can do likewise when they index the topic. Or, an indexing program can calculate the importance of keywords by what degree they are unique to the topic. In one test, varying the weight of the keyword based on its frequency in the individual topic relative to its frequency throughout the document increased precision 40 percent or more [67].

Calculating the degree of match can be improved likewise. *Vector-space techniques* gauge the degree of match between the keywords of the user's query and those of the topic. They calculate a cosine product of the vector formed by the two sets of keywords [67].

Provide hints

When listing keywords or index terms, show the number of matches in the document. Distinguish matches by where they occur: in the body, title, abstract, or keyword list [166]. That way users can avoid terms with too many or too few matches.

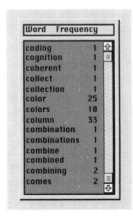

Confirm a query before carrying it out

Feedback should start before the query is launched, especially if the user pays by the query or the query will take more than a few seconds. Before carrying out a user's query, display the query as interpreted by the system and request the user to confirm it. Do not merely repeat the user's input. Display it in a different form. If the user poses the query in a language, display feedback visually. If the query is specified graphically, give feedback verbally.

Make the confirmation optional. Let experienced users turn off the confirmation step.

Let users reuse past searches

Let users reuse and combine earlier queries by selecting them from a list. The following shows a user searching for hardware problems common to two different models of a device:

Saving queries has another benefit. Users often repeat them verbatim. One study of information retrieval at Boeing Aircraft Company found that the majority of retrieval requests were repeated [68].

Base search on seed topic

Once the user finds one useful topic, let that serve as a specification for finding more. Use the characteristics of this *seed topic* as a query to retrieve like topics. Doing so lets the user say, "Here's a good match. Now go find some more like it."

Preview matches

Do not force users to examine each of the topics retrieved individually. Instead, in a single window display enough of each of the destinations for the user to decide among them.

A *keyword-in-context* (KWIC) display is an alphabetical list of all matches to a search word in the document. Each word is shown as it appears in a topic, that is, surrounded by preceding and following words.

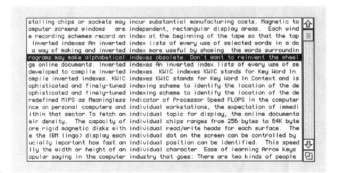

Although KWIC indexes can be generated automatically, they are not always helpful. Showing only a few words fore and aft of the target word may not provide enough context for the user to evaluate the relevance of the match. One study of full-text search found that showing 65 characters around the match sufficed in only the simplest cases [214]. For large documents KWIC indexes display too much information, simply because large documents contain so many words. Common words occur many times, and the user must scroll through hundreds of lines to find unique terms. In this case, use KWIC just for titles, descriptions, abstracts, or sum-maries [144].

When there are too many matches to a search word, display all the phrases that contain the word and let the user pick one [166]. Sort the list by frequency, ignor-ing whether the other word came before or after the sought word.

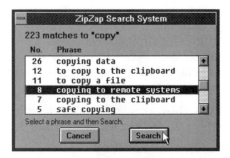

Give feedback on success

For queries that identify more than a few topics, provide feedback on the number and degree of matches. In one test a document providing feedback outperformed conventional fill-in-the-blanks query mechanisms [4]. Some techniques for provid-ing feedback on search results:

- List titles in order of apparent relevance, especially if the list will not fit in a single scrolling zone [127].

- Show the degree of match either as a percentage match with the search terms or as a number of matches.

- Use graphic shading to show the degree of match. Shade an icon or fill a geometric shape that represents the matched topic [4].

- Give the user a two-dimensional display of the matches with each match positioned by its value along two scales. One system plotted books by Library of Congress and Dewey Decimal numbers [166].

- In full-text searching, display the first occurrence of matched terms. Highlight them. Highlighting the search terms helps users focus on the important part of the information [76].

Let users refine searches

In an approach variously called *query by reformulation* or *retrieval as conversation,* the user goes through several cycles of critiquing retrieval results. The retrieval system uses the critique to sharpen the query and to generate the next retrieval for the user to critique.

In *query-by-example,* the untrained user describes the information sought by manipulating a representation of the database [277]. The system presents an example of what it guesses the user wants. The user next critiques, or adjusts, the system's example. The refined description is then used to retrieve another example [198].

Let's look at an example in action. Here the user starts by requesting articles on waterproofing and roofs published in 1980 or later.

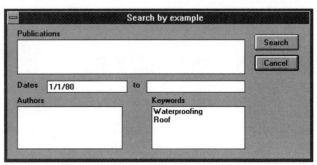

The system displays the titles and authors of such articles. Notice that it has revised the dates to show the earliest and latest dates for articles found. It has also added keywords.

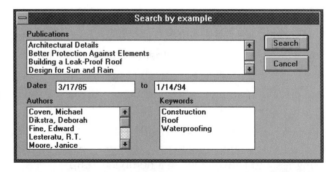

The user now changes the earliest date and deletes one of the keywords. The system will now refine the list of articles displayed. This dialog continues until the user has identified the topics of interest.

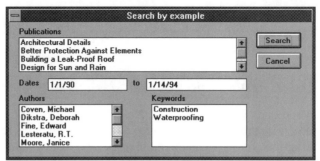

Retrieve more topics

In searching, recall is typically low, especially for novice and occasional users. One way to retrieve more relevant topics is to broaden the search beyond that initially requested by the user.

Extend words of the query

Broadening the set of keywords used to retrieve data improves recall [175]. There are several ways a system can extend the search terms entered by the user:

- **Grammatical variants**. A word can have various forms depending on how it is used in a sentence. *Stemming* attempts to extend a word to include such grammatical variants. Stemming would extend a word like *copy* to include *copying, copies, copied*. Stemming is possible because the English language uses only about 75 prefixes and 250 suffixes. A brute-force stemming algorithm works by repeatedly stripping away prefixes and suffixes to uncover a root word (at least three characters). This can fail for words like *catering,* which are reduced to *cat.* A more sophisticated approach uses a dictionary of words and their roots. It is slower and takes more memory, but is more accurate [216].

- **Synonyms**. Synonyms are words that mean the same thing as one another. Most languages have lots of synonyms. To account for the fact that the author and the searcher may have used different synonyms for the same concept, some systems enrich the user's query by adding synonyms to the words chosen by the user. To *copy* they add *duplicate, replicate, reproduce*. To broaden search, use a thesaurus to supply semantically equivalent keywords. Using a thesaurus to match synonyms typically increases matches by 10 percent [67].

- **Related words**. Find related words that are more general or more specific, more abstract or more concrete, than those specified by the user. It sometimes helps to search for words that mean the opposite (*antonyms*), because such topics may be cross-linked to their counterpart.

- **Alternative spellings**. In the U.K., it is *colour*, but in the U.S., it is *color*. Such differences as *program* vs. *programme* seldom cause people a problem, but they can thwart literal-minded computer programs (or is it programmes?). Maintain a dictionary of known spelling variants and extend the user's spelling to include other possibilities. I came across one online document with the terms *highlight, hilight, highlite*, and *hilite* intermixed. Poor editing, to be sure, but that is the kind of problem a search system can handle for the user.

- **Homonyms**. Let users specify the phonetic spelling with a "sounds like" command.

Online dictionaries apply these techniques. The online version of the *American Heritage Dictionary* lets users broaden searches by including different inflections (do -> doing) or derivations (do -> redo) of a word. The *Perseus Project* includes a morphological parser, named "Morpheus," which helps inexperienced students of ancient Greek to find the dictionary entry for a word even though the form of the entry differs from that of the word in question [14].

Find related documents

Another strategy is to retrieve not just the topics that matched the user's query but others related to the matching topics. Compton's *Knowledge Browser*, for instance, retrieves related topics and presents them to the user. How can a search system recognize related documents?

- **Designated groups of related documents**. Group related topics into sets so that a query that finds one finds them all. Organize these related online topics into "books" and "pamphlets" by subject so users retrieve all related topics as a set [112].

- **Same author**. You can also broaden a query by looking for other works by authors specified by the user. An author who has written one article may have written several or may have published a book on the same subject.

- **Same words in title or abstract**. Also look for other documents that use the same words in the title or abstract. For instance, if you find a topic titled "Spreadsheets for Physicians," also look for other articles with *spreadsheet* or *physician* in the title. Such a strategy would snare titles such as "Physicians Turn to Spreadsheets for Reports" and "A Physician's Spreadsheet Notebook."

- **Same words in body text**. If two topics contain several of the same important words (for example, words found in the index) or synonyms of those words, then those two topics are probably related. Such a strategy can fail when incidental words (such as units of measurement) are frequently repeated in a topic [216].

The Dynamic Medical Handbook extended matches by taking into account not only the index terms matched by the topic itself (its intrinsic part) but the matches of its subtopics (its extrinsic part). This procedure identified topics whose lower-level subtopics match the search terms. If topics I.A.1, I.A.2, and I.A.3 all match the index terms, then topic I.A is a promising starting point, even though it may not match the index terms at all [91].

Adjust keywords to match usage

Information retrieval systems can improve their performance over time by making the fullest use of information entered by the user. Have the system gradually adjust the keywords of a topic so they better match the keywords entered by users to retrieve the topic [116]. Always make the best guess possible given the information available. In one test, such a strategy increased successful retrievals from 10 to 20 percent to 40 to 60 percent [95].

Match the meaning of topics

Full-text retrieval and concordance indexing face two common problems. First, a text passage may fail to mention the subject of the passage. A paragraph on iron, copper, titanium, gold, and silver may not contain the word *metal* because the subject is obvious from the context or because it was mentioned in a preceding introductory section. When such documents are converted to modular online documents, this context is removed. The second problem is the opposite of the first. Some passages contain words but are not about those words. For instance, this sentence contains the word *elephants* twice but is not about elephants.

Some advanced systems attempt to overcome these problems by matching the meaning of the user's query and that of the text in topics. *Semantic analysis* tries to select topics based on the meaning and associations, not just the forms, of words.

For example, the Semistructured Intelligent Navigation System (SINS) calculates the similarity between the user's query and information contained in topics. It does so by comparing values specified by the user (a *ruleprint*) to corresponding values representing the content of each topic (its *fingerprint*). The system helped users find in-formation in 25 percent less time and with 50 percent as many jumps as a conventional system [92].

Retrieve only relevant topics

Users of information retrieval systems frequently retrieve everything available on a subject for fear that they will miss something. They then slowly and painfully sift through their findings, discarding most of what they found. If the number of candi-dates is large, the user cannot easily judge which is relevant. Improving precision requires selecting only relevant topics, usually by filtering out the irrelevant.

Let users fine-tune search

Give users control over how the search is performed. Without overwhelming them with features, provide controls that let them specify precisely what they want. Let users:

- Decide whether to match upper- and lower-case characters.

- Specify that the search string must be, may be, or may not be a whole word.

- Specify that the string occurs in a sentence.

- Require that the string starts a word, ends a word, or is included in a word.

- Insert wild card characters that match any character or character in the corre-sponding position.

- Assign weights, positive or negative, to various retrieval criteria. Let them desig-nate some as "must have" and others as "nice to have."

- Vary the priorities for searching titles, keywords, abstracts, and body text.

Knowledge Finder by Aries Systems Corporation, for example, lets users disengage stemming (word variants in their terminology), set the trade-off between quality and quantity, and even specify the maximum number of topics to retrieve.

Retrieve at different levels of abstraction

Abstraction involves storing and retrieving information at various levels of detail and from different viewpoints. To improve precision, let users filter information at various levels of abstraction. In a Help facility, for example, let users retrieve infor-mation on commands, related groups of commands, or the program itself. Notice how each of these queries requests information at different levels of specificity:

```
copy                    information about the Copy command
copy format             information about the Format option of the Copy com-
                        mand
copy format RLE         information about the RLE parameter of the Format op-
                        tion of the Copy command
```

Use proximity operators to sharpen search

Let the user search for pairs of words that occur near one another. Such proximity searching allows for intervening words and rules out matches when words are not close enough to be associated. For example, to search for the words *computer* and *music* only where they occur within five words of each other:

```
Keywords ==> "computer <5W> music"
```

Let users specify:

- Maximum number of words between search terms

- Whether terms must occur in a particular order

- Whether terms must be in same sentence or same paragraph

Provide additional criteria for retrieving

Give users more ways to describe the information they want, letting them narrow the search using any criteria possible. Consider letting users search by these criteria:

- **Special subject-specific codes and conventions**. In special-purpose systems, adopt the conventions of the user's discipline. Scholarly systems for examining classical manuscripts should, for instance, follow the standardized citation schemes unique to each manuscript [61]. Let biblical scholars request "Genesis 3:12," for example. *CD/Corporate Information* lets users search by CUSIP, Disclosure, D-U-N-S, Forbes, or Fortune numbers. Dun's *Million Dollar Disc* lets users search by Standard Industrial Code (SIC) or Standard Metropolitan Statistical Area (SMSA).

- **Structure**. Spatial memory is very acute and can help us find topics by recalling how they are organized or how they are related to other documents. You may, for instance, remember that the information you sought was at the bottom of the hierarchy and had two sibling topics.

- **Meta-information.** Let users retrieve by the characteristics of the topic itself, such as the date added, dates revised, author, media used, length, and so forth.

- **Circumstantial associations.** Items in human memory are "tagged" with circumstantial or incidental associations. These include when something was learned, what it was next to when last seen, who was present, and so forth. Online documentation systems should let users request information by incidental particulars as well as characteristics of the content. "Let me see the report I looked at early last month . . . on a Monday, I think . . . I looked at it just after I scanned the news wires for articles on skin diving . . . oh yes, it was displayed in yellow text on a dark (blue, I believe) background."

- **Graphical or audio data.** How do you search for a picture, a sound, a melody? Sketch it? Hum a few bars? Research in pattern-matching using neural-net computers promises progress in carrying out these searches. IBM's Ultimedia Manager/2 can retrieve pictures based on the color, shape, texture, and layout of objects in the picture. However, we must still come up with easy ways for users to specify the visual or sound pattern to search for.

- **Nonwords.** Let users search for abbreviations, acronyms, words containing punctuation, phrases, and other nonwords, such as part numbers [116].

```
Keywords ==> NRC TMI melt-down U238 "nuclear accident"
```

PUTTING THESE IDEAS TO WORK

Essential ideas of this chapter

➡ Access is essential for online documents. Either make information twice as accessible as on paper or leave the information on paper.

➡ Practical systems require several different access mechanisms to accommodate different types of users performing different kinds of searches. Let users mix and match access strategies and techniques.

➡ For novice users, provide all the access mechanisms found in paper books: table of contents, index, paging, bookmarks, and so forth.

➥ Provide retrieval mechanisms for large documents, but work hard to make them easy to use. Also work to ensure that users find all of what they want and nothing of what they do not.

➥ Invest in a good index. All users benefit from a well-designed index. And index terms can be used as search keywords.

For more ideas and inspiration

Bielawski, Larry and Robert Lewand. 1991. *Intelligent Systems Design: Integrating Expert Systems, Hypermedia, and Database Technologies*. New York: John Wiley.

Dumais, Susan T. 1988. "Textual Information Retrieval." In *Handbook of Human-Computer Interaction*. Amsterdam: North-Holland. 673-700.

McGrew, P.C. and W.D. McDaniel. 1989. *On-Line Text Management: Hypertext and Other Techniques.* New York: McGraw-Hill.

Reisner, Phyllis. 1988. "Query Languages." In *Handbook of Human-Computer Interaction.* Amsterdam: North-Holland. 257-280.

Salton, Gerard. 1989. *Automatic Text Processing: The Transformation, Analysis, and Retrieval of Information by Computer.* Reading, MA: Addison-Wesley.

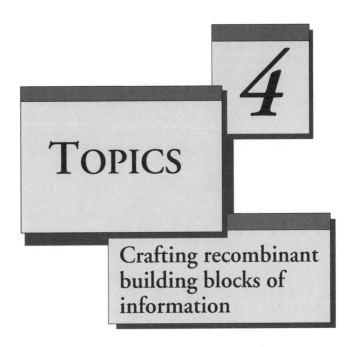

TOPICS

Crafting recombinant building blocks of information

If good online documentation is a question-answering machine, then *topics* are the answers to the user's questions. Creating good topics requires understanding how and when users ask questions and what it takes to answer them.

WHAT ARE TOPICS?

Human beings work best with discrete chunks of information. We can handle only so much at a time. The scope of perception and the capacity of human working memory are limited. We demand clearly defined units of information that we can attend to and understand before moving on to other units of information.

Throughout this book, I have used the term *topic* to refer to just such a unit of information. Other terms are *chunk*, *node*, *module*, *unit*, *piece*, *fragment*, *article*, *block*, *section*, and *card*.

Topics are semantic units representing a concept or thought rather than arbitrary units of presentation (screen, window, frame, page, or panel). A topic is a unit of thought akin to a scene in a play, a shot in a movie, or a third-order heading in a technical manual.

The topic may contain several media elements, including paragraphs of text, step-by-step lists, charts, pictures, animations, sounds, music, and video clips. All of these elements, however, work to answer the same basic question, to make the same point, and to accomplish the same purpose. A topic thus is the unit of information that:

- Fully answers the user's question

- Is read entirely

- Can be accessed individually

- The user thinks of as a unit

Writing a good topic is hard. My experience over dozens of projects is that it takes two to three years for skilled writers of business and technical documents to master the art of designing and creating effective online topics. This chapter outlines some of the things they had to discover.

I find that the learning time is much less for writers trained in modular writing methodologies such as Structured Documentation [284], the STOP (Sequential Thematic Organization of Publications) procedure [281], or Information Mapping® [134].

WHY DISCRETE TOPICS?

Much of our educational system teaches us to write long, flowing passages. Up through the university level, students are instructed to begin by capturing the reader's attention and then to gently lead the reader through prose so silky smooth and seamless that the reader is propelled magically along to the end where the writer delicately and tactfully releases the reader. This model has two problems: It does not work for impatient readers of business and technical information, and it definitely does not work when presenting information in small screens and windows.

People do not read long passages

In business and technical documents—even those on paper—readers seldom read from the beginning to the end. They skim, they scan, they skip, they flip, they hop, they bounce. They jump all over the place.

> Another aspect of the re-definition of writing and writer dictated by online documentation systems is the assault on a central concept of Western culture—the book itself: a linear narrative moving in time, occupying real space, with a beginning, middle, and end [18, p. xv].

Traditional rhetoric decrees that a work have a beginning, middle, and end. But an online help document can have many beginnings, and it ends as soon as the user is satisfied or gives up. The middle is just what occurs in between. If users can read online documents in any order, the writer cannot rely on the user's reading path to provide prerequisite information.

The image of a document as a series of pages or a long continuous scroll where the reader starts at the beginning and continuously reads to the end is inappropriate for online documents. A better model is a table covered with slips of paper over which the reader jumpily searches.

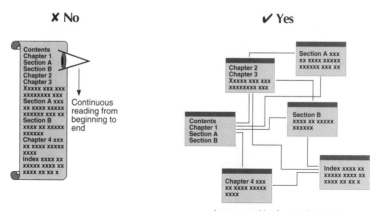

Jumpy searching from topic to topic

The reader of a business document typically starts at the table of contents, scans down to find a heading of interest, flips to that heading in the text, reads a little, discovers it is too specific, flips back to the start of the chapter and begins skimming forward, gets frustrated, jumps to the index, looks up a subject, flips to the first entry for that subject, skims the text there, jumps back to the index and from there to the second entry for the subject, reads a little, finds it too general, scans for a more specific subheading, finds it, reads the text in detail, understands, and is satisfied.

Whether on paper or on screen, business and technical documents are seldom read smoothly from beginning to end.

The myth	The reality
The document appears like scroll or series of pages	The document is more like separate cards or slips of paper
Information read from beginning	Items read in any order the reader finds them
Author determines the order in which ideas are presented	Reader's pattern of searching determines the order
The reader reads all of the document	The reader jumps a lot, scans and skims a little, and reads even less

Online displays are smaller

Online documents typically display the equivalent of one-third of a page at a time. Such tunnel vision blunts reading patterns honed for paper documents. Consider how a user finds information in a technical manual. Pretend our user is looking for information on Command Y, which has two options, A and B. On paper the information about Command Y might appear on a two-page spread with the description of the command and its options on one page and an example of using the command on the facing page.

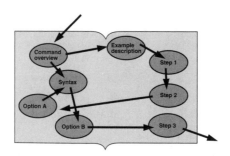

The user might start by glancing at the overview. He or she might then notice the example in peripheral vision and shift to the right-hand page and start reading the example. In reading about Step 2, the user would be instructed to use Option A. The curious user might glance over at the description of this option on the facing page. There he or she might notice the syntax diagram, which lists Option B. The user might then jump down and start reading about Option B before noticing that Option B is used in Step 3 of the example on the facing page. When reading on a two-page spread, our eyes flick back and forth with such effortless freedom that we are seldom conscious of how much our gaze shifts and how many pieces of information we examine.

Let's consider what happens when we put this information online. Now the pieces of information that were spread over the two pages are each a separate topic or appear in a separate window. The user who chooses to read the overview topic sees only the overview. The other topics are invisible. Unless the author of the online document explicitly mentions those other pieces of information, the reader may never know they exist.

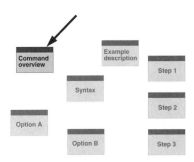

To go to another piece of information, the user must now move a hand to the mouse or keyboard, move the screen pointer to the cross-reference, and select it. This takes a lot more thought and effort than merely moving the eyes. It interrupts the user's thought processes. Now when the chosen topic appears, it replaces the overview. To reread the overview the user must repeat the selection process—yet another interruption.

While reading from paper, the user can quickly move from one piece of information to any other related piece. When reading online, the user can only move along paths expressly enabled by the author and then only with considerable conscious effort. This is why many users liken the experience of reading online documents to reading a newspaper through a toilet-paper tube.

The implications for us as designers are:

- Write discrete topics, not sprawling passages.
- Make each topic as complete as you can. Include or cross-reference all relevant related topics.
- Provide explicit pathways to related pieces of information, especially any necessary to understand the current topic.
- Do not depend on the user reading a long series of topics in a particular order.

HOW TO CREATE A GOOD TOPIC

Because users seldom read long passages online, we must create short, independent, self-contained topics that can be read in the order selected by the user.

Make topics coherent

Effective topics are coherent and clearly focused throughout. The benchmark of a good topic is that it:

- Answers **one** question
- About **one** subject
- For **one** purpose

The question may be general or specific, the subject may be abstract or concrete, and the purpose may be local or global—but all are clearly defined.

The easiest way to ensure coherence in a topic is to first write out the single question the topic is to answer. Then judge every aspect of the design and writing of the topic by whether it helps answer that question. When editing the topic, ask, "Does it answer the question clearly and fully?" When testing topics, observe whether the topic truly answers the user's question without wasted effort or confusion.

Craft recombinant building blocks

No writer can anticipate all the possible ways a user can reach a given topic in an intricately structured online document. How, then, do you design so that the user can start reading anywhere in the document, as if pulling a card from a well-shuffled deck?

Make topics self-contained

Make each independently accessible topic of the document complete in itself. At least ensure that the user who reads one out of sequence is not misled but is clearly directed to missing information. Include enough information for the first-time user to comprehend accurately. To make up for lost context, repeat contextual information each place it is needed and provide links to related information. Phrases like *as we saw above* are dangerous because they presume a single reading path. Make such assumptions explicit.

I like to tell writers to pretend they are writing recipe cards. You can take a stack of recipe cards, toss them in the air, and when you pick them up off the floor, they still make sense. Sorting them out by main ingredient or by which meal they complement will add value to the cards, but they still make sense, no matter in which order you read them.

Write, edit, and review topics in random order. Left to their own devices, well-organized writers will write topics in a very logical order. Unfortunately, they forget that readers will not be reading in such a logical order. Writing topics in random order requires the writer to consider each topic as if it were the first, just the way the user experiences it. Likewise, have reviewers read topics out of order. Otherwise you get comments such as, "You already told them this twelve screens ago." Be sure to explain to reviewers why you are presenting topics out of order.

Keep topics rhetorically neutral

In documents where the writer controls the purpose and order of material, the writer takes a "rhetorical stance" relative to the reader. This stance determines the writer's choice of presentation and style. However, in online documents, writers often cannot predict exactly when and for what purpose the user will read a topic. The user may read Topic A then Topic B and then Topic C at one time for one purpose. The same user may later read Topic C and then Topic B and then Topic A for a different purpose. Because of this unpredictability, writers are often advised to make online topics "rhetorically neutral."

Make fewer presumptions about the user

Take care in what you assume about the reader of a particular topic. Make your topic work for a wide range of assumptions.

- **Degree of interest**. The user may be totally absorbed in the subject matter of the topic, slightly interested, frustrated beyond rational thought, or bored to tears. The subject matter may be exactly what the user wants to know, merely a curiosity, or an annoying distraction.

- **Purpose for reading**. The user may be reading to perform a task immediately, to learn how to perform a task later, to decide whether to perform a task, to see what kind of information the topic contains, or just to pass the time.

- **Prior knowledge**. The user may read this topic before reading any of the topics that present prerequisite or background information.

Avoid stylistic whiplash

Users who lithely jump from topic to topic, scanning and skimming as they go, find arbitrary inconsistencies in style distracting and sometimes confusing. The experience of reading many different styles is called *stylistic whiplash* and is a common complaint about online documentation.

Use a transparent style

A writing style that draws attention to itself burdens an already overloaded reader. In online documents, if the reader notices the style of writing or presentation, that style is suspect. Strive for a simple, professional, transparent style that keeps the user focused on the information you are presenting and not on how you are presenting it. (Chapter 9 makes recommendations for writing style in online documents.)

Eliminate unnecessary material

Because the user never sees the complete document, the writer can include all the topics needed for clarity and completeness. Conciseness, though not necessary at the document level, which the user never sees, is needed in individual topics, which the user does see.

Because screen size is smaller than page size and larger fonts are required for legibility, you must express information in online documents with greater succinctness and brevity than in paper documents. Including potentially useful or merely interesting information in a display increases the time required to search or read the display and further loads the user's memory.

Where possible, trim words or use tables, charts, and graphics to express concepts more compactly and with more interest. Erect bypasses for noncritical, nice-to-know information. Do not waste users' time by telling them all the things they are going to learn, how lucky they are to learn them, and how cleverly you have organized the information. A task-oriented table of contents will suffice.

Most online documents contain too much information, not too little. To detect information that you can omit, remove selected pieces of information and test the effect on users. If the users can complete the same tasks in the same time, then the removed material is not necessary. Or create an optimistic, skimpy first draft and let testing tell you where to add material and where not to.

Do not repeat what the user already knows

An online document should not tell users what they already know. Paper documents can afford the luxury of such verbal throat clearing, but online documents cannot spare the space. Start at the very edge of the user's ignorance. If you assume too much knowledge, the user won't understand the explanation. If you assume too little, you fill the document with useless words. How then can you predict what the user knows? Consider:

- **User's education**. Do not teach users what they already know. You can assume, for example, that mechanical engineers understand concepts of stress and strain and thermodynamics. Graphic designers have a basic knowledge of design grids and layouts and an understanding of measurements in points and picas. You cannot, however, assume that a mechanical engineer will understand points and picas.

- **User's work experience**. If a program replaces a manual procedure, you can usually assume that users are familiar with the manual work procedures. But verify this assumption early into the project. Many companies believe that the computer system contains the skill and expertise necessary to perform the task and that any untrained user can do what used to require skilled technicians. As a result, novice computer users are often expected to master not only the computer system but the manual procedure it automates as well.

- **Previous portions of the program**. Use of a program demonstrates some knowledge of the program. For a message, you can assume the user had the knowledge to take actions to produce this message. For a context-sensitive help system, you can assume the user knows how to get to the context associated with each message.

- **What is visible on the screen**. Don't repeat information that is displayed elsewhere on the screen. Do not tell the user, "The 'Enter first data point' prompt means to enter the first data point" as if adding a definite article would enlighten the befuddled. If icons and menus remain displayed on the screen alongside the help window, why repeat them in the small help window? Instead, refer to them. One system I've seen used arrows in the help window to point to menus on the rest of the screen.

Cross-reference rather than include

In paper documents, we tend to explain each new term, concept, or acronym where it is introduced. In online documents this is not only wasteful, it is dangerous. Online documents are seldom read in a predictable sequence, so there is no way to tell where the user will first encounter a new piece of information. And, with electronic cross-referencing, the user is never more than a button-press away from an explanation. In each online topic cover only one idea. Do not embed related information, but do make it accessible.

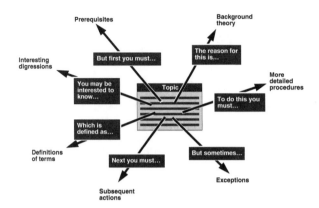

Complete the main idea in each topic

In each topic, answer questions fully. Do not leave the user hanging. Imagine that you jump to a topic whose title suggests that it will answer your question. You read the first scrolling zone of information and it covers the right general subject. You scroll down and read more information. You get more excited because it seems headed in the right direction. You scroll down again and get really excited because the topic seems poised to answer your question. So you hit the scroll-down button and nothing happens. Huh? You try it again before you realize that the reason nothing happens is that you are at the end of the topic. Many users compare this frustration to the feeling they get when they are engrossed in an evening TV drama and "TO BE CONTINUED" comes on the bottom of the screen.

So answer the user's question. Do not leave the user hanging. Sometimes, however, you cannot answer the question fully. The question may be too vague or too complex. In these cases give the user a partial or provisional answer and tell the user how to proceed to fully answer the question.

CHUNKING STRATEGIES

Chunking is the process of dividing information into separate topics. It is one of the most difficult tasks in writing online documents. How large should you make topics? How do you divide a body of information into separate topics?

> One common but subtle difficulty in hypertext systems is that sometimes it's unnatural to break your thoughts into discrete units, particularly if you don't understand the problem well and those thoughts are vague, confused, and shifting [22, p. 260].

In sizing topics, you must balance conflicting needs. With small topics, users can access specific facts and writers can combine topics in more ways. On the other hand, large topics simplify the design and make navigating among topics easier. Also, a few larger topics generally display faster than many small topics. Dividing a subject into discrete topics is as much art as science and requires compromise and judgment.

Common chunking strategies

There are two main strategies for chunking information into topics. With a *fixed-size* strategy, you make all topics about the same size—usually the size of a paper page or of a computer screen or window. In a *variable-size* strategy, you let the size of the topic vary to fit the content of the topic.

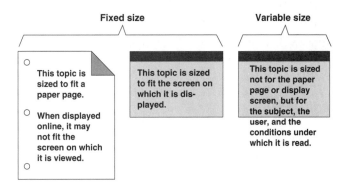

Size online topics to fit paper pages

Putting the equivalent of one paper page into each online topic may seem silly at first—and it *is* often a silly idea—but there are cases where this strategy has merit.

- **When converting one-page-per-item paper documents**. Existing paper documents are often organized with one unit of information per page. Catalogs and technical reference manuals frequently use this structure. Many computer command references allot one paper page per command. On many versions of the Unix operating system, for example, the help document consists of *man pages*, which started out as individual pages in paper manuals.

- **For documents that will be read from paper**. In many hybrid online-paper systems, users search for information online and then print it out before reading it in detail. In these cases, it makes sense to format the online display to resemble the eventual paper pages.

- **For users familiar with the layout of paper pages**. Frequent users of a paper document often learn the page layout of heavily referenced pages. Chunking information as paper pages can preserve the spatial layout such users depend on.

Provided the chunks are meaningful units of information and not arbitrary divisions of an ongoing flow, chunking to fit paper pages is not dangerous. Page-sized chunks are usually more than most people will read online, however. If creating page-sized topics, make sure users are well motivated to read and get to the point early in the topic, not at the end.

Size online topics to fit a screen or window

There are definite advantages to sizing all topics to fit entirely in a single screen or window. The user does not have to scroll down to read all of the topic. The display does not waste space on a scroll bar or next-screen buttons.

This strategy works well in products for children and novices. Information kiosks and CBT lessons for beginners cannot rely on the user knowing how to scroll the display.

Let the size vary

Often you have no choice but to let the size of topics vary and to provide ways for users to scroll or page through all of the topic. Variable-sized topics are necessary when:

- **Units of information vary widely in size**. Life does not always come in evenly sized chunks. In the *Oxford English Dictionary,* the shortest entry is 5 words long and the longest is 250,000 words long. Some parts of a product are simple while others are complex.

- **The display size is unknown**. The designer of the document may have no control over the size of display. Users may have screens of different sizes. If the document appears in a resizable window, the user can resize and reshape that window to fit in with other windows on the screen.

How much can you include?

Make topics long enough to answer the user's question but short enough so that the user will actually read the topic.

Resist arbitrary limits

Size topics to best accomplish your purposes. Beware of arbitrary limits on the length of topics.

- **Challenge editorial standards**. At least, question editorial rules. I have seen one rule that limited the length of topics to seven paragraphs and another that decreed no topic may exceed 60 words in length. All of these rules have their place, but you must ask whether they are valid in your particular situation.

- **Don't write to fill the hole**. On one online project, writers who reviewed their drafts in page-sized printouts consistently produced page-sized topics. When printouts were changed to the length of a single scrolling zone, the average size of topics dropped to about one-third of a page.

- **Break old habits**. Often, we write out of habit. Writers accustomed to writing large-format paper manuals tend to write longer online topics than do newspaper reporters. Shorter still are the topics written by those experienced in preparing slides and overhead transparencies.

- **Remove software limits**. Topic size sometimes depends on the tools you use. In the Rexx project, for example, limitations of the authoring tool forced designers to split some topics and combine others to fit within the limits of 200 articles per document and 10,500 characters per article [165]. Ensure that your software does not impose arbitrary limits on the size, number, or organization of topics.

Size for the purpose of the topic

Limit the amount of information in each topic and display, depending on the audience, the difficulty of the material, and the conditions under which it will be read.

Size for the user

How much can and will the user read? That depends on who the user is. A document for children must present small topics of a single simple concept. Topics for adults can be longer. Someone with good reading skills can handle longer topics than someone with poorer skills or someone who reads in a language other than their first. A novice user will be burdened by just navigating through the online document and will have less attention or working memory to apply to understanding a topic. For such a novice, topics should present one idea at a time. On the other hand, a training program for an expert computer user on basic system commands may include several related commands in a step.

Size for the material

Some kinds of information divide naturally into small, simple chunks. Other kinds of information seem a hopeless tangle of related facts.

It is often tempting to chunk information by repeatedly dividing a subject to get it to the small size that the writer, reader, and computer can easily handle. Seymour Papert warns against this "balkanization of teaching with computers" [203, p. 180], that is, the unnatural division and subdivision of knowledge into small, easily taught recipes for performing elementary tasks.

Knowledge is more than a collection of facts; it also involves seeing connections and understanding trends and themes. Viewing separate displays, the user must struggle to infer and understand the relationships among them. Complex subjects may require larger and more complex topics than simpler subjects.

Size for the reading conditions

The user's reading span depends on the conditions under which he or she reads. Topics that can be read leisurely in a quiet setting can be longer than those that must be read in a noisy setting during a crisis.

- **Noise.** Is the user reading in a noisy environment with frequent interruptions and continual distractions? Or is the reader in a quiet, private office with the phone off the hook and soothing music playing? The noisier the environment, the shorter the topic must be.

- **Stress.** What is the user's state of mind while reading this topic? Calm and relaxed? Or anxious and pressured? Topics on troubleshooting and problem-solving are typically read only after the user is thoroughly frustrated and angry. Make topics shorter if they are read during stressful situations.

- **Pace.** Can the user take as long as necessary to read the topic? Or is the user required to read, understand, and respond to the topic immediately? Size the topic to the time available for reading it.

Design topics for convenient display

Topic size also depends on the display size and format. Divide information into easily scanned chunks. Do not make users search for information in long displayed passages. Having to repeatedly scroll down or flip to the next frame to find an answer is a symptom of a poorly structured document. This is why you must often redivide information that has been organized for paper pages. In preparing the 45 reference manuals for the RISC System/6000 to go online, IBM restructured the information to produce smaller, more modular topics—more like encyclopedia articles than book chapters [64].

Sizing for convenient authoring

The needs of the author should never come before the needs of the user of the on-line document, but do consider the effect of topic size on the productivity and sanity of authors. My experience is that it is better to start out with topics larger than seem ideal. This reduces the number of separate topics and links the author must create and manage. It also gives you time to test these topics to see which ones really are too large and how they should be divided.

Rules of thumb

In designing topics, I apply two rules of thumb: First, each topic can contain the equivalent of one-third to one-fifth of a paper page. Experience with a number of conversion efforts found that each page could contain three to five online topics [10, 291].

Second, users will read no more than three windows or screens of information to answer a question [229].

"Ah ha! Got ya!" you think. "How does computer-based training ever work if nobody reads more than three screens?" The answer to that question puzzled me until I noticed what skillful CBT authors do. They trick the student into asking a new question every screen or two. In essence, they remotivate the user.

WHAT GOES INTO A TOPIC?

Creating a topic requires more than writing the words or drawing the pictures that appear to the user. To author a topic, you have to provide three kinds of information:

- **Content**. The words, pictures, and other media the user experiences when reading the topic. Content includes the title, introduction, and body of the topic.
- **Meta-info**. Information about the topic. This is the information that is used by the developer of the topic to plan, specify, and track the topic but that the end user may never see.
- **Access aids**. Ways to get to this topic from elsewhere and ways to get to related topics from this one.

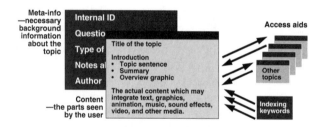

Content

The content of a topic is what the user experiences when the topic is displayed. The content comprises the words, sounds, and pictures that answer the user's question. It includes the body as well as the introduction and title of the topic.

Body

In deciding the content of a topic, consider the kinds of questions a user might ask or the ways a user might want to receive information. Does the user need a definition, a picture, a procedure, an example, advice, rules, exceptions, or sources of additional information?

With the advent of multimedia computers, we can often include more than just printed words in online documents. Online documents can now include displayed and spoken words, static and moving pictures, music, sounds, animation, and video. Just because you can include a media element, though, does not mean you should. We must include "appropriate" elements, that is, those that help answer the question by providing information or by motivating the user. Omit media elements that merely draw attention to themselves. Here are some recommendations.

Question	Words	Graphics	Other media
How do I _____?	Numbered list of steps	Pictures of each step	Animation or video showing procedure
			Procedure spoken aloud
When do I _____?	List of conditions	Picture of condition recognized visually	Sound of triggering condition
			Video or animation of pattern of motion
What is _____?	Definition	Pictures of examples	Moving pictures of item in action

Question	Words	Graphics	Other media
What's wrong?	Explanation of problem Procedure for fixing it	Diagram of problem Flowchart for troubleshooting	Animation of conflict Video of corrective procedure
Why did _____ happen?	Explanation	Diagram or flowchart	Animation of actions causing results
How does _____ work?	Explanation	Annotated picture, diagram, or flowchart	Narrated animation or video
Which is better?	Table comparing alternatives Procedure for comparing List of criteria	Chart comparing	Video of performance tests
Why do _____?	Explanation of purpose, goals, results List of benefits	Picture of desired results	Animation or video of results Video testimonial
Why not do _____?	List of costs, risks, difficulties	Picture of undesirable results	Animation video of undesirable results
Why believe _____?	Evidence Rationale	Visual evidence	Sound or video providing evidence Video of authority saying so
How else can I _____?	List of alternatives	Pictures of alternatives	Animation, video, or sound of alternative procedures
How are _____ and _____ related?	Statement of relationship Table comparing	Picture making relationship apparent Diagram of relationship	Animation showing dynamic relationship
Why is _____?	Conceptual explanation List of reasons	Diagram of reasons	Animation showing conceptual basis
Where is _____?	Explanation of how to find it	Map or picture with item highlighted	Animation or video zooming in on item

Question	Words	Graphics	Other media
What does _____ contain?	Simple list of parts	Picture of parts	Sound recording of its sounds Animation or video of its motions
How is _____ organized?	Indented list of components	Organization chart Exploded parts diagram Block diagram	Animation or video of assembly and disassembly
What can I do with _____?	List of uses	Picture of potential results	Video case studies of successful uses
What do I do next?	Procedure (Link via Next button)	Picture of step	Animation or video of step
What must I do first?	List of prerequisites (Link via Previous button)	Picture of prerequisites	Animation or video of prerequisites
How do I recognize _____?	List of characteristics	Picture pointing out visual characteristics	Sound or video of recognizable features
What happens if _____?	Explanation of results	Picture of results	Sound recording, animation or video showing results
Is _____ true?	Confirmation or denial Procedure for testing hypothesis	Picture of true and false conditions	Sound or video recording of true and false conditions

Chapters 9, 10, and 11 present guidelines on designing various media elements included in a topic.

Introduction

The *introduction* is a concise graphic or brief paragraph that prepares the user for the content of the topic. It tells what the topic is about and lets the user decide whether it is relevant to the task at hand [89].

Most users will read the title of a topic, look at its pictures, and scan a sentence or two of the introduction before deciding whether to continue reading or to move on. Even with the need to keep topics short, a brief introduction is more than an unnecessary luxury. In general, if a topic is longer than one screen or scrolling zone, a *brief* introduction can make it more effective.

- **Provide a smooth transition**. If users are jumping from topic to topic, they may find the going rocky. A brief introduction can smooth out the jumps by providing a transition into the content of the topic rather than jumping right in. Think about how often you begin a paragraph or a sentence with a transitional phrase, such as, "For example" or "On the other hand." Writing a transition for a topic is more difficult because we often do not know where the user is coming from. In these cases, we have to provide a generic transition that relates the title of the topic to the content.

- **Put the topic in context**. In each topic, clearly establish the context. Make clear what question is being answered [251]. Introductions in online documents must communicate a greater "global awareness," that is, a perspective and context that makes clear how the current topic fits into the overall document or library of documents [19].

- **Let the user decide whether to read the topic**. Make the meaning and importance of a topic obvious so that the user can quickly decide whether to read or skip it. The first thing a user wants to know upon arriving at a topic is "Does this topic answer my question?" Do not make users read the entire topic to find out it does not. Let them back out of the topic while they are still motivated to continue the search elsewhere. The introduction should also make prerequisites explicit [251].

- **Present the gist of the subject**. A well-crafted introduction can provide a concise summary of the full content of the topic. Such a summary may fully satisfy an experienced user who is reading to verify a fact or to refresh a recollection.

- **Prepare the user to understand**. If the content is at all complex, the introduction should prepare the novice reader to understand it. Such an introduction serves as an "advance organizer" to alert users on what the topic contains and give them a framework to understand what will be presented.

Note how this topic introduces its subject, relates it to other topics, and provides enough information for the user to decide whether to read the entire topic:

```
Send Global Delayed

Send Global Delayed, like other Send Global commands,
broadcasts a message to all users on the network, but
does so only when the network is not busy, typically at
night. Use the Send Global Delayed command . . . .
```

There are several ways to introduce a topic:

Graphical overview

Probably the most popular introduction is a picture. A user of one online document with graphical overviews for all topics said, "I like using this system because whenever I call up a new topic I'm rewarded with a picture." But graphical overviews can do more than please users, they can show at a glance how separate pieces of information are related.

Some examples of a graphical overview include:

• Organization chart showing how the subject is organized

• Syntax diagram for a command in a programming or macro language

• Picture showing procedure

Elaborate the title

If the title is just a name or brief phrase, the introduction may restate it as a complete sentence.

Title	Introduction
SendDelayed	The SendDelayed command sends your mail message at a later time.
Customizing environment	You can tailor your work environment to suit your needs.
Defaults	Defaults are the settings used by commands when you leave a setting blank.

The elaboration should clarify the title and make clear the kind of information the topic contains. It should not merely repeat the title, as in

```
SendDelayed     SendDelayed send message after a delay.
```

Summary of the content

Another style of introduction provides a brief preview of the contents of the topic. Before plunging into a detailed step-by-step procedure that may span several scrolling zones, give the user a one-sentence summary, for example:

```
To copy a file, select its icon and chose the Copy
command from the Edit menu.
```

Such a succinct summary may be all that an experienced user needs. For the novice, it gives an overview of the entire procedure, combating the tunnel-vision effect of seeing only one step at a time.

Another way to summarize is to list the components of the topic. A simple bullet or indented list will usually suffice. However, if your topic is so complex that it requires an indented list to describe, perhaps you should divide your topic into multiple topics.

Title

At the top of every topic include a concise title that tells the user what the topic contains and lets the user gauge the aptness of a topic and decide immediately whether to continue reading it. Titles are especially important in online documents because the user must frequently select a particular topic from a list of topic titles. Unless such titles clearly and accurately represent the content of the topic, the user wastes time examining irrelevant topics.

Make titles context free

Don't depend on the topic or other surrounding information to make sense of the name. The title may appear in an index, in a list of retrieved topics, or in a list of cross-references. Without the body of the topic to clarify a context-dependent title, the user cannot easily decide which topic to select.

In the command reference manual for a certain programming language, each command was listed in 60-point type at the top of the page. Each page also contained headings such as Syntax, Options, and Examples. On paper these headings were clear because the name of the command was always present in peripheral vision at the top of the page. When the document was converted to online documentation, each heading became a separate topic. There were 350 topics titled *Syntax*, 350 titled *Options*, and 350 titled *Examples*.

Make titles understandable

Phrase titles so users, even novices, can understand them. Use standard grammar and terms meaningful to the user. Forgo jargon and unnecessary technical terms. Unless space is tight, do not write in a telegraphic style that omits articles, punctuation, and other small words.

✗ No	✔ Yes
SortRecing data	Sorting the records
Copy file disk tape	Copying files from a disk to a tape cartridge

Make titles scannable

Make the meaning of the title obvious in a glance without further reading. Often users must scan a list of titles and quickly select the one that answers their question. Phrase titles so that they can do this without excessive eye movement and rereading. One of the best ways to make titles scannable is to put the most important words at the front of the title. Such front-loaded titles can usually be scanned in a single vertical eye movement.

✗ No	✔ Yes
How to copy a file	Copying files
How to copy a directory	Copying directories
How to move a file	Moving files
How to move a directory	Moving directories

Each topic should have a unique name. In any list of topics, the user should clearly see the differences between titles and hence topics. Too-similar names can prove confusing to users. Remember, users tend to select titles that promise specific answers to their questions.

Make titles thematic

Have the title summarize or preview the topic. *Thematic titles* summarize the topic and prepare the user to notice its key points. They also suggest how the user is to interact with the display. For instance, the title "Creating a new job ticket" tells users that they will learn to create a job ticket and prepares them for step-by-step instructions.

Meta-information

Meta-information is information about the topic. It is usually not seen by the reader of the topic. It is the information of interest to the author of the topic and the manager of the online documentation project. It includes the specifics about the topic, its revision history, and identification number. Meta-information may be stored in the same file as the contents of the topic but is more often stored in a separate project-management database.

Question to answer

Before specifying the content of the topic, record exactly what question the topic is to answer. This question becomes the standard against which you judge the design of the topic. Every element must contribute to answering this question. What is the user's goal in reading a topic? Does the user want to recall a name, apply a rule, follow a procedure, solve a problem, or understand a concept?

Internal ID

The *internal ID* is a number or code unique to the topic. Unlike the title, it does not change as the topic is rewritten or translated. This internal identifier may be assigned automatically by the authoring tool or may be assigned by a human author. The internal identifier may also be the name of the file containing the content of the topic.

Systems that reference topics solely by name fail when someone renames referenced topics. For this reason most systems internally refer to topics by some hidden identification number that does not change when the topic is renamed or translated to a foreign language.

If you are assigning a code, try to make it understandable by the author and project manager. Ideally, the author should be able to guess the title of the topic from the code. Usually the best way to achieve this is to make the ID reflect the type of question being answered (how to, when to, why), the category of the item being discussed (procedure, menu, form), or the name of the specific item. For example:

Title	Identifier
Copying files	proc_cop_fil
Moving files	proc_mov_fil
Deleting files	proc_del_fil
Form for copying files	form_cop_fil
Menu for copying files	menu_cop_fil
Commands for copying files	comm_cop_fil

Whatever scheme you use, set up and zealously enforce conventions for assigning IDs.

Topic type

Topics come in two varieties: typed and untyped. *Typed* topics are categorized by type and can contain only a particular kind of information; *untyped* topics can contain any kind of information.

Typed topics can make documents more predictable as users learn what kind of information to expect in each type of topic. Allowing different types of topics, however, increases the number of concepts the user must learn [5] and forces the writer to fit all ideas into an existing set of concepts [22].

In general, use typed topics for special-purpose systems where users can take advantage of them. For example, the gIBIS system, developed to support collaborative design projects, contains three kinds of typed topics: *issues* (the question designers want to answer); *positions* (proposals or opinions on how to resolve the issue); and *arguments* (reasons for a position) [22]. Xerox NoteCards provides 50 specific types of topics.

Type topics by the question they answer. For each type of topic, create a template or style sheet that specifies the content and style of presentation appropriate for that type of topic. Make the type of topic clear to the user. Give each type of topic a distinctive icon, graphic design, and phrasing of title ("How to . . ." vs. "Why should I ...").

Position in reading sequence

If you are designing clusters of topics or encouraging users to read a series of topics, record whether a topic is one the user is likely to encounter when first entering the document, while following a trail of topics, or at the end of a trail just before leaving the document. Although you may not completely control how users read the document, knowing likely reading patterns will help the author design the topic.

If the topic is the . . .	Then make it . . .
start of a reading trail	present a preview or overview of the trail
middle of a reading trail	develop a new idea consistent with preceding and following topics on the trail
end of a reading trail	summarize or recap the reading trail

You may also need to identify valid contexts for the topic. Specify for what users and situations the topic will provide useful information. A topic could have different names in different contexts.

Chapter 6 provides more advice on designing topic clusters and reading trails.

Audit trail

Online documentation projects can be quite complex, involving hundreds or thousands of topics. You will need to record information necessary for scheduling and budgeting topic development. For each topic, consider recording such items as:

- **Accounts**. Charge for the author and media specialists' time.
- **Costs**. Include both budgeted and accumulated.
- **Schedule**. Include milestones, due dates, and deadlines.
- **Security restrictions**. Specify who can modify, delete, and examine this topic.
- **Author**. List who created and modified the topic, and who is currently responsible.
- **Dates**. Show when the topic was created, last modified, issued, approved.
- **Version**. State the current revision level.

On a small project, tracking such details may seem a waste of time, but on a project with 250 topics or 2,500 topics, determining who should revise or rewrite a topic is a serious concern. For multimedia documents, you will want to record similar details for all text, graphics, animations, music, sound effects, video clips, and other media elements.

Access aids

Access aids help the user find the correct topic. They are the parts of a topic that direct the user to *this* topic from elsewhere and point the user from this topic to related topics.

Keywords

Many systems let users retrieve topics by typing in *keywords* that describe the content of the topic but may not actually occur in the text of the topic. For example, you may have a topic that mentions gold, copper, silver, and iron but does not contain the word *metal*. By assigning the keyword *metal* to this topic, you let users retrieve it using the word *metal* even though that word does not appear in the topic itself. For instructions on assigning keywords, see page 279.

Cross-references to this topic

The value of a topic is partly in the number of topics that can cross-reference it. A topic helps answer questions not solely by its content but by how it makes other topics comprehensible and valuable. While authoring a topic, maintain a checklist of other topics that should cross-reference this topic. Ask yourself: In what other topics will the user form the question answered by this topic? Ensure that these other topics provide links to this one.

List of related topics

You cannot include everything every reader might need to know. You can, however, provides links to much more information than is contained in the topic. When writing a topic, list other topics containing information relevant to the reader of the current topic. List the topics that provide information that you considered including but did not, such as:

- More detailed versions of the information in the current topic
- Background theory and prerequisite concepts
- Previous and following steps in a procedure or process
- Other ways of doing the same thing explained in this topic
- Definitions of terms used in this topic

Take care when you present these cross-references. Presenting cross-references too early can tempt users to jump before understanding where they are jumping from. Putting cross-references too late, especially if not in the first scrolling zone, can cause users to ignore potentially useful links.

PUTTING THESE IDEAS TO WORK

Essential ideas of this chapter

➥ Write small, self-contained modules, not long, flowing passages.

➥ Make each topic fully answer one question but keep it short enough that users will read all of it.

➥ Size the topic to the complexity of the subject, the experience and motivation of the user, and the tranquility of reading conditions. In general, put about one-third to one-fifth of a page of information in each topic.

➥ Cross-reference rather than include nonessential information.

➥ Start by deciding what question the topic answers. Design the content, title, and all other components with that question in mind.

For more ideas and inspiration

Barrett, Edward, ed. 1988. *Text, ConText, and HyperText: Writing with and for the Computer.* Cambridge, MA: MIT Press.

Bolter, Jay David. 1991. *Writing Space: The Computer, Hypertext, and the History of Writing.* Hillsdale, NJ: Lawrence Erlbaum Associates.

Horn, Robert. 1989. *Mapping Hypertext: Analysis, Linkage, and Display of Knowledge for the Next Generation of On-Line Text and Graphics.* Lexington, MA: Lexington Institute.

Shneiderman, Ben and Greg Kearsley. 1989. *Hypertext Hands On!: An Introduction to a New Way of Organizing and Accessing Information.* Reading, MA: Addison-Wesley.

Weiss, Edmond H. 1991. *How to Write Usable User Documentation.* Phoenix, AZ: Oryx.

LINKS

5

Informational pathways

Links are the highways, back roads, and sidewalks of information. With the click of a mouse or press of a button, the user of an online document can select a link to summon new information. Links present an opportunity to stop reading in one place and resume reading somewhere else in the document or in some other document. But links do more than provide pathways from topic to topic. They show relationships and unite separate topics. They let users interact with the document.

WHY CREATE LINKS?

Links take time to create, use up computer memory and storage, and can prove distracting to the user. So, why create them? Let's look at some practical reasons to put links in your online documents.

Show relationships

Links weave topics into a fabric of ideas. They represent relationships among separate concepts. They combat the fragmentation of information that occurs when ideas are fit into many separate topics.

Every link defines a specific relationship between the topics it connects. It may show that Topic B is a subtopic of Topic A and that Topic C is an alternative to Topic A. As such, links represent information, just as do topics. Links let the author express concepts that cannot fit into a simple modular topic. Weaving topics together into patterns and clusters is sometimes called *writing in the large* because it is how the author of a document expresses large strategic issues. The reader of a document without links is left to infer the relationships among many separate pieces of information. With links, the relationships are made clear.

Connect related facts

Links can tie together related facts from different parts of a document. Often documents are partitioned into different types of information. Sometimes the user needs one kind of information, sometimes another. And often the user needs both. Consider an example. Computer documentation is commonly of two types: task- and feature-oriented. A t*ask-oriented* document provides instructions for commonly performed tasks. It tells users how to do what they want to do. *Feature-oriented* documentation tells what the product can do. It typically describes the individual capabilities of the product such as its commands, menus, messages, and so forth.

Many users need both types. Task-oriented documents help users get started performing common procedures. However, creative users frequently want to do more than just the procedures documented. They need to use additional options and to combine capabilities in new ways. These users need feature-oriented documents. With links, you can provide both types and cross-reference them.

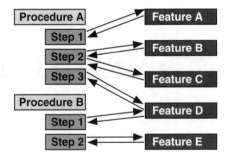

Cross-reference how-to-do-it information with how-it-works information so each can elaborate the other as needed [50]. In steps of task-oriented procedures, cross-reference the commands or other features used in those steps. Users following a procedure can select such a link to see what else they can do or investigate alternative approaches. Users can adapt an almost-right procedure to make it work in their unique situation. The reader of the feature-oriented description can follow a link to satisfy a craving to see how the feature is used in a realistic procedure. Each type of documentation can be the best of its type, and the user can find the other type of information when needed.

Links can connect other types of information. These cross-reference links are handy in connecting:

Overview	↔	Details
Tools	↔	Procedures using tools
Elementary procedures	↔	Complex procedures using the elementary procedures
Facts	↔	Commentary on the facts
Defaults	↔	Options
Simplest way	↔	Most powerful way

Cope with scatter

Scatter is a problem that occurs when a subject is discussed in several different locations in a document or separate documents. Rather than occurring in one digestible chunk, essential facts may be scattered throughout a library.

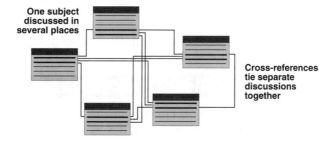

Scatter is a problem in paper documents but is worse online. With paper documents, much of the scatter occurs across a two-page spread. Headings, graphics, and formatted text are usually sufficient to attract the scanning eye to all of the pieces of information on a subject. When the same information appears online, the separate pieces may reside in different topics. Links can connect such topics so users can find all of them.

Share topics

Links let topics appear at more than one place in the document. Rather than repeat information needed in different locations in the document, you write it once and link it wherever it is needed. Sharing topics reduces the number of topics you must create, ensures consistency, saves disk storage space, and makes documents easier to update.

In this example, a topic is shared between two clusters of topics. To readers of Cluster A, the topic appears part of Cluster A. To readers of Cluster B, the topic appears part of Cluster B.

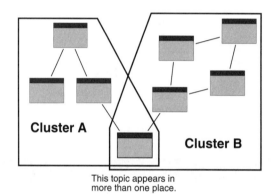

This topic appears in
more than one place.

Candidates for shared topics include these kinds of information:

- Elementary procedures repeated as parts of more complex procedures

- Conventions and policies that apply widely

- Warnings and cautions repeated throughout the document

Design flexible organizations

The ability to connect topics lets authors create hypertext. It gives authors total freedom in organizing documents. No longer is the author limited by the word-by-word, page-by-page, scene-by-scene restrictions of other media. Hypertext will, it is claimed, "break the 'linear straightjacket' of ink on paper" [57, p. 271]. Links let the writer express the nonlinear aspects of a body of information that are now imperfectly represented by rhetorical devices such as cross-references, sidebar articles, digressions, parenthetical remarks, flashbacks, bibliographic citations, glossary terms, footnotes, hierarchies of headings, numbered headings, tables, and boxed warnings. With links you can shape the document to fit the information instead of forcing information into an arbitrary structure.

Give users more paths to information

Links give users more paths to information. Users can move in any direction they feel appropriate in their quest for information. They can follow up on an interesting point, look up a definition, check a bibliographic reference, or see a contrasting viewpoint. They are free to navigate what Geri Younggren calls "n-dimensional information space" [294].

Links allow for different levels of background knowledge and let users adopt their own learning strategy. When users use links to explore related information, they learn more from online than from paper documents [218].

Links put the user in control. They give users choices as to how to read documents and make the experience of using the document more like playing a videogame than reading a textbook.

LINKS IN PAPER DOCUMENTS

Links are not unique to hypertext and online documents, but are common in paper documents as well. In fact, much of this chapter could be applied to designing paper documents. In creating online documents, it is important to understand the kinds of links in comparable paper documents. Users are familiar with these links and will expect to find them in the online equivalents of their favorite paper documents.

Some links are explicitly marked and have exact boundaries. We can tell precisely where they begin and end. Some examples of explicit and exact links include:

- Page references in the index, table of contents, list of figures, or list of tables
- Footnote references
- *See also* . . .
- *See* Figure XX
- Bibliographic references
- Hierarchy of headings

These are easy to convert to online links. In fact, products such as SmarText by Lotus do just that [216].

Other links are implied but not stated directly. Often the beginning, end, or relationship expressed by such an implied link is fuzzy. These implicit and loose links include:

- Sidebars or secondary articles that appear on the same page or on a facing page as the main article
- Phrases like *as shown above* or *will be explained later*
- A general policy of defining technical terms in a glossary
- Proximity on a two-page spread, or putting things close together on a page

These links require more work to convert to online links because all online links must be explicit. One handy way to gauge the amount of rewriting and redesign necessary to convert paper documents is to compare the number of explicit and exact links to the number of implicit and loose links. Unless almost all links are explicit and exact, the conversion effort will involve much redesign and rewriting.

SCOPE OF LINKS

Think of a link as an arrow pointing from one unit of information to another. You could draw it as an arrow connecting two circles. The circle at one end shows what the link points from and the one at the other end what it points to.

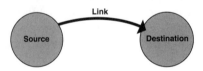

The from end is called the *source* and the to end is the *destination*. The size of each circle is its *scope*. The scope can be a whole topic, a block within a topic, or a single point within a topic.

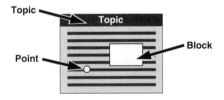

What do we mean by these units?

Unit	Description	Examples
Topic	The entire topic, not just a part of the topic	All the words, pictures, and sounds of the topic
Block	Part of a topic	A paragraph or passage of text
	Blocks may vary in length, overlap, nest inside one another, mix media, and drape over screen boundaries	A complex graphic or an area in a graphic A passage of music or a series of sounds
Point	An indivisible element of information	A word or phrase
		Name of a person or thing
		A simple graphic, such as an icon or a part of a larger graphic
		A frame or short segment in a video or animation sequence

Do not confuse the scope of the source of the link with the size of the link's trigger. The *trigger* is the icon or phrase the user selects to activate the link. It may or may not indicate the full extent or scope of the link. A link that refers from a whole topic cannot easily use the whole topic as a trigger, not if the author wants to include any other links within that topic.

Point-to-topic links

Point-to-topic links are the most common form of links. Most hypertext, presentation graphics, and computer-based training packages let authors create point-to-topic links.

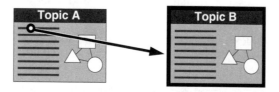

Such links relate an individual item to a whole topic about just that item. They are especially helpful for zooming in on more detailed information. For example:

Point	Topic
Word →	Definition
Item in picture →	Explanation or enlargement
Name of a person →	Biography
Mention of a tool →	Details on that tool
Item in a list →	Details on the items

Topic-to-topic links

In *topic-to-topic* links, everything in the destination relates to everything in the current topic. Topic-to-topic links are quite common. They are usually triggered from buttons or icons around the border of the window displaying the topic.

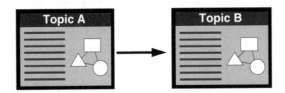

Topic-to-topic links let users:

- Follow a sequential trail of links (next, previous, back, first, last) that connect events in chronological sequence, such as the steps of a procedure or process

- Compare and contrast objects or concepts

- Navigate to common reference topics: home, top, menu, index

- Consider alternatives, contradictory arguments, and other ways of doing the same thing

- Jump to sibling topics, that is, other topics that are subtopics of the same parent topic

Point-to-block links

Point-to-block links refer the reader to a block inside a topic rather than to the whole topic.

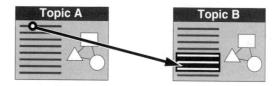

Why not make the block a separate topic? The cited information may not be important enough to warrant a topic of its own, or too few people may need to refer to it. The block may not be independent enough to stand alone. Many users may need to see it in context to understand it fully. Any of these reasons may compel us to refer to a block within another topic.

Some examples of point-to-block links include:

- Term linked to an explanation of that term in context

- Part of a graphic linked to a paragraph of text explaining that part

- Word linked to a definition within a one-topic glossary. Seeing other words that start with the same letters may prove helpful to the user looking up the definition of a particular term.

- Bibliographic citation linked to the full reference in a citation list. The user may benefit from seeing other references, especially those by the same author.

Jumping into the middle of a topic has risks. The user may become disoriented. An inexperienced user may not fully understand the context of the information cited [251], especially if users cannot tell what part of the information is cited or where it occurs in a larger unit. This is especially difficult if the start of the topic is not visible in the window.

Point-to-point links

Point-to-point links connect one small item to another. They can connect individual words, phrases, icons, or other elements.

Point-to-point links are often used to connect multiple occurrences of an item:

- Images of a part that occurs in multiple diagrams

- All mentions of a person or occurrences of a character in a work of fiction
- All usages of a particular command or tool

Point-to-point links are often generated by search mechanisms that find a particular word or phrase in text. Such mechanisms often provide a button or command to let users quickly flip from one occurrence of the word or phrase to the next occurrence and the next and the next. This trail of occurrences is really a series of point-to-point links. However, linking all occurrences of a word can lead to so many links that they clutter screens and bog down the system [216].

Block-to-topic links

Like point-to-topic links, *block-to-topic* links let users zoom in for more information on an item in the current topic. A user can select a paragraph or graphic, for example, and immediately see a whole topic on the same subject.

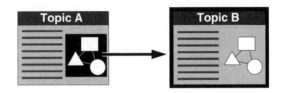

Some examples of block-to-topic links:

Block		Topic
Step in a procedure	→	More detailed version, perhaps including substeps
Subsystem in a diagram	→	Enlargement of that subsystem so that its components and subcomponents are clearly visible
Mention of an event	→	Cause of that event
Passage in music, animation, or video	→	Commentary on that passage
Mention of a problem	→	Remedy

Block-to-block links

Block-to-block links connect individual paragraphs, graphics, or segments of complete topics.

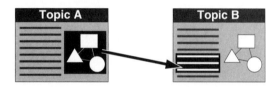

Block-to-block links most often connect multiple occurrences of blocks of information. These may be blocks that provide secondary or supporting information for the topics that contain them. Or they may be blocks that have no meaning out of context. Blocks that occur over and over again include common:

- Warnings and cautions
- Notes and tips
- Illustrations
- Reference tables

Block-to-block links are also useful for connecting something shown in one topic but explained in another or vice versa.

Block-to-point links

Block-to-point links are the opposite of point-to-block links and serve mirror-image purposes. Block-to-point links are for zooming out and shifting context at the same time. They are rarely necessary.

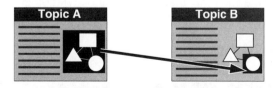

Topic-to-point links

Topic-to-point links let the user zoom out for a broader view of a subject. They are the opposite of point-to-topic links.

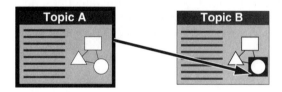

Some uses include these:

Topic		Point
Part	→	Whole
Subtopic	→	Parent topic
Local information	→	Global view
Details about an item	→	Overview of that item in context

Topic-to-block links

Topic-to-block links are for zooming out but not so much as with topic-to-point links.

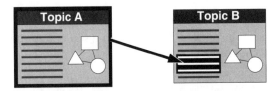

Use topic-to-block links to:

- Jump to where the subject of the current topic is discussed (not just mentioned) in another topic

- Connect a topic to a summary that recaps it along with others

- Show where a concept applies

DIRECTION OF LINKS

A link is like a street. On some streets traffic flows in one direction only. On other streets traffic flows both ways. Links, likewise, can be one- or two-way pathways. This simple distinction between one-way and two-way links seems to cause more confusion than almost any other issue about designing links, not because it is hard to understand, but because systems and writers have been inconsistent in how they apply the terms *one-way* and *two-way* to links. Here's how the terms are used in this book.

Definitions (of a sort)

Here, a *one-way* link from Topic A to Topic B means that in Topic A the user will find a link trigger that can be selected to jump to Topic B. A *link trigger* is an icon, button, or highlighted word selected to jump to the destination. After jumping to Topic B, the user does not see an identical link trigger to return to A.

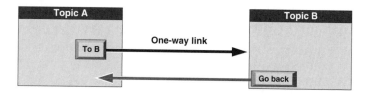

Here's where the confusion starts. The one-way link does not mean that the user is forever stranded in Topic B with no way to get back. Most systems provide a generic Back command that takes the user back to the previously viewed topic. Creating a one-way link does not mean that users cannot travel the link in both directions, only that they must go down it the forward direction before they can return in the opposite direction. One-way links thus imply a strong sense of direction that two-way links do not [204].

What then are two-way links? A *two-way* link has a link trigger on each end to take the user to the opposite end of the link. A two-way link between Topic A and Topic B would put a link trigger in Topic A to take the user to Topic B and another link trigger in Topic B to take the user to topic A.

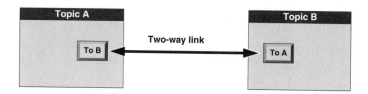

Two-way links appear like two one-way links pointing in opposite directions. On most systems the user cannot tell the difference between a two-way link and two one-way links pointing in opposite directions. Many systems create only one-way links. If you need a two-way link, you just create two one-way links.

One-way or two-way links?

When are one-way links (with implicit return) better than two-way links (or two mirror-image one-way links)? Do what city planners do when deciding whether to make a street one-way or two-way. Ask how many users will want to go from Topic

A to Topic B and how many will want to go from Topic B to Topic A. Also ask how many will want to go from Topic A to Topic B and then immediately return to Topic A.

Use one-way links when most users will go in one direction only or else will jump to a topic and then return to the current topic. Such step-and-back links are especially useful for topics cited from multiple locations in the document. Some examples:

Term	→	Definition
Diagram	→	Conventions used in the diagram
Concise warning	→	Complete warning
Procedures	→	List of common shortcuts

One-way links to topics with no further links are called *step-and-back* links, because they let users step into a new topic and then immediately return where they came from. They provide a way of sharing information needed in many locations (definitions, conventions, warnings) without letting the user stray into unrelated and irrelevant information. The user who jumps to such a shared topic is unaware (and undistracted) by the links to the topic from other topics.

Use two-way links to promote two-way movement between a pair of topics. Use them to represent reciprocal relationships between topics of roughly equal importance, for example, every "See XXX" link implies a "Cited by YYY" link in the opposite direction. Some other examples:

Topic	↔	Subtopic
Overview	↔	Details
Previous	↔	Next
Summary	↔	Amplification
Abstraction	↔	Instance
Generic form	↔	Specific form
Alternative 1	↔	Alternative 2
Item	↔	Its opposite

ACTIONS TRIGGERED BY LINKS

What happens when the user selects a link? Usually new information appears on the screen. Some links trigger an external program while others merely refer the user to a paper document.

Reveal new information

How is the new information revealed? The answer depends on the type of link. Several variations are common.

Type link	How new information appears	Typical uses
Replacement or jump	Destination replaces the source topic	Moving on to an entirely new unit of information when the user is finished
Comment, note, or pop-up link	The destination topic appears in a small window that pops up over the source topic. This window must be dismissed before continuing.	Present brief definitions, notes, comments, and tips
Swap or reference link	The destination topic is injected into the current topic at the point of the link trigger. The rest of the display makes room for the new information.	Spelling out abbreviations or expanding outlines of headings to complete topics

The merits of each of these ways of displaying new information are discussed in Chapter 8.

Run an external program

An *external* link activates an external process or runs some other computer program. External links are important because they let online documents do things not possible with the online documentation software alone. External links could, for example, command a videodisc player to display a video segment on a television monitor next to the computer.

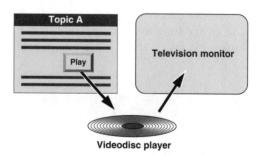

When the user selects an external link, that link triggers another program. This program then displays new information to the user before ending and returning control to the online documentation software. The user sees the new information but may be unaware that it was provided by another piece of software.

External links are limited only by the capabilities of the computer. With external links, a user can:

- **Perform calculations**. You might have the document perform calculations for the user.

- **Exchange data with other programs**. The document can retrieve information from a remote database, for example. This way the document can display up-to-the-minute information, such as stock prices or airline schedules.

- **Issue commands to the computer**. The document can trigger commands in the operating system. A help facility can actually carry out actions for the user by sending commands back to the base application.

- **Control external equipment**. External links can control videodisc players, CD-ROMs, audio CD players, printers, and external monitors.

- **Add multimedia elements**. An external link can run animations as if they are an integral part of the online document.

- **Practice new skills and techniques**. An external link can start up an application and open a training file for the user to practice applying concepts presented in the online document.

External links let developers of online documentation systems selectively add capabilities, choosing the best software to provide each capability. Disk space and memory are not squandered on unneeded features.

External links, however, add complexity to the design effort. They typically require a multitasking or multiprocessing operating system with effective interprocess communication. They may require custom programming. They definitely require the author to understand the technical concepts of how programs can be run cooperatively. External links require more different pieces of software and perhaps more hardware, and you must ensure that all users will have the components required to use external links. Finally, external links require extensive testing for usability and reliability.

Virtual links

Virtual links point out potentially useful information but do not provide a way to jump to this related information electronically. A reference to a particular page or section of a paper document is one kind of virtual link. Another is a mention of a related section of the online document that does not include a button or icon to jump to that location.

The Help for Microsoft Word for the Macintosh 4.0 and Apple's *Macintosh Human Interface Guidelines* companion CD-ROM both referred to page numbers in related paper documents—as does this example.

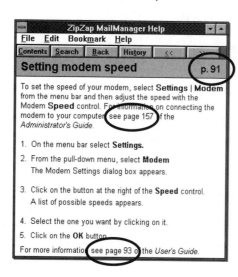

References to pages in related paper documents.

Virtual links let you put information on paper or online depending on which medium best presents the information. These links let the user refer to more information at the same time, since the paper document does not use screen space. With virtual links, the user avoids the onerous task of searching through the index of the paper document. Virtual links are necessary for users who refuse to allocate the disk space required to put all documents online. And virtual links are helpful when documents contain graphics that cannot be displayed online.

Don't forget, however, that this approach requires revising and reissuing the online document every time you republish the paper document. Be sure to allocate enough time to update and verify the virtual links. While preparing the online document, put in distinctive dummy page numbers, something like "page XX." After the page layout of the paper document is done, replace the dummy page numbers. Next, have someone else verify every page reference twice.

Be aware that virtual links are passive. Users may not notice the page reference or may consider it too much work. Try to make the reference as specific as possible, and refer to a specific page or heading rather than a book or chapter.

Online and paper documents work well together. A mixed system of paper and online documents may provide users the greatest access to information. Tie the two forms of documentation together by using paper documents to explain how to access online documents and online documents to refer users to specific pages in the paper document.

In general, avoid virtual links to other online information. Users expect real links for such cross-references and become confused when virtual links do not respond to their mouse clicks.

TRANSITIONS INTRODUCE THE DESTINATION

In books, in movies, and in online documents, *transitions* can help us understand what we are reading and seeing. Think how many times you encounter a transitional phrase such as *on the other hand, for instance*, or *furthermore*. The next time you watch a movie, pay attention to the dissolves, fades, and changes of camera angle that mark the divisions between scenes.

Transitions are especially important in online documents because users can easily become confused as they jump from topic to topic along links. By putting transitional clues into links, however, we signal the user that they are leaving one topic and entering another. And we clarify the relationship between source and destination, especially in systems that combine separate parts into a "seamless" display.

Verbal transitions

Verbal transitions give the user a sentence or short paragraph that previews the destination. Intermedia, for instance, lets the user preview a link by popping up a brief explanation of the link's destination.

This verbal transition can appear in three places:

- **Current display.** The transition typically appears in a one-line message area at the bottom of the display.

- **Intermediate display**. The transition appears in a separate pop-up window. The user may dismiss this window or it may disappear automatically when the destination topic appears.

- **Destination display**. The transition may actually appear as the first paragraph of the destination topic, right below the title.

One use of verbal transitions is to bridge delays caused by long response times. Display the verbal transition immediately. While the user is reading the transition, the system retrieves and formats the destination topic. If the system displays the destination by the time the user finishes reading the transition, the response time seems faster than if the user has to wait for the destination to appear.

Should you automatically display the destination topic or pause after the transition to give the user a chance to change his or her mind? For example, you could display the verbal transition and let the user decide whether to continue to the destination topic or return to the source topic.

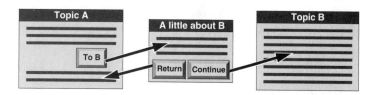

Many users would find having to confirm every selection a nuisance [251]. There are circumstances, however, where letting the user reverse direction makes sense.

- **Retrieving a topic takes a long time**. Warn users of the delay and let them decide whether the information is worth the wait.

- **The user must pay for viewing the topic**. Many commercial databases charge users by how many records are retrieved. If viewing the destination of a link costs money, tell users what the cost will be and have them OK the cost before proceeding.

- **Many will not want to proceed**. If your testing shows that many users select this destination in error, use the transition to explain what the topic concerns and give users a chance to reverse direction gracefully.

Write verbal transitions so that they tell the user how the information at the destination relates to the source. Provide just enough information so that the user can start reading at the destination.

If the transition does require the user to take an action to continue on to the destination, make that action simple and easy. Make it the default. Let the user select it by pressing the Enter key or the space bar or by tapping the mouse button anywhere except on the Return button.

Visual transitions

Visual transitions include wipes, zoom ins, dissolves, and the like. Use such transitions when displaying the destination of a topic if you want to:

- Reinforce a spatial metaphor by suggesting movement up and down, left and right, and in and out.

- Lessen the visual shock when displays differ dramatically.

- Signal appearance of a new topic when displays are very similar.

See Chapter 11 for more on visual transitions.

Sonic transitions

Sound effects can help clarify relationships between pieces of information, especially for those with poor eyesight. We rely on subtle sounds in everyday life to help us understand where we are and how we are moving. Consider these sound effects:

- Opening and closing doors
- Turning and flipping pages in a book
- Advancing a slide projector
- Footsteps
- Automobile starting up, approaching, and receding

Such sounds can be used analogously in online documents. Music can also signal movement from one piece of information to another. For example, a series of notes rises when moving up to more abstract information and falls when going down to details. See Chapter 11 for more on using sounds in online documents.

LINK TRIGGERS

Link triggers are the words, icons, buttons, or other objects the user selects to have the link display its destination. We must make link triggers apparent to users without cluttering the screen. Users must recognize which parts of the screen are active and which are not. At the CHI'89 InfoBooth, 21 percent of users tried to select items from a bulleted list even though the items were not selectable [236].

Make clear what the link does

To decide what a link trigger must signal, think about the questions users ask about the link. Where does this link go? Can I get back? Will it erase what I'm looking at now? Users may not know exactly what they will see at the end of a link but should not be startled by what does happen. Link triggers must make clear:

- **Scope and extent**. Where are the links? What can I jump from? Is the link just this word or the entire sentence or the entire topic?

- **Current condition**. Users must be informed of changes in the condition of the link. A link may be temporarily unavailable, perhaps because its destination is inaccessible, has been deleted, or has not been added yet. You may also need to show which link is currently nominated, that is, which one the default action will select. If multiple windows are displayed, you may want to indicate which link in one window was selected to display the topic currently viewed in another window.

- **Whether already selected**. Flag links to topics users have already visited. These may be topics they want to revisit or avoid. The Xmosaic tool from the National Center for Super-Computing (NCSA) shows links that have been traversed in blue with a single underline and those that have not in red with a double underline. Other systems use checkmarks to flag links to topics the user has visited already [195].

- **Results**. Flipping back and forth in paper books is easy and safe. Doing so online is more difficult because the current display is often replaced or overlapped by the new one. Thus, the user must plainly understand the result of selecting an option. Users assume that options represent useful information and are frustrated if, after selecting the option, they find the information useless. Let people know ahead of time what will happen when they select a link, especially if the link activates a multimedia element, takes more than a second or two to display the destination, erases or covers up part of the current display, or is hard to reverse.

Because displaying everything users need to know about a link may hopelessly clutter the screen, decide what information is essential and what is not.

Make link triggers apparent

Users cannot select a link trigger if they do not notice it or cannot find it on the screen. Make triggers conspicuous without cluttering the screen or disrupting legibility of text. Here are some techniques.

- **Highlight the trigger**. Make link triggers more prominent than other items on the display. Put the trigger in a distinctive color or draw a box around it. To flag link triggers in text use *italics*, <u>underlining</u>, **boldface**, or other emphasis mechanisms. See Chapter 8 for other recommendations. Remember, however, that anything that emphasizes an individual word or phrase disrupts reading of the paragraph.

- **Use a special mark**. For graphics you can superimpose a brightly colored or three-dimensional button. You may choose to design special punctuation marks to go inline with text to designate link triggers. For example, you could identify footnotes with a mark like this ✱. Symmetrical inline marks could indicate where link triggers begin and end. HyperWriter employs marks like these around a ◀ link trigger ▶ Such marks are especially helpful when triggers consist of phrases, not just single words, and when trigger follows trigger.

- **Display triggers beside source**. One solution is to put the link trigger in the margin beside related text. Such triggers are readily apparent without disrupting reading. However, for sparsely linked documents, this technique may waste valuable screen space. For graphics, you can make triggers of the labels for parts of the graphic.

- **Display on menu**. Some systems do not embed links within the content of the topic but gather them together onto a single menu. Typically, each topic would have a "Related topics" menu. This approach works well for links from the topic as a whole but does not let you create links from points or blocks within the topic.

- **Change cursor when over trigger**. To show that something is a link trigger, you can have the cursor change when over the trigger. The shape of the cursor can indicate the type of link or information at the destination. Although this technique works well to supplement others discussed here, it is seldom sufficient. Users should not have to point to everything on the display to find all the links.

Word triggers clearly

Phrase textual link triggers so they clearly tell what information resides at the destination of the link. If the text trigger stands by itself, for example, in a list or menu, use the title of the destination topic (or an abbreviation of it). If the link trigger is embedded in a sentence, balance the need to make the destination clear against the danger of disrupting the flow of the sentence. Hyperties, for example, lets abbreviations, synonyms, and pronoun references act as link triggers to the same destination [251].

```
The Model XJY Gizmoframus .... Your XJY can .... It can
also ....
```

Allow multiple destinations

What do you do when link triggers overlap, that is, the same phrase or graphic is linked to multiple destinations?

Consider changing the symbology of the link to indicate the overlap. Intermedia, for example, distinguishes overlapping areas by drawing a thin border around single regions and a thick border around overlaps.

If you cannot distinguish overlapping links, you must give the user a choice of destinations. When the link is triggered, take the user to a stepping-stone topic that lists possible destinations and lets the user select one.

Reduce clutter

If link triggers unduly clutter the display, take steps to reduce the visual disruption. Techniques include:

* Highlight links only when pointed to.

* Display the topic with the link triggers hidden and then let the user turn them on after reading the topic.

* Highlight only the first link to a topic in a display. Other links may occur, but do not highlight them.

* Highlight the area after it is selected and display the destination on the same screen without covering up the link trigger.

Make selecting links easy

If selecting links is easy, more users will use links to search for information. On the other hand, if selecting links is difficult or unreliable, users must search by other means. In designing link triggers, consider the experience, typing abilities, and eye-hand coordination of users as well as the number and type of links.

With mouse or other pointer

Most hypertext systems let users trigger links by pointing to them with a mouse and pressing a mouse button. Other point-and-click devices are trackballs and joysticks. Still other systems let users point with a finger or stylus on a touchscreen. Point-and-click selection works well for users comfortable with the mouse or other pointing device, provided you make the link trigger large enough that the user can reliably select it. Here are some common recommendations [13, 179, 292].

Pointing device	Minimum size (smallest dimension)		
Mouse	0.25 in.	7 mm	20 pixels
Trackball	0.25 in.	7 mm	20 pixels
Stylus	0.13 in.	4 mm	15 pixels
Finger	0.50 in.	13 mm	40 pixels

The best size depends on the eye-hand coordination of the user and the gain of the pointing device. If you must make link triggers smaller than these, separate them with "dead" space and provide feedback to tell users when they are indeed pointing at the link trigger. Several systems highlight the link trigger to show that clicking the mouse button now will activate the link.

By skipping to it

Other systems let users repeatedly press the Tab or arrow key to move among link triggers on the screen. The currently nominated link trigger is highlighted to show that pressing the Enter or Return key will activate it.

This simple way of selecting links is especially effective for untrained users or ones who cannot reliably use a mouse or other pointing device. Experiments with hypertext systems created with Hyperties showed that users could navigate complex documents using just the left and right arrow keys to move among link triggers and the Enter key to activate them [250]. This skip-and-confirm technique is not so effective for selecting among more than about a dozen link triggers per display.

With key or button

Still other systems let users select links by pressing keys or buttons on the keyboard. Each link trigger corresponds to a key or button on the keyboard.

This technique is good for touch typists and other experienced users who can press keys and buttons without taking their eyes off the screen. However, you must display the name of the key that activates the link. Displaying which button triggers each link is not too distracting when the selectable items are displayed as a vertical list. However, it can disrupt reading when the link triggers are embedded in a paragraph of text.

```
Notice [F2] how distracting [F3] these function key
[F7] labels [F5] are when included [F8] inline [F4]
with text [F6].
```

Another way to show the trigger key is to underline the letter that triggers the link.

```
For example, some words of this sentence are link
triggers You would select one by typing the underlined
letter, typically while holding down some other key.
```

The trigger key usually requires holding down some modifier key, typically ALT on a PC keyboard, when pressing the trigger key.

DEFINE SPECIFIC TYPES OF LINKS

Like topics, links can be restricted to specific types of relationships. A system for scholarly debate, for instance, might use a different type of link to direct the user to topics that support, refute, elaborate on, exemplify, and restate an initial argument. *Typed* links let users retrieve information based on the types of links, but add complexity to the system. Typed links make navigation more predictable by suggesting clearly what kind of information lurks at the other end of the link. Having different link types lets the system perform consistency checks; for example, looking for matching subtopic and parent-topic links [150]. Like typed topics, typed links are best reserved for specific-purpose systems. *Untyped* links, on the other hand, place no restriction on the type of relationship signified by the link. They are simpler to use and are necessary for any general-purpose system.

Each type of link expresses a distinct relationship between its source and destination. Each type also answers a distinct type of question that may occur to the user reading the source of the link. The link provides a pathway to the answer.

Relationship	Questions answered
Prerequisite information	What do I need to know before I begin?
Prerequisite action	What do I need to do first?
Next step	What do I do next?
Subtopic	Can you be more specific?
Parent topic	How does this fit in the overall scheme?
Support	Why should I believe this idea?
Counterargument	Why should I doubt this idea?
Definition	What does this term mean?
Summary	What are the main ideas I should remember?
Parts	What are the components of this item?
Whole	How do these pieces fit together?
Contents	What's here? What can I do with this?
Example	How is this used?

Standardize the symbology of links so that it reveals the relationship of the destination to the source. The user should be able to look at the link trigger and guess whether the destination is a subtopic of the current topic or the definition of a term or an example of a concept. Standardize your choices to eliminate arbitrary differences among the links of a single type. Standardize such decisions as:

- Wording
- Style, size, and font
- Icon
- Colors
- Verbal, visual, and sonic transitions
- Scope of source and destination
- Direction (one-way or two-way)
- How new information appears
- How to return

WAYS OF CREATING LINKS

Although the focus of this book is on design rather than production, one production issue warrants special attention. That issue is the way links are created. You can create links manually, one at a time, or you can generate them en masse from a source file. You can also define them by policy. The *Columbus: Encounter, Discovery and Beyond* multimedia project, for example, uses no manually created links. Instead, links trigger retrievals from the underlying database. Your choice of method is important because it can make a big difference in the amount of effort required.

Manually construct links

With *manually constructed* links, the author individually handcrafts or hard-codes links between one location and another.

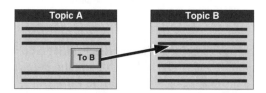

The procedure is simple. There are many variations, but they generally include these steps:

1. Select the Create Link command.

2. Identify the source of the link.

3. Identify the destination of the link.

4. Specify the transition, label, icon, and other characteristics of the link.

Manually constructing links provides great flexibility. You can link any chunk of information to any other. This method handles information that does not easily fit into a more rigid scheme. Manually construct links where relationships are unusual or unexpected or where automated techniques fail; for example, for abstract subjects where keywords are not sufficiently precise [6].

Authors can easily learn to construct links manually. With most systems it takes no more than five minutes for authors to learn to construct links. Although constructing links manually is easy, it is still time-consuming. After you have decided what pieces of information to link, you may still require two to three minutes to make the link, specify its characteristics, and verify that it works. On a small project, spending a few minutes per link is not too costly. However, on a project involving hundreds or thousands of links, the amount of effort required to create links becomes formidable.

Handcrafted links often prove difficult to maintain. Each time you add a new topic, you will need to construct links to and from the topic. Every time you delete a topic, you must delete any links that pointed to the deleted topic. Any time you change a topic, you must consider all the links that point to the topic. Is the revised topic still a fit destination for these links? Or is some other topic now a better destination? Errors are hard to detect with handcrafted links.

Handcrafted links may be easy to create, but they are not always easy to manage on a large ongoing project. One of my clients found that producing the second version of their handcrafted hypertext took as much effort as the first version, even though the second version added only 10 percent new information.

Write, publish, and enforce standards to ensure consistency among handcrafted links. The consistency of handcrafted links seems to vary inversely with the number of hands crafting the links and the proximity of the deadline. On large, rush projects, almost superhuman efforts are required to ensure consistency among the way links are used, the way they appear to users, and what happens when users select them.

My advice is to manually construct links as a last resort. Use them for free-form connections not easily handled in other ways.

Compile links from tagged files

Another way to create links is to automatically generate them from an existing source document, typically a word-processing file with embedded tags.

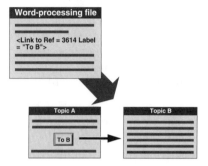

To create links, the author embeds codes in text to mark the source and destination of each link. The source file is then run through a process that generates a file for the online documentation delivery system. This file includes the links. The user never sees the embedded codes. Such embedded codes are at the heart of the Standard Generalized Markup Language (SGML) and other schemes for representing the structure and content of documents independent of the actual display format.

This scheme of automatically generating links is just as flexible as handcrafting links: You can connect any chunk of information to any other. With embedded-code systems, you need no sophisticated tools. Links can be specified with a simple text editor. Rules built into the converter can ensure that links are consistent in appearance and performance. And, because the document is in a simple format easily read by other computer programs, some forms of error-checking can be automated. The real advantage of this approach, though, is that it can generate multiple versions of the document. From a single source, you can produce both online and paper versions of a document or multiple online versions.

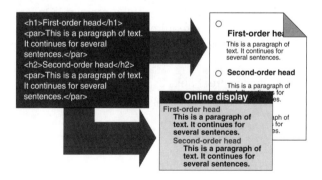

The scheme of automatically generating links from a coded source file has its drawbacks. It is even more time-consuming to create links this way than to do it manually. And errors are more likely. Although most errors are simple typos or syntax errors, they are difficult to track down and correct. Because the source file must be run through a converter before the document can be tested, authors lack the immediate feedback they have become accustomed to with WYSIWYG systems. Experienced technical writers tell me that it takes them twice as long to create links this way.

Automatically generating links seems practical for big projects, especially projects that involve converting documents already in word-processing formats and those that require producing both paper and online versions of the same document.

If you are using such a scheme, make sure authors understand the scheme and the reasons for it—otherwise, morale plummets. Also, automate the insertion of tags or use a tool that puts a graphical-user interface in front of the process of inserting codes. Today, no human being should waste time typing awkward codes or memorizing cryptic ID numbers.

Infer links from the content

One way to create links is to leave the work to a computer program. Programs like SmarText by Lotus infer relationships between parts of a word-processing file and create hypertext links to represent those relationships.

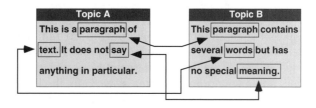

Such programs use two techniques. One technique relies on explicit signals of structure. This technique looks for headings and explicit cross-references and creates the equivalent hypertext links. The second technique generates cross-reference links automatically by comparing the similarity of meaning between two topics as inferred from the words present [237].

Letting the computer make links is certainly convenient, but seldom perfect. The quality of inferred links depends on the consistency and precision of the original text. Sloppy writing produces sloppy links. The speed, consistency, and thoroughness of automatic linking, however, may outweigh the occasional inconvenience of a few misaimed links [6]. Allow time to check and correct incorrect links.

Create computed links

Programmatic or *computed* links do not point anywhere until they are selected by the user. Selecting such a link causes the computer to calculate what to display to the user next. Behind such a link is a program. This program may be called a *script, macro,* or *procedure*. This program selects the destination that best matches criteria encoded in the program.

Computed links are cross-references whose targets change with the content and organization of the document. Computed links are cross-references whose destination or even existence depend on some condition. For example, the online edition of the *Oxford English Dictionary* contains lexical or implied links between each word and its definition [215].

Imagine a current-events database used around the world. It might contain a link like this one:

When the user selects the link, it runs its program. This program finds a biography of a prime minister. In particular, it finds the current prime minister of the user's home country. Users in the UK will fetch a different biography than users in India. If an election is held and a new prime minister is sworn in, the link still works because now the new prime minister's biography matches the current date.

The advantage of computed links is that you can create them once and plug them in whenever they are needed. Write a generic procedure that senses where and when it is activated and retrieves information appropriate to that situation.

Computed links are especially valuable in indexes. To keep from having to recompile the index each time the document is changed, have index entries point not to the location of the topic but to a query or procedure that will find the topic.

Such links require some programming ability. The amount varies from system to system. At a minimum it requires the author to master the syntax of the language, the logical flow and constructs (if-then-else, repeat-while, repeat-until, AND, OR, NOR), and the data objects accessible from within the language.

Computed links work well for easily expressed generic relationships but not for free-form or unique relationships. Use them, for example, to provide an Up button or to let the user look up a term in the glossary. Computed links are well suited to complex, frequently changing documents, especially those with multiple authors who cannot be trusted to follow guidelines for consistency.

Computed links are limited only by what you program. They can query a database or invoke an expert system. One simple use of computed links is to find the topic whose keywords best match the keywords of the link. Links that search for the best possible match always find something, even if it is a default topic. If a better destination is added, the link will take the user to that topic the next time it is activated. If the best match is deleted, the link just finds the next best match. Clever link-makers can thus create self-maintaining links that anticipate and compensate for changes in the destination.

BEFORE YOU LINK ...

Do not include links for superficial or circumstantial associations. Include links only if the association is one the user will understand and consider important. Before adding a link, ask:

- Will a significant number of users want to stop reading here and start reading at the destination of the link?

- Do users need the information at the end of this link? If the primary users are novices, reduce links to obscure uses of commands, unlikely errors, and advanced procedures.

- Will users expect a link here? Learn from users. If you notice many users following a path of links A to B to C to D, then put in a link from A to D.

- Will users understand the information they find there? Do not link to information in a different language. If you must, warn the user before displaying the new information.

PUTTING THESE IDEAS TO WORK

Essential ideas of this chapter

➡ Include links only when users will want to stop reading in one place and continue reading somewhere else. Do not include links for incidental associations or insignificant relationships.

➡ Use links to simplify access between related documents and related kinds of information.

➡ Make link triggers apparent without cluttering the display or disrupting reading.

➡ Use verbal, visual, and sonic transitions if necessary to clarify the relationship between source and destination information.

For more ideas and inspiration

Hashim, Safaa H. 1990. *Exploring Hypertext Programming: Writing Knowledge Representation and Problem-Solving Programs.* Blue Ridge Summit, PA: Windcrest Books.

Nelson, Ted. 1987. *Dream Machines.* Redmond, WA: Tempus Books.

Nelson, Theodor Holm. 1987. *Literary Machines.* South Bend, IN: The Distributors.

Nielsen, Jakob. 1990. *Hypertext and HyperMedia.* San Diego: Academic Press.

Seyer, Philip. 1991. *Understanding Hypertext: Concepts and Applications.* Blue Ridge Summit, PA: Windcrest Books.

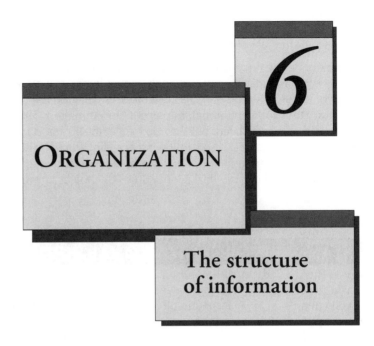

ORGANIZATION

The structure of information

Organization is so fundamental that we take it for granted. But new forms of communication and new media have challenged our habitual assumptions. The rhetoric based on a beginning, middle, and end no longer applies to context-sensitive help messages, search databases, hypertexts, and other documents that have no predictable reading order.

Organization concerns itself with how information is divided into separate topics. It determines the order in which these topics are presented and establishes the interrelationships among them. Organization determines that one topic is a subtopic of another or that one topic precedes another. For paper documents, organization determines where information goes; for online documents, it determines when it appears as well.

Online documentation, which encourages multiple, complex organizations, challenges the linear narrative as the sole way of organizing a document. Argentinean Jorge Luis Borge's "Garden of Forking Paths," a labyrinthine detective story, has been translated to interactive fiction by Stuart Moultrop of Yale University. The story's rich structure consists of 100 segments linked by 300 connections [27]. Such imaginative structures hold great potential for communication—and for confusion.

The writer of online documentation must accept the burden of making the organization and structure apparent.

Writers of online documents cannot abdicate the responsibility to lead. Writers may feel tempted to forgo the difficult analysis that linear writing requires and throw the decision of what is important and what to know first onto the user. But users expect the writer to lead them through the jungle of information. They may not like being controlled or manipulated, but they do expect the writer to blaze trails for them. Experience has shown that users follow trails easily and enjoyably, but has not established that they can forge useful trails with little guidance [276]. Users don't want to have to hack their way through hundreds of choices at every juncture.

STANDARD ORGANIZATIONAL STRUCTURES

In all cultures, in all ages, and in all disciplines, certain ways of organizing and presenting information have been popular. These patterns include sequences, hierarchies, grids, and webs as well as simple variants and combinations of these structures. They are popular because they are conceptually simple and hence easily learned and remembered [136]. These structures offer ways to craft intuitive, obvious organizations for online documents.

Sequence

The simplest, true organization is the sequence. Word follows word, step by step, paragraph after paragraph, page by page. In this structure, the user has two choices: forward or backward. It is perfectly reliable and monotonously predictable. This safe, sane sequential structure is the backbone of most paper documents—this one included.

> It may be that the "linearity" of print derided in the hypertext literature is less constricting for the reader than the blind loops and directional links of subjective hypertext [6, p. 359].

The sequence is the simplest way to consider multiple items. It is the natural result of focused attention and the flow of time. It is the way we examine a set of things: one after another. Any number of items in any specific order can be considered a sequence.

The sequence is fundamental to our language, even our experience of life. We progress through a succession of days, reason through a chain of events, pursue a train of thoughts, solve a string of crimes. Lists help regulate our lives and jog our memories. Who has not relied on laundry lists, shopping lists, wish lists, or to-do lists?

Sequential organizations present the ideas of the online document in a sequence of topics or displays. They shepherd the user down a prescribed path. Pure sequential structures are essential for teacher-directed learning. They may be too restrictive, many would argue, for student-directed learning. Sequential organizations are also appropriate for:

- Step-by-step instructions
- Passive demonstrations
- Detailed arguments

Do not be afraid of linear segments to develop an idea. Pausing every 15 seconds to force the user to make a decision is the surest way to break concentration. Some users prefer reading in a predictable sequence. In one study, females and those with greater English skills followed a more linear path whereas others explored more [21].

Designing a sequence

How do we design a good sequence? Though a collection of separate topics, the sequence must appear as a unit to the reader.

Select by user and purpose

Unless users are familiar with the items, it is unlikely they will identify them as a sequence or understand the order of items. For instance, most people would recognize red, orange, yellow, green, blue, indigo, violet as the colors of the visible spectrum. But what of the following sequence: tibialis anterior, peroneus longus, peroneus brevis, triceps surae, flexor digitorum longus, flexor hallucis longus? Medical doctors and avid runners may recognize these as the primary muscles of the lower leg. But it is doubtful that many nonspecialists would recognize or comprehend the sequence.

Select items of the same class

A pure sequence contains items of a single class. Violation of this rule can produce confusion . . . or humor, as in Mark Twain's classic summary of his life:

> I have been in turn reporter, editor, publisher, lawyer, burglar. I have worked my way up and wish to continue to do so.

Violation of this rule is not so humorous for readers of online documentation buffeted through a sequence of unrelated topics.

Complete the sequence

The sequence must contain all related elements—or it must be obvious which items are missing and what they are.

Putting topics in order

The other crucial design element of a sequence is the order of items. Arbitrary order or no order is do-it-yourself order. The reader will find meaning in the order, even if it is random.

Spatial order

Often the arrangement of physical objects in space or in our field of vision suggests an order. When describing knobs and switches on a control panel or icons on a menu, you can use *spatial* order. Take care however, because we do not all scan a display in the same way. Most scan top to bottom, but only those with languages reading left to right scan horizontally in that direction.

Chronological order

Chronological sequence propels the reader steadily forward in time. It is the essence of the novel and the campfire yarn. It is not bad for processes and procedures either. The success of this order is that it is simple and straightforward—literally *straight forward*.

Logical order

Logical sequence arranges topics by causes and effects. Essential to philosophical tracts and legal briefs, this order sometimes makes an appearance in sales brochures, technical proposals, and scientific papers that draw conclusions from experimental results.

Logic can proceed in two directions: from cause to effect or from effect to cause. Reasoning from cause to effect is used to predict the effect of some change. The logical sequence can also proceed backward from effect to cause at each stage successively answering "Why?"

In the logical sequence we must forge a chain of reasoning free of knots and breaks. Each cause must clearly imply its effect and each effect must in turn supply a subsequent cause.

Associational order

The *associational* sequence is common in the fiction of William Faulkner, James Joyce, and Virginia Woolf. In a stream of consciousness, the mind leaps from one idea to the next with no propulsion except that the first idea somehow suggests the next. (As a rule of thumb, if you can clearly explain the link between ideas, it is logical order.)

Though valuable for verbal impressionism, this order is difficult to employ in scientific and technical exposition. Association could be useful, however, in a description of the visual appearance of a scene or object where the description reveals the subject in the same sequence as the observer's darting eyes would see it.

Climactic order

Items of a sequence can be ordered to increase their rhetorical impact. In *climactic* order items proceed from least important to most important, from casual to essential, from dull to striking. It is good for building up to a sales pitch or for increasing motivation gradually.

Anticlimactic order

Anticlimactic order puts the more important items first. It is like the inverted pyramid organization used in newspaper reports since the Civil War. Reporters then were taught to put the most important facts first in case the telegraph should fail before they could finish transmitting.

By putting important items first, they get first attention and hence are more likely to be remembered. They are also more likely to be read by impatient readers. Use anticlimactic order, also, to present ranked items so users can examine the best candidates first.

Clincher order

Even in lists arranged in anticlimactic order, you may want to end the list with a clincher. A *clincher* is a motivating item that impels immediate action or leaves a sweet taste in the reader's mouth. Consider this note I once got from my boss: "The reasons for meeting the deadline are: (A) It is essential to maintain credibility with the customer base. (B) It saves having to reschedule other projects. (C) If you don't, I'll fire you." I think he was just kidding, but I met the deadline.

Indexed order

Items of a sequence can be arranged by some familiar characteristic. Such a sequence is said to be *indexed*. The most common indexed order is alphabetical.

Encyclopedias and command-reference manuals are often arranged alphabetically by titles of topics. On paper this makes sense because it makes finding a particular topic easier. However, in online documents with nearly instantaneous access, flipping through a sequence of topics to get to one in the middle makes no sense at all.

Varieties of sequence

Even a structure as simple as the sequence comes in several varieties and can be combined in many different ways.

Pure Sequence

Pure sequential organizations have a beginning, an end, and a single path in between.

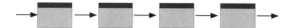

This is the ultimate in simplicity and predictability—reliable and dull. The user cannot get lost but neither can the user explore. Use the pure sequence when you are sure all users need to read all of the same topics in the same order.

Two-way sequence

In the *two-way* sequence, users can go in both directions along the sequence.

Use the two-way sequence when some users will want to go in both directions. Some like to reason from cause to effect and others from effect to cause.

Sequence with alternatives

Not all sequential documents consist of a rigid sequence of topics. Some offer the user alternative paths while still retaining an overall sequential flow.

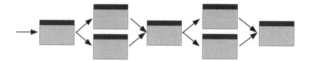

Here the path branches and then rejoins. Use this sequence to describe alternatives so the reader does not have to skip over irrelevant information.

Sequence with optional steps

A related structure allows controlled digressions, like footnotes and sidebar articles in paper documents.

The user can read an optional topic or two before resuming the main path. Use such optional digressions to provide access to details needed by a few readers. This structure lets impatient users skip over information they already know. It keeps the path short for some users and complete for others.

Sequence with side excursions

A similar structure attaches side topics to the main topics of a sequence.

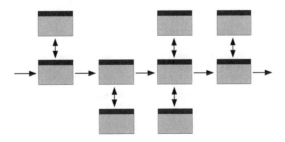

If the reader wants more details, he or she can jump out of sequence to a topic providing such details. After reading the topic, the user returns to the original topic. This is the fundamental structure of an annotated book.

Loops

Loops, or circular sequences, are useful for cycling through information.

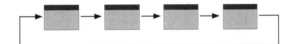

They describe cyclical processes and procedures. Use circular sequences for information that has no definite beginning or ending and for information that is repeated continually, such as an unattended demonstration.

Grid

I live in a town near 40 degrees north latitude and 105 degrees west longitude. My home is in square 5A of my city map, near the intersection of Spruce Street and 9th Avenue. The calendar on my wall tells me that this is the third day of the second full week of the month. By a grid of rows and columns we pinpoint ourselves in space and time.

Grids, those rectangular arrangements of rows and columns, pervade our working, playing, thinking lives. Grids are so common because they enforce a simple, comprehensible organization onto separate pieces of information, integrating them into a familiar and readily accessible matrix.

A grid is a permanent and familiar part of our psyche. We see the ubiquitous grid in spreadsheets, tables, game boards, street plans, and marching bands. This familiarity makes it a popular way of adding another dimension to the document's structure without great loss of predictability. With a grid, each topic has an easily remembered address: the combination of its row and column positions. Just as a regular pattern of streets helps drivers navigate a city, a consistent pattern of links will help users navigate an online document [204].

Classic grid

The *classic* grid or *orthogonal structure* organizes and presents information along two logical dimensions. A *table* is an example of a grid structure. We look up information in a table by zeroing in on the intersection of the selected row and column.

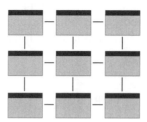

Not all grid structures look like a table. Imagine a reference manual for a programming language. Each page contains information on one command. These commands are like the rows of the grid. For each command there are headings such as Synopsis, Format, Options, Notes, Examples. The same headings appear on every page. These headings form the columns of the grid. The user can read an entire page to learn everything about a particular command or can scan under a particular heading on each page to compare, for instance, the format of various commands. Reading all about a particular command is like reading across a row. Scanning particular headings is like reading down a column.

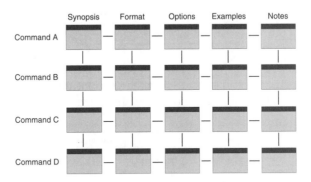

The user finds information by selecting a command (Copy in the scrolling list on the left) and a subtopic (the Examples button along the top). Information then appears in the large area in the center. This information represents the intersection of a row and column of the grid.

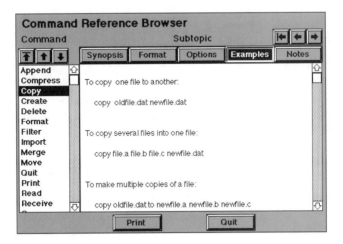

Looping grid

In some grids, rows or columns are not lines but loops. They can even loop in both rows and columns.

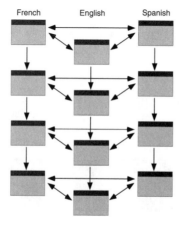

One innovative use of the grid structure links the various translations of segments of a document. The resulting structure looks something like this:

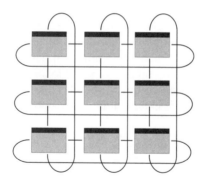

Users read down the column for their language. Translators, however, shuttle back and forth along the horizontal links. The French translator, for example, compares the English and Spanish versions.

3D grid

Grids are not limited to two dimensions. They can be three-dimensional.

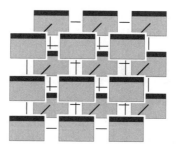

Three-dimensional grids give another dimension for organizing information. The prototype for the Living Constitution used a data cube to present information in the Time Gallery. Information was arranged chronologically along one edge, alphabetically along another, and thematically along the third. The user could view timelines, time slices, time-category slices, and other specific views [85].

Grids are not limited to three dimensions, but users cannot easily envision structures of more than three dimensions.

Hierarchy

The Pentagon, the Vatican, and IBM all have one thing in common: a hierarchical management organization. The *hierarchy* is a common and powerful way of organizing both information and people.

The simple hierarchy is the basis for classification and management. We see it in the numbered headings of technical manuals and the genealogy charts of royalty.

The hierarchy is the basis of a parts classification. Complex mechanisms include assemblies, which include subassemblies, which include components. In biology, plants and animals are classified in a vast hierarchical scheme known as a *taxonomy*. Under this scheme, you are a member of the Sapiens species of the Homo genus of the Hominidae family of the Primate order of the Mammalia class of the Chordata phylum of the Animal kingdom.

Hierarchies emphasize top-level generalities and overviews, thus providing the user with a preview of what lies below. Users readily learn a hierarchical organization and reliably recall the location of topics within the hierarchy [258]. A hierarchical list of topics helps users form a more accurate understanding of the structure of a document than an alphabetical index [182]. Technical users especially prefer hierarchical organizations [59].

Like the grid, the hierarchy provides each topic with a unique address. In the hierarchy, this address is formed by the path from the top of the hierarchy to the current topic. This address is also the recipe for navigating to the topic. A topic designated

2-3-1 can be found by selecting the second topic at the top level, then the third on the next, and the first on the third level.

How to build a hierarchy

There are two ways to create a hierarchy:

- **Top down**. Repeatedly subdivide the subject into finer and finer parts. Use the top-down scheme to establish a classification scheme of your own devising and to check for missing categories in information organized bottom up.

- **Bottom up**. Start with the lowest level of parts and repeatedly sort them into categories. Repeat for the categories, until you reach the top level with a small number of supercategories. Use bottom up to make a large number of diverse topics comprehensible and accessible.

Tell users how items are classified, especially if the scheme is one users would not expect or if items are included in multiple categories [67].

Limiting depth and breadth

In designing hierarchical structures, you must balance the number of choices on each level (breadth) against the number of levels (depth) of choices.

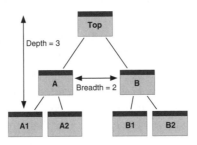

Let's start with the easy cases. If possible you should:

- Display not more than five to seven options per topic so you don't overload the user's working memory.

- Allow only three levels so users can access topics economically.

How then do we design for a vast database containing thousands or even millions of topics? Normally, we use a moderately broad structure to avoid having more than a few levels. Users perform better with a broad hierarchy than with a narrow one [274]. Though users will spend more time scanning menus for choices, they will get lost less often. Increasing depth decreases performance more than increasing breadth. In a test of hierarchical menus of various breadth-depth combinations

(2-6, 4-3, 4-1 & 16-1, 16-1 & 16-1), the best performance resulted from eight options on each of two levels (8-2). The least-preferred menu was the deepest (2-6) [158].

The following table shows the total number of topics possible with various combinations of breadth (columns) and depth (rows). The numbers in boldface represent preferred combinations of depth and breadth. Shaded numbers represent marginal (light) and unacceptable (dark) combinations.

Depth	Breadth				
	5	**7**	**10**	**15**	**25**
1	5	7	10	15	25
2	**25**	**49**	100	225	625
3	**125**	**343**	1,000	3,375	15,625
4	625	2,401	10,000	50,625	390,625
5	3,125	16,807	100,000	759,375	9,765,625
6	15,625	117,649	1,000,000	11,390,625	244,140,625

For example, a three-level hierarchy with seven subtopics per topic can provide access to 343 topics. Notice that only moderate depth is necessary, even for a large number of options.

Varieties of hierarchy

Hierarchies vary from very regular and symmetrical tree structures to more free-form structures. Each has its place in online documentation.

Pure hierarchy

In a *pure* hierarchy, all items at the same level are the same type. Divisions occur at definite, consistent levels. All branches run to the same depth.

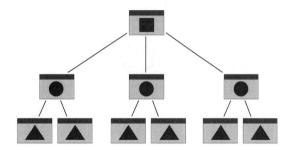

Use true hierarchies for subjects that are themselves true hierarchies. Use them also for large documents that need the extra predictability of true hierarchy but not the flexibility of the general-tree organization.

General-tree structure

In a *general-tree* organization, items are arranged into categories, subcategories, sub-subcategories, and so forth. Topics at the same level need not be of the same class and branches can go to different depths.

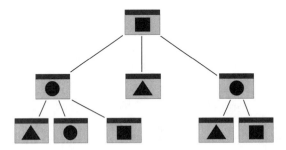

The general-tree organization works well for any classification system.

Lattice

In a *lattice* hierarchy, some topics may have two or more parent topics.

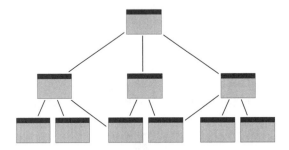

The lattice is a general form of a directed acyclic graph (DAG). In a DAG, one-way links connect topics in a pattern in which paths fork and rejoin but do not form cycles.

Use the lattice structures for classification schemes where a topic can be a member of multiple categories. One such example is object-oriented programming systems with multiple inheritance whereby an object inherits characteristics for more than one object class.

Hierarchy with cross-references

Some hierarchical documents provide cross-references to let the user jump directly to a relevant but organizationally distant topic. *Cross-referencing* makes scattered information accessible without duplicating it unnecessarily.

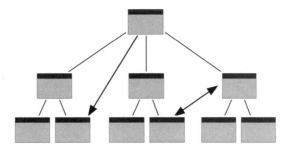

There is a fundamental difference between topic-subtopic links and cross-reference links. The topic-subtopic links define the hierarchical organization of the document. The cross-reference links merely provide shortcuts. Another way to think about this difference is to realize that cross-references do not appear in the table of contents, but topic-subtopic references actually define the table of contents.

Web

In the *web* or *network* structure, any topic can be linked directly to any other topic. The web structure places no restriction on the pattern of connections among topics. It is a free-form organization. The web structure offers the ultimate in expressive power.

One value of the web structure is its ability to mimic associational thought. People rarely think along strictly linear or hierarchical lines. Certain things remind us of other things and send our thoughts off in new directions. The web structure thus promotes the kind of exploration that occurs during the development of new ideas.

Pure web

In a *pure* web structure, every topic is directly linked to every other topic.

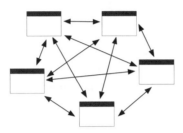

Linking everything to everything else would seem to solve the organization problems.

> It is conceivable that the linking power of hypertext packages will encourage some authors merely to link everything to everything else, or keep adding further nodes of information according to some vague philosophy which espouses associations as "natural" and hence desirable, leaving the reader to decide what they want to access [182, p. 85].

Free-form web structures can either provide knowledge or just propagate the creator's confusion. Remember, raw facts may be highly interrelated, but knowledge is well organized.

Complete web structures pose other problems.

- **Overhead**. The number of links increases dramatically with the number of topics. In a large system the overhead of storing and maintaining the large number of links can result in sluggish performance and an enormous appetite for storage space.

- **Too many choices.** Web structures present the user with an unbearable number of choices at each juncture. In all but the smallest documents, the complete web is impractical for online documents.

Partial web

Not surprising then, most documents that use a web structure do not include all possible connections. Most web structures are quite sparse, linking each topic to no more than a few other topics. The most common form of a *partial* web in online documentation is the hierarchy with cross-references. Such structures logically fit in both categories.

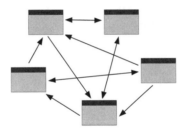

All other structures are subsets of the complete web and are forms of the partial web. From the web structure, the designer can construct the other simpler structures, as well as special ad hoc structures. For example, from this web structure

you can construct all these other structures:

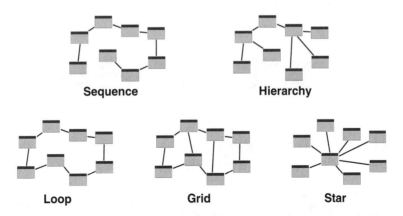

WHAT ORGANIZATION IS BEST?

Picking the right structure for an online document involves trading expressive power for predictability. Organizations that are simple and predictable often seem restrictive to creative writers and expert readers. Structures that allow full expressive power are often bewildering to novices or occasional users.

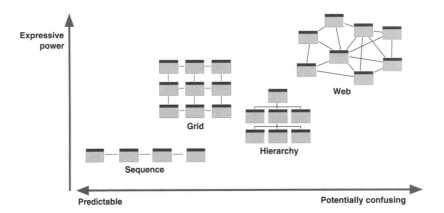

Selecting an organization also requires matching the organization to the purpose of the system. In general: For learning, provide a strong sequential path with possible side excursions. For browsing, organize information in a cross-referenced hierarchy. For fact-finding, organization doesn't matter. Just make it quick.

ORGANIZE TO MEET USERS' NEEDS

Several organizational strategies have resulted from research into how people actually process new information and from experience with paper and online documents. These strategies are discussed in this section.

Center on the user's task

One strategy is to organize a document about a product by how the user plans to use the product. You can organize such task-oriented documents by:

- Phases of use
- Tasks the user performs with the product
- The user's conceptual view of the product
- Phases of learning the product

Although such task-oriented documents take more time to develop than product-oriented documents, they improve the productivity of users significantly and are strongly preferred [199].

In preparing task-oriented instructions, organize topics to tell users what to do in the order in which they must perform the steps. Avoid flashbacks and digressions.

Mirror the organization of the subject

Let the data shape the database, not vice versa. If the information is chunky, divide and display it as chunks. If a task is primarily sequential, train for it with a linear sequence. Don't tangle it up in an intricate web of possible orders. If it is hierarchical, access it through a tree of menus. Use the flexibility of online media to fit the organization to the natural structure of the information. Do not force sequential information into a web just because you want to create a hypertext.

In applying this strategy to documents about a product, organize the document the way the product is organized. For each part of the product, create a topic in the document. This organization is simple to create and to maintain. Automated tools can then generate an outline or table of contents. Because each topic of the product has a corresponding topic in the document, the online documentation system can use context sensitivity to display topics that correspond to the part of the product in use at the moment.

Organizing the document to mirror the product's organization can cause problems, however, especially for novice users. If the user's conceptual view does not match the organization of the system, the document may seem awkward, and the user may have trouble finding information. Organizing the document to resemble the product is best reserved for cases where no other organization is practical. If you are using this strategy, organize the document to resemble the outward appearance of the product, not its deep, mysterious inner workings.

Organize as a paper document

To make online books familiar and understandable to novices, you can organize them like equivalent paper books. Divide the document into chapters, sections, and subsections, and let users find topics through a table of contents and an alphabetical index. Organize online glossaries like an alphabetical dictionary, complete with menus that take the place of thumb tabs. You can organize general-purpose documents as an encyclopedia, consisting of a single layer of topics in alphabetical order by title. When following this strategy, provide all the familiar access techniques present in paper documents, and supplement them with computer retrieval and search techniques.

Map general questions to specific answers

Because users' questions are often vague and ill formed, developers experience problems in organizing online documents to meet their needs. The document must lead the user from a vague, general question to a specific answer. This style of or- ganization is extremely sophisticated and requires great knowledge of the user's psychological state while using the online document and the ability to anticipate the kinds of questions the user will ask.

To organize a document this way, start by collecting questions. Brainstorm, collect trouble reports, and observe actual users. Classify these questions into general cate- gories and combine similar ones. Then arrange these questions from general to specific and provide answers for each of them. If a question is too general to have a specific answer, come up with actions or tests the user can perform to narrow the question to one that does have a definite answer.

LAYER DOCUMENTS

Online documents should not inundate the user with facts or leave the user adrift in an ocean of information. They should provide layers of information that the user can consume at will. *Layering* documents means designing them so that they can serve different users for different purposes, each user getting just the information needed for the task at hand. We must convert the sequential flows occasioned by paper organization to the layered structure permitted online.

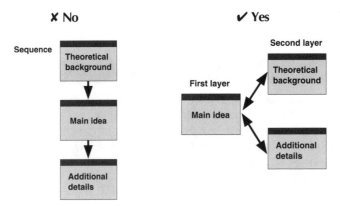

Paper has a single surface on which we can place text and graphics, but it lacks depth. All information must be on the same level or layer. With hypertext, however, the screen can have deeper reserves of information. These deeper layers do not clutter the screen but are available if needed. With layered information, the user can get a little information and then a little more and a little more. Experts tend to use links to access related ideas. Novices use them to access background information [191].

Here, Topic A is the top layer. It is concise and to the point, written with the level of detail and generality appropriate for most users.

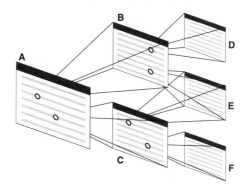

If this surface explanation is sufficient, the reader need look no deeper. However, Topics B and C lie just below the surface and may be brought forth by selecting their references within the text of Topic A. These deeper topics might contain more background information for novices or more detailed information on advanced features for experts. Even deeper layers of information are in Topics D, E, and F. Notice that Topic E serves both Topic B and Topic C. It contains information needed in more than one place but stored and maintained in one place only.

Paper documents are all on the surface. Everything is visible all the time. With on-line documents you can have hidden reserves of information. What you might put later in a paper document, you would put deeper in an online document.

Layering is especially effective in annotating authoritative works. The surface layer is the work itself, and subsequent layers provide commentary and analysis. This is the structure of such ancient works as the *Talmud* and *The Art of War*. Electronic versions have applied this technique to the music of Beethoven, Mozart, and Stravinsky, to the writings of Lewis Carroll and Virginia Woolf, and to the movie *A Hard Day's Night*.

Progressively disclose information

Progressive disclosure is the technique of successively revealing more detailed information about a subject. It is sometimes called the help-me-harder technique because it lets the user request ever more detailed explanations [282].

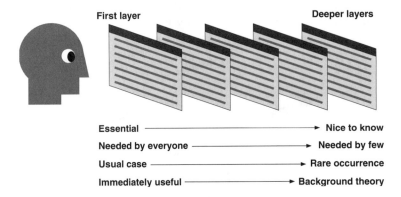

Layering for progressive disclosure is simple: Put the information most people need most of the time on the surface layer. Put the information people may need rarely on deeper layers.

Make the first response to the point

Answer the most common question first. To minimize the number of displays and operations necessary to complete a task, put the required actions and inputs on the first display the user sees. Format the document so that experts can skip over the information they do not need. Irrelevant information is costly in time, effort, and frustration. Therefore, resist the temptation to interject extraneous information. When one company applied a filter to remove irrelevant information from an online repair manual, the time required for tasks was cut in half [175].

Because users of technical documentation do not read documents cover to cover, and because our audience includes users with varying experience, we face a dilemma when preparing instructions. Do we explain everything at the level of detail necessary for the novice and hope that the expert will see the concepts through the forest of details?

Online you can provide information at various levels of detail and link them to show interdependencies [78]. The instructions on how to select commands can refer to the instructions on selecting from menus which can refer to that for pointing and clicking with the mouse.

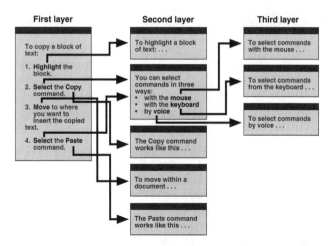

Provide hints before help

Let the user request information in various amounts and at various levels of detail. Provide different commands for requesting progressively more detailed information.

Another approach is to respond to the user's first request for help with a short message. If the user immediately requests help again, the system displays a concise help display. A third request opens the full online reference document.

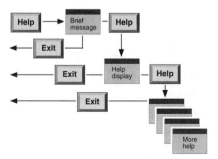

Provide a shortcut for users who want to jump directly to the detailed information since pressing two or three buttons for help will deter many users. One system I worked on had three buttons:

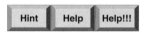

Show synopsis before details

Before plunging into the details, give users the gist of your message. This will help them form a correct conceptual model of the system. To ease access, present an overview and then let the user zoom in. For example, start by displaying a map or table of contents. The user can then select the topic and go right to detailed information. Another way of layering information in a hierarchical document is to let the user say how many levels of headings to display in the table of contents. To reduce the density of displayed information, keep the same number of items but reduce the amount of detail displayed for each. Let the user selectively request more detail on individual items. Explain only how to perform the current task. Link to, but do not initially present, the reasons behind a diagnosis. Make all elaborations, digressions, and comments optional.

Summarize first

Another approach is to present a summary first. For example, the Andrew help system created an "expert" version of UNIX documentation by rearranging the sections in the "novice" version so that experts saw the quick-reference section first [161]. For many users this summary will suffice. If not, they simply will request more information.

Make each version a separate layer

Many technical products evolve rapidly through a series of versions or releases, each with its own documentation. Maintaining separate documents for each version can require large amounts of storage and barrels of midnight oil. One advantage of layering is that if the documents are stored online, writers can graft new information onto the current document to form new versions. Information that does not change is not duplicated.

For example, this figure shows the organization of a document that has two versions and some field notes. The first version is the path shown by the solid arrows. The next version is shown by the gray arrows. Note that topic 1.2A replaces 1.2 and that 1.3.1 and 1.3.2 have been added. The field notes show the kind of information that an end user can add to the online document.

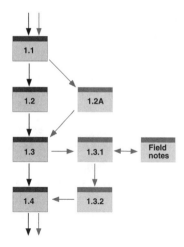

The value of multiple versions of a document goes beyond maintaining product documentation. Multiple versions let researchers, writers, and teachers explore alternative representations for the same facts. Systems vary widely in the way they provide for multiple versions of a single document:

- Change Control, a hypertext system from Context Corporation, stores multiversion documents as a base document together with a collection of named changes, called *deltas*, to that document. Writers can combine these deltas to produce many different versions of the document.

- KMS handles versioning by letting users define the contents of the database at a particular moment as a version [5].

- Some systems define a snapshot of the document at a particular moment in time. Such snapshots are called *version sets* [124].

- PIE defines a version layer as a consistent group of changes to the document. A particular version is just a series of version layers added to the base document [124].

One reason there are so many approaches to handling multiple versions is the difficulty of representing each of them consistently and unambiguously.

> In particular, a reference to an entity may refer to a specific version of that entity, to the newest version of that entity, to the newest version of that entity along a specific branch of the version graph, or to the (latest) version of the entity that matches some particular description (query) [124, p. 848].

AVOID COMMON ORGANIZATIONAL PROBLEMS

Improper organizations can lead to problems in online documents. This section reviews some of these common problems and suggests remedies.

Russian-dolls structure

Layer information moderately. Avoid a *Russian-dolls structure* with endless layers of topics within topics within topics. Don't make the user burrow through many layers to get to a simple piece of information. Each additional action is another chance for the user to make an error or give up. Balance layering with shortcuts to tunnel through layers and go directly to specific facts.

Fire-hydrant syndrome

Many online documentation systems suffer from *fire-hydrant syndrome,* so named because getting a bit of information from one of them is like trying to take a sip of water from a fire hydrant. They force the user through an excessively long sequence of displays. These structures often result when the writer fails to take into account the small display size of the computer.

The fire-hydrant syndrome overloads memory so that by the time users finish reading the document, they have forgotten why they read it or what they read. If you must spray the user with long sequences of displays, use these techniques to combat fire-hydrant syndrome:

- Put a preview or overview at the beginning of the sequence.

- Start the sequence with a menu from which the user can jump to a specific topic in the sequence.

- Let users skip backward and forward in the sequence, for example, to skip or repeat topics in a training sequence:

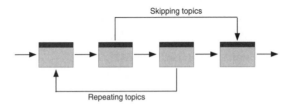

- Summarize at the end

Premature organization

Online documentation requires writers to record their thoughts in separate named topics and join these topics into structures. This process leads to the problem of *premature organization* when ideas are classified and structures assigned before the writer knows enough to do the job well [124]. Once recorded, such ideas are difficult to reorganize, so an ill-formed or incomplete structure perpetuates itself. Ideally, the document's organization should change as effortlessly as the writer's mental conception. In developing online documents, consider the need to revise the organization. Authoring systems for online documents should also make reorganizing the document as simple and quick as possible.

ENGINEER A READING SEQUENCE

Presenting information in the wrong order hampers learning, yet in intricately organized online documents, that order is entirely in the hands of the unguided user. As a writer of online documents, you cannot anticipate all the possible ways a user can reach a given topic in an intricate document. You can, however, define a preferred reading sequence that presents information in a coherent order that ensures context.

Design topics so they are understandable—or at least not confusing—if read out of order. At the same time, design them to encourage and support reading patterns that will help users.

Design topics for combining

When designing a topic, ask yourself where users are likely to encounter this topic: at the beginning, middle, or end of a reading session. The answer will lead you to design three kinds of topics.

A *start* topic is one where the user is likely to begin reading. It is the topic the user encounters by pressing a Help key in a context-sensitive help system or by specifying a query in an informational database. Generally start topics provide an overview or preview of the suggested reading trail.

Body topics provide the content of the trail. They communicate a small idea and contribute to a larger idea. They answer a specific question fully while participating in the answer of a larger, more complex or more abstract question. Body topics typically build on information provided earlier in the reading trail.

End topics are good places to stop reading. They say to the reader, "It's OK to stop reading now." They signal the end of information on one subject. End topics typically summarize or recap the reading trail.

These different types readily combine to form reading trails. The simplest has a start, a body, and an end.

More complex combinations require careful design.

Set up recommended reading paths

Trying to design a reading trail for every question of every user leads to informational gridlock—a structure so complex that no one an find the answer to any question. My recommendation is to set up a primary path for mainstream users, your largest or most important group. Then add two or three alternative paths for other users with special needs.

For example, your mainstream people may be occasional users of a computer who need succinct procedures with a moderate level of detail. Alternative paths may be required for novices who need more background information and very explicit procedures, or for impatient experts who want shorter paths to more advanced information.

Begin with an overview

At the beginning of the reading trail, welcome the reader and prepare him or her to understand information that will be presented along the trail. Funnel the reader's thoughts to the ideas discussed on the reading trail.

One way to orient and prepare the reader is to give the reader a mental model of coming facts and a structure in which to organize details as they are presented.

Notice how this topic uses analogy to explain the concept of electronic mail in terms a novice is likely to understand:

```
Electronic mail is like a note passed from one user to
another by the computer. The note may pass from com-
puter to computer on its way from the sender to the
recipient. The note consists of a file of text. The
note is delivered to the recipient's computer and
written there, where it can be read at leisure by the
recipient.
```

Build along the path

Build on information earlier in the reading trail [251]. Add to the reader's growing knowledge and understanding. Notice how this topic adds a new twist to an idea the user presumably acquired from experience or from topics earlier on the reading trail:

```
Sending electronic mail to a user in another office is
like sending to a user in your office, except that the
address must include the office of the recipient. To
include the address office of the recipient . . .
```

This topic appears to violate the very strong recommendation of Chapter 4 to make each topic so self-contained that it might be read in any order. This topic illustrates a situation where you must compromise between the need for independent topics and the need to explain complex ideas.

To resolve this conflict, design the topic for readers with the prerequisite information but make sure that those without the prerequisite information can get it easily. First, be clear about the information you are assuming and, second, provide links to topics that provide that information. Notice that in the example the underlined phrase is a link to an earlier topic on the reading trail. If you make this compromise, even users who jump into the middle of a reading trail are not confused.

Summarize at departure points

At the end of a reading trail, put a brief summary. A summary does three things for the user:

- **Marks the end of the reading trail**. It says, "You have read all of the information on this subject." It gently and politely urges users to go back to work and apply the information gained.

- **Refreshes the reader's memory**. This ensures that the user remembers the main points when returning to the task at hand.

- **Ensures all users see the critical ideas**. Even users who jumped into the middle of the reading trail or who skipped over topics get one last chance to see the main ideas of the trail.

Format the summary as a checklist or table. The following example is clearly a summary, and it invites users to scan rather than read in detail.

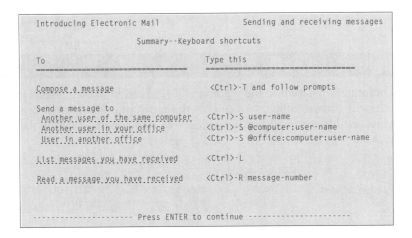

```
Introducing Electronic Mail            Sending and receiving messages

            Summary--Keyboard shortcuts

To                                   Type this
================================     ================================

Compose a message                      <Ctrl>-T and follow prompts

Send a message to
  Another user of the same computer   <Ctrl>-S user-name
  Another user in your office         <Ctrl>-S @computer:user-name
  User in another office              <Ctrl>-S @office:computer:user-name

List messages you have received       <Ctrl>-L

Read a message you have received      <Ctrl>-R message-number


-------------------- Press ENTER to continue ----------------------
```

Include links from each summary item to the topic that discusses the item at length. That way users can jump back for a refresher on types they do not understand.

STANDARDIZE COMMON TOPIC CLUSTERS

If groups of the same kinds of topics occur over and over throughout your online document, standardize how you organize them. This consistency makes navigation easier for the user. Let's look at how you might organize different kinds of information common in business and technical documents.

Overview and introduction

To introduce a new product or capability, we must provide an overview and brief details about it. Here is a cluster of topics to do that:

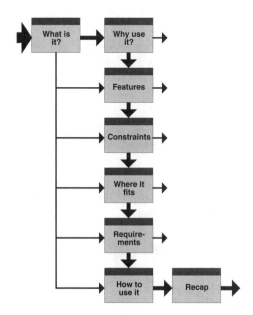

Most first-time readers start with the "What is it?" topic and then flip through each of the subsequent topics until they reach the recap. This path provides a sequential trail. Impatient readers, or those who just need to confirm a specific detail, jump directly from the introductory topic to one of the specific subtopics and exit from there. This structure thus provides two kinds of reading trails: one sequential trail for complete reading and a hierarchical trail for jumping to a specific topic.

Step-by-step procedures

How-to-do-it procedures usually have a sequential backbone with possible side excursions. Normally, the user who wants to perform the procedure starts with the overview, proceeds through the prerequisites and the steps of the procedure, reviews the results, views a recap, and is done. That is the main path.

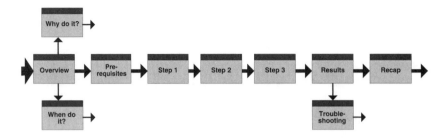

Other users, however, may encounter results they did not expect. These users are routed to a side topic on troubleshooting. Still other users may not need to perform the procedure now. They may just want to know what it does or when it is performed (daily, weekly, yearly, only in certain circumstances). For them special topics are available directly from the overview.

Multilevel procedure

A more complex procedure may have several levels. The user typically starts with an overview of the entire procedure. The user can then proceed through a series of high-level steps. Each of these steps would be explained in more detail in topics covering the substeps of each major step.

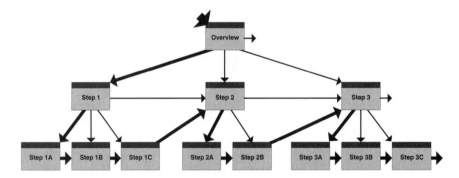

You might route novices through each detailed step but guide more experienced users through the procedure at a higher level, making excursions to the lower level optional.

Command reference

A *command-reference cluster* tells all about a particular command in a programming, macro, or scripting language. Here the user starts with a synopsis. He or she can then jump to examples to see how to use the command, jump to a topic on syntax to see the format of the command, or jump to a topic on the purpose of the command to learn exactly what it does. From the syntax topic, readers can see a list of options from which they can read about a particular option. Options and examples are cross-referenced, so that someone reading about an example can learn more about the option used in that example and someone reading about an option can see a practical application of that option.

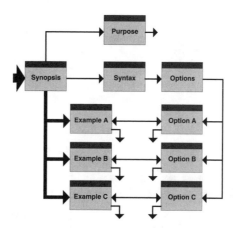

Glossary entry

Glossary or dictionary entries have an unusual two-level structure. Most users will just want to see the term and its definition. A few, though, may want to call up examples, a list of synonyms, or a list of related terms. Those items are optional, as they could prove distracting to most readers.

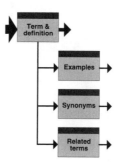

Troubleshooting procedure

Troubleshooting procedures help users identify and fix problems. From an overview, users follow a branching structure to isolate the exact problem.

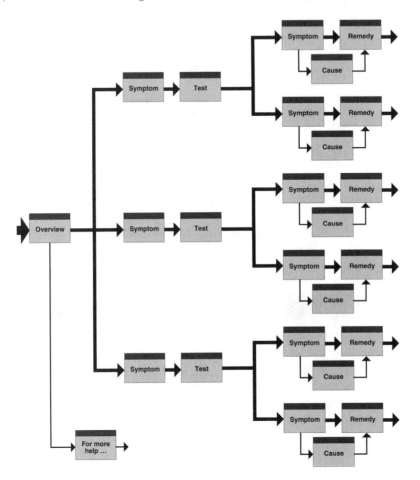

Typically, users start by selecting a general symptom. They are then instructed to perform a test to further narrow the list of possible problems. Testing to narrow possibilities may be repeated many times. Once users confirm a specific problem, they can proceed directly to the remedy or can review the cause of the problem first. Impatient users will go directly to the remedy. Those trying to understand the product will read about the cause of the problem before completing the repair.

Training lesson

Training lessons commonly have a linear structure. This ensures that prerequisite concepts come before dependent ones. (Do not confuse this linear structure with the larger structure whereby a learner selects a particular lesson. That larger structure is typically hierarchical.) Along the path, the user alternates between reading about concepts and practicing the concepts. Concepts usually proceed from known to unknown, general to specific, whole to parts. At the end comes a summary or recap and an opportunity for the learner to prove his or her mastery of the lesson.

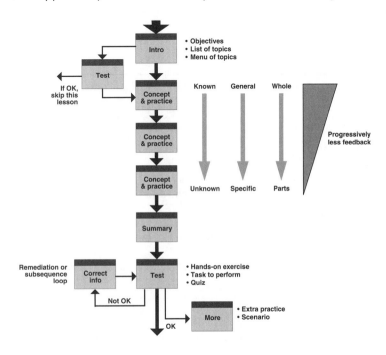

This straightforward linear structure may prove too restrictive for some learners. They may not want to shuffle through the whole lesson, and may jump directly to a test to see if they know enough already. Only if they are convinced that they do not understand the material do they start at the beginning of the learning path in earnest.

Chapter 13 discusses online documents for learning.

PUTTING THESE IDEAS TO WORK

Essential ideas of this chapter

➡ Most documents are organized as variants of four elementary structures: the sequence, the grid, the hierarchy, and the web.

➡ In general: For learning, provide a strong sequential path with possible side excursions. For browsing, organize information in a cross-referenced hierarchy. For fact-finding, just make it quick.

Type of document or information	Primary organization
Less than one page of information	Single topic
Detailed argument	Sequence
Training lesson	Sequence with backtracking, skipping ahead
Step-by-step instructions	Sequence, possibly with alternatives and skipping ahead
Demonstration program	Sequence. If unattended, use a circular structure.
Topics, each with the same subtopics	Grid
Typical technical book	Hierarchy with cross-references
Collection of randomly related topics	Partial web

➡ Organize the document the way the user thinks the information is organized and the way the user applies that information. Do not impose an arbitrary structure on the information.

➡ Design clusters of topics to answer complex questions. Design a short, simple sequence of topics for mainstream users. Then add extra entry points and paths for other users, such as experts who need deep detail and novices who need background information. Finally, add extra points for impatient readers and for those reading as a refresher.

➡ Progressively disclose information, one layer at a time. Start with a small amount of simple information and, as users request, display more complex, detailed information.

For more ideas and inspiration

Barrett, Edward, ed. 1989. *The Society of Text: Hypertext, Hypermedia, and the Social Construction of Information.* Cambridge, MA: MIT Press.

Berk, Emily and Joseph Devin, eds. 1991. *Hypertext/Hypermedia Handbook.* New York: McGraw-Hill.

Martin, James. 1990. *Hyperdocuments and How to Create Them.* Englewood Cliffs, NJ: Prentice-Hall.

McKnight, Cliff, Andrew Dillon, and John Richardson, eds. 1991. *Hypertext in Context.* Cambridge, England: Cambridge University Press.

Nelson, Ted. 1987. *Computer Lib.* Redmond, WA: Tempus Books.

DIALOG

7

The electronic conversation between user and document

When we have a question, most of us prefer to ask another person. Often, if our question is complex, a conversation ensues whereby the person answering our question gives us partial answers and helps us refine our question. This give-and-take conversation is similar to the dialog between a user and an online document. With proper design, the dialog with the document can be as successful as one with a human.

ENGINEER EFFECTIVE DIALOGS

Online documentation is software, and like all interactive software it works by exchanging information with the user. This section provides characteristics of an effective dialog between user and document. It does not rehash general user-interface issues covered in other books, but instead concentrates on the issues crucial or unique to online documents.

Interact with the user

Make the user an equal partner in the dialog. Contrast the plight of the passive viewer of TV and movies . . .

> Relatively little difference exists between an anesthetized patient on the operating table and the aesthetically illiterate television or film viewer. Neither person can do very much about what is happening to him or her [295, p. 13].

with that of the user of some ingenious online documents:

- In the *MarsBook*, the user can rotate a model of the Mars station to any of hundreds of viewpoints and then see an enlargement of that view.

- *Palenque* lets the user explore an ancient Mayan ruin. The user can see what it looks like to walk trails through the jungle and climb stairs of the pyramids. From points of interest the user can pan around a 360-degree view [223].

- The *Ulysses Project* includes an Interpret option that lets the user select a passage of the poem and see it performed by one of six actors. For some segments, the user can specify the emotion (frustration, pride, joy) of the actor [154].

Interactivity should not, however, be viewed as a form of physical exercise or a test of manual dexterity. Interactivity is mental involvement with the subject matter. It should mentally challenge the user to ask and answer questions. Unnecessary button-pressing and mouse-clicking interrupt that involvement and break the spell. Remember that users without experience using a mouse will require some practice before becoming proficient and comfortable with using mouse clicks for selecting topics [176]. Also avoid *hyperinteractivity*, which requires the user to make a decision and press a button or click an icon every few seconds.

Do not overload the user

Most online documentation systems would work fine if users could give them their full study and attention. Unfortunately, many online documents are used by users who are tired or frustrated, are in the middle of a difficult task, are trying to solve an unexpected problem, and know nothing more about online documentation than how to press the Help key. If accessing information requires disrupting the user's thought process, he or she is likely to continue without needed information.

Online documents that require users to make too many branching decisions can actually add to a user's mental load and distress. In general, require no more than three to five decisions to answer any question. A decision may be selecting a command, pressing a function key, clicking on an item in a menu, scrolling a window, or looking something up on a reference card. If finding information takes too many decisions, users will seek simpler techniques—such as asking an equally ignorant colleague, calling your customer-support hotline, or adding to their frustration by trial and error.

For impatient readers, minimize the steps between question and answer. Context sensitivity and retrieval are two mechanisms to let users go directly to an answer without intermediate button-pressing or mouse-clicking. Use hypertext branching, which requires the user to jump from topic to topic in search of information, for more leisurely browsing [271].

Make consequences predictable

Users should be able to predict the general result of every action they take. They should recognize which items they can interact with and what each provides. The sudden appearance of unrequested information can startle, annoy, and distract users. For predictability, test the document. Ask test subjects, "If you click here, what should happen?" Then make that happen.

Of course, online documents should be reliable. They should not unexpectedly quit, hang up, or crash the system. Pressing the Escape key in one multimedia encyclopedia froze the entire PC, not just the program itself. After such experiences, users are reluctant to use online documents at all.

Documents need not be totally predictable. In fact, some "expected unpredictability" can be fun. Games and products for casual use often include an easter egg. An *easter egg* is a surprise—a blurb of text, a sound effect, or an animation—hidden in the display and revealed by clicking with the mouse on a nonobvious part of the display or pressing some unusual combination of keys. *Kaa's Hunting* by Ebook includes illustrations with hidden sound effects. Selecting an animal causes it to growl or roar. Illustrations can spring to life as moving animations. In *Arthur's Teacher Trouble*, many items in a scene can be selected to trigger amusing animations or sounds. Remember, however, surprises that entertain in a game will annoy and frustrate in a tool.

Make dialogs efficient

Do not waste time. Do not make users press three buttons when they could get the same results with two. Avoid requiring long, repetitive actions, such as having to page monotonously through a series of topics because you did not put in direct paths to individual topics. Likewise, do not force users to scroll through a long alphabetical list to find an individual word. Autoscroll lists. As the user types letters, scroll the list to the first entry that begins with those letters.

Integrate smoothly

Create a seamless information source, not a cluttered, compartmentalized library. Users do not understand why they must go though intricate rituals (different in every case) just to find a fact related to the one they are reading. Most users do not understand the concept of separate online books. To them, there is only one book and it is the computer.

Likewise, do not isolate graphics and other media elements from text. Avoid requiring users to issue a command just to see a list of related graphics they still must select from.

Do not try to outsmart the user

Experiments with intelligent documents have shown the potential of inferring the user's need for information and delivering information that meets that need. However, such systems often seem capricious and unpredictable to users.

> There may be a rather high cost to systems in projecting "intelligence" to users. Intelligent entities are expected to be responsible; they can be "blamed" for troubles with greater impunity. Intelligent help systems can be experienced by users as *making commitments* to render assistance [50, p. 1076].

Recognizing users' plans is almost impossible. Users pragmatically change plans whenever they feel the current plan is not working [47]. The problem with intelligent documents is that by the time they adapt to the human being, the human being has adapted to the way the document was. Reading a document that is continually adapting to you is like commuting on an expressway where the exits change from day to day.

Let the user control the dialog

We have all had the experience of trying to ask a question of someone who would not shut up, listen, and understand us before giving an answer. Many online documentation systems are like that. Instead, they should let the user control the dialog.

Snippets of information continually popping up can drive users to distraction. Many refused to use Apple's Balloon Help for just this reason. Better to let the user take a definite action and trigger the display of the note or comment.

Provide a way users can ask questions, make comments, and perform other actions at any point in the document. Also let users express comments, such as: "too hard," "too easy," and "boring" [238]. Here are some common requests users make as to how a system can respond to them.

Request	Response
Let me comment on this	Annotation facility
Let me complain	Electronic mail to developers
Do it for me	Wizard that steps the user through the process
Let me try it	Create special work area
Teach me	Jump to CBT lesson
Show me that again	Backtrack link
Show me more	Continue button
Show me that a different way	Cross-references between concepts and instances, abstract and concrete information
Show me more detail	Link to deeper details
I'm lost	Display map, Home button
Evaluate me	Provide test or task that lets user demonstrate skills
Give me a hint	Pop-up window with one-sentence clue
Show me how	Run animation that demonstrates procedure
Tell me why	Link to conceptual reasons, causes
Let me change my mind	Undo command, backtrack link
Let me quit	Quit button always available
Let me skip this	Next button
Show me an example	Link to example

Simplify access to the document

A book open on your desk is more accessible than one on the bookcase across the room. The bookcase is more accessible than a library across town. To encourage use of online documents, make installing and opening the document as easy and natural as possible. Let the user summon the document and identify a topic with a minimum of effort.

- Provide an installation program that verifies the user has the resources to store and view the document, and then sets it up so the user can jump directly into the document.

- Provide a simple command to open the document. Let users issue this command by selecting it from menus, clicking on an icon on the screen, tapping a function key, or typing in the command.

- Let users open documents both from within and without the program described by the document. Do not require users to start up the application before opening the help file or tutorial on that application.

- Let users arrange their online library to suit their needs. Let users rename and move documents (or copies of them) from directory to directory.

Let users close the document at any time

Let users quit at any time. Often users will say, "I don't know and I don't want to know." Let them quit before they become that frustrated. Almost nothing is more terrifying to a user of an online system than being trapped inside the system, unable to exit. Novice users have been known to yank the power cord out of the wall in frustration.

Online documentation systems must let users exit gracefully at any time and, where practical, should return them to what they were doing before opening the online document. Systems typically require the user to issue some command to leave the online document. Make the command obvious (Quit, Exit, End, Done) and use it consistently throughout the system. Better still, include it on all displays, for instance as an icon on the screen.

LET USERS DO MORE THAN READ

Readers by nature like to interact with documents—even paper documents. People highlight and underline text. They scribble notes in the margin and write letters to the author. They tear out pages or photocopy them. They quote passages or include them in their own writings. Users of online documents like to do the same things. They can even improve online documents.

> Even its paper form, a manual is rarely ever error-free and often a person using a manual can find better ways of performing a task than is specified in the maintenance manual. Providing a means of identifying, capturing and then re-distributing this information can significantly improve the hyperdocument [222, p. 103].

In many traditional online documents, users can only read the document. Others provide separate authoring and delivery systems. But with some hypertext systems, the reader is the writer, and readers are encouraged to annotate, restructure, and even rewrite such documents. Systems vary in the degree to which readers can:

- Add links between existing topics

- Add new topics and create links to them

- Edit or even delete existing topics

Let users add annotations

Allowing users to annotate online documents lets them "make notes in the margin" just as they do in paper books. They can add comments ("This lesson takes about an hour!") or customize the document to their needs ("Specify 'A4' for letters printed in the Paris office."). To help users overcome the deeply drilled prohibition on writing in the margins, include margin notes in the document to show where and how to place margin notes.

Typically, the reader adds an annotation by selecting an Annotate command from a menu and then typing the annotation onto a form on the screen. The system then places an icon in the margin or beside the title of the topic to indicate the presence of an annotation. To read the annotation, the reader selects this icon with the mouse.

There are two problems that prevent widespread use of annotation facilities in systems that provide them. First, they are too hard to use compared to making or reading an annotation on paper. To read an annotation online, the user has to notice the icon indicating the annotation, find the mouse, point to the icon and click on it, wait for a window to appear, read the annotation, then click another icon to dismiss the window. Reading an annotation on paper requires nothing more than a flick of the eyes.

The second problem with annotations in most online documentation systems is that they are lost each time the user gets a new version of the document. The need for frequent updates conflicts with the need for persistent notes. Until designers simplify the task of annotating documents and transferring notes to a new version of the document, annotation facilities will not have the utility of margin notes on paper.

Let users talk back

Interactive systems can provide a valuable feedback channel from users to developers. When readers have the ability to annotate and index, you can refine documents by simply putting the raw material online and observing how users amend, how they index, and what parts they do not read at all [48]. The Andrew help system at Carnegie-Mellon University, for instance, encourages users to suggest improvements. From its first release, the Andrew help system has provided a "Send comment on help" option that lets the user type in complaints, suggestions, or even praise. These comments are automatically routed via electronic mail to the staff that maintains the system [119]. The Airlift Deployment Analysis System (ADANS) developed at Oak Ridge National Laboratory let users of its Hyper-Help system send electronic mail messages to suggest improvements [35].

By analyzing such feedback you can decide what information to feature and what information to remove. Emphasize information that is read frequently by many users. Reduce the number of steps required to reach this information. Eliminate information that is seldom or never read, if it is not critical.

Let users copy and print

Users will want to copy and print out information in your document. Let them do so, but ensure they get information in a useful form and that they respect your copyrights.

Print out topics as properly formatted paper pages, not as literal images of computer screens complete with menus, icons, and jagged type.

Give users a choice of what to print. Let them print an individual topic, a media element, a cluster of related topics, or the whole document. Provide ways to print out dynamic and sonic media.

For this medium	Print out
Animation	Key frames, pauses between continuous movements
Video	Still photographs of key scenes
Sound	Description of the sound
Voice	Transcription of the words

Remind users that you hold copyright to the information in the document and spell out what they can and cannot do with information they copy or print. *Microsoft Encarta* spells out the user's copyright responsibilities when copying information. Text cut and pasted from *Compton's Multimedia Encyclopedia* automatically includes Compton's copyright notice.

Let users modify documents (sometimes)

These additional ways of interacting with documents raise other issues: how to encourage proper use and protect valuable documents at the same time. Before you allow users to rewrite, relink, or delete parts of the document, get answers to these questions:

- Will careless or inconsiderate readers delete information, making the document incomprehensible or misleading to the next reader?

- Will dishonest readers change the meaning of a document or reassign credit or blame for ideas expressed in it?

- What is my legal liability if warnings are deleted or procedures made unclear by users?

- Who holds copyright to the modified document?

- How can you make sure that intelligent, well-considered changes have been made?

- How can you update a document after it has been modified by users without totally replacing it?

Allow multiple authors

Multiple writers can cause another difficult problem. What happens when two writers working on a document simultaneously try to save their changes? Several policies for controlling access are possible [5, 124, 276].

- Break the document into separately editable pieces small enough so that two writers will rarely need to work on the same piece at the same time.

- Allow the second author to read a document but not alter it.

- Allow annotation and other nondestructive changes simultaneously, but prohibit deletions and alterations of existing test.

- If the changes made by the second author do not overlap those of the first, save the changes.

- Let both authors save their changes as alternative versions of the same topic. Notify them that an inconsistency exists. KMS allows multiple authors to open a topic at the same time, but only one can save changes to it. The others are given the option of saving.

USE FAMILIAR METAPHORS

Designers often use metaphors to make the computer system look and act like something the user knows and likes. Such metaphors make systems easier to learn by letting users apply what they know about the familiar system. The visual and verbal cues of the metaphor give the user landmarks to navigate by. Metaphors also gain acceptance for new technology by making it seem familiar. If there is a widely known schema (book, journal, TV), then use it. If not, do not force a metaphor on the user. Several metaphors are possible for online documents.

Book metaphor

Users inexperienced with online documents benefit from online documents designed to be analogous to familiar paper documents. They want the table of contents and index to look and work pretty much like the ones they are familiar with [159]. Users of the HyperHolmes hypertext strongly preferred access methods that paralleled those in paper books [167].

Using the book as a metaphor for online documents is like using the typewriter as a metaphor for electronic publishing systems. Book metaphors, however, fail to suggest the rich interconnections possible in online documents. The book metaphor may mislead users into believing the document is organized as a familiar paper book. It may also disguise the true size of the document.

Point out the metaphor to the user. Users may not use the table of contents or index unless these features are pointed out. Teach users how to apply what they know about finding information in books to finding information in the online system. Even with a book metaphor, not all techniques will be obvious.

Spatial/travel metaphor

Using books and manuals as a metaphor for online documents may have short-lived benefits. A better metaphor may be a transportation network where items are connected by a somewhat logical system of pathways through which, with effort, the user can get anywhere in the system. Given that we all have experience navigating physical space, spatial metaphors should provide familiar models for navigating online documents [191]. Users often remember the physical location of information in paper books. "It was about two-thirds of the way through, on a right-hand page, about halfway down, just below a coffee stain shaped like Italy."

- The Book House project to help library patrons find books uses the metaphor of a building arranged much like a real library [195].The Bughouse project used rooms of a house to organize information on insects. Over 80 percent of users said they felt the use of a house as an organizational metaphor helped them find the information they needed [107].

- The prototype for the *Worldview* electronic atlas arranged views by latitude, longitude, and scale (degree of zoom) [85].

- The *Interactive Encyclopedia of Jewish Heritage* uses the City of Knowledge metaphor in which information is organized on the layout of an ancient walled city. The four gates represent the four ways of accessing information [251].

Avoid arbitrary positioning in a spatial metaphor. Arbitrary position assignments are rapidly forgotten. Users are more likely to remember what an object is than where it is [67]. Make the spatial metaphor relevant to the data and familiar to the user.

For physicians and surgeons, organize information as anatomical diagrams. For electronic technicians, organize it as electronic schematic drawings. For business managers, as a corporate organization chart.

Organize spatially by concept. Put similar concepts closer together and less related concepts farther apart. Put abstractions and general concepts above concrete and specific facts. Arrange chronological events along a timeline with time flowing left to right. Show more relevant information at the surface and less relevant information on deeper layers [260].

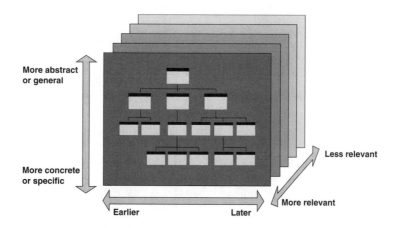

Other metaphors

Ingenious designers have made use of several familiar objects and systems as models for online documents.

- **Control panel**. Use a control-panel or instrument-panel metaphor for high-tech subjects. Allied-Signal used a display resembling the cockpit of a military aircraft to display trade-show information about aircraft products. The *Space Shuttle* CD-ROM by Software Toolworks uses a TV remote control metaphor, as does *Microsoft Cinemania*.

- **Photo album**. Organize collections of photographs as a photo album or vacation slides. Pedro Meyer's CD *I Photograph to Remember* resembles a loving photo album chronicling the last years of his parents' lives. It combines 100 black-and-white photographs with a narrative by Meyer in Spanish and English. The vacation-slides metaphor gives structure to the CD version of *From Alice to Ocean,* combining Rick Smolan's photographs and Robyn Davidson's account of her trek across the Australian outback.

- **Television**. For moving pictures, use a TV metaphor, letting the user select a channel to view a particular motion sequence. Or use a VCR-and-tapes metaphor in which the user selects a subject by dragging a tape to the slot in the VCR with the topic appearing on the screen of a simulated TV set.

- **Games**. Adventure and quest games bear a natural resemblance to the task of tracking down information in an online document. Dr. Warren Moseley of the University of Alabama at Huntsville styled a tutorial on the Software Engineering Standard 2167 on the popular computer game *Where in the World Is Carmen Sandiego?* In his game, learners must ferret out information from the online version of this software standard.

- **Showroom**. Online sales catalogs can use the model of the product showroom. Steelcase's *Sales Improvement System* uses the metaphor of a showroom where users can see and examine images of office furniture.

- **Magazine**. For periodic information, the metaphor of a magazine or newsletter may work better than that of a book. IBM's *Computer Sciences Electronic Magazine* used the metaphor of a paper magazine in which to imbed interactive multimedia elements. IBM's designers struck an analogy with popular scientific magazines such as *Scientific American* and *Popular Science*. The metaphor was expressed in the terminology used to describe the organization: magazine, cover, departments, article, sidebar. Users found the metaphor of a magazine familiar and friendly [159].

- **Pile**. The pile metaphor represents collections of information arranged by informal categories [174]. The size of the stack indicates the amount of information it contains.

ANSWER QUESTIONS QUICKLY

When we ask a question, we expect a prompt reply—especially when we ask the question of a computer. It makes no difference to us that the computer must find the answer in a database on the other side of the globe.

Respond rapidly

Finding information online must be twice as fast as finding it on paper. Unless it is significantly faster online than on paper, users won't search online.

If response is sluggish, users will retreat to the fast, safe world of static text and static pictures [12, p. 266].

A rapid response is essential for navigating and browsing online information. Manual searching can prove frustrating on computers with response times over a second or two. Users expect to move between displays with the same speed and fluidity as flipping pages. These same users, however, underestimate how long it takes to find information in paper manuals, probably because they are actively searching for the information and do not notice the passage of time. With online documentation, the time spent waiting for the system to retrieve a document is painfully obvious [282].

The Help command on the Xerox Star typically required several minutes to display the first Help topic requested. Few users tried more than once [282]. Slow access speed from CD-ROM will frustrate the Nintendo generation. One multimedia encyclopedia took 75 seconds to begin to play an eight-second bird call. Neil Armstrong's 26-second "One small step" took over three and a half minutes to begin playing.

Whenever I ask users how fast online documentation systems should respond to requests, they either say "instantly" or "faster than it does now." Recommended maximum response times vary, but the following are typical [13, 100, 179].

Action	Maximum response time (sec)
Start the computer	30
Start a program	15
Log on to a remote system	5–30
Move the cursor	0.1–0.5
Select or type a command	2
Scroll a list	1
Request a simple document	1–2
Perform a complex search	2–10
Request an archived document	20–90

Acceptable delays seem to depend on how much work users think the computer must do to carry out their request. Instantaneous response is not the solution either. Response time must match users' expectations and perceptions.

- **Do not respond too quickly**. Can response be too fast? Some research suggests that reducing response time below one-half second offers no real advantage [5, 226]. Response times faster than human perception are definitely too fast.

  Without some explicit cue, 0.05 second response may be too fast—we had trouble noticing whether or not the screen had changed, especially if we blinked at the right time [5, p. 830].

- **Respond consistently**. Unexpected delays frustrate users. Often users will tolerate delays if they are predictable. Uncertainty about the length of a delay seems a greater source of anxiety than the delay itself [179, 192]. Try to keep response times within 50 percent of the mean response time [46].

- **Explain delays**. If the user requests a lengthy action, begin the request immediately, but tell the user how long the process may take and give the user a way to cancel the request in progress. While the request is being processed, periodically report progress. Explain seemingly inactive displays ("Loading job specifications").

THE "LOST IN HYPERSPACE" PROBLEM

Developers of hypertext and other online documentation systems must combat what Andries Van Dam has called the classic "lost in hyperspace" problem [276].

> The biggest problem in hypertext systems, which most of us admit in footnotes toward the end of papers extolling the virtues of our systems . . . is getting lost [39, p. 39].

> Disorientation is virtually universal for people encountering a hypermedia document for the first time [263, p. 62].

Symptoms of being lost in hyperspace

Readers in complex online documents often lose track of where they are or where they have been. In a field study of a hypertext document, 56 percent of users said they were unsure about where they were and 44 percent doubted they could find a topic they visited earlier [195]. Prowling through vast sprawling systems of linked topics, users frequently become lost and discouraged. They waste time reading irrelevant information while missing the information they seek. Then they panic. This disorientation takes several forms:

- **Where am I?** How did I get here? How can I get back to my starting point?

- **Where do I want to go?** Where is the information? How do I get there? What must I do to find specific topics?

- **How much have I seen?** How much more is there? Is there something I am missing? Readers of hypertext often spend too much time backtracking and following alternative paths just to make sure they haven't missed anything.

- **How do I get out?** Can I quit now? How? Users get lost in vast hierarchies and networks of information and then they panic.

Letting users structure their own documents is no solution to the problem of getting lost. What we gain in self-tailoring documents, we lose in confidence and predictability.

> If the reader is allowed to choose his path through the narrative, then the stability and certainty inherent in a printed text disappear [27, p. 44].

Without a predictable reading sequence, the problem of getting lost only increases.

Is it really a problem?

There are some signs the "lost in hyperspace" problem is just a natural occurrence of readers and authors confronting a new medium with which they have no experience.

Adults are more prone to complain of disorientation in hypertext networks than are children. Children seek actively with little fear of getting lost [30]. Perhaps adults expect relationships between pieces of information to be more logical and consistent than they are [194].

The "lost in hyperspace" phenomenon appears to be more a symptom of a poorly designed document than a characteristic of online documents in general.

> Hypertext disorientation is indistinguishable from bad writing [23, p. 42].

Despite millennia of research and development, we still do not know how to produce good linear documents. How then can we have confidence in our abilities to produce complex, richly linked, nonlinear hypermedia that inexperienced readers can navigate effortlessly? With careful design, though, our documents should be able to overcome the "lost in hyperspace" problem just as they overcome typos and dangling participles.

Keep the design simple

Elaborate hypertext systems are hard to learn and tricky to operate. Keep the system simple, or at least make it appear simple to the user.

- Do not provide all possible features in the first version.

- Let users get started with just a few access techniques. Do not require them to learn them all.

- Layer the interface so that rarely used optional controls or features do not obscure the most used and necessary ones. Let users perform common actions with a single mouse click or button press.

- Organize the document in a regular structure, such as a hierarchy or grid. Add cross-references for flexibility.

- Limit the number of different types of topics and links. Many systems get by with simple body and note topics and just subtopic, cross-reference, and annotation links.

Link moderately and methodically

Merely adding links does not make a document more useful or comprehensible. Danny Goodman, author of *The Complete HyperCard Handbook*, had this to say about the lure of links:

> Some people get so hung up on the idea of hypermedia and nonlinearity that their stacks just go wild. They want to cram a million buttons on each card, until the buttons outweigh the information on each card, and it's hard to figure out where you are [115].

Use hypertext as a means, not an end

Hypertext is like cayenne pepper—a little goes a long way. It provides endless possibilities for exploration, but offers endless possibilities for getting lost.

Except when the intent is to deceive or mystify, nonlinearity should not be our goal. Murder mysteries have nonlinear twists and turns. So do mazes and the conversations of the scatterbrained. Human memory is a sparse web of the most important associations, not every possible association between ideas [191].

Not too many links

Link moderately. If you include too many links, users may get lost or become annoyed by irrelevant information. If you include too few links, users have to visit too many topics to find the answer to their questions [33]. The proper number of links depends on the types of links, the subject, and the user, but 2 to 8 links per topic seems a common recommendation [250]. In one test, an online document with an average of 10.2 links per topic outperformed the same one with 4.3 links per topic [33]. A hypertext based on the *Grolier's Encyclopedia* averages about 2 links per topic; 80 percent of the topics have fewer than 10 links. The online edition of the *Oxford English Dictionary* averages only 2.26 cross-references per entry [215]. In other experimental hypertexts, links ranged from 2 to 10 links per topic [200].

A more sophisticated approach considers the type of link and how predictable it is to the user. I classify links into three categories: standard, routine, and special.

Several standard links

Standard links are ordinary and predictable, and are the same for every topic in the document. They are triggered by buttons labeled Next, Previous, Back, Up, Contents, Index, Map, Home, Lesson, and Help. Usually these buttons are arrayed around the border of the document's window or displayed in locations that do not change from screen to screen. Because such links go to well-known destinations and the triggers occur in fixed locations, users learn them readily. Frequent users of a system will have little trouble with as many as 15 such links.

A few routine links

Routine links may appear in different locations in different topics but they signal the same kind of relationship in each case. These are the links that take the user to sub-topics of the current topic or to definitions of a highlighted term. If such links follow simple conventions, users can predict the kind of information at the end of the link, if not the exact destination. Allow up to 7 or 10 routine links depending on the experience of the user.

Not many special links

Special links are the least predictable ones. They can appear in different numbers and in different locations in different topics. They include links for related topics, see-also references, footnotes, and cross-references. They typically present informa-tion unexpected by the user or information quite different from that in the current topic. Try to limit special links to 3 or 4 per topic.

Keep the user oriented

Help users develop a mental map of the organization of the document. Otherwise, they must rely on memorized routes and sparse landmarks to keep from getting lost [182]. Paper documents clearly signal the reader's place in the document with page numbers, page headers, tab dividers, and the height of the stacks of pages to left and right. Online documents must provide comparable clues to keep users from getting or feeling lost. This requires making the document's organization obvious, the user's place in it clear, and methods of navigating it easy.

Display the topic name and path to it

Label the display with the name of the displayed topic. If the display is scrollable, do not scroll the topic name off the top of the display. Some systems label each topic by joining the name of the current topic with all its ancestor topics. Such a label shows the path from the top of the document hierarchy to the current topic. It lists all the subtopic selections necessary to get to the current topic. For example:

```
ZipZap➜Word Processing➜Change➜Delete➜Delete Paragraph
```

To get to this topic, the user picks the ZipZap item from the top menu, the Word Processing item from the next menu, Change from the next, Delete from the next, and Delete Paragraph from the next.

Number each topic and display

Give each screen or topic a short identification code, for example:

```
Item 74

Page 2 of 4

Topic 65C

Card 7 of 12
```

Frequent users often jump directly to an individual topic by ID or code number [67]. In any sequence of displays, tell users where they are in the sequence, for example: "Screen 5 of 10" or just "5/10" if space is cramped. You may also want to timestamp topics to show users when they last visited a topic. Display this timestamp in an unobtrusive corner of the topic [195].

Display a *You are here* icon

One system used the icon for the Display Map button to show the user an approximate location in the document. It consisted of a simple organization chart with a block for each major area of the document. The user's position was highlighted. Watch as the user navigates from the table of contents to a specific low-level topic.

Show a roadmap of the document

Give new users a map or diagram of the organization of the system. Such graphical organizers show interrelationships spatially and graphically. They depict the current topic and its relationship to other groups of topics. The user can go to another group of topics by selecting it on the map. For tips on designing maps, see page 215 later in this chapter.

Give users a clear starting point

Designate one topic in the hypertext as the root or home topic. This topic serves as the starting point for novice users. Design this topic to introduce the document, show how it is organized, and provide convenient access to key topics. To let the user jump to key topics:

* Include a table of contents for the document

* Include an alphabetical index of key topics

* Make the topic the top level of a hierarchical menu leading to key topics

MAPS IN ONLINE DOCUMENTS

Over and over again in usability testing I have heard users cry out, "If I could just see how all this fits together, I'm sure I could find what I need!" Maps showing the overall organization of the document provide a global context for users [107]. In online documents, users can spot a topic and jump to it by selecting it on the map. The map becomes a visual menu of available topics.

Maps should be used when the organizational plan can be presented clearly. Remember, a bad map is worse than none at all. Some maps do a poor job helping users learn the system. In one study, users with a map performed worse than users who learned by navigating the system [261]. A map can hinder learning if users rely on it instead of getting actual experience navigating the document. If the map is abbreviated for clarity, the user may believe that only the links and topics shown on the map exist or that only these are important. Maps that show relationships not related to the user's question are frustrating at best. They are like trying to find buildings in London using a map of Paris.

Maps can provide valuable feedback. For a navigation aid, show an iconic map of the structure of the document. Highlight the icon that represents the current topic. For searches, highlight topics with a high number of matches and let users select from the icon to jump to that topic.

One effective way to introduce an online document is to combine a map with a guided tour. Use the map to provide an overview and a guided tour to point out essential information and to give the user some experience in navigating the document [191].

Paradoxically, the larger and more complex the structure of the document, the more users need a map to navigate it successfully; yet the more complex the structure, the harder it is to make a map that looks like anything but the antics of a neu-rotic spider. The value of map displays becomes questionable for documents of more than about 5,000 topics [103].

Complex systems often display a neighborhood view, which shows only closely re-lated topics. One way is to show a fish-eye view. A *fish-eye view* shows the area of interest large and in detail and less related areas in progressively smaller and less detail. Fish-eye views can show both context and details in the same view [94, 235].

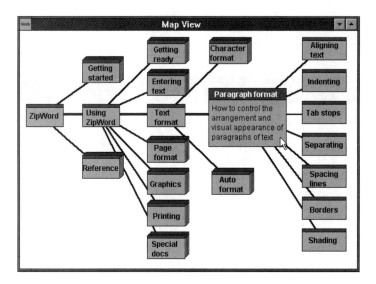

Other experimental maplike displays include:

- **The Perspective Wall**. This is an animated, three-dimensional display of a large two-dimensional layout, such as a timeline. It arranges information on three panels. The center panel parallel to the screen shows the current area of interest. The two side panels, drawn in perspective extending away from the user, show the context of the center display [172].

- **The Tree Map**. This technique represents a hierarchy as a mosaic of overlapping tiles. Tiles for topics contain the tiles of subtopics [146]. The Tree Map divides the screen first into vertical sections for each top-level category. Each of these sections is divided horizontally for the next level of categories. The division con-tinues for all levels of the hierarchy alternating vertical and horizontal division. Size and color can represent topic size, type information contained, when last visited, frequency of visits, or matches to the current search query [224]. The tree map technique can represent hierarchies of over 1,000 topics on a 13-inch monitor [146].

- **The Cone Tree**. This scheme displays large hierarchies in three dimensions. Topics are represented as small rectangles, like index cards. The top of the hierarchy is the apex of a cone with its subtopics arranged in a circle around the base of the cone. Each of these topics is in turn the apex of another cone that includes its subtopics. The angle of cones is adjusted to fit all topics into the display. Cones are translucent so that they reveal structure behind them. Cones also cast shadows on a horizontal base plane at the bottom of the display. When the user selects a topic, the cones rotate to bring that node to the front [225].

TOUCHSCREEN-KIOSK DESIGN

An *information kiosk* is a computer system used to deliver information in a public location. You see such systems at airports and in hotels, where they provide information about local restaurants, entertainment, government, and so forth. They also appear in museums, where they provide information about exhibits. Kiosk systems have been used at trade shows to provide information on a company's products.

Such systems consist of a free-standing computer that a user can walk up to and operate in order to gather information on a particular subject. Such systems typically use a touchscreen to let the user select among displayed options. Others may provide a trackball or other pointing device, and even a keyboard if the user must enter names, addresses, and numbers.

For the Nintendo generation, touchscreens are a natural. However, designing touchscreen information kiosks requires attention to the special problems of the touchscreen and of computers exposed to the general public.

Show people how to select. Tell users to touch. Display instructions in large, clear text. Speak it aloud: "To select an item, touch its label." People have pushed monitors off stands, cracked screens, pressed with their palms and fists, and touched the monitor case. Some continue pressing for minutes on end. If you are using a capacitance-sensitive (instead of pressure-sensitive) screen, remind users they cannot point with fingernails, pens, or pencils.

Make buttons large enough to touch: at least 3/4-inch high and 1-inch wide. Surround each with a 1/4-inch dead zone.

Provide a reset command to prepare the document for a new user. You may provide an "I am done" button so a polite user can "close the book" so it is ready for the next user. You should also have a "start" button for users who walk up to a document open in the middle.

Nail or glue down anything you do not want stolen. Mice and keyboards will disappear. Even things screwed down will go. Lock up the controls users should not adjust. Often users will try to turn off the system when they are through.

PUTTING THESE IDEAS TO WORK

Essential ideas of this chapter

➥ Online documentation is software and needs the same attention to user-interface design as does any interactive program.

➥ Metaphors make the document look and act like something the user likes and understands already. Pick a metaphor that makes the document more attractive to users and lessens the amount of learning required by letting them apply what they know already.

➥ Provide ways for users to add annotations to documents and to send comments to the creators of documents.

➥ Let users copy and print out online documents or parts of documents. Remind them of copyright restrictions but simplify the process of selecting and reformatting the information.

➥ When designing touchscreen kiosks for use in public places, remember that such systems must survive the ravages of the general public. Provide explicit instructions and protect the hardware from accident or vandalism.

For more ideas and inspiration

Bailey, Robert W. 1989. *Human Performance Engineering: Using Human Factors /Ergonomics to Achieve Computer System Usability.* Englewood Cliffs, NJ: Prentice-Hall.

Carroll, John. 1990. *The Nurnberg Funnel: Designing Minimalist Instructions for Practical Computer Skill.* Cambridge, MA: MIT Press.

Helander, Martin, ed. 1988. *Handbook of Human-Computer Interaction.* Amsterdam: North-Holland.

Mayhew, Deborah. 1992. *Principles and Guidelines in Software User Interface Design.* Englewood Cliffs, NJ: Prentice-Hall.

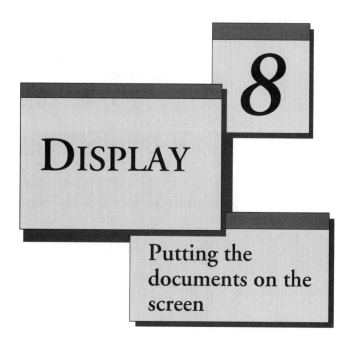

DISPLAY 8

Putting the documents on the screen

Online documentation is primarily a visual medium. Except where the subject is sound or music, communication takes place through displayed words and pictures. Good visual design and legible display largely determine how and what the online document communicates.

> In designing displays, remember the needs of visually impaired users. Do not shy away from using visual design to communicate information, but do provide alternative ways that visually impaired users can get the same information. See Chapter 11 for some ideas on using voice output and audible alarms in online documents.

A SCREEN IS NOT A PAGE

The display screen is fundamentally different from the printed page in both obvious and subtle ways, posing challenges and demanding difficult choices of designers.

Why not display page facsimiles?

Displaying facsimiles of pages from the paper manual avoids the bother and cost of reformatting the manual but presents the user with "serious readability and communication problems" [282, p. 236]. The following series of displays shows one problem with displaying page-formatted documents online:

This is the first display of the series. It is an exact replica of a page from the paper manual. After reading it the user presses the Enter key.

```
COPY                    XY_OPS5                    DOC-285

NAME

    COPY - duplicates files and directories


FORMAT

    COPY source [destination] [options]


DESCRIPTION

    The COPY command duplicates files and directories.
    It makes an exact copy of the source file or directory,
    giving the copy the name specified for the destination.
    Options control how the copy is made.

    source - the file or directory being copied. Source is
             the only required parameter and has no default.

Press <ENTER> for more.
```

The page header disappears but otherwise all is well. The user reads and then presses the Enter key.

```
destination - the name for the copied file or directory.
              Destination is optional and defaults to the
              name of the source with ".2" appended. For
              example, "COPY MYFILE" names the copy "MYFILE.2".
              If a file with the name specified for destination
              exists, XY_OPS5 displays a warning and lets
              you decide whether to overwrite the existing
              file or directory

    options - modifiers to control how the copy is made.


OPTIONS

    /VERIFY - check the copy against the original to ensure that
              the copy exactly duplicates the original

    /AT=time - delay copy until specified time. Useful for bulk
               copying and for backing up entire disks or large
               directories.

Press <ENTER> for more.
```

At this point the novice user gets confused. The document says "Page 1" but this is the third display.

```
        /COMPRESS - write the copy in a compressed format.
                    Useful when making backup or archival
                    copies.

        /UNCOMPRESS - make an uncompressed copy of a compressed
                      source. Necessary when restoring a compressed
                      backup or archive file.

        /ENCRYPT=key - encrypt the copy using the key specified.

        /DECRYPT=key - decrypt the copy using the key specified.


     EXAMPLE

        To compress and verify the file "MYDATA" and name the result
        "MYDATA.Z":

                COPY MYDATA MYDATA.Z /VERIFY /COMPRESS

     Page 1

 Press <ENTER> for more.
```

This display, like the first, has a page header. The second and third did not. But now the page number is missing.

```
     COPY                 XY_OPS5                DOC-288

     CAUTIONS

        COPY does not check for space available before beginning
        to make the copy. If it runs out of space, it displays
        an error message to this effect.


     RELATED COMMANDS

        MOVE, DELETE, ENCRYPT, VERIFY, COMPRESS






 Press <ENTER> for more.
```

Here the
novice panics.
The sight of a
blank screen is
a sure sign that
something is
wrong.

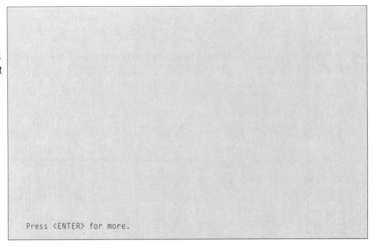

Press <ENTER> for more.

At least this
page has
something on
it, even if it is
only the page
number.

Page 2

=>

The user may give up before guessing what is going on. Each display shows one-third of a paper page. The name for this disorienting effect is the *peephole effect,* for it is like reading through a peephole.

The screen is not a page. In many ways it is more like a TV or movie screen than a paper page. The similarities and differences must guide us as designers as we go from paper to electronic media.

Online displays are smaller than pages

Online documents are displayed in an area smaller and more horizontal than a paper page. As a rule:

1 page = 3 to 6 screens or windows

A standard industrial-grade alphanumeric monitor typically displays 24 lines of 80 characters. Filled with text, it can display only about 320 words. Allowing room for titles, recommended blank space, page numbers, and other required information, the capacity of the monitor is less than 200 words. That is about half a page from a paperback novel or one-fifth of a page from a technical manual or engineering handbook. One page of a newspaper would require 20 to 30 screens or windows.

On large, high-resolution graphics monitors, the online page is potentially as large as a paper page. However, this potential is seldom realized because, on such systems, online documents are typically displayed in windows that cover only part of the screen. The small page has profound effects on the behavior of users.

> Users, unable to see where they are in a large procedure, tend to follow instructions blindly [173, p. VC-74].

Online displays are shaped differently

Most paper pages are shaped as *portrait* or taller-than-wide rectangles. Television and movie screens have a *landscape* orientation—as do most computer monitors.

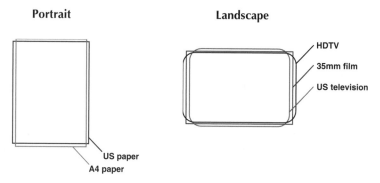

Portrait   **Landscape**

HDTV
35mm film
US television

US paper
A4 paper

Which shape is best for online documents? First, what shape do users prefer? Studies comparing preferences for rectangular shapes find that people prefer *golden rectangles*; that is, those 1.618 times wide as tall [98]. This is the same ratio preferred by users who could reshape windows on a screen. The second shape to consider is the human field of vision. This is elliptical, about 1.65 times as wide as tall, which explains the preference for horizontal golden rectangles. These ellipses put the maximum amount of information in clear focus so it can be examined with the minimum of eye movement. Why then are paper pages taller than wide? One answer is that this shape distributes the stresses of binding so that pages do not fall out. The other answer is that we do not view a single page at a time but a two-page spread, which has a shape very like a golden rectangle.

This is why most online documents, especially those in resizable windows, appear as landscape rectangles.

Some online displays reverse light and dark

Paper documents commonly display dark text and graphics on a light background (negative contrast). Some screen displays, however, reverse this convention.

Negative contrast has been found to reduce errors and the time required for a task, to increase understanding, and to improve subjective feelings of reading comfort and legibility [179]. Negative contrast, thus, is better than light characters on a dark background—but not to any great degree. The most potent difference between the two forms of display is that users strongly prefer dark characters on a light background [275], perhaps because this form more closely resembles the familiar display of paper pages.

Positive contrast has its place too. Use positive contrast for online documents that contain fine lines or subtle colors which would fade against a light background.

Screens are grainier

Even the resolution of high-resolution computer screens is low compared to typeset paper pages or even laser-printed pages. Compare the relative size of pixels:

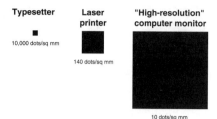

Compare text and graphics as they appear on paper and on screen.

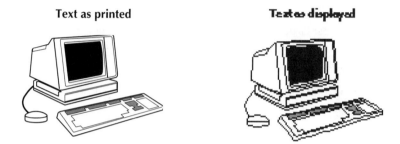

Remember that online graphics cannot show any feature smaller than a single pixel or any line less than 1 pixel wide. Gradations must be in whole multiples of pixels.

Screens display color differently

Online and paper documents may have different sets of colors available, and even when the same colors are available, colors may appear different on screen.

Displayed colors are produced by a different process than printed colors. On the screen, colors are produced by adding varying amounts of three primary colors: red, green, and blue. On paper, colors are produced by subtracting various amounts of cyan, yellow, and magenta and by adding black as a fourth color. On color monitors, small objects formed using a combination of primary colors may appear fuzzy because of misregistration, especially near the edges and corners of the screen. Additive colors can produce only those colors that lie between their primaries. Hues between these primaries will appear less saturated than the primaries.

Computer displays vary in the number of colors they can display. Although 16 or 32 colors prove more than adequate for color coding, 256 colors may be required to make colored objects recognizable. Showing subtle colors, such as facial tones, will require a palette of thousands of colors. Keep in mind that some users may not have the maximum number.

DESIGN SCREENS METHODICALLY

Taking these differences into account, how do we design screens for online documents? To design a screen decide what, where, and how to display items.

1. **List items to display**. These include the content of the document, that is, the title, introduction, text, graphics, animation, and other visual elements. They also include the controls and indicators necessary for the user to operate the online documentation system. These controls include buttons for navigating and manipulating the display.

2. **Organize the items**. Group similar items and assign priorities. What should the user notice first in the display and what should be present but not prominent?

3. **Lay out the display**. Decide where each item goes in the display.

4. **Emphasize important items**. Assign visual characteristics such as blinking and color to make primary items most prominent.

5. **Test**. Can users find and read information effectively?

6. **Revise**. And test again until your display works.

Because every decision affects every other, the design process is cyclical and requires trade-offs. The rest of this chapter discusses the design issues involved and provides guidance on the decisions you must make.

DECIDE WHERE DOCUMENTS APPEAR

As a designer, you must decide how to present information on the screen. Where does the document appear on the screen? As the user requests new information in the document, where do you display that information? If the system lets the users create multiple windows of information, how to you keep them from cluttering the screen and covering up other valuable information?

Display documents in the most useful location

With limited space to display documents and programs, you must choose whether to display documents as complete screens, in a fixed area on the screen, or as a resizable, reshapable window.

Over whole screen

Many systems display the online document over the entire screen.

This document uses the entire screen as one large display.

Doing so provides the maximum amount of display space, so the user does not have to decide among separate displays. If users must scan more than a single scrolling zone of text, paper will be faster [182]. This approach also removes distracting information from the user's field of view and allows the user to concentrate on the document exclusively. This is ideal for kiosk systems and tutorials where the document stands alone. Unfortunately, it is just that distracting information that is often needed to understand and apply what the online document contains. Often users need to compare information in the document with something else on the screen. Users avoid help systems that completely cover the application they support. Systems that display only one view of the document at a time make it hard for users to compare information from two parts of the document.

In a fixed area on the screen

Another way to display the online document is to divide the screen between different documents or between the program and the document, either by splitting the screen or displaying side-by-side, tiled windows.

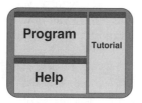

Tiled windows and split screens are a natural way to let the user view and work on more than one type of information at a time, just as in noncomputer work [108, 196]. No special actions are necessary to switch back and forth between them. Because the online documents always appear in the same location, users quickly learn where to look for different types of information and are less likely to miss or ignore a message. For help or tutorials, however, the fixed area takes space away from the program. Experienced users who rarely refer to such online documents may resent this "waste" of space. Writers may omit important information in order to fit topics in the available space.

Separate, overlapping window

A third possibility is to display the document in an independent window on the screen. Users can locate windows to suit their particular needs: they can move windows about on the screen, shrink and expand them, collapse them to an icon and later re-expand them, and overlap them.

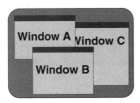

With overlapping windows, the user can interact with multiple documents or with the document and the program at the same time and can control the size and position of the online document on the screen. Tests have shown that both novice and expert users prefer overlapping windows [179]. However, these same tests have found that users who do not know how to manipulate windows waste considerable time.

Reveal new information predictably

Deciding where the document goes on the screen is only half the job. How is new information added to a document already displayed? When the user selects a link, presses the Help key, or performs a retrieval, how is the new information revealed? There are many possibilities, but most are variations of a few common techniques.

Replace the current display

One way to display new information is to erase old information. The old topic or window disappears from the screen and the new one is displayed in its place.

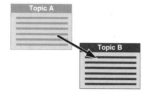

Completely replacing the current display avoids cluttering the screen with potentially distracting information. It can keep the user focused on the task at hand. It signals a complete change of subject and is appropriate when the user is finished with one piece of information and ready for a different one. It can, however, make it harder for users to compare information in different topics. The sudden change of the whole display can startle users, causing them to momentarily forget the question they were trying to answer.

Some tips for replacing one display with another:

- Make it easy for users to flip back and forth between two related topics. Provide a convenient Back command or use two-way links between topics users will need to compare.

- Avoid arbitrary differences in the visual appearance of subsequent displays. Strive for a consistent background color, predominant color, and overall light-dark balance.

- Use visual transitions (see Chapter 11) to announce the change and to give the user a few milliseconds to adjust to the changing display.

Add independent windows

Each request for new information can add a new window to the current display without erasing the existing window. Users can move such windows around, close them, and stack them independently.

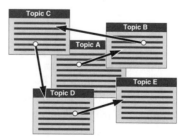

This approach maintains the context of previously viewed topics. It lets the user decide how to arrange the screen, where information goes, and what information remains on the screen and what information is erased. However, multiple windows can clutter the screen like a messy desk. By moving and closing windows, the inexperienced user may lose track of the relationships among windows of information.

Splitting a continuous text into separate windows slows reading, but simplifies retrieving relevant pieces for users with experience manipulating multiple windows [272]. It is especially helpful when examining complex subjects that require comparing small pieces of information.

Pop up a temporary window

New windows of information need not clutter the screen. You can display new information in a temporary new window that the user must dismiss before continuing. The window containing the new information typically overlaps the one the user is reading.

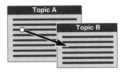

Temporary windows provide a simple mechanism for displaying small chunks of auxiliary information without much risk of sending the user off on a tangent. They are prominent enough to capture the reader's attention and ensure that the information is noticed. They can, however, prove distracting, especially if they cover up critical information in the original window.

Temporary windows are ideal for presenting small amounts of new information that the reader needs to understand before continuing with the current topic. These include definitions, short explanations, simple examples, warnings, and cautions. Probably the most common use is to present definitions. When users encounter a strange term, they may be reluctant to abandon the current display to search for a definition. In this case, they can pop up a definition right over the current window.

Design temporary windows to deliver simple messages without disruption. Use temporary windows only for short messages, and keep the new window small. Position the new window so it does not cover up the item it defines or explains. The user may need to compare the item in the main window with the information in the new window. Make the temporary window easy to dismiss.

Inject information into the current display

Instead of replacing the current display or adding a new window, you can inject the destination information into the current display. Existing information makes room for the new information, typically by sliding down in the window. This is the technique used by *swap links*, which replace the link trigger with the destination of the link.

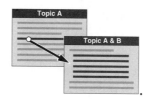

Adding new information to the current display maintains the reader's context. The reader sees how the new information fits in with what he or she has seen already. It lets the reader selectively reveal detail, and minimizes disruption by maintaining the illusion of a single, unified document. In this way the reader can gradually wade into a subject by selectively expanding and contracting subtopics in the current display.

Injecting new information, however, can become disruptive when the chunks injected into the current display are large or the relationship to the existing information is not clear.

The authoring tool Guide provides a particularly elegant way to traverse a hierarchy. When the user selects a subtopic reference in text, the reference disappears and in its place appears the referenced text or graphics. Such expandable references are called *replacement buttons*. The replacement occurs in place. Material below the reference is not covered up but is pushed down. The user sees the replacement in context. In the following example, each of the headings is a swap link:

```
Composing electronic mail messages

Sending electronic mail messages

Receiving electronic mail messages
```

Selecting the middle heading replaces it with its explanation. The other two headings remain. For clarity, the replacement also includes the heading.

```
Composing electronic mail messages

Sending electronic mail messages
You can send electronic mail messages to other users of
this computer, to users on other computers in your
office, and to users in other offices—even offices on
the other side of the globe. Sending electronic mail is
simple. To send a message you have written, simply
select "Send" from the main menu and then, when the
"Sending Mail" menu appears, fill in the name, office,
and computer of the recipient.

Receiving electronic mail messages
```

The user can leave the expanded topic in place or undo the replacement and "fold" the topic back under its button. Ted Nelson called this "stretch text" [190].

Swap links also work well to spell out abbreviations that occur throughout a document. The abbreviation is highlighted to tell the user that it is selectable:

```
To forward all  EMAIL  messages, select the Transmit
Command.
```

Selecting the highlighted term replaces it with its full form:

```
To forward all  electronic mail  messages, select the
Transmit Command.
```

The user can toggle back and forth between the expanded or collapsed forms.

Scroll new information onto display

Many systems, especially those with unformatted alphanumeric displays, scroll all prompts, messages, and online documents onto the display from the bottom of the screen. New lines of information push old information off the top. The advantages of this technique are that short messages leave the most recent parts of the previous display intact and information appears at the user's center of attention. But if online documents are of different lengths, users may have trouble finding the start of the document because documents do not always begin at the same position on the screen. The longer the message, the less of the previous display remains on the screen. Adding a line or two to the online document may shove vital information off the top of the screen. Not knowing how much the online document will displace the previous display, users are reluctant to request online documents. My advice is to use this as a last resort.

Manage window proliferation

If users can create multiple windows of information, you must take care that the windows do not obscure more information than they reveal.

How many windows is too many?

How many windows of information can readers of online documents use effectively? The answer, of course, depends on the skill and knowledge of the user. It also depends on how much information users need to compare. You must weigh this need against the danger of too many windows. Learning to manipulate overlapping windows can prove tricky and take time away from the task at hand. Large numbers of windows can thwart the users' attempts to use skills and habits developed from years of reading paper documents. Seeing the relationships among separate items of information is especially difficult with many small windows. As a result, putting the application, its tutorial, a help facility, and an online reference manual on the screen at the same time can make learning the product harder than actually using the product.

As a rule of thumb, users can handle three to five windows of information before they start to become confused and annoyed. If you have good reasons, exceed that limit, but take special steps not to overwhelm users.

Fixed-page vs. scrolling window

If a topic does not fit entirely in a single display, provide the user a way to move about within the topic. In doing so, you should clearly distinguish between actions that move within a topic and those that jump to another topic [206]. There are two ways to handle information that will not fit in a single display. You can format the topic as a series of fixed-size windows or pages, or you can display information in a single scrollable window.

Use fixed-size displays for . . .	Use scrollable displays for . . .
Novices not accustomed to scrolling displays	Users experienced with scrolling displays common in graphical user interfaces
Information easily divided into window-sized chunks	Information in various-sized chunks, especially when tables or graphics would be separated from related body text
Systems that do not provide scrolling	Windows the user can resize

If you format the document as fixed-size displays, provide commands or buttons to flip to the next display of the topic. Also, do not split sentences between separate displays, and avoid splitting a paragraph unless it is longer than a single display.

If you present the topic in a scrolling area, let the user scroll up and down by lines and by entire pages. Given a choice between scrolling by function keys and scroll bars, users in one test strongly preferred the scroll bar [125].

Managing multiple windows

To control the problem of windows cluttering the screen and covering up useful information, minimize the amount of the screen covered and let the user arrange windows.

Open windows in best locations

Ensure that new windows open where the user would expect them and want them.

- Do not unnecessarily cover up existing windows. Position new windows over blank areas of the screen.

- If users do not need the information in previous windows, place new windows so only the title of the previous window is visible.

- For multiwindow displays, align the horizon line of a scene continued from one into the others [295].

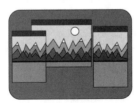

- Initially display the document in a shallow window. Put the summary at the top of the topic so that it is visible when the document first appears. Users who need more information can then scroll the topic or expand the window.

- If possible, position windows so they show relationships among topics. As the user proceeds down a hierarchy, stack windows upper-left to lower-right with titles showing. Users infer that overlapped windows show a hierarchical relationship [196]. (You may need to reverse the left-to-right orientation for readers of Hebrew and Arabic who read right to left.)

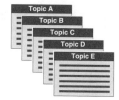

Let users rearrange windows

Let users combine and rearrange windows of information. This way they can try out different groupings and can compare related pieces of information.

- Let users collapse unused windows to icons.

- Provide commands to arrange windows in simple patterns.

- Let users position windows off the edges of the screen. *Compton's Multimedia Encyclopedia* displays a *virtual workspace,* letting users position and manipulate windows of information off the edges of the screen. It works much like a large desk on which the user might spread open books and magazines.

Cover as little as possible

Do not cover more of the screen than necessary and let users easily remove un-needed windows.

- Shrink the online document's window to fit its contents so that as little as possible of the work display is covered.

- Let the user set a limit to the number of simultaneously displayed windows. Once the limit is reached, each new window causes the oldest window to disappear.

- Make closing unneeded windows easy. Let users select several windows and issue a single Close command to close them all. Or let users close all but the most recent windows.

DO NOT PACK INFORMATION TOO TIGHTLY

Television programs never display a full screen of text. Why then do writers of online documents believe that users, whose expectations are set by thousands of hours of watching television, will read screen after screen of margin-to-margin text? Several studies have shown that the time to find information in a display increased with text density [275]. Another reason to lower display density is to allow room for translations.

Several authorities on technical writing, based on research on alphanumeric menu screens, have recommended covering online documentation screens with no more than 25 percent text and graphics. Although sparse screens are easier to scan, there are problems with following this recommendation too rigidly. Doing so may purchase a 10 percent increase in reading speed with a 300 percent increase in the number of screens. Hardly a good trade.

The research on which this recommendation is based ignored how well the screen was organized. Most such research has been based on menu screens which people search for a particular item but never read in full. Screens that display online topics are quite different. Once users find the topic that answers their question, they read in detail. They do not want to have to plod through three or four screens to read what could be presented on one. Here are some better guidelines:

If the user . . .	Make the display
Reads, rather than scans	Dense but well organized. Allow text and graphics to cover up to about 85 percent of the available space.
Scans, rather than reads	Sparse. Cover no more than about 25 percent of the available space.
Both scans and reads	Moderately dense (65 percent covered) and very clearly organized.

Simplify the display

New users are easily overwhelmed by a number of objects competing for their attention. Eliminate unnecessary information and options, pruning the purely decorative elements. Repeated logos and other devices reduce attention span up to 2 seconds per visual in business presentations [186]. Layer the design so that the initial display offers just the most important information and the most common options [43]. Provide a "See also . . ." button to reveal more information.

Simplify the display of text, too. Limit the number of fonts in text and graphics. Generally limit type sizes, styles, and colors to three sizes, three styles, and three colors per display and five sizes, three styles, and four colors per document.

Replace text with graphics

Where possible, say it with pictures. Replace long paragraphs with lists, tables, charts, diagrams, and other visual displays. Visually code related items in the display. Information coding, such as color, labels, repeated symbols, flashing text or objects, orientation, shape, and intensity, helps the user handle more information without reducing performance. Consider *structured writing*, a hierarchical, visual style of writing that uses indentation and typography to show how the text is organized [137].

Use visuals for primary communication and not just for summarizing or supporting text. Use text to elaborate on and flesh out details not possible in the graphics.

Condense text for continuous reading

Condense blocks of text that are intended for continuous reading, not as scanning targets. Higher density may actually increase reading speed for continuous text [275]. Condensing text for continuous reading frees space for text that is the target of scanning.

Use blank space actively

The unused space on a paper page is called *white space*. The online equivalent is called *blank* or *quiet space*. Almost all books and courses on document design advise the graphic designer to use white space. Few, however, clearly distinguish between active and passive white space. *Active white space* helps to organize the information. *Passive white space* merely separates information from its surroundings. Outside margins are passive white space. Active white space separates parts and reveals their relationships.

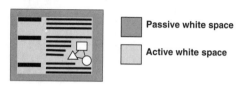

Passive white space

Active white space

Wide margins are necessary for paper documents to visually separate the text from surrounding objects in the reader's field of view. Margins are also necessary to give the reader somewhere to grip the document and turn its pages without covering up the text. Wide margins are not necessary for online documents. On the computer screen the window border or screen bezel adequately frames the display. Too wide a border steals space better used for the content of the document.

ARRANGE THE DISPLAY LOGICALLY

Haphazard design or no design results in cluttered displays. The users' initial impression of a cluttered screen is "This is going to be a lot of work" [99]. They are often right. Research with structured and unstructured screen displays found a 30 percent higher error rate for unstructured displays [275].

Divide the display into functional areas

Divide the screen into functional areas, each for a different type of information. Consistently display each type of information in its assigned area. If necessary, shrink and enlarge areas to handle special cases but do not vary the relative locations of the areas [173].

Shape functional areas to fit their content

Make functional areas rectangular and size them to fit their content. For example, use wide and shallow areas for displaying short messages, and make areas for displaying graphics square or slightly rectangular. Irregular shapes may provide novelty, but are less practical for displaying information. For each area, consider the type and amount of information it must display, and design the area accordingly. Allow functional areas to shrink and grow as needed but keep them in the same relative positions [13].

✘ No   ✔ Yes

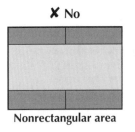   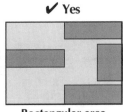

Nonrectangular area   Rectangular area

Put smaller functional areas around the edge

Place smaller functional areas around the perimeter of the display. Doing so frames the text and graphics of the online document and provides a margin to separate the document from other displays on the screen. Putting small areas around the edge of the display also keeps them from intruding into the area for the main text and graphics.

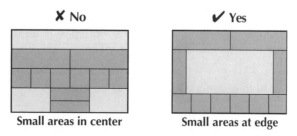

✗ No   **✔ Yes**

Small areas in center   **Small areas at edge**

Balance the display

Balance displays symmetrically—left vs. right, top vs. bottom. Spread out information and use blank space to organize and group displayed items.

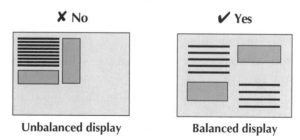

✗ No   **✔ Yes**

Unbalanced display   **Balanced display**

Group related items

If you must present many separate pieces of information, present them in a few small groups. Distinguish different types of information in the display. Make sure controls for the content are distinct from controls for the system presenting the content [236]. Also, clearly distinguish procedural from conceptual information [289]. To group related items:

• Cluster them together, surrounding the group with blank space.

• Draw a box around a group of related items.

• Display related areas using similar visual characteristics, such as color, font, or reverse video.

Also, place close together items that are frequently compared or contrasted, or that the user must examine in sequence. Remember that visual acuity decreases by half at 2.5 degrees from the center of the field of vision [275].

Arrange items in a familiar, logical pattern

Our experience in reading books and newspapers and watching TV gives us certain assumptions about how information is arranged in space and time. We scan from top to bottom and left to right (if our language is written in that direction). We expect more important information to be more prominent in the display. Some suggestions:

- Arrange items used in sequence in a straight line from top to bottom or left to right.

- Place alternatives side by side in equal positions.

- Place the most important items in the most conspicuous and most easily viewed area of the display. Place less important and less frequently viewed items around the periphery.

- Users prefer buttons on the side of the hand used to control the mouse: left if they are left-handed, right if right-handed. The placement of buttons (top and right vs. bottom and left), however, does not significantly affect performance, regardless of gender or handedness [176].

- Users may overlook small windows or other items displayed at the bottom of the screen.

Arrange items consistently. Consistency is essential in complex systems with many displays, since users learn such systems one display at a time. Meaningless differences between displays distract users from learning important information and significant relationships.

Anticipate and guide the user's eye movements

Design the display to direct the user's gaze to important information. Except for placing more important and more general information above or to the left, we have no universal rules for arranging items. The order in which people scan items in a display varies. Contradictory studies have found scanning patterns of upper left to lower right, clockwise from upper left, in rows from upper left, and U shaped. Other studies found that scanning patterns varied from individual to individual. I suspect that the real scanning pattern is determined more by the arrangement of objects in the display and the user's interest in them. We start with the most prominent item in the display and jump to the next most prominent object and so on. If objects are equally prominent, we start in the upper left corner and continue jumping to nearby objects, especially if the jumps continue in the same direction. If you want users to read in columns, then arrange items in columns. If you want them to read in rows, arrange items in rows.

Vary the prominence of objects and use blank space and vertical lines to direct the user's eye to items in the right order.

Put action areas near the center of attention

Place selection areas where the user is looking when the decision to select is made. That way, the decision can be quickly followed by an action.

- Embed cross-references in the text of the topic.

- Place the next-page, scroll-down, and next-topic controls near the last line of the topic display.

- Either embed subtopic references in the text of the topic or place them at the end of the topic.

USE COLOR TO COMMUNICATE

In online documents make color functional first, last, and always. Where possible, make colors pleasant and appealing—but never at the expense of clear communication.

Use color functionally

Avoid irrelevant and unnecessary color. If color is not relevant to the task, it interferes with performance of the task [270]. Do not let colors draw attention to unimportant information on the screen, such as the borders between adjacent areas, topic numbers, or marginal annotations. Avoid a purely decorative use of color. Instead, use color to:

- **Differentiate and join**. Color helps users isolate and separate different items in a display. In gIBIS, adding color coding to visually distinguish different types of links and topics made identification "a rapid, reflexive activity" [22, p. 262]. In online documents, colors are typically used to distinguish text, examples, highlighted text, selections, and function keys.

- **Focus attention**. Use color to focus attention on information you want the user to notice and remember. We remember material we pay attention to, and when color is used to direct attention to material, it increases recall [72]. Color pictures are recalled more accurately than black and white [270]. Color makes presentations more persuasive [1] and in one test increased attention span from 8 seconds to 11 seconds per visual in a business presentation [186].

- **Speed up search**. Color coding helps the harried operator find specific information on a dense, unformatted display . Color coding can reduce search times up to 80 percent when the item sought is a distinctive color [72]. The greater the density of the display, the greater the potential of color coding to reduce search time [13].

- **Express a range of values**. You can also use color to express quantities of values along a range. A spectrum of colors can represent a range of values between two extremes. For example, you can represent temperatures with a scale from deep blue to bright red.

Select color carefully

To select colors for use in online documents, you may have to balance conflicting functional and aesthetic goals. Forgo purely personal and subjective preferences and select colors that help users accomplish their goals.

Pick color for a purpose

Pick your colors deliberately and thoughtfully. For grouping items, select colors that users can easily distinguish. Use contrasting colors to emphasize difference; use similar, but distinguishable, colors to show similarity. To make colors easier to discriminate, select spectrally different colors, use purer or brighter colors, and reduce the number of different colors [252].

When using color coding, keep these guidelines in mind:

- **Use only a few color codes**. Although a computer can display millions of colors and the eye can distinguish thousands of colors, the mind can remember only a few color codes. If the user must recognize a color displayed alone, limit colors to three or four. If the user must distinguish among colors displayed together, allow six or seven colors [252, 270].

- **Make colors distinct**. Avoid colors that are too similar in brightness or hue. Select conspicuous colors that stand out in peripheral vision [72].

- **Use natural color associations** to make learning the color codes easier. For example, use green for vegetation and blue for water.

Use the same color scheme and color codes on all displays of a document. Unless codes are obvious or few, define them on the display. Try to establish a single palette for all color in the document, including animations and video—otherwise, the screen will flash annoyingly as the palettes change.

Apply the user's color conventions

Every domain has its own color conventions. Online documents should respect these conventions to avoid confusing users. For example, in Western societies, the following color conventions are widespread:

Field	Red =	Other color associations
Finance	Loss	Black = gain
Politics	Radicalism	
Temperature	Warm	Blue = cool
Mapping	–	Blue = water, green = vegetation
Traffic signs	Stop	Yellow = caution, green = go
Safety	Danger	Yellow = caution, green = safety

Balance colors

Balance colors for any display the user sees for more than a few minutes. Staring at one predominant color for a long period of time shifts color perception toward the complementary color. Complementary colors are those that yield gray when mixed together. This aftereffect may last seconds or even days and is known as the *McCullough effect* [266].

Use a neutral background color for color-coded information. Remember that each color alters our perception of other colors: pure color shifts adjacent colors toward its complement [142]. In a test comparing red, blue, green, yellow, violet, and gray backgrounds, the gray background was the only one with consistently low error rates for red, blue, green, yellow, and violet color codes [210].

Avoid garish colors

Garish colors cheapen the display and the user's opinion of you. If your document is intended for adults, avoid overuse of primary colors when more subtle and pleasing colors are available. Avoid trendy colors. Especially avoid pinks, purples, and pastels, which few computer monitors can display faithfully.

Avoid conflicting colors

Avoid putting spectrally distant pure colors—such as red and blue—side by side. The optics of the human eye are not color corrected. The lens of the eye brings different colors into focus at different distances behind the lens. Blue objects come into focus nearer the lens than red objects. As a result, red objects appear closer than blue ones. This effect is called *chromostereopsis* and creates an illusion of depth on the screen [270].

Likewise, do not overuse opponent colors such as yellow and blue, red and green, green and blue, or red and blue. Such opponent colors leave afterimages and suggest shadows.

Don't compromise legibility

No color combination has the contrast and, hence, legibility of black and white. People read colored text more slowly and with more errors than black-and-white text [179, 270].

Use primary display colors or black and white

For best legibility, display text in a primary screen color. Most computer screens display colors by combining dots of red, green, and blue of varying intensities. These three pure colors are called the *primary colors* of the screen, and they appear sharper than other colors. Characters formed of a combination of primary colors may appear fuzzy because of misregistration, especially near the edges and corners of the screen. Generally for a black background, green proves the best choice on a red-green-blue color display because red is too intense and blue is too dark.

Maintain contrast

For legibility make foreground and background colors different in lightness and hue. Especially avoid combinations that are the same lightness level, such as yellow on white or navy blue on black. Visual acuity for brightness is about 10 times that for color. Legible combinations include:

Background	Use	Avoid
white	blue	yellow
	black	cyan
	red	
black	white	blue
	yellow	red
	green	magenta

For other legible color combinations, use opponent colors, such as yellow and blue. If you use a pure blue, use it as a background. Many people cannot clearly focus on blue objects. If you must use blue as a foreground color, mix green with the blue. The green component will make the object easier to focus upon without shifting its apparent color [252], but the mixture will not have as sharp an edge as pure red or pure green alone.

Do not depend on color alone

Use color to repeat a message encoded in black and white or as a way of making reading more efficient. Never use it as the only conveyor of a critical message. About 8 percent of men and 0.4 percent of women do have trouble distinguishing red and green. However, even people with total color blindness can still discriminate between light and dark.

Also, consider whether some users will view the document on a monochrome monitor, such as the screens of popular laptop computers. For example, Microsoft's Quick Basic 4.0 for the IBM PC displays Help screens with bright text on a dimmer background on monochrome monitors. On laptop models with LCD screens, which have but one level of brightness, these Help displays are white on white [62].

There is no international standard color monitor. Monitors vary from manufacturer to manufacturer, from model to model, and even among the units of a single manufacturer. Colors also vary as the monitor ages and users adjust display colors to suit their personal preferences.

Colors seen by the user depend on environmental lighting as well as on light projected by the screen. Background illumination and glare often make displayed colors appear less saturated, that is, washed out [252].

MAKE TEXT LEGIBLE

Make text for continuous reading legible, not just recognizable. Remember that displayed text, however, is generally less legible than printed text. Reading from the screen is typically 20 to 30 percent slower, slightly less accurate, and more variable in speed than reading from paper. This is especially true for users with little experience in reading from the screen [125, 218]. Reading from the screen is also more tiring than reading from paper. In one proofreading test, online displays did as well as paper for the first 10 minutes (25 percent vs. 22 percent error rate), but after 50 minutes the error rate for online displays rose significantly (39 percent vs. 25 percent [288]. But with careful design of screen displays, reading speeds and accuracy can approach those of paper [118, 201]. When text was displayed using antialiased fonts at 91 dots per inch in one test, users read with about the same speed and accuracy as they did from paper [118]. Improving the legibility of text requires attention to letter shapes, type size, display contrast, and the layout of text.

Use well-formed character shapes

Most of the difference in reading speed between paper and online documents results from the low legibility of displayed characters compared to printed characters [117]. By displaying text in well-formed characters, we can improve the legibility of displayed text.

Simple shapes

Simple character shapes display more faithfully and are more legible than complex shapes. For online documents, favor simple functional letter shapes.

✘ No	✔ Yes
Cursive typefaces	Sans serif typefaces
Decorative typefaces	Slab-serif typefaces
Serif typefaces at small sizes	

For small type sizes, avoid serif typefaces altogether, or use typefaces with square, rather than tapered, serifs. Such faces are called *slab-serif* faces. Make sure the serifs are at least one pixel high and wide. Fonts with smaller serifs may display irregularly because serifs that fall on pixel boundaries may not display at all.

Familiar proportions

Pick fonts with well-proportioned characters. For fixed-width fonts, the ANSI specification for screen displays prescribes width-to-height ratios of from 0.7 to 0.9. For proportionally spaced fonts, the specification recommends an M width-to-height ratio of 1.0 [138]. Such proportionally spaced type is read faster with fewer and wider eye fixations than fixed-width type and is rated higher in visibility, ease of reading, and contrast [131].

Large dot matrices

Character recognition is very sensitive to the size and design of the dot matrix. The smallest dot matrices generally recommended [138] are:

- 4 x 5 for subscripts, superscripts, and perfunctory notes, such as copyright notices

- 5 x 7 for numbers

- 7 x 9 for continuous reading or when users must recognize individual characters, such as in proofreading tasks

Matrices of 9 x 11 or larger with true descenders are preferred.

Distinct strokes

Avoid weak, spindly characters. Make the width of stalks and arms of characters (*stroke width*) at least 1/12 the character height [138]. Remember that strokes appear thicker when drawn light on a dark background and thinner when dark on a light background, because light appears to flow from the bright to the dark areas of the screen.

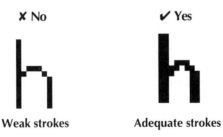

Weak strokes   **Adequate strokes**

Fuzzy fonts

Paradoxically, we can often make screen fonts more legible by making their boundaries less distinct. So-called *fuzzy fonts* use four to eight gray tones in a technique called *antialiasing* to smooth out the staircasing effect of angled and curving strokes.

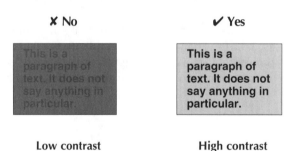

Fuzzy fonts increased the performance of one group of proofreaders from 60 percent to 98 percent of proof speeds with paper, and achieved reading speeds comparable to paper in another test [117].

Increase contrast

Legibility depends on adequate contrast between text and background. Accuracy and response time improve with increased contrast, and increasing contrast can compensate for small character size [179, 275]. Keep in mind that no color combination has greater contrast than black and white.

✘ No   **✔ Yes**

This is a paragraph of text. It does not say anything in particular.   **This is a paragraph of text. It does not say anything in particular.**

Low contrast   **High contrast**

Take care when text appears over a background color or picture. Brightly colored backgrounds, though attractive initially, become tiresome as they compete with the foreground text and graphics. A subtly colored and textured background can give the document the rich feeling we get from books printed on expensive paper, but it can also play havoc with legibility. When using photographs or textures as a background, keep them quiet. Use black-and-white photos scaled to either light or dark grays only.

Avoid ALL UPPER CASE

Use full capitalization sparingly, especially in the body of text. Words in ALL CAPITAL LETTERS are harder to recognize and are read more slowly than the same words in lower-case letters. In one test, reading and proofreading were 30 percent more efficient with upper- and lower-case text than with fully capitalized text. [247]. The reason is that lower-case letters give the word a more distinctive shape. This is another reason to prefer a typeface with longer ascenders and descenders.

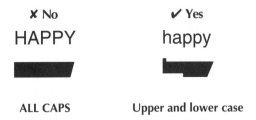

Increase line spacing and blank space

If line spacing is too small, the reader may miss the beginning of the line, repeating a line or skipping one. Also, small line spacing crowds foveal, or central, vision with text from lines above and below the one you are reading. Increasing line spacing increases reading speed and reduces the number of fixations per line [275]. As a rule, make line spacing at least [138]:

- 1/30 of the line length (This gives a 2-degree downward angle for finding the next line)

Make sure the minimum space between the bottom of one line and the top of the next is:

- 2 times the stroke width of characters
- 15 percent of the character width

Do not, however, make spacing too great. Double-spacing text will double the total number of displays and destroy the integrity of paragraphs.

Keep lines short

Long lines are harder to read than moderately short lines. They require more eye movements to read a line and make it harder for the user's eyes to find the start of the next line. Longer line lengths are tiring to read. Newspapers, especially those that use small type sizes, print information in narrow columns. Limit lines to 40 to 60 characters or about the length of the 26 upper-case and 26 lower-case letters as displayed in the alphabet [275]. If possible, let users adjust line lengths to their personal preferences.

Left justify text

Left justify rather than fully justify the text. Fully justified text, as used on paper books, requires elements of fine typography not available on most computer systems. Fully justifying online text usually requires putting extra spaces between words. This results in uneven word spacing and occasional rivers of white flowing vertically through paragraphs of text. Not surprisingly, full justification reduces reading rates about 10 percent [275].

<table>
<tr><td align="center">✘ No</td><td align="center">✔ Yes</td></tr>
<tr><td>This is a paragraph of text. It does not say anything in particular. It is here merely to show what text looks like when it is displayed this way. You may stop reading now. Please stop reading. Still here? Wish you would read everything this carefully.</td><td>This is a paragraph of text. It does not say anything in particular. It is here merely to show what text looks like when it is displayed this way. You may stop reading now. Please stop reading. Still here? Wish you would read everything this carefully.</td></tr>
<tr><td align="center">**Fully justified text**</td><td align="center">**Left-justified text**</td></tr>
</table>

Do not overemphasize reading text

Emphasize text that the user scans for but does not read continuously. However, use emphasis only lightly in text the user must read and not just recognize. Set headings and instructions off from the body of text by blank space. If you must emphasize key words in the body of text, highlight only a few and use only subtle emphasis mechanisms, such as <u>underlining</u>, **boldface**, *italics*, or a slight difference in color.

SIZE TYPE FOR PROMINENCE AND LEGIBILITY

The proper size for text depends on several factors, including the reading distance; screen resolution; contrast between text and background; visual acuity of the user; and whether the text is scanned, read word-by-word, or read character-by-character. Display text large enough so that users recognize characters, and yet small enough so that they can see entire words or phrases at a glance. Between these two extremes is a zone of optimal legibility.

Question any simple recommendation for a specific point size, character height, or dot-matrix dimensions. Legibility depends on both the character size and the viewing distance. For paper documents, the viewing distance is not critical because it is relatively constant and easily adjusted by the user. Reading distances for computer screens are more variable and less adjustable by the user. Doubling the reading distance reduces the effective size of type by half. For these reasons, display sizes are best specified as visual angles, rather than absolute sizes.

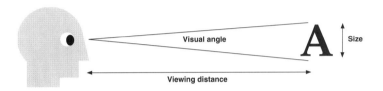

Visual angle, screen size, and viewing distance are related by this formula:

Screen size = viewing distance x tangent (visual angle)

For relatively small angles, say, less than 5 degrees, you can simplify the formula without great loss of accuracy:

Screen size = 0.01745 x viewing distance x visual angle

The ANSI/Human Factors Society Standard [8] recommends making characters:

- about 0.35 degrees for continuous reading
- at least 0.5 degrees for scanning targets

For example, for a display viewed at 20 inches, a 0.35 degree visual angle requires a character size of about 0.12 inch. At a screen resolution of 75 dots per inch, each character will stand 9 pixels high.

Viewing distance	Reading text		Scanning targets	
in.	in.	pt.	in.	pt.
12	0.07	5	0.10	8
14	0.09	6	0.12	9
16	0.10	7	0.14	10
18	0.11	8	0.16	11
20	0.12	9	0.17	13
22	0.13	10	0.19	14
24	0.15	11	0.21	15
30	0.18	13	0.26	19
36	0.22	16	0.31	23
42	0.26	18	0.37	26
48	0.29	21	0.42	30
60	0.37	26	0.52	38

Remember, though, that these figures are for ideal readers under near-perfect conditions. Other factors can reduce legibility, and remember that even with corrective glasses or contact lenses, most people have less-than-perfect vision.

EMPHASIZE SCANNING TARGETS

Only a robot reads all of an online document. Most human beings spend a lot of time scanning and little time reading. These two activities are closely related. People often scan for the item they want to read and don't start reading until they find the single item they are seeking. If they do not find the item they are seeking, they never read the display. So, scanning is a prerequisite for reading. Often, however, techniques used to make an item easy to find make it and other items in the display harder to read.

Easy to spot ≠ Easy to read

As designers, we must continually find effective compromises between scannability and legibility. We must use the highlighting mechanisms at our disposal to guide the user's attention.

Use these available emphasis mechanisms	To highlight these types of objects
Dynamic display	The cursor
Color	Headings and other targets of scanning
Reverse video	Critical information: abnormal values, values that have changed, warnings, and cautions
Intensity	
Boxing	Terms searched for in text. Selectable items, buttons, and icons that the user can activate
Size	
Blank space	Things the user does not expect or will not predict
Capitalization	Key words, figures, and other information you want the user to remember
Underlining	
Font differences	

Remember to use highlighting with finesse. Highlight no more than 10 to 15 per-cent of the items on the screen at one time [179]. Highlighting one object in a dis-play draws attention away from other objects, and any emphasis device loses its effectiveness if overused.

This section catalogs the emphasis mechanisms you can use. It also recommends when and how you use them so as not to greatly reduce legibility. They are ar-ranged from most to least powerful.

Dynamics

If something blinks or flickers or moves in our field of vision, we notice it. Dynamics is the strongest attention getter and the only emphasis mechanism effec-tive in peripheral vision. Any change of sensory input draws attention [130].

Change the display

Unexpected change (or the absence of expected change) is a powerful attention getter. Use change to draw the user's attention to critical information. Some exam-ples:

- Display the horizontal scroll bar only when information stretches off the right of the window. The sudden appearance of the scroll bar alerts the user to the addi-tional information available through scrolling.

- Change the shape of the cursor to indicate what happens if the user selects the item pointed to.

- Pause before displaying the prompt for the user to act. This gives the user time to read the display [208].

Blink

Blinking means to continually alternate the display characteristics of some object on the screen. To blink, alternate between:

- Displayed and hidden
- Bright and dim
- Normal and boldface
- Two contrasting colors

Blinking is so powerful that it is easily overdone. Never blink more than one item at a time. Use blinking to draw attention to emergency conditions and special exceptions. For a single blinking rate use 3 Hz [41, 275]. For two rates use 2 Hz and 5 Hz, and use no more than two blinking rates in a program [138]. Make on-times equal to or longer than off-times.

Dynamically display text

To draw attention to text, display it one word at a time or continuously in small blocks. If the text is displayed slightly slower than the users' reading rate, they will be drawn to read it—for a while. One study found that students preferred a very slow display rate of about 30 characters per second, which is slower than the normal reading rate [31]. One explanation for this preference is that it let the students feel in control. However, most people who read text online for extended periods of time prefer the fastest possible display rates. Experimenters have periodically paused a text display to let students catch up [31].

Avoid visual distractions

Changes to the display can easily add noise. Take steps to ensure that changes are comprehensible and predictable.

Make changes distinct and clear. Users may not notice a small change to an existing display. They may also fail to recognize an item that appears and then immediately disappears.

Present new information in the expected way. Fill screens top to bottom and left to right. If text and graphics cannot be displayed instantly, display the graphics first and then the text—otherwise, the display of the graphic would distract the reader of the text.

Change only one thing at a time. Users cannot attend to two moving objects at once. Nor can they watch animation or video while reading related text.

Reverse video

Displaying text or objects with the foreground and background colors reversed is called *reverse video*. The first- and second-level headings of this book are reversed from the colors of the body text. When displaying a word in reverse video, add extra spaces around the word and display the spaces immediately before and after the word in reverse video too.

✗ No   **✔ Yes**

the ▮highlighted▮ word   the █highlighted█ word

Reversing light and dark can often reduce the legibility of text as the thickness of letters appears to change as they reverse lightness. Also, excessive use of reverse video on a display leads to the *crossword-puzzle* effect, the mottled appearance of a display with many reverse-video blocks.

Color

Color is effective in highlighting essential information, aiding search, and grouping objects in the display. It is so important and so difficult to use well that I have included a complete section on color starting on page 241.

Brightness, boldness, line width

Making a word bolder or brighter than surrounding text calls attention to it.

Normal   **Bold**

Use this technique **in moderation** to emphasize words embedded in a paragraph of text. Likewise, to emphasize graphical objects, you can draw them in wider or brighter lines.

Boxes and borders

Boxing words or other objects sets them off. If they are links, boxing them can make them look like buttons and can show the extent of their selection zone. Boxing does not work, however, for words in a closely spaced paragraph because the space between words and lines may leave little room for the box. The lines of the box may clip the tops, bottoms, and edges of characters or force the lines farther apart. When displaying text inside a box or border, leave enough space around the text to separate it from the border of the box.

Use boundaries to differentiate areas. Changes in boundaries call attention to specific areas. To call attention to the information in an area, draw its border with a thicker line or a bright color. This focuses attention on the information in the area without reducing its legibility. But don't overdo boxes, as they reduce blank space and can lead to a checkerboard effect.

Size

Some systems can display text and other graphical objects at various sizes. Most people readily notice a 30 percent difference in size even when objects are in separate parts of the display.

Although larger objects are easier to spot and recognize, keep search targets smaller than a 5-degree visual angle, which is the largest size that the user can read in a glance. This angle covers an area about 1.7 inches in diameter at a reading distance of about 19 inches.

Blank space

Use space before, after, around, and within text

to make it stand out on the screen.

Capitalization

Capitalization can emphasize individual words and short phrases. Printing a word in ALL CAPITAL letters makes it stand out in a paragraph or as a heading. However, those words are read more slowly than the same words in upper and lower case. Furthermore, capitalization robs words of the distinct shape that makes them easier to find. As with other emphasis mechanisms, do not overdo capitalization. If your text contains acronyms, avoid capitalization as an emphasis mechanism.

Underlining

Underlining is widely available, even on many alphanumeric displays. Underlining works well to emphasize titles and headings, but can hinder reading <u>in a paragraph of text</u>, <u>especially if the lines are so close together that the underline appears to cap the following line or the underline cuts through descenders</u>.

Italics

An italic or slanted type style adds a subtle emphasis to words and phrases in text. It can thus attract attention without overpowering the surrounding text.

Normal   *Italic*

Do not overdo italics. An entire paragraph in italics serves no purpose. An entire topic in italics will prove tiring to read. Remember that some systems create the italic version of a font by slanting normal character shapes. This distortion can make italic text harder to read.

Different font

A subtle form of emphasis results from changing from one typeface to another. Can you `recognize` which `words` in this sentence use a **different** font? One use of this technique is in instructions to distinguish words displayed by the computer or typed by the user. Using different fonts for emphasis requires a high-resolution display and a moderate or large type size. Make the two typefaces about the same size but distinct enough in shape that the user will notice the difference. In general, use no more than three different fonts in an online document.

PUTTING THESE IDEAS TO WORK

Essential ideas of this chapter

➡ The online display is about one-third as large and one-twentieth as sharp as the paper page. It is also shaped differently and may reverse the background/foreground contrast found in paper documents.

➡ Display the document in a way that minimizes the disruption to the user's work. If possible, display the document in a small, fixed message area or an independent window the user can position and size on the screen.

➡ Substitute screen design elements, such as blinking, color, and reverse video, for print emphasis mechanisms not available on the screen.

➡ Divide the screen into large, primary display areas in the center and smaller, secondary areas around the edges. Use these areas consistently. Standardize the format and location of titles, display IDs, text, graphics, labels, options, and other items that appear in several displays.

➡ Use lists, tables, visual coding, and progressive disclosure to avoid cluttered, tightly packed displays. Condense text for continuous reading.

➡ Do not highlight more than a few items in a paragraph of text. Use subtle emphasis mechanisms, such as underlining, all caps, or italics in a paragraph of text. Do not display an entire paragraph in all caps.

➡ Use color to speed up searches, to separate closely spaced items, to link separated items, and to focus attention. Do not use color just for decoration.

➡ For legible text, follow these guidelines:

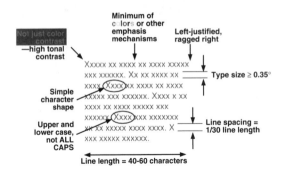

For more ideas and inspiration

Banks, William W. and Jon Weimer. 1992. *Effective Computer Display Design.* Englewood Cliffs, NJ: Prentice-Hall.

Dumas, Joseph S. *Designing User Interfaces for Software.* Englewood Cliffs, NJ: Prentice-Hall, 1988.

Durrett, H. John, ed. 1987. *Color and the Computer.* Boston: Academic Press.

Galitz, Wilbert O. 1989. *Handbook of Screen Format Design.* Wellesley, MA: QED Information Sciences.

Rubenstein, Richard. 1988. *Digital Typography: An Introduction to Type and Composition for Computer System Design*. Reading, MA: Addison-Wesley.

Thorell, Lisa G. and Wanda J. Smith. 1990. *Using Computer Color Effectively: An Illustrated Reference.* Englewood Cliffs, NJ: Prentice-Hall.

Tullis, Thomas S. 1988. "Screen Design." In *Handbook of Human-Computer Interaction.* Amsterdam: Elsevier Science Publishers B.V. (North-Holland). 377-411.

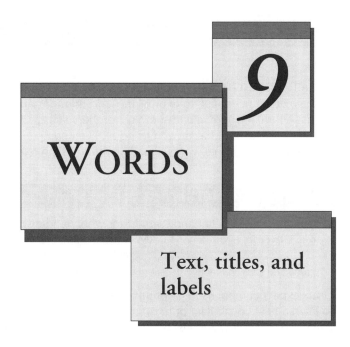

9

WORDS

Text, titles, and labels

The principles of good writing are the same for online documents as for paper, but applying these principles is more difficult. The perceptions and psychology of the reader differ. Many users read online documentation in the middle of some other task and then only as a last resort after they are confused, tired, and frustrated. The online "page" is smaller, fuzzier, and less legible than the familiar paper page.

Online documentation is just like writing paper documentation—only more so. Without clear and simple writing, online documents fail [29, 236].

> The tenets of good technical writing seem to apply ten-fold to online documentation [128, p. 437].

Online documentation is a new medium, and many online documents are not effective because the writer fails to account for the differences. Online is like a second language to writers whose experience has been writing for paper. Online documentation embodies new idioms and requires new rhetorical strategies. It tolerates less self-indulgent writing.

To write online documents, we must apply with a vengeance the principles of good clear writing while attending to the differences between paper and online documents.

USE SHORT, SIMPLE, FAMILIAR WORDS

In the 1930s, C. G. Ogden defined a *Basic English* vocabulary of 850 words, which he claimed were enough to express most descriptions and procedures. Though this list has alternately grown and shrunk over the years as Ogden's technique has gone in and out of favor, it has proved its point. Even complex concepts can be communicated in short, simple words already familiar to the reader.

Use concrete terms

We all understand better and learn faster when reading concrete and specific words. Developers of the GM-CAMS touchscreen system observed

> The message here is that abstract, obtuse words used in touch areas can lead to errors, and slow interactive decision making [173].

Users expect computers to communicate in everyday language. They do not want to learn a new vocabulary or grasp new forms of old words. Writers should especially avoid *nominalizations*, that is, turning verbs into nouns.

✗ No	✔ Yes
the program's drawing of	the program draws
hardcopy output device	the printer
physical interface device	a cable
status indicator LED	warning light
option selection mechanism	a list of choices

Avoid unnecessary computer terminology

Many users find computer jargon confusing, annoying, and frightening. Unless all of your users have extensive knowledge of the architecture and operations of computers, avoid computer terminology in messages and online documents. Use the reader's vocabulary and refer to tasks and objects at the reader's level of understanding.

Jargon is fine—the user's jargon, not yours. Jargon unites members of a specialized field and, used with those who understand it, adds precision and color. If you can speak the jargon like a native, go ahead and use it. If you can't, stick to standard English.

For example, these terms are OK for programmers but not for inexperienced operators:

byte	parameter
data	pathname
directory	response
input	root
output	system

Explain in the user's words. Use terms, units, and names from the user's work.

✗ No	✔ Yes
The parameter is invalid.	Pick: 1, 2, 3, or 4.
Comm session is not bound.	Phone link broken.
Print Manager error code 21	Please turn on the printer.
Syntax error 43	Shorten the name to 8 or fewer characters.
Return code -1	The file exists but is empty.

Beware secret jargon

If you must communicate an entirely new concept, invent a new word or borrow a word from another field. Do not use a word from the user's everyday vocabulary with a new, unfamiliar meaning. Beware everyday words that have a special meaning with respect to computers:

application	execute	option	screen
argument	field	output	scroll
branch	file	parent	server
button	font	parse	session
child	help	power	status
click	interactive	procedure	support
client	invalid	process	syntax
command	keyword	program	terminal
default	library	prompt	terminate
disk	link	query	toggle
drag	macro	record	trigger
elegant	menu	recover	tutorial
enabled	metaphor	root	utility
enter	mouse	routine	window
environment	object	run	

This secret jargon baffles users who interpret the words with their everyday meanings. These words create special problems where they have still other meanings in specific professions. For instance, don't use "invalid" in a document for nurses, "terminate" in one for personnel managers, or "default" in one for bankers.

Call things what the user named them

Express ideas in terms of the objects the user is manipulating, not in terms of the computer's internal representation of those objects. Identify variables by the names users give them.

✘ No	✔ Yes
The input data value is out of range.	Fonts can range from 10 pt to 24 pt.
The file was not found.	The file PLAN.95 not found on disk Server_95.

ENSURE ACCURATE READING

Because text displayed on the screen is less legible than the equivalent text printed on paper, take special precautions to ensure that the user does not misread displayed words and phrases.

Take care with small important words

In English the meaning of a sentence or phrase often turns on a single small word. Often-overlooked words include:

all	if	not
and	is	one
any	may	or
can	no	yes

Unfortunately, such small words are the ones most likely to be ignored or not read online. To ensure that such words are not overlooked, display them with underlines, in reverse video, or in ALL CAPS. Since emphasized text is harder to read and emphasis loses its effect if overdone, emphasize <u>only</u> key words and phrases, <u>NOT</u> entire passages.

Also consider rewriting sentences whose meaning turns entirely on one such word. Say the same thing in two complementary ways or repeat the critical information graphically.

Do not omit relative pronouns. "The program reformats the data you entered" is harder to understand than "The program reformats the data that you entered."

Take care with prefixes

Prefixes can change the entire meaning of a word. Negative prefixes reverse the meaning of a word and often an entire sentence. Especially troublesome are short, easily overlooked prefixes, such as:

an	in
de	non
dis	un

Problems often arise if the prefix is separated from the root word when the term is hyphenated at the end of a line. Problems also occur if the prefix is also a word itself and the spacing between words is too small. For example

> The result was incompatible data files.

> The result was in compatible data files.

Avoid overabbreviation

Because space is scarce, it is tempting to abbreviate wherever possible. Over-abbreviation, however, can confuse the user. Abbreviations are easily misread. If you use abbreviations, use them consistently and stick to familiar, common, standard abbreviations.

Contractions can lend an informal and chatty tone to messages, but they are often a problem on low-resolution computer screens. The apostrophe is only a few pixels in size. Often the part contracted is vital to the meaning of the message, for instance the words *not* or *will*. The same problem applies to possessives formed with an apostrophe.

✘ No	✔ Yes
Don't	Do NOT
It'll	It WILL

Use only standard, easily read symbols

Use only letters, numbers, punctuation marks, and standard symbols ($, *, @, %, &). Avoid special characters that not all of your users can display. Stick with standard symbol sets and fonts that come installed on the computers and terminals of your readers. If you are writing documents on one computer system that will be read on another, double-check to ensure that all characters are translated properly.

Do not rely on punctuation

The most easily misread marks are punctuation marks. The difference between a period and a comma or between a colon and a semicolon is usually only a pixel or two—a difference that can easily hide behind a speck of dust. Avoid colons and semicolons especially. They are hard to recognize on the screen, and many users do not know the difference between them anyway [243].

To test the vulnerability of your text to the misreading of punctuation marks, prepare a sample with all punctuation marks removed and see whether readers can figure out the meaning. If they can, albeit slowly, your text is safe. If not, rewrite it so that the meaning does not depend on any individual punctuation mark.

SPEAK SIMPLY, DIRECTLY, AND ACCURATELY

Users do not turn to online documents for grandiloquent prose, flowery phrases, or poetical flourishes. They expect the computer to speak simply, directly, and accurately.

Write simple sentences

Write simple sentences. Two studies comparing computer tutorials written at various reading grade levels found that users of all levels of verbal ability preferred the simplest (fifth grade) version. They performed equally well with this simple version and did not find it condescending or insulting [230].

Write active sentences

Where possible, write in the active, not the passive voice. Active sentences are easier to process and remember than passive sentences [179].

✘ No	✔ Yes
An option is then selected by the user.	Select an option.
. . . are sorted by the program	The program sorts . . .
Limits are adjusted manually by the user.	Set limits manually.

Notice too that the shift from the passive voice saves words.

Make positive assertions

Write simple affirmative sentences [100]. Tell people what is true rather than what is not false. Where you have a choice, tell people what to do rather than what not to do. Instead of saying "Do not exit the Report Menu without first selecting the Verify option" say "Verify the data before you exit the Report Menu."

Keep sentences simple

Deciphering complex, formal language distracts users from the task at hand and further taxes their memory. Favor simple declarative and imperative sentences.

✘ No	✔ Yes
The user should by now have established the chemical balance.	Set the chemical balance.
It is recommended that you now ...	Please ...
The text height, which is the page height minus margins, can be set on Panel P4.	Text height is the page height less margins. Set page height on Panel P4.

Especially avoid embedded clauses. When sentences containing embedded clauses fall on the boundary between two scrolling zones, the poor user must read the first half of the outer clause, read the first half of the inner one, stop reading and find the scroll-down button or icon, find the continuation at the top of the window, read the rest of the inner and outer clauses, and then make sense of it all. Shorter sentences mean fewer sentences are split between windows.

Express ideas precisely

The computer is the symbol of logical and mathematical precision. Users expect more precision and tolerate less ambiguity in online documents than in paper documents.

Speak directly to the user

Tell users clearly and directly what to do and what not to do. Do not say that they *may, can,* or *are allowed to.* Avoid the vague words *could* and *should,* especially for readers who speak English as a second language.

✘ No	✔ Yes
You should back up your files.	Back up your files.
Bending the disk could damage it.	Do not bend the disk.

State quantities exactly

Users expect computers to give precise information, especially when expressing quantities.

✘ No	✔ Yes
a little while	4 or 5 seconds
increases	doubles
shown above	shown on Panel M-22
somewhat	25%
insufficient	4 pages too few

If you cannot give an exact quantity, consider giving a range, such as "This process will take 3 to 10 seconds." But avoid pseudoprecision, such as "Please wait 2.50 seconds."

Do not make the computer sound human

Avoid *anthropomorphism*, having the computer impersonate a human being. This erroneously implies that computers can think, know, understand, and sympathize as people do. Such deception can temporarily fool or amuse novice users, but the effect is short-lived. The danger is that imitating a human establishes an unsound conceptual model in the mind of the user [247]. Do not pretend that the computer is not a computer. Help the user understand and anticipate how it operates.

✘ No	✔ Yes
I will begin when you press Enter.	Press Enter to begin.
My memory is overloaded.	Too many items to process.
What do you want me to do?	Please retype your command.

Avoid the voice and viewpoint of a human being. Do not address the user in the first person. Consider the following error message displayed late one night by a large commercial information database:

```
I don't understand that
```

Who is the person speaking here? Is there a little person hidden inside the computer? Is someone listening in on the conversation with the system? Is Big Brother watching? And what about this one:

```
I must have amnesia. The date can't possibly be cor-
rect. We'd both be really happy if you'd fix it with
the Control Panel.
```

This program seems mentally ill. Not only does it admit to forgetfulness, it shows a split personality. Note the shift from *I* to *we* . Or is it trying to act friendly by including me in the message?

When describing the computer or speaking to the user, avoid words that attribute human characteristics to the computer:

Words that apply to people	Words that apply to computers
know	process
think	sort
understand	store
remember	retrieve
ask	use
tell	operate
speak	direct
	control
	calculate

One study found that students preferred mechanical computerlike messages, such as "Response correct," to casual, chatty messages, such as "Nope," "You bet," and "Wait a second!" [42]

Write for the literal-minded user

The increased anxiety many users feel may lead them to interpret online documents literally. New users of UNIX on the Andrew system frequently typed in the square brackets used in standard UNIX online documentation to denote options [161]. Such literal-mindedness can require modifying standards common in paper documents.

Traditional usage puts terminal punctuation within quotation marks. Many users will type the quotation marks and any included punctuation. Better to omit the quotation marks altogether and surround the phrase with blank space, or use a distinctive color, type **style,** or `face` for what the user is asked to type. For example:

✘ No	✔ Yes
Enter "DELETE."	Enter:
	DELETE
Enter "DELETE".	Enter **DELETE**

Avoid wisecracks

Writers often try to relieve tension and make the system more enjoyable by including humorous messages. What they forget is when and how often those messages will appear. What is funny the first time is boring the tenth time and positively annoying the twenty-seventh time it is seen. Not only that, but some users won't get the joke, or won't find it funny even the first time. People's senses of humor differ— and some people don't have one. A user who has just lost four hours of work is not likely to find anything funny in a message that makes light of the predicament. Avoid messages like these:

```
Drat an error occurred while reading or writing!


Nearly Fatal Error ID = -4.5
Illegal or Rude Command!


The memory allocator is in deep, deep trouble. Close a
file immediately!


Why did you click on "Help"? This stack is so self-
explanatory that you can't possibly need any help!
```

Unless you want to project a wisecracking personality, avoid humor, or use it with due moderation. **Never** poke fun at the user. **Never** make jokes about the product.

APPLY A CONSISTENT STYLE THROUGHOUT

Inconsistent language confuses users and destroys confidence in the product. Users read meaning into every change of phrasing and each different grammatical pattern. Variety for the sake of variety or artistic expression inevitably leads to confusion when applied to online documents. The problem of consistency becomes critical with the large, web-structured collaborations possible with hypertext.

> [Unless] each author writes clearly and completely, while you might understand the individual nodes, it's hard to follow the thread of thoughts as it winds through several dozen nodes [22, p. 260].

If you phrase, format, and display information consistently, the user quickly and painlessly learns the conventions used throughout the document. You can then use such conventions to make the document more concise and dependable.

A consistent style makes information more accessible. All indexes, whether generated manually or automatically, face a fundamental problem: people use different
words to describe the same objects. In one study covering several subject domains,
80 to 90 percent of the time users guessed different words for the same topic [95].
Defeating these odds requires consistency and forethought.

If indexes are to be used to access a document, the writer and editor must use terms
consistently. Elegant variations may satisfy the writer's creative urge but will thwart
the reader not clever enough to use the same phrase when retrieving information
[237]. Remember, such unique phrasing creates informational orphans.

What aspects of the style of online documents, then, should you make consistent?
The answer is to make all differences of language intentional and meaningful.

Words

If you call it a *widget* in one place, don't call it a *gizmo* in another. Such variations
annoy experts and confuse novices. Consider these terms from a single online document. They all refer to the date the stored information was last changed:

```
Modification date
Update date
Date of last modification
Date of latest change
Most recent access
```

Consider the plight of the poor users who must use several programs on different
computer systems. Here is a sample of the variety of names for common operations:

Enter a system	Leave a system	Print out something
log on	exit	print
log in	log out	printout
logon	logoff	pr
login	off	lp
hello	bye	output
sign in	quit	list
sign on	cancel	display -p
knockknock	xit	copy to print
	99	hardcopy
	terminate	

Grammatical structures

Because messages and online documents are seldom read as long passages, variety of expression is of no use in making the messages more interesting. Arbitrary differences in grammatical patterns imply different meanings to most users of online messages.

✗ No	✔ Yes
Color = blue	Color is blue.
The current font is Block #78.	Font is Block #78.
Line spacing set to double.	Line spacing is double.

In general:

- Use simple, imperative sentences for directions.
- Use simple, declarative sentences for descriptions.

Abbreviations

Because space is scarce, online documents, especially messages, must sometimes abbreviate words and phrases. Use abbreviations that are obvious (*ft* after a number to indicate *feet*) or else very common (NASA, IBM, ZIP code). Avoid those that users must learn or guess. If you must use obscure abbreviations, follow a consistent scheme for forming abbreviations, such as omitting vowels or selecting the first few letters of the word. Also allow only one abbreviated form per word. If you use many abbreviations, include an online glossary where the user can look up the meaning of all abbreviations. For easier reading omit periods from abbreviations. (CRT, not C.R.T.) [100].

Spelling

Because online documents use many technical terms, they are unusually prone to misspellings. Many computer systems form technical terms by combining ordinary words using unusual forms of capitalization, variations of word spacing, and non-standard characters. Consider the following ways of referring to the name of a file:

```
file name
file's name
filename
fileName
file_name
```

For online documents, standardize all such special terms.

Special conventions

Also standardize space-saving notations and conventions such as:

/	Use a slash to separate alternatives; for example, "and/or"
[option]	Surround optional items with brackets
...	Use ellipses to indicate a range or continuation
\<Return\>	Surround a label of the key with angle brackets
\<Ctrl\>-X	Indicates pressing the X key while holding down the \<Ctrl\> key

The exact conventions you adopt are less important than explaining them clearly and following them faithfully.

ASSUME NONSEQUENTIAL SCANNING

Users do not so much read an online document as search it. They encounter topics in an order writers cannot predict and often skim these topics looking for a specific fact. Our writing style must accommodate jumpy searching as well as complete perusal.

Keep paragraphs short

Paragraphs viewed on the computer screen or in a window on that screen seem longer than they do on paper. Paragraphs that seem short on a large page seem to go on forever when viewed on the small computer screen or window. Therefore, write shorter paragraphs, more like the three-line paragraphs in newspapers than those in textbooks of philosophy. Especially avoid paragraphs that span several displays.

Emphasize the new, the novel, the surprising

People perceive most easily information that confirms what they already believe and tend to ignore or misinterpret information that is contrary to their beliefs. Hence, the more something differs from the user's expectations, the more you must make it explicit and visible. Never bury such information in the middle of a paragraph where a scanning reader will fly right past it. If something is unexpected, highlight it:

```
When you send an electronic mail message, you can
specify whether you want automatic error checking and
what type of checking you want. NOTE: Character
checking is the default. Before version 4.2, the
default was no checking.
```

Or put it at the start of a paragraph. Or make it a separate paragraph.

Avoid the as-shown-above syndrome

The *as-shown-above* syndrome is the tendency of many writers to write as if read-ers would read the online document from beginning to end. You recognize this syndrome in such phrases as:

"As shown above . . ."; ". . . below"

"Earlier you read that . . ."

"By now you have learned how to . . ."

". . . will be explained later"

You also see it in the policy of spelling out abbreviations or defining terms the first time they appear. It is also evidenced by placing warnings, cautions, notes, and conventions in the front of the book. The problem is that readers do not read online documents cover to cover from front to back—online documents do not even have covers. Many do not even have a start and an end. Most are a collection of topics the reader may encounter in any order. Write accordingly.

Avoid blind references

Because the amount of information visible at any one time is less for the online document than for the paper document, avoid the paper-documentation habit of assuming that other information is immediately visible. What appears on the same paper page may hide offscreen in the online document. For example, pronoun an-tecedents may lurk on a previous display or may scroll off the top of the screen. The phrase "This fact means . . ." communicates little if the antecedent to "This" is no longer visible on the screen. Telling the user to "Repeat the preceding steps . . ." can be dangerous if the preceding steps have scrolled off the top of the current dis-play. Make references explicit. Forward references suffer from a small page size too. Finding the "following" item, for example, may require flipping electronic pages. Do not assume that the user can see two separate items at the same time.

WRITE GLOBALLY

If your document will be translated into other languages or used by people of widely different cultures, take steps to preserve meaning and avoid confusion.

Write for translation

When writing your document, consider the problems you may be creating for translators and for those who read in a language other than their first. Some tips follow.

- Avoid prepositions in short phrases. Prepositions are difficult to translate accurately, especially when they appear in short phrases out of context, such as phrases on a menu [213].

- Minimize abbreviations, acronyms, and mnemonics in documents to be translated [10].

- Leave room for English to expand to twice in height and three times in length when translated [10].

- Write in a neutral, businesslike tone. Avoid a cutesy or stuffy tone.

- Avoid slang and jargon.

- Categories, and the uses of categories, are culturally determined. Do not depend on a deep understanding of logical constructs.

- Use a simple vocabulary and conventional syntax. Follow the same conventions that someone studying your language would learn first.

- Use a standard typeface, especially for readers unfamiliar with the Roman alphabet.

- Give extra feedback. Provide frequent checks of the user's knowledge or tests of mastery. Include online glossaries with examples, and, if possible, include language-to-language dictionaries.

Take care with spoken words

If your document uses spoken words, take care that they are understandable both before and after translation. Keep the use of speech predictable.

- Avoid surprising or unanticipated text.

- Use only one narrator. Include spoken text only where users will expect it.

- Cue users before starting the text or let them control when spoken text plays.

- Provide a written transcript for all spoken text.

Select a narrator who speaks slowly and distinctly, with a standard American or British accent. These speakers are more understandable to those with another first language. Speaking slowly also allows time if more words are required in the target language.

For the foreign-language version, use a native speaker of the language who is familiar with how terminology is used. Make sure the gender and accent are those of someone who could deliver this message in the target culture. A woman speaking Arabic with an Egyptian accent would not be credible in Iran or Saudi Arabia [10].

Localize other things too

Remember that words are not the only things you have to translate.

Localize these items, especially if they are used in retrieving topics:

- Format of numbers, especially the decimal point and thousands separator (1,000,000.00 vs. 1.000.000,00)

- Format of dates and times (4:30 PM vs. 1630, 3/31/94 vs. 31.03.94)

- Format of addresses and phone numbers

- Format of amounts of money ($123.45 in US vs. 123$45 in Portugal)

- Units of measurement

- Order of family and given name and forms of polite address.

- Names for generic person (John Doe vs. Pierre Dupont)

INDEXING LARGE DOCUMENTS

In many paper and online documents, users look up topics in an index. Several types of indexes are possible, some manually created and others automatically compiled by the computer. In online documents, users can also search by specifying keywords describing the information they seek. In many online documentation systems, the same terms serve as both retrieval keywords and index entries. The procedures for compiling these terms are the same. The index might contain an entry *files, copying*. The user could find the same information by searching for *files and copying*. For online documents, the process of indexing includes both assigning search keywords and preparing a directory where the user can select from those words to jump to the associated topic.

Improving the indexing and keywording is one of the best ways to make documents (paper or online) more accessible. In one test, increasing keywords from 2 to 32 per topic increased search success rates from 21 percent to 76 percent [67].

Automated indexing

Automated indexing methods extract keywords and index terms from the text of the document itself. Techniques include *concordance* indexes, which include all words of the document, and *limited-word* indexes, which restrict which words become keywords or index entries.

Automated indexing is convenient and sometimes just as effective as indexing by human indexers [237]. The effectiveness depends on the suitability of the method chosen and on the quality of writing in the document. In my experience, automatic indexing works best with documents written by professional writers (journalists, copywriters, technical writers) but not so well for documents written by people for whom writing is a sideline or part of some other more important activity (scientists, engineers, programmers). It also works better for documents written by a single author than those with multiple authors.

Concordance indexes

Concordance or *uncontrolled-vocabulary* indexes are automatically compiled lists of all the words in a document, showing where each occurs. Such lists are typically displayed for the user to select from to see the text where the word occurs.

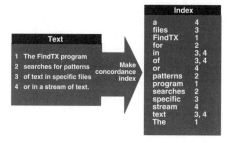

Software to create uncontrolled-vocabulary indexes is readily available, but these indexes suffer from several problems. Such indexes are large, typically half the size of the text file they index, and they suffer if the document contains many synonyms or misspellings [90]. Also, many ideas are not limited to a discrete passage of text.

Other ideas, because they are alluded to obliquely or are significant by their absence, are difficult to recognize automatically.

Limited-word indexes

Limited-word indexes reduce the size of concordance indexes by using *negative masking* to eliminate irrelevant words or *positive masking* to index only known, relevant terms.

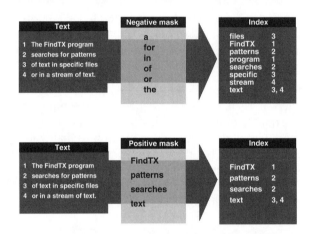

In general, words that occur very often or very rarely are of little interest to searchers. However, many middle-frequency words are also of no interest and some low-frequency words are of great interest [216].

Typically, negative masking leaves too many words and positive masking includes too few. *Word-frequency* indexing combines them to produce a complete, yet concise, index. First, words are counted and listed by frequency of occurrence. A negative mask is used to remove irrelevant function words, such as articles (a, an, the), prepositions (of, on, to), and conjunctions (and, but, yet) as well as other common but irrelevant words. Many concordance indexing systems ignore any words found only once in the document on the assumption that these are probably misspellings. After removing these words from the list, the most common of the remaining words are used as a positive mask.

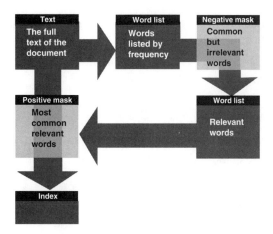

When you cannot use a true limited-word indexing technique, you can still limit the size of the concordance index by eliminating common words (negative masking) and removing suffixes (-s, -ed, -ing). Advocates of this approach claim that, for most cases, it is as effective as using a limited-word index [90].

Manual indexing

In *manual indexing*, a human being decides what words best describe each topic. Manual indexing can account for the subtleties and inconsistencies of language better than automated techniques. Manual indexers can sometimes substitute more precise terms for ones used by a sloppy or unskilled author. However, manual indexing is time-consuming and the quality of the result depends on the skill of the indexer.

Indexing procedure

The process of keywording a topic is much like indexing a paper document. Here is the general procedure for indexing a topic [28, 67].

1. List all the user's questions that the topic answers (How do I . . . ? Why should I . . . ?). Phrase the questions the way users would ask them.

2. Select the principal words and phrases of these questions.

3. From the title, introduction, and content, select the primary nouns and verbs.

4. Add entries for graphics and tables.

5. For the terms selected so far, add terms that are more general and more abstract.

6. For each term, include two or three synonyms. Try to anticipate what users would call these concepts.

Index generously. Remember, most users will try only three or four terms for a concept before giving up [28].

Checklist for index entries

When you are done, your index (and keyword list) should contain entries and synonyms for the primary items in these categories:

- Words and phrases
- Names of things, places, people
- Acronyms and abbreviations
- Tables, diagrams, and pictures
- Segments of animation, video, music, and sound
- Concepts and ideas
- Warnings, cautions, and other restrictions
- Procedures
- Rules, guidelines, standards, and policies
- Definitions of terms

Rules for indexing

Make the keywords for each topic distinct. Include less common but more precise words as these better discriminate between similar concepts [95]. Index each topic with multiple distinct terms and ensure that terms are well distributed among topics [90]. Using a variety of terms well distributed among topics makes each easier to identify.

In general, make concrete concepts plural and abstract ones singular (files, menus, directories, but communication, storage). Phrase actions as gerunds (copying, moving, deleting).

Provide multiple entries for each concept. Index under both the infinitive (To copy files), gerund (Copying files), and object (files, copying) forms. Invert verb-object entries ("deleting parameters" and "parameters, deleting"). Alphabetize numbers as numbers and as if spelled out (76-8 as if "Seventy-six eight")

Index concepts under both their technical and nontechnical names. For example, index a passage of music by the terms musicians would recognize (*allegro, forte*) and those an average listener would recognize *(fast, loud).*

Indexing nonverbal media

Take special care to index tables, pictures, animations, video segments, sounds, music, and other such media. Users cannot use full-text search to find such items, yet these items may be the very ones users seek. To assign keywords to such media, ask these questions:

- What questions does this item answer? Why would someone view or listen to it?

- What is unique about this item? What distinguishes it from others of its type?

- What does it contain? What objects (people, equipment, menus, voices) does it include and what are their characteristics (number, size, shape, color, motion, tempo, loudness)?

- What is it about? What does it represent or symbolize (safety, anxiety, beginning, ending)?

- What kind is it? Tag items by genre or type. Music may be classical, rock, jazz, country, or folk. Photographs can be portrait, landscape, x-ray, microscopic, underwater, and so forth.

Remember to index by media-specific characteristics, such as the running time of music or animation or the number of colors in a graphic.

Standardizing terms

Inconsistent keywords are worse than wrong ones. If the search finds nothing, the user may at least try other keywords. But if the search finds some topics, users assume that the topics found are all the document contains on that subject. To prevent a mismatch among the keywords of different indexers, standardize keywords for information retrieval [237]. Also, standardize how you will express units of measurement such as dates, times, and dimensions.

For establishing keyword lists, start with general indexing categories such as those found in the *Library of Congress Subject Headings*, the *Facts On File* news headings, and the *Reader's Guide* headings. For documents in specific disciplines, use the sauruses and glossaries for those fields, for example:

- *Engineering Index*

- *Chemical Abstracts*

- *Communication Abstracts*

- The Library of Congress's *Thesaurus for Graphic Materials*

- *Social Sciences Index*

- *Thesaurus of Sociological Indexing Terms*

- National Library of Medicine's *Medical Subject Headings* (MeSH)

Also consider the terms used in indexes of authoritative reference works in the field.

List all possible indexing terms before you begin indexing. If you are manually indexing the document, work from this standard list. If you will use automated full-text indexing schemes, have writers and editors use these terms [237]. Give indexers the list of approved keywords in two forms. Give them an alphabetical list so they can verify that the term they want is on the list. And give them a list organized in a hierarchy of categories so they can find the term for a new concept and can specify information at various levels of abstraction and generality [95]. Standardize on this set of terms and change it only grudgingly.

PUTTING THESE IDEAS TO WORK

Essential ideas of this chapter

➥ Use short, simple, familiar words. Avoid abstract terms and computer jargon.

➥ Keep sentences short and simple. Make positive assertions, using the active voice.

➥ Speak directly to the user in a neutral, not chatty or stuffy, tone. Do not speak in the first person or use terms that imply that the computer is human.

➥ Avoid or take special care with small words and punctuation marks that are easily overlooked or misread on the computer screen.

➥ Standardize terms, grammatical patterns, abbreviations, spellings, and special conventions used throughout the system.

➥ Express just one main idea in each topic. Eliminate unnecessary information and electronically cross-reference (rather than include) related topics.

➥ Write topics so they can be read in any order. Avoid phrases such as "as shown above."

For more ideas and inspiration

Barnum, Carol and Saul Carliner, eds. 1993. *Techniques for Technical Communicators.* New York: Macmillan.

Rubens, Philip, ed. 1992. *Science and Technical Writing: A Manual of Style.* New York: Henry Holt.

Wright, Patricia. 1988. "Issues of Content and Presentation in Document Design." In *Handbook of Human-Computer Interaction.* Amsterdam: North-Holland. 629-652.

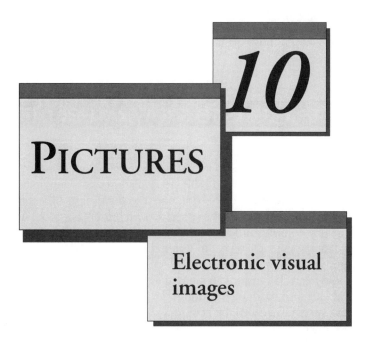

PICTURES

10

Electronic visual images

Online documentation is an inherently visual medium. The computer monitor looks a lot more like television or a video game than a book. Although few would dispute the value of pictures in online documents, many online documents today lack pictures or use illustrations sparingly. Whenever words would fill a screen or window, consider whether your message could be presented as a list, table, diagram, icon, graph, outline, flowchart, or some other graphical form.

✗ No	✔ Yes
At the "Command" prompt, type the word "DELETE" and press the Enter Key.	Command ==> DELETE [ENTER]
From the Text menu select the style choice. This reveals the Style submenu. From this submenu, select Bold.	

Text	Effects	Setup	Object	Shortcuts
Font	▶			
Size	▶			
Style	▶	Plain	⌘ P	
Justification	▶	**Bold**	⌘ B	
Spacing	▶	*Italic*	⌘ I	
Position	▶	Underline	⌘ U	
		✓Shadow	⌘ W	
Search & Replace		Outline	⌘ O	
Spell Check	▶	Small Caps	⌘ \	
Type...	⌘T			

This chapter suggests where and how you should use pictures in online documents—even those displayed on low-cost alphanumeric terminals.

USE PICTURES TO SHOW RATHER THAN TELL

The ability of graphics to improve communication, especially for technical subjects, is well documented [137, 191]. Pictures can draw attention to essential information, especially if it is unfamiliar to the user or differs from what the user expects. Pictures increase the speed at which users carry out actions and help them imagine complex processes. Pictures show trends, illustrate abstract concepts, clarify complex issues, reveal multiple dimensions in data, and can more effectively present dense information. Graphical organizers, such as maps and diagrams that show interrelationships spatially and graphically, improve recall of learned material, increase productivity, and reduce errors. Adding pictures to menus in a videotext system increased the accuracy of selections [217]. Not surprisingly, in one test, presentations with visual aids were 43 percent more persuasive than those without [279]. The conclusion is that, for paper and for screen, graphics work—if you design them well.

Where should you use graphics and what type should you use? Consider the questions that graphics can answer.

Show why to purchase this product

Before users can install, operate, or repair the computer, they must know the computer exists, understand its advantages, and decide to buy it.

User's question	Type of graphic to answer the question
Do I need this product?	Dramatic photograph or drawing showing problem and solution offered by the product; picture of results possible with product.
What is available?	Eye-catching photograph in advertisement.
Which products should I consider?	List of benefits and features of the product; table of specifications of the product; diagram of interdependencies and compatibilities with related products.
Which one is best?	Tables or charts comparing performance of comparable products; tables comparing features of comparable products.
Should I buy now or wait?	Attractive pictures of the product, of results of using it, or of satisfied users.

Show how to install the product

The user has bought the product. How do we get it out of the box and into service?

User's question	Type of graphic to answer the question
How do I unpack the product?	Exploded-part diagram showing how product is packed in the box; wordless instructions for unpacking.
Do I have all the parts?	Checklist of components; picture of all components, with close-up views of critical details necessary to identify components.
How do I put it together?	Exploded-part diagram, phantom view, or translucent view showing assembly; numbered list of required actions; sequence of pictures showing how to open cabinet, insert circuit boards, connect cables; table or picture of switch settings.
How do I customize it?	Decision table for selecting configuration options; pictures of inserting disk; picture of sample screen showing dialog with user.
How do I test it?	Troubleshooting tree, table, or flowchart.

Show the user interface and operating system

Before users can run application programs, they must learn the operating system and its user interface.

User's question	Type of graphic to answer the question
What are the keyboard commands and special keys?	Picture of keyboard highlighting special keys; pictures showing how to use modifier keys such as Shift, Option, Alternate, Command, and Control; visual symbols for special keys and key combinations.
How do I operate the mouse, trackball, or other pointing device?	Sequence of pictures or animation showing how to move the pointer and how to click, drag, and double-click.
How do I issue commands?	Syntax diagrams for commands; decision table for selecting commands.
How do I use windows?	Sequence of pictures or animations showing how to create, move, resize, uncover, and delete windows; visual symbols for mouse and keyboard actions.
How do I select commands from menus?	Pictures showing example of selecting from menus.
How do I enter data on menus?	Sequences of pictures or animations showing how to select gadgets, enter data into slots, and activate screen buttons.
How does the file system work?	Tree diagram of file system, using visual symbols or analogs.

Show how to run application programs

For productive work, users must learn to start and operate application programs.

User's question	Type of graphic to answer the question
What can the product do? Why bother learning it?	Attractive photo or drawing on cover and at start of each chapter; before-and-after pictures that clearly show the results of each command, list of benefits, capabilities.
How do I perform common tasks?	Visual symbols for tasks and commands; flowchart of procedures; map of menus; numbered list of steps; sequence of screen snapshots for confirming location in procedure.
Which feature do I use?	Decision table or tree relating goal to command or option.
Where is command _____ in the menus?	Map of menus; table relating commands to location in menus; picture of menu with command highlighted.
What is the format of commands?	Syntax diagram; list of available keywords and symbols.
Are my results OK?	Annotated pictures of typical results; checklist or table for evaluating results.
How do I recognize errors?	Icons and color to highlight warnings and cautions.
How do I avoid errors?	Diagnostic troubleshooting flowchart, table, or tree diagram; table of common problems and their solutions.
How do I do it quicker and easier?	Visual symbols for flagging tips and shortcuts; visual symbols for keyboard shortcuts and accelerator keys.

Show how to program the product

Writing programs, as opposed to running them, requires abstract knowledge and skills. Programming is not restricted to writing programs from scratch in assembly language or in a high-level programming language. Today, word processors, databases, spreadsheets, and even microwave ovens allow end users to program their actions. These users need much of the same information that developers of products need.

User's question	Type of graphic to answer the question
How is the program organized?	Structure tree diagram; bracket diagram; architecture diagram; action diagram; logic box; structured English, or pseudocode.
What is the format of commands?	List of available commands and keywords; syntax diagram.
How do I find and fix a bug in my program?	Troubleshooting table, tree, or flowchart; table of common problems and their solutions.

Show how to repair the product

Someday something in the product will break or wear out, and someone must know how to fix or replace it.

User's question	Type of graphic to answer the question
What is the problem?	Troubleshooting table, tree, or flowchart relating problem to cause to solution.
What are the dangers?	Visual symbol and color to flag safety warnings and cautions; checklist of precautions.
How do I replace defective parts?	Checklist of required tools, including pictures or visual symbols for tools; picture sequence or animation showing how to locate defective component, remove it, and install replacement, which will require images of circuit boards, cables, switches, knobs, dials, and so forth.

INCLUDE GRAPHICS IN ALL DOCUMENTS

Illustrations in online documents vary from ultrasimple typewriter graphics to sophisticated film clips. The types of illustrations you use depend on the display system, storage space available, and the creative and artistic talent you can muster to the task.

Even documents displayed on alphanumeric monitors can include pictures. You can combine standard letters, numbers, and punctuation marks to form simple but effective illustrations. I call such illustrations *typewriter graphics*. You can use them to draw two- and three-dimensional boxes and shapes.

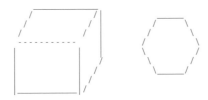

You can form arrows to show movement or flow, to highlight an object, or to guide the user's eye about the screen.

Online documents continually tell the user to push this button or press that key. Such documents often use key symbols to represent the special-purpose keys on the keyboard. Key symbols alert the user that the document is referring to a key.

```
+----+
! F7 !          [Return]        <Enter>
+----+
```

Using typewriter graphics, you can create tables complete with vertical and horizontal rules.

```
+=======+===========================+
| Stubs | Main headings             |
|=======|=======+=======+=======|
|  stub | item  | item  | item  |
|- - - -+- - - -+- - - -+- - - -|
|  stub | item  | item  | item  |
|- - - -+- - - -+- - - -+- - - -|
|  stub | item  | item  | item  |
|- - - -+- - - -+- - - -+- - - -|
|  stub | item  | item  | item  |
|- - - -+- - - -+- - - -+- - - -|
|  stub | item  | item  | item  |
+=======+=======+=======+=======+
```

You can also draw simple bar and column charts, scatter diagrams, area graphs, and histograms.

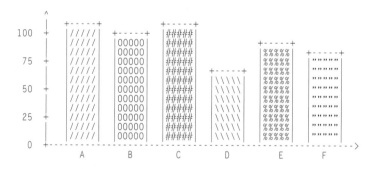

You can draw simple diagrams.

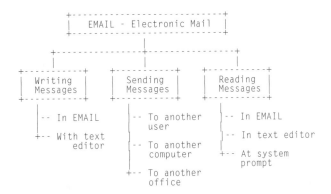

You can even create simple representations of the human figure and face.

DESIGN FOR THE SCREEN, NOT PAPER

Visual designers unaccustomed to the differences between paper and screen are faced with new decisions and compromises as they incorporate pictures into online documents.

Speed of display

Illustrations should display quickly and consistently. Text containing illustrations should scroll smoothly. The speed with which illustrations display depends on several factors:

- **How the illustrations are formatted**. Simpler formats generally display faster.

- **Size of the illustrations**. The time required to display a graphic generally depends on the area of the graphic if it is a raster graphic, or on the number of objects if it is a vector graphic. (See page 294 for a discussion of raster and vector graphics.)

- **Whether illustrations are embedded in the online document or stored in separate files**. For graphics stored in separate files, the file must be located, opened, and read, before display can begin.

- **The medium on which the illustrations are stored**. Illustrations on a slow floppy disk will take longer to read in and display than those on a fast hard disk. Illustrations that must be fetched from another computer's disk over a busy communications network may take even longer.

- **Any decoding, deciphering, or decompressing required before displaying the illustration.**

Storage requirements

A picture is worth a thousand words, but it may take up even more storage than a million words. To lessen the memory and disk space required for graphics:

- **Use fewer illustrations.** Cut out the purely decorative and those that merely repeat what the user already knows or what he or she is looking at elsewhere on the screen. Store repeated graphics once, but have them appear in multiple locations.

- **Shrink illustrations**. The storage required for raster graphics is roughly proportional to the area of the graphic multiplied by its resolution. Crop these tightly and create them at screen resolution. For vector graphics, the storage depends on the number of objects in the graphic. Eliminate unnecessary details.

- **Use fewer colors**. The wider the choice of colors, the more bits required to store the color of each object or pixel in the graphic.

Type graphic	Number of colors required
Text and line drawings	Black and white
Drawings of familiar objects	16 colors
Photographs of familiar objects*	256 colors
*(Except for) photographs of faces and foods	32,000+ colors (or a specially crafted palette of 256 colors)

- **Compress graphics**. Techniques such as CCITT, JPEG, and MPEG can greatly reduce the storage required for graphics, typically by a factor of 2 to 10. Take care though, some of the compression schemes are *lossy*, that is, compressing and decompressing the image alters it slightly. Lossy compression is generally fine for moving pictures because people seldom notice defects in images they view for 1/30 of a second [207].

Displaying graphics with text

Some designers use separate windows for text and graphics; others display both text and graphics in the same window. Which is best? When there is enough space, display graphics and related text adjacent to one another in the same window. Many users fail to view graphics if pictures are not placed near the corresponding text or if the user must press a button or issue a command to make the graphic appear. When users fail to view graphics, they miss critical information [141].

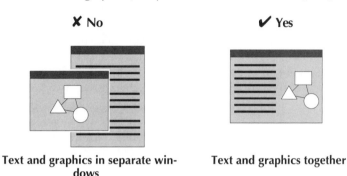

✘ No	✔ Yes

| Text and graphics in separate windows | Text and graphics together |

Except for cueing symbols or icons, place graphics to the right of text, since we read from left to right [129]. (You may need to reverse positions for languages such as Arabic and Hebrew, which read right to left.)

If the graphic and related text will not fit in the same scrolling zone, display text and graphic in separate windows and let the user scroll the text while leaving the graphic fixed. If the graphic contains critical information, make its window appear automatically, but use a visual transition to avoid startling the user. If the graphic contains only secondary information, provide a link the user can select to make the graphic appear. Make links to these nonincluded graphics prominent to prompt users to select them.

Included vs. referenced graphics

With an *included* graphic (a static view), the illustration is copied into the online document and there it resides. *Referenced* graphics (hot views) do not actually copy the illustration into the online document but let the document display the original illustration, which is stored separately.

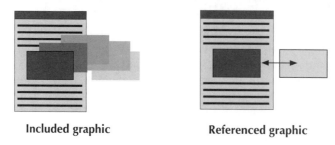

Included graphic   **Referenced graphic**

Use included graphics when the graphic is not likely to change or when changes to the illustration require corresponding changes to the text. Use referenced graphics when you want to maintain or change the graphic without having to reinsert it into the document. Referenced graphics save storage when the same graphic must appear in several places in the document. Updates and changes to the original graphic are reflected in the copy in the online document. However, avoid referenced graphics if the link to the separately stored graphic may be easily broken, as when the user moves the online document to a new directory.

Graphic formats

Computer graphics can be created in either vector or raster format, depending on how the data is represented on the computer.

Vector graphics are sometimes called *draw* graphics. They are made of separate lines, polygons, arcs, and other geometric shapes defined by the coordinates of the ends and edges. Vector graphics are stored as the drawing commands necessary to re-create the image. When a vector graphic is displayed, the entire image is re-created from scratch. In *raster* or *paint* graphics, the individual pixels that make up the image are stored as a bitmap.

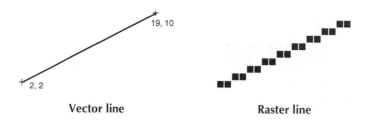

Vector line   **Raster line**

Use vector graphics for simple, regular objects, especially for illustrations that are shrunk, enlarged, or rotated on the screen. Vector graphics are also easier to change and update. Use raster graphics for detailed, irregular objects, such as photographs and rough sketches. For the sharpest display and least distortion, match the resolution of the raster graphic to the resolution of the screen.

Photographs

Photographs with a wide range of gray tones and color photographs do not display well on moderately priced computer displays. Medical x-rays will require a gray-scale monitor capable of displaying many levels of gray. Color photographs require monitors capable of millions of colors. Remember that the resolution of the screen is 20 to 100 times less than that of a clear photograph. To create gray tones, black-and-white monitors simulate gray with patterns of dots. This technique, called *dithering*, trades screen resolution for a greater number of simulated gray levels. Notice how it is used in this halftone photograph shown with an enlarged portion. Notice how the gray tones are really a tight pattern of black and white dots.

Consider alternatives to photographs. Often a simple diagram or line drawing will work better. Designers of ADAM, the interactive anatomy system, discovered that realistic photographs made small crucial items, such as nerves, harder to recognize than stylized drawings [10].

The dreaded jaggies

Staircasing, or *the dreaded jaggies*, is the ragged appearance of curves and diagonal lines on the computer screen. To minimize this effect, draw with vertical and horizontal lines. If you must use diagonal lines, use multiples of 45 and 30 degrees as these minimize the raggedness. Avoid the near-vertical and near-horizontal lines that show the largest degree of staircasing.

On color and gray-scale displays, we can use in-between tones to round off edges and smooth lines and curves. This process is called *antialiasing*.

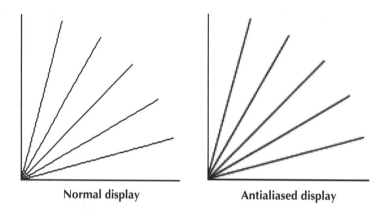

Normal display   **Antialiased display**

KEEP PICTURES SIMPLE

Because online pictures are displayed at a lower resolution in a smaller area than paper documents, you must keep them as simple as possible. Reduce the number of parts in each illustration and avoid fine lines and tiny text.

Make pictures easy to recognize

Make all pictures simple and easy to recognize. Show objects the way people are used to seeing them, avoiding stylized illustrations, distorted views, and unusual perspectives. Show the whole object, not just an isolated part, and show objects as viewed from an eye-level viewpoint of a typical viewer. If possible, show a conventional three-dimensional view. Solid, realistic images are recognized quicker, understood more easily, and recalled more reliably than flat, static abstractions [135].

Eliminate unnecessary information

Purge the graphic of nonfunctional elements and objects best shown elsewhere, such as the following:

- **Objects shown elsewhere on the screen**. Point to things outside the frame of the online document, provided its window always appears in the same location relative to other objects on the screen.

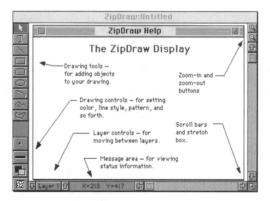

- **Unnecessary parts of examples.** Split the display area and show the example on one half and the annotation for it on the other half.

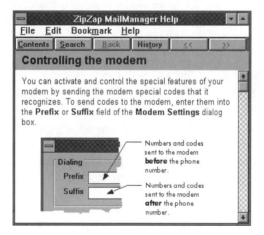

- **Decorative elements.** Remove all embellishments such as frilly borders and textured backgrounds.

Reduce detail

Many graphics that work well on paper must be simplified for use online.

Detailed graphic on paper   **Detailed graphic online**   **Graphic simplified for online display**

The resolution of the screen limits fine details and often requires redesigning graphics for a more streamlined image.

- **Include fewer layers of detail**. Online documents can display fewer layers or levels of detail. They have a shorter visual hierarchy than paper documents. Although a paper document can include as many as four or five levels of detail in a display, few online documents can display more than three levels of detail and even this requires using color and varying degrees of brightness.

- **Limit tiny details**. Reduce reliance on fine details, points, lines, textures, and patterns. Limit the smallest size to one pixel and gradients to those possible in one-pixel increments.

- **Reduce the size**. If you can do so without reducing legibility, make the graphic smaller by shrinking it or by reducing the size of text or other elements. If users are not required to read text in the example, use a smaller typeface for example screens or use a graphical editing program to shrink the example.

HANDLE LARGE GRAPHICS WITH CARE

If necessary, divide a complex illustration into several separate, simpler pictures. Include an overview picture from which the user can zoom in to these component pictures for more details.

Use multiple pictures

You can divide a large graphic into a series of smaller graphics, such as the individual maps of an atlas.

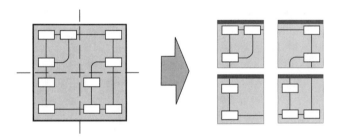

Use this technique with caution as viewers can easily get lost or discouraged before they find the graphic they need.

- Put the more important and more frequently used parts of the graphic early in the series.

- Do not split a diagram that must be viewed as a whole between separate displays. Use some other technique, such as zooming in.

- Overlap the coverage of the separate graphics, say by 10 percent.

Provide a scrolling view

If the graphic is continuous, put it in a window and display part of the graphic at a time. Let the user scroll or slide the display to bring different zones of the graphic into view.

- If movements are primarily horizontal and vertical, provide scroll bars.

- If diagonal movements are common, provide a control to move the graphic vertically, horizontally, and the in-between diagonal directions.

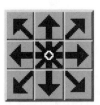

- If small precise positioning movements are needed, let the user drag the graphic within the window.

Let users zoom in

Another way to handle oversized graphics is to give a *zoomable* view. Start with an overview with sparse detail. When the user selects a region of the graphic, this region expands to fill the complete display. As it does, more details become visible. The viewer can continue to zoom in for more details of a smaller area or zoom out for a wider view with fewer details.

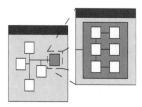

Selectively display detail

Limit the amount of detail shown at any one time. Let users selectively request and see details. Online illustrations can be self-annotating. The user simply selects an object in the illustration, and an explanation appears in a reserved area on the screen or in a pop-up window.

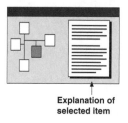

Explanation of selected item

Combine an overview with a close-up view to show both context and details. Let the user select a part of the overview to see an explanation or close-up view of that part.

ELECTRONICALLY LINK TEXT AND GRAPHICS

Electronically link text and graphics. When users select part of the text, the related graphic appears. When they select part of the graphic, the related text appears.

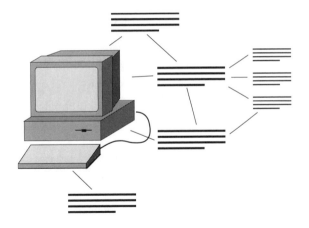

Link this . . .	to this
body text	supporting figure
graphic	related text
graphic	caption, legend, annotation, notes
part of graphic	annotation or description of the part
overview, picture of whole	detailed views of each of its parts
picture of an object or component	pictures of assemblies that include it

Consider all the ways users will want to read your document and provide the links they need.

PUTTING THESE IDEAS TO WORK

Essential ideas of this chapter

➥ Even alphanumeric terminals can use simple typewriter graphics to display diagrams, maps, charts, and key symbols.

➥ Pictures work best when combined with words. Include labels, annotations, and comments to help users understand the purpose and meaning of pictures.

➥ Simplify online graphics. Remove nonessential elements and reduce unnecessary detail.

➥ Divide large graphics into an electronically linked series of simpler graphics.

➥ Use only as many colors as necessary to make objects recognizable.

➥ Select graphic formats, compression schemes, and numbers of colors to control the storage costs of graphics.

For more ideas and inspiration

Bertin, Jacques. 1983. *Semiology of Graphics.* Green Bay, WI: University of Wisconsin.

Horton, William. 1991. *Illustrating Computer Documentation: The Art of Presenting Information Graphically on Paper and Online.* New York: John Wiley.

Horton, William. 1994. *The Icon Book: Visual Symbols for Computer Systems and Documentation.* New York: John Wiley.

Martin, James and Carma McClure. 1984. *Diagramming Techniques for Analysts and Programmers.* Englewood Cliffs, NJ: Prentice-Hall.

Nelms, Henning. 1981. *Thinking with a Pencil.* Berkeley, CA: Ten Speed Press.

Tufte, Edward R. 1983. *The Visual Display of Quantitative Information.* Cheshire, CT: Graphics Press.

NEW MEDIA

11

Adding sound and moving pictures

We live in a dynamic, changing environment, and we instinctively notice and attend to sounds and moving objects. Television and film are dynamic, visual, and audible media. They combine still and moving pictures, music, sound effects, spoken and written words. Online documents should do the same, as people's expectations are shaped as much by television and the movies as by books.

ONWARD TO MULTIMEDIA

The door is open to designers. Today even modestly priced personal computers can show cartoons, say "Good morning," and play a Beethoven symphony. Designers can use techniques ranging from simple visual transitions and builds to stunning animation and video.

The *MarsBook* lets viewers stroll through the interior of NASA's proposed Mars station, opening doors and examining furniture and equipment. The University of Washington's *ArchiMedia* library of architectural case studies uses photographs to show the appearance of the building, diagrams to show its mechanical and structural systems, animation to show patterns of sunlight and wind, text for the history and commentary, a series of photographs to show construction techniques, and music to demonstrate the acoustics [197]. *Sculpture Interactive* at the Tate Gallery in Liverpool gives visitors a multimedia preview of the exhibit of sculpture by Henry Moore. It lets visitors view Moore's working drawings, watch televised interviews of Moore, simulate a walk through his studio, and view his sculpture from different perspectives—all from the computer [60]. What will your online document do?

What are the advantages of multimedia to designers, communicators, and users? Where should we use it?

- **To communicate more directly**. With a wider choice of media, you can pick the medium that best represents a concept. Playing music is more direct than reading words about music. A video clip can better convey the emotion of a speaker than written or spoken words alone.

- **For complex subjects**. Use multimedia when information is complexly layered, that is, when you need to give information about information [101]. You can combine media to communicate different parts of the message. You can also use complementary media to overcome the biases or weaknesses of a single medium.

- **To meet users' needs**. Users with strong preferences for one medium or another learn better when information is presented in their preferred medium [130]. Human beings try to maintain a comfortable level of sensory stimulation. If our office is too quiet, we turn on some music. If it is too noisy, we don earplugs [130]. Multimedia gives users a choice of media and control over the level of stimulation.

- **To reach nonverbal learners**. For many, especially the young, the written word is not the medium of choice. Multimedia, by its resemblance to TV and video games, may be a more natural language [186]. About 60 percent of the users of a multimedia museum exhibit were under eighteen [52].

- **For better learning**. Information presented by multimedia is two or three times as likely to be recalled as information in a static presentation [10]. Presenting the same information visually and audibly improves understanding and retention [52]. Multimedia may produce broader forms of learning than those measured on standard verbal tests [145].

Avoid media madness, or the gratuitous use of media that is sometimes called *whoopee-cushion* multimedia. For every media element, ask two questions: Does it effectively communicate the most important message, and, is it the best way to communicate this message? Do not fear being entertaining in what you do, but do not create entertainment for its own sake. The more you use different media and the more powerful the media, the more important it becomes to embed these media elements in a simple, clearly organized structure [207].

SOUND

Printed pages are mute and silent, but many computers can produce simple beeps, musical tones, melodies, and even polyphonic harmony. Others can store and play back ultra-high-fidelity digitized sounds—everything from revving car engines to bird songs at dawn.

> Do not forget the needs of hearing-impaired users. Use sound where appropriate, but do not rely on sound alone to communicate critical information. Provide visual analogs for sounds. For instance, let users select between audible signals, blinking signals, or both.

Why use sound?

From earliest history to state-of-the art technology, sound has proved a potent communication medium. Video and film producers speak of the almost mystical ability of realistic background sound to breathe life into a visual scene. The power of voice and sound effects was proved convincingly by Orson Welles' radio broadcast of *War of the Worlds*. Some uses for sound in online documents include:

- **To support visuals**. Sound can provide context and credibility for visuals, and the right effects can punctuate and emphasize the action. Without sound effects, most science-fiction movies would fail to convince us that what we are seeing is real. What would the shower sequence in Hitchcock's *Psycho* be without the shrieking strings of the orchestral score? Because users can listen while reading or performing other tasks, sound is especially valuable for communicating additional layers of information.

- **To attract attention, interest**. Sound is almost impossible to ignore [7]. It can attract attention to the computer from across a room. Sound can increase involvement by users, especially younger ones raised on TV and video games. Sound can also provide light humor and secondary entertainment—if not overdone. Sound and music can heighten emotional involvement when its tone fits the feeling and mood of visuals.

- **To improve perceptions of quality**. The overall impression of the quality of a multimedia work is often influenced more by the quality of the sound than the quality of the display. Researchers at MIT's Media Lab found that test subjects viewing identical TV displays consistently said that the one with better sound had a better picture [10]. Rather than show low-quality video, substitute high-quality sound accompanied by a series of still pictures.

- **To represent things not shown**. Sound can help us see in the mind's eye things not visible on the screen. Sound tells us where and when a scene takes place. It can also indicate a specific situation. Realistic sound can create the impression that the scene continues outside the small window on the screen.

- **To provide feedback**. Sound can acknowledge actions by users and report on the status of an ongoing process. The SonicFinder used audible feedback for actions in a graphical user interface [104]. Sound can provide navigational cues. Sonic transitions can tell the direction the user is moving and how new information relates to old. Clusters of topics can have distinctive background music or sound. Predictive sound can signal an upcoming event or change, just as ominous music warns of impending disaster in the movies [295].

- **To aid memory**. Presenting information visually and aurally improves recall. Few would deny that rhythm and rhyme aid memory. In an information kiosk in Canada's Jasper National Park, information presented as spoken words accompanying pictures was better retained than the same information presented as text displayed alongside the pictures [217].

- **To preserve continuity**. Sound can be a positive distraction. You can use it to distract users from irrelevant information or flaws in the visual display. It is especially effective in preserving continuity through a series of disparate visuals. Off-camera narration can bridge gaps in a sequence of visuals. A regular rhythm of music and sound helps conceal an uneven rhythm of visuals. Sound can also fill in empty time while the user is waiting for the computer to respond.

Many authors, especially those from the mute world of ink and paper, claim that any sound is too much. To them, all sound is annoying. No doubt loud, purposeless sound annoys users, but when used well, sound is strongly embraced by users. When audio was removed from a multimedia museum exhibit, the completion rate plummeted [52]. IBM's silent typewriter was a flop because typists wanted a quiet typewriter, not a mute one [130]. Initial skepticism about the use of sound soon becomes acceptance.

> Corporate officials were initially skeptical of the "cute" sounds, asking how to turn them off. Now that they are regularly using the database, we get nothing but glowing reports about how important the sounds are, how much visitors love the sounds and even a request for a "more interesting sound for QUIT." Once a user has used a piece of software with variable sound feedback, the application feels broken with the sound off [130, p. 260].

In one test, users unanimously preferred different, distinct sounds for feedback instead of a single sound. Almost 90 percent preferred different sounds to no sounds [130].

Audible signals

Audible signals are brief sounds that convey specific messages to the user. These signals range from simple bells and beeps to complex buzzes, honks, clacks, clicks, chimes, warbles, and chords. Signals can also include realistic sounds. Audible signals are sometimes called *auditory icons* [105] or *earcons* [26, 106].

You can use audible signals to draw attention. For example, you can alert the user that some lengthy process is complete or that the program needs specific instructions before continuing [69]. Audible signals improve response time in signal-detection tasks and clearly work better than visual displays alone for certain tasks and kinds of data [58].

Use audible signals for these tasks:

- Prompt for an activity
- Signal the completion of a task
- Provide a positive or negative comment
- Attract attention
- Warn or caution
- Signal a specific condition
- Confirm input

Use simple tones for simple messages

Simple beeps, bells, and buzzes have been used for decades in computers and video games to signal problems and accomplishments. Most computers can generate simple tones and melodies. However, because there is no natural association between the signal and its meaning, users must learn the meaning of each such signal. Although you can combine pitch, intensity, and tempo to produce thousands of signal sounds, learning more than a few requires lengthy training and periodic retraining [152]. Remember that many users are tone deaf and cannot easily recognize complex melodies. Thus, for simple signals:

- Limit the number of audible signals to four or five and make each distinct from the others.
- Limit melodies to two or three distinct notes at least a whole step apart. Do not rely on nonmusicians to recognize differences between complex chords.

- Design all the signals for a family of related messages from the same pitches or rhythms [26].

Use sound effects for complex messages

Sound effects can be used as a signal or symbol. Users readily learn and retain the meaning of a complex system of sounds—provided the sounds are meaningful and logically connected to the concepts they represent [106]. Environmental sounds are interpreted as indicators of the characteristic of source events (size, speed, rhythm, force, material) rather than of the sound itself. Attributes of environmental sounds can thus represent attributes of computer events [106].

Examples of sound effects include:

- A word processor makes typewriter sounds as you type. Keys go klack, klack, klack and a carriage return sounds like zzzzzzz-bing!

- Icons make a whooshing sound as they are moved on the screen. The volume and pitch of the sound depend on how fast the icons are moved.

- In the HyperCard edition of *The Writer's Pocket Almanack*, my two co-authors and I used page-turning sounds as transitions between closely related displays and door-opening and closing sounds between more distantly related displays [37].

Sounds can be quite complex. Sound *morphing* is the process of blending two or more sounds to create a unique sound. The sounds of the dinosaurs in the movie *Jurassic Park* were created from the sounds of dozens of animals [10].

In complex systems, sounds can provide feedback users could not attend to if presented visually. Sound effects can reveal dimensions or values of the events or objects they represent. They can tell us the size of a file or the speed of a process [105]. The ARKola simulation of a bottling plant used distinctive sounds to represent the status of each machine. The bottle dispenser clanked, the heater-blower whooshed. The rhythm indicated the speed of the machine. If a machine stopped, its sound stopped too. Spilling liquid produced a splashing sound and breaking glass alerted the operator to bottles being wasted [106].

Make sound effective

Get attention but don't distract. Sounds should be distinctive and discriminable, so that the user can hear them as an overall sound pattern and still attend to them individually [106]. Make the signal louder than background noise, but not so loud and sudden that it startles or annoys. Avoid or moderate the use of signals in public places. Signals are distracting in open offices and embarrassing in public areas. No one wants their errors announced to everyone else in a large room, and no one wants to listen to someone else's beeps and bells [245].

Select sound effects that the user associates with the condition being signaled. Use sounds as audible analogs of physical or logical actions. Do not be afraid to use clichéd or stereotyped sound effects. Realistic effects may be too dull. Exaggerate slightly but do not let sound effects get silly. Use *cartoon sounds*, sounds that, like caricatures, simplify the real thing and emphasize its salient characteristics. Some recommendations [105, 106]:

To signal or represent this . . .	Use this kind of sound effect . . .
Large object	Lower frequencies
Small object	Higher frequencies
Large, empty room or other enclosure	More reverberation
Ongoing processes	Repeating sequences of sounds separated by brief pauses, not continuous sounds
Complex objects or concepts	More complex sounds
Urgency	Rapidly change the volume or character of the sound
Unpredictability	Irregular pattern of sounds
Dependability	Regular repeating rhythm
Moving upward, toward more abstract or general information	Rising frequencies
Moving downward, toward more concrete or specific information	Falling frequencies
Moving forward	Simple melody repeated
Moving backward	Same melody as for forward, but played backward

Background sound

Every environment has its own distinctive background sounds. On a city street you hear honking horns, passing cars, the yells of street vendors, footfalls of walking crowds, the distant wail of an ambulance. In a restaurant you hear the clatter of dishes, the murmur of conversations, doors opening and closing, the shouts of waiters. In a hospital you would hear the muffled steps of orderlies and nurses, doctors being paged, carts and wheelchairs rolling down a corridor.

These sounds are not consciously listened to but are sufficient to evoke recollection of the environment. Such sounds are called *background* or *environmental* sounds.

In online documents background sounds serve as a backdrop for other sounds such as voice or subject-matter sound. Use background sounds to suggest a place or time. To suggest a particular geographic locale or historical period, use sounds and music commonly associated with that location or period. To suggest particular kinds of events, use sounds and music often heard at such events (sports contests, weddings, religious services).

Make sure that when background sounds are played back, they are played at a level slightly above that of the background noise of the user's environment but lower than other sounds in the document.

Sound as subject matter

In some online documents, sound is not an aid or a signal but the subject matter itself. For example:

- Medical doctors are learning to recognize heart and respiratory disorders from an electronic stethoscope [285].

- Mechanics compare engine sounds under the hood with those recorded in a catalog of mechanical sounds. Disk-drive technicians learn to diagnose problems by the distinctive chatter of the read/write head as it seeks information on the disk.

- Travelers learn to pronounce foreign phrases by listening to a sound lexicon.

- Computer science students can listen to the rhythm of a sorting algorithm as it puts data in order.

Such documents must reproduce sound in high fidelity. Record the sound with the right equipment and the right professional staff. Here, realism counts. Reproduce what it will sound like to the user. Record the sound directly, but add in environmental sound. Or, provide the environmental sound on a second track and let the user decide whether to listen to the subject-matter sound with or without typical background sound.

Playing sound

The success of sound depends on playing sounds at a natural volume level and letting the user control playback.

- **Let users control sound**. Always let users turn off sound, but make sure the topic still makes sense without sound. Give users a control panel to set the volume and to play, pause, and replay subject-matter sound. You may also want to let the user choose between different coordinated sets of sound depending on setting and mood [10].

- **Set volume level carefully**. Many objections to sound can be overcome by setting the volume correctly. Strive to make sounds louder than the background noise of the user's environment, but lower than the voice of someone speaking to the user. Within this range adjust the volume of different kinds of sound accordingly:

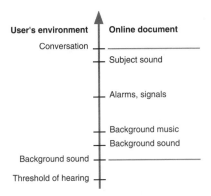

- **Use silence to prompt and emphasize**. To emphasize something, mute the sound. This removes distraction and prompts the user to act or to pay attention to something in the display. To focus attention on one sound, stop all other sounds. In suspense movies, the background music stops only at the dramatic climax. The cessation or absence of a sound, however, is not a good alarm, especially in a noisy environment [106].

Remember, sounds in online documents need add no more sound to an environment than a whispered conversation [130].

MUSIC

When was the last time you saw a movie or television program without background music? Music is an omnipresent accompaniment to visual entertainment, and even news programs have theme music. Although you don't need a soundtrack for your help file, you can use music to:

- **Augment feedback**. A musical reward is especially effective in training materials for children.

- **Grab attention**. Music grabs and holds the user's attention and is very useful in demonstration programs.

- **Gently alert users.** Musical tones can alert users to noncritical situations without distracting them from their current task.

- **Provide an emotional context**. Music effectively sets the emotional tone for visually depicted events.

- **Maintain continuity**. Music can smooth over gaps and inconsistencies in visuals and other sounds and fill idle time.

MIDI vs. digitized music

There are two ways of storing music on computers. One is to record the actual sound waves and is called *digitized* music. This can provide highly realistic reproduction but can require extensive storage, typically 10 megabytes per minute of music. The other technique is called MIDI, which stands for *Musical Instrument Digital Interface.*

MIDI does not store the actual sound waves for the music. Instead it stores the instructions necessary to cause a synthesizer to generate the sounds of the music. MIDI records information about the individual notes, when they begin and end, how hard they are played and held, what instrument plays them, and how the native pitch of the note is modified or bent. Typically, musicians create MIDI scores by playing them on an attached music keyboard and then editing the results on the computer. For nonmusicians, there are libraries of editable MIDI music for sale or license.

Editing MIDI music

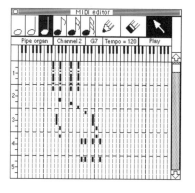

Editing digitized music

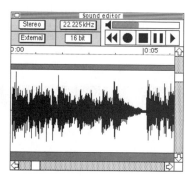

MIDI requires 100 times less storage than high-fidelity digitally recorded performances. However, to play back MIDI music, users must have a MIDI synthesizer and the software to control it.

Selecting music

Music cannot convey a specific literal meaning. It is a purely abstract language, which makes it ideal for representing emotions and mental states. Here are some general recommendations for using music:

For this purpose . . .	Use music this way . . .
Positive feedback	Short happy melody in a major scale. Vary it so that it does not get stale.
Negative feedback	Melody with a neutral tone. Avoid fog horns, nah-na-nah-na-nah-nah tunes, groans, boos, raspberries, Bronx cheers, and other forms of aural abuse [245].
Alert users to noncritical condition	Simple tune.
Grab attention in a promotional piece	Play the company's theme or other inspiring melody. When I first started up an IBM ThinkPad 750, it greeted me with the opening measures of Beethoven's Fifth Symphony.
Set emotional context of a visual display	Play melody of the appropriate tone: happy, sad, ominous.
Show mental state of a character in photograph or video	Play melody consistent with that state.
Warn the user of a change for the worse	Melody in a minor scale.
Preserve continuity	Play a long continuous passage, consistent with the tone of visuals and other sounds.
Cover for slow response time	Play a pleasant melody. Bach's Brandenburg Concertos seem to work well.

Music and pictures

Music tells us what we cannot see in displayed pictures. It can tell us whether the people shown are really happy. It can tell us that the product shown is a triumphant breakthrough, that it is powerful, that it is fun, that it is dangerous. Use music to show whether a character is happy, sad, nervous, afraid, or unbalanced. In the CD-ROM game *The Madness of Roland,* each character has a distinct musical theme consistent with the thoughts of that character.

VOICE

Words can be displayed or spoken. Spoken words have a different character to users and evoke a different response than displayed text. Each has its place on online documents.

Uses for voice

Reproducing the human voice is not easy. When is it worthwhile?

- **When speech is the message**. The *American Heritage Dictionary* in Microsoft Bookshelf, 1993 Multimedia Edition, includes audio pronunciations of over 65,000 words. On the same CD-ROM, *Bartlett's Familiar Quotations* includes quotations, some spoken by their authors.

- **For complex subjects**. Use speech to narrate simulations and demonstrations and to present instructions. The user can easily attend to spoken words while watching and interacting with the screen. Spoken words, unlike printed words, do not clutter the screen or take the user's eyes away from the task at hand [231]. Present instructions audibly and data visually. Doing so reduces errors and increases performance, primarily by clearly separating the subject matter and information about the subject matter [71].

- **For nonreaders**. Speech makes online documents available to the blind and visually impaired. It also makes words available to those who cannot read or will not read.

- **To convey emotion**. A tone of voice can tell us whether to take words as a warning, a hint, or a joke.

However, avoid turning the computer into a chatty pal. Talking cash registers and automobiles failed dramatically.

Synthesized vs. recorded voice

Voice in computer systems can be synthesized or recorded. The difference is analogous to that between vector and raster graphics and that between MIDI and recorded music. With *synthesized* voice, the computer generates the sounds corresponding to the words to be spoken. It does not store the actual sound waves.

Users unanimously prefer realistic recorded speech to robotic synthesized speech, but synthesized speech can be made quite understandable. With synthesized speech, you can store the text once and have it displayed, spoken, or both—with no extra storage cost.

Text-to-speech synthesis comes in three levels of quality. The lowest level of quality converts the text directly to speech. It converts combinations of characters or letters into corresponding sounds. Because of irregularities in spelling and pronunciation, the results are sometimes laughable. The next level of quality uses a *phonemic* transcription of the words to be spoken. The phonemic input specifies exactly how each word is to be pronounced. The highest level of quality is with *allophonic* transcription of the text. Here the input tells the synthesizer exactly how to generate the specific sounds of each syllable.

Unless the synthesized speech is perfectly clear, give users the alternative of displaying text, especially if they work in a noisy environment.

Let users read or listen

Forgo *read-along* narration that merely reads aloud the text presented on the screen. Reading text aloud on the screen can hinder comprehension when the user reads faster than the speaking voice. You can speed up the playback of voice segments 20 to 30 percent without loss of understandability. Or, let users choose among displayed, spoken, and printed text.

If reading aloud the text of a document, use a simple beep or other sound to alert the user that a term or phrase is a link trigger [16].

Write for the spoken word

When writing words to be spoken, take as much care with the sound and rhythm of the words as with what they mean.

- Use standard grammar and complete sentences for spoken messages. This normal style actually reduces errors and improves response time over a telegraphic style, mainly because the extra words provide needed reinforcement [253].

- Prefer short common words. Few words over three syllables long sound natural when read aloud. Extensive use of acronyms brought hysterical laughter to one group of users.

- Use short, simple sentences. Avoid complex sentences, especially sentences like this one, that have embedded clauses and phrases.

- Rely on tone and inflection rather than punctuation to shade the meaning of words.

INTERACTIVE PICTURES

In online documents, pictures are not limited to passive, look-but-do-not-touch images. Pictures can change in response to the user. Users can build up complex graphics one layer at a time or can peel away layers to simplify and customize a display.

Builds

The simplest form of dynamic display is called a *build*. You build up an image by sequentially adding to the display.

You might start by display-ing only Step 1 of a pro-cedure.

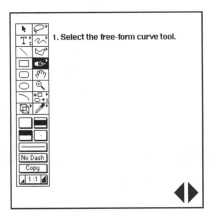

Then, when the user re-quests more information, you add Step 2 of the pro-cedure.

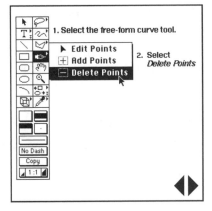

Then Step 3.

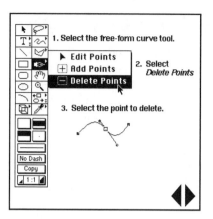

And finally, the end result.

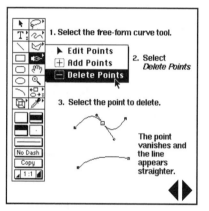

The resulting display is too crowded to be effective if presented all at once. However, it works online because the eye is drawn to the new information introduced with each step. Adding information is less distracting than putting each stage on a separate display, and the user can see all the stages together. Use builds to:

- Progressively reveal more detailed information.

- Show a path on a map, a flow through a chart, or progress on a project tracking chart.

- Depict the stages of a process or steps of a procedure.

Design builds with care. Add a significant, but digestible, piece of information with each step, and try to complete the build in four to seven steps. Let users decide when to go to the next step or whether to back up a step or start over. Remember that builds enforce a particular sequence. This may mislead or frustrate users when components could be viewed in any order the user chooses.

Filters

Rather than build up complex graphics, we can start with a dense but comprehensible display, and let users remove details as if removing layers of acetate on which different kinds of information are printed. With *filters,* users can remove layers of information in any order or combination they desire. For example, this display lets users see what hardware is required for various combinations of media:

Here all options are selected to show all components and connections.

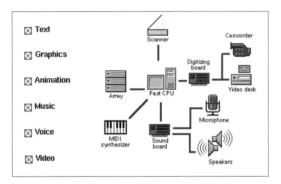

Here the user has selected one subset of media.

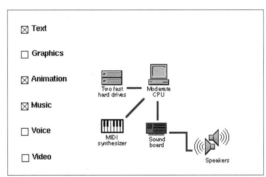

And here the user has selected another combination.

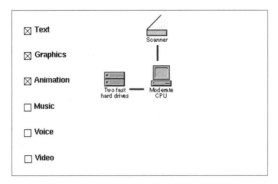

Here the use of filters lets one dynamic picture replace the 32 separate pictures that would be required to show every possible combination of components.

VISUAL TRANSITIONS

Visual transitions are special visual effects that express the flow from one idea to another. They control how one image replaces another. Transitions are visual conjunctions. They are the *and, but, or*, and *however* of visual language.

Uses of visual transitions

Visual transitions in online documents are more than decoration. You can use them to:

- **Show relationships.** Use visual relationships to show the user how the new information relates to or differs from the old. Transitions can mark the boundary between one idea and the next.

- **Focus attention**. Transition effects can emphasize and deemphasize images. Use them to guide the user's eye to a specific area of the screen. In *static* media, we must point to the critical item. In *dynamic* media, we can zoom in on it. One especially effective combination is to use a transition to prefocus the user on the general message and animation to direct the user to the salient feature of the topic [1].

- **Maintain continuity**. Transitions can preserve coherence when shifting from one context to another. A visual transition can lessen the shock of sudden changes to the visual display.

- **Reinforce metaphors**. Use visual transitions to support a metaphor presented in visuals and sounds. For example, a transition can simulate pages turning and movement in space.

Use transitions with care and restraint. Unless used logically and consistently, they can detract from understanding, particularly when they distract the user from the primary focus of the information [1]. Avoid elaborate transition effects between plain static images.

Glossary of visual transitions

Many transitions are possible. Sadly, their names are not used consistently. What one authoring program calls a *wipe*, another calls a *scroll*, and still another calls a *push*. Here are some of the more common functional ones.

Cover

In a *cover* effect, the new image moves into the frame covering the old. Or, the old moves out of the frame uncovering the new information.

Push

In the *push* effect, the new image displaces the old. As the new image moves into the frame from the side, the old one slides off in the opposite direction.

Wipe

In a *wipe*, the new information is painted over the old. Neither new nor old move.

Peel

In a *peel* effect, the old information is peeled back to reveal the old. This presents the illusion that the old information is on a sheet of paper or plastic covering the new information.

Iris

The *iris* effect simulates the opening of the iris of a camera lens. The new information is painted onto the screen in a widening circle, like the opening of the iris.

Dissolve

One of the smoothest and most natural transitions is the *dissolve*. Here the old information seems to become progressively more transparent, thereby revealing the new information.

Fade

In a *fade,* the entire image becomes gradually darker (fade to black) or lighter (fade to white). Likewise, the image can gradually appear from solid white or black. Although less common, some other solid color can be used instead of white or black.

Zoom

Zooming in makes one object or area expand to fill the screen. *Zooming out* causes the display to shrink to one item in a larger display.

Barn door

In the *barn-door* transition, the old image splits in the middle and the two halves slide off to left and right revealing the new information underneath. This simulates the opening of a barn's sliding doors or of the opening of curtains at the beginning of a play. The effect can be reversed with the new information sliding on from the sides to cover the old information.

Page turn

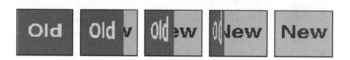

In *page-turn* transitions, the old information seems to expand and shrink in perspective to create the appearance of one page tilting up from one edge of the frame. This also looks like a door opening.

Rack focus

Rack focus starts with the subject out of focus and gradually brings it into focus. You can simulate out-of-focus by applying a gaussian blur to the image.

Communicating with transitions

Use transitions the way they are used in well-directed movies: to clarify, not decorate. Stick with functional transitions and avoid the purely decorative. The viewer should understand the relationship between new and old information, but not consciously notice the transition. Use transitions predictably and keep them relatively quick.

When you want to do or communicate this	Use this visual transition
Begin a primary sequence	Fade in from black
End a primary sequence	Fade to black
Move forward one topic or other discrete chunk in a series	Push or wipe new information onto the display from the right
Move backward one topic or other discrete chunk in a series	Push or wipe new information onto the display from the left
Move forward in a continuous topic or long passage	Scroll information from bottom to top of the display
Move backward in a continuous topic or long passage	Scroll information from top to bottom of the display
Show more specific information on an item in the current display	Zoom in on the item
Show the context of the currently displayed information	Zoom out from the current display, collapsing it to an icon or label
Suggest a smooth, gentle transition of ideas	Dissolve or fade from one display into the next
Advance to a new scene without implying that the previous one ends	Use a wipe or push [1]
Indicate a break in a sequence	Slowly fade to black and then fade back in [45]
Bridge a gap in time	Dissolve from the old to the new
Suggest continuity between disparate scenes	Dissolve slowly from one to the other
Simulate the contraction of a person's field of attention	Zoom in on the object of attention

Morphing

Morphing is a precise dissolve in which key features of one object transform into equivalent features of another. Morphing equates the two objects. It is a visual metaphor that says "These two may not look alike, but they share essential characteristics."

Use morphs to link old and new forms of an object. Urban planners can show the development of a city. Archaeologists can contrast current-day ruins with an artist's conception of the original scene. Advertisers can show the evolution of a product.

For morphing, ensure that the starting and ending image match as closely as possible. They should have the same size, orientation, color scheme, viewpoint, and lighting conditions.

In morphing, match the most important features of the starting image with the equivalent features of the ending image. For people, the most critical features are the profile, corners of the eyes, corners of the mouth, top and bottom of the ears, and the sides and bottom of the nose.

Use a simple background. Morphing warps the entire image—including the background. You can avoid any noticeable distortion by using a plain, monochrome background. Another solution is to perform the morphing against a single-color background and then to substitute an unchanging background scene for this area of color. Begin and end the morphing dissolve slowly but speed through the middle part. Complete the transformation in a second or so.

Moving pictures (animation and video)

Moving pictures are powerful. So strong is the effect of motion in holding the eye that a cameraman "can simply center a moving image in his finder and regardless of poor composition, improper placement in the frame, unsatisfactory background or numerous other pictorial faults, hold the viewer's attention through sheer movement alone!" [177, p. 198]. But merely holding the viewer's attention is only the first step in communicating. Communicating requires good technique. This section discusses design principles that apply to both moving drawings (animation) and moving photographs (video).

Control pace

The pace or tempo of a scene can excite or calm the viewer. To change the pace of a scene, alter the length of the shots. Idle time seems to pass more slowly than time filled with activity. Short shots make action seem to go faster, and long shots make it seem slower. D. W. Griffith perfected the technique of the cross-cut—jumping back and forth between two concurrent events—to increase the excitement of a chase scene. For a quiet, serious, or sad mood, use long scenes with slow, steady movements. For an excited, agitated, or happy mood, use short scenes and shots with fast movements.

Do not show static scenes for longer than about six seconds. If the scene takes longer than that to comprehend, it is probably too complex. If you show a simple scene without movement for longer than six seconds, the viewer gets bored and looks elsewhere. If you have nothing else to show, then show the same object in different ways. Zoom in to reveal details; cut to a new viewpoint to reveal a different facet of the subject.

Preserve continuity

The viewer should see a series of related images as a coherent whole. That requires attention to continuity. Continuity concerns not just events occurring continuously in time but with events as part of a logical unit. Each image should flow visually and logically from the previous one. Some guidelines:

- Avoid abrupt and unnecessary changes in a continuous scene. Do not shift lightness, color balance, or viewpoint except in small steps.

- Use visual transitions to bridge gaps in time and location.

- Carefully ensure that people and objects in one shot are the same as in previous and subsequent shots taking place at the same time and place.

- Keep the viewer's eyes moving in the same direction. Maintain the general direction of vectors from shot to shot. Keep moving objects moving in the same direction, or else show them change direction. If one shot shows someone pointing to something offscreen to the right, the next shot should show the object at the right of the frame [295].

- Use music to bridge gaps. Do not worry too much about matching beats in the music to movements in the visuals. If the tone and mood are right, viewers will find the correspondences [295].

- Use cutaways to different but related scenes, such as an audience-reaction shot.

Signal the end

Clearly signal the end of a segment of animation, video, or music. Movies typically end with the cowboy riding off into the sunset, with lovers kissing, or with the newlyweds waving good-bye. Show smiles and successful results, fade to black, play a resounding triumphant chord. If the segment ends with the final frame displayed, make sure it is one that provides an adequate review or conclusion. Achieve closure.

Keep motion segments simple and predictable

Keep motion segments simple. Dynamic media cannot carry a legend or key to define colors. And users cannot read lengthy explanations while watching moving pictures.

Show one thing at a time. Move only one major object at one time, and put slight pauses between major phases of movement. Create no major event or change in the middle of the movement of a major object. Do not rely on viewers noticing any small or subtle detail in a moving object.

In general, the triple-step structure produces the clearest scenes. Start with a wide establishing shot showing the scene of the action. Then go to medium shots to introduce the characters and equipment. Then go in for a close-up of first one and then another character or component.

Design for interactivity

If the user controls which motion segments to play and when to play them, you must design them for interactivity.

Keep segments short, typically no more than 20 to 30 seconds. Video segments longer than 20 to 30 seconds turn the viewer into a passive spectator [32].

Remember that video and animation are subject to the as-shown-above syndrome just as much as is text. Do not assume that users will view all motion segments or view them in any particular order. Ensure that each makes sense by itself.

Provide links to and from dynamic media

Link to the beginning of segments of a dynamic medium. Users may want to jump to the beginning of a speech or the beginning of a particular movement in a symphony, or to the beginning of Act II, Scene 2. In a dynamic sequence, you can signal branching options with a flashing icon, a button, or a label that appears for a time. However, link triggers in dynamic media should not appear and disappear or move around too rapidly for users to select them [207].

One caution: Users will not spontaneously interrupt continuous playback of animation, video, music, and voice sequences. Prompt them to do so. Remind them periodically that they control playback.

Let the user control the action

Let the user control motion segments. In an interactive program, never arbitrarily erase information after a fixed time. Let the user signify when to erase or replace information in a display or when to move to the next display. Users should control speed so they can see rapid fluctuations in detail [262] and spot patterns of movement and change not apparent at normal speed [187]. Remind users that they control the action. Give them prompts or a control panel.

Give users VCR-like controls for playing video, animation, and sound, since these are either familiar or readily learned [159]. Use the same basic controls for similar media, such as sound. Make the response appropriate for the particular medium. Common controls include these:

Control	Icon	Function
Play	▶	Play the segment
Pause	❚❚	Freeze a particular frame. Halt play temporarily. To resume play, press Play or Pause again.
Next	❚▶	Move forward to the next segment.
Previous	◀❚	Move backward to the previous segment.
Fast forward	▶▶	Play at faster than normal speed.
Slow motion	❘▶	Play at slower than normal speed.
Rewind	❘◀◀	Move to the beginning of the entire sequence.
Loop	↻	Loop the segment so it automatically starts over when it reaches the end.
Reverse	◀	Play the segment backward.
Eject	⏏	Quit viewing the segment.

To reduce the risk of confusing the user, display the first frame as a static illustration and let the user trigger motion. At the end, leave the last frame displayed until the user dismisses it or chooses to replay the segments. Do not loop a segment unless the user requests it.

Animation (in particular)

Animation is the illusion of motion. Animation makes exploded diagrams explode, procedures proceed, and working models work—all in front of the user's eyes.

> By nature, animation builds on other characteristics of a presentation or visual. Animation tends to amplify whatever else is occurring in terms of visual impact. If the visual is logically clear, animation in the appropriate places adds emphasis and focus. However, animation added to an unclear visual or in the wrong place or in a way that is inconsistent with the message of the visual may be more distracting than useful. For example, if the animation is inappropriately focused or too clever, people may only remember "dancing cows," not "how milk can be good for you" [1, p. 18].

Animation need not be complex. Simple moving line drawings are often more effective than complex shaded animations or fully detailed video segments [12]. Here are a few frames from an animation showing how to replace a faulty circuit board.

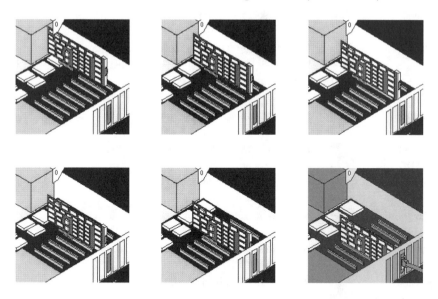

Uses for animation

Use animation to communicate, not to decorate. Use it to convey change, movement, and progress. Use animation to:

- **Show things that move and change**. Use animation to explain a complex mechanical device with many moving parts, such as a laser printer. Because they unfold over time, processes and procedures are naturals for animation. Also use animation to show increase, decrease, or change in some physical variable.

- **Analyze processes**. Animation can reveal repeated patterns of action, bottlenecks, and the relative speed of processes. Use animation (or video from an unusual viewpoint) to help viewers step back and look at a common experience in a new way. Give them a new frame of reference.

- **Explain abstract concepts**. Animation can show ideas and abstractions present only in the mind. Animations have been used in computer-science courses to explain introductory programming concepts, data-communication protocols, program logic, and data structures. They have also been used to analyze and design algorithms and to tune and debug computer systems [38].

- **Improve comprehension**. Animation can explain. For improving the comprehension of business presentations, animation (without transitions) outperformed text, static graphics, transitions, and their combination [1].

- **Increase interest**. Animation stimulates interest [241]. Animation increased interest and was strongly preferred by computer-science students studying algorithms [262]. In business presentations, animations combined with transitions increased the audience's attention and it's appreciation of the presenter and the presenter's message [1].

- **Focus the viewer's attention**. Animation draws attention and increases attention span [1]. Use animation to emphasize important aspects of a graphic. The animated or moving object is foreground—everything else is background. If you see an arrow in a static graphic, consider replacing it with a simple animation to direct the user's attention and prompt the user to act.

- **Handle sensitive subjects**. Animated characters are better than videotaped real characters for sensitive subjects such as sex education, ethnic relations, and other subjects where the animated characters let the viewers concentrate on the idea and not on the identity or appearance of the actors.

- **Show dangerous subjects**. Animation lets you create a world of hazards without danger to the user or to the cameraman. Because of their indestructibility, cartoon characters are ideal for showing the negative consequences of dangerous actions.

  They could fall 2000 feet, be electrocuted, blown up, cut into sections, burned, flattened, drowned, even frozen in a cake of ice, yet be right back in fighting shape in a matter of seconds [269, p. 521].

Types of animation

Cel animation

In classic *cel animation* you produce a separate drawing for each frame of the animation. (*Cel* is short for cellophane, the material early animations were drawn on.) Each drawing differs slightly from the previous one [245], as in this sequence for turning pages.

Sprite animation

Sprites are two-dimensional images that move in front of a fixed background. These sprites can change their appearance to simulate movement within the sprite. Sprite animation is probably the most common form of computer animation as it is simple and economical. With sprite animation, the turning pages would look the same, but the page that turned would be a sprite in front of a background drawing of the other pages of the book. Here is the background and turning pages.

Color cycling animation

Color cycling creates an illusion of motion by repeatedly redefining the colors in a static graphic. Color cycling is easier to do than to understand. It relies on the fact that computer colors are just numeric codes. A palette or color look-up table specifies what color each numeric code actually represents. With color cycling you draw one picture that shows the moving object in successive positions. In each position you draw it in the color of a different numeric code. In the palette, however, all of the codes used by the moving object are defined as the same color as the background, except the one that shows the object in its starting position. For example, in this end view of a book, all of the page positions are defined as different numbers. All but one of these numbers is defined as the background color.

Drawing showing the colors assigned to each position

Color palette. The numbers for all positions except the first are light gray, which is the background color.

To simulate motion, the codes for successive positions of the moving object are redefined as the visible color while all others are the background color. Here's how the animation appears to the user at various stages.

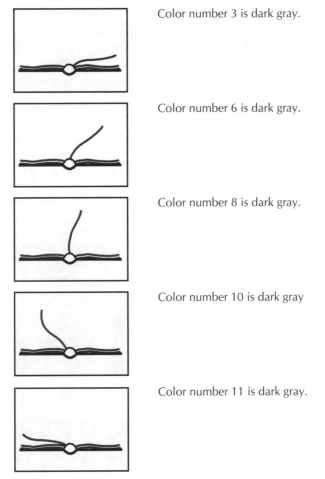

Color number 3 is dark gray.

Color number 6 is dark gray.

Color number 8 is dark gray.

Color number 10 is dark gray

Color number 11 is dark gray.

Color cycling is especially effective for animating repetitive movement in an enclosed area as long as successive positions of the moving object do not overlap. It works well for showing flames or flowing liquid. Because it does not require storing and displaying many separate drawings, color cycling is economical.

3D model animation

Three-dimensional models are sometimes used to create animations. They start by the designer constructing a detailed model of the objects to be shown in the animation. The computer then calculates what the scene would look like from a particular viewpoint and with particular lighting conditions. This is called *rendering* the scene. The model or the viewpoint is shifted slightly and the process repeated to generate the next frame of animation.

Rendering richly detailed 3D scenes requires vast computer resources. Creating the models for a one-minute 3D animation can take three to five days [10]. Rendering one minute of ray-traced animation at 600x480 can take 50 hours and require 200 to 300 MB to store the results. Film-quality rendering (3000x2000 pixels) can require 15 gigabytes per minute [10].

Stop-motion animation

In *stop-motion* animation, you photograph real objects, shifting or modifying them slightly between photographs. Stop-motion animation can show the assembly or disassembly of a complex piece of machinery. It has a magic, comical feel as inanimate objects spring to life.

Making motion credible

In animation, make movements clear, distinct, and energetic.

Obey laws of momentum and inertia

Animated graphical objects are subject to the laws of physics. Graphical objects are perceived as having mass. In motion, they acquire momentum, preserving the direction and speed of any movement. Objects overcome resistance. Speed represents high power or low resistance. Acceleration is attributed to the power of the object; slowing down, to friction [11]. Objects do not burst into motion. They accelerate into a movement and decelerate out of it. This is called *slow in and slow out* [269]. Nor do they suddenly change direction; they round corners.

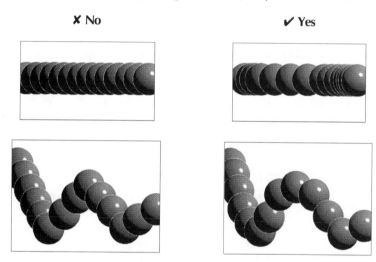

Show characteristic patterns of movement

In designing animations, pay special attention to patterns of motion, especially repeated motions. A pattern of motion is sufficient to endow a graphical object with human characteristics, such as aggressiveness, persistence, nervousness, and fatigue [11].

Make mechanical movements straight and uniform in speed. Make human movements cursive and fluent. Human movements include not only movements of people and animated characters, but also inanimate objects moved by them [269].

Unvarying, symmetrical reciprocal motion can prove hypnotic or annoying. It communicates a mechanical, nonhuman feeling. Asymmetrical reciprocal motion creates a feeling of syncopation, rhythm, and swing [17]. For smoother movement, draw and erase images smoothly and keep the distance between drawings small.

To simulate vibration, repeatedly show the same image, shifted slightly back and forth between frames.

Keep animation simple

Do not overload the viewer with meaningless animation by showing too much too fast [1]. The display becomes distracting when we try to show too much spatially by crowding the display, or too much temporally by changing too rapidly or abruptly [12]. Remember that users can pay attention to only one moving object at a time. If the animation includes simultaneous movements by separate objects, let the user cycle or repeat the scene.

Do not put a busy background behind animated characters. Leave large areas with a plain background on which animated characters can move. Avoid intricate details, bright colors, high-contrast figures, or anything else that will draw attention away from the animated character.

Also, users cannot attend to intricate details in moving objects. In animation, pay more attention to the overall contours of shapes. If these are right, few interior lines will be needed. Make all critical events clear from outline contours alone. Do not disguise pertinent information in a tangle of lines. Remember that single-pixel lines may not display correctly after the image has been compressed and decompressed [10].

Prepare the viewer for changes

Signal any movements that might be unexpected or might be overlooked. Baseball pitchers wind up for the throw. Golfers and bowlers have a distinctive backswing before sudden movement. In classic Disney cartoons, the character rears back to the left before charging off to the right [269]. Do not suddenly propel objects into motion, especially small objects or things the user is watching.

Prepare the viewer for sudden changes. If you do not, he or she may not notice the change or may be shocked by it. In animation, use a change of color, motion, or sound to prepare the viewer for a sudden or dramatic change of the visuals. Gradual changes can prepare the viewer for a new style of presentation or a new type of content [241].

To sneak something unnoticed into the display, move one or two other objects jerkily and quickly in a different part of the scene as you glide the new object smoothly and slowly into place. Stage magicians have used this trick for centuries.

Video (in particular)

Video is the most powerful and most expensive medium for online documentation.

> If a picture is worth a thousand words, a dynamic picture of time-varying objects is worth a thousand static ones [276, p. 893].

Of course, producing video requires specialized equipment, an extensive team of expert professionals, and an ample budget. For interactive video, design costs and times are about seven to ten times those of simple video production and require over 300 hours of authoring for each hour of interactive video [93]. When are these costs justified and how do we reap the benefits of video?

Uses for video

Video is ideal for showing images of real moving objects. Use video to:

- **Show how things move**. Video is the easiest and most natural way to show movement of solid objects. It is effective in demonstrating physical procedures, teaching psychomotor and athletic skills, and revealing patterns of movement and action. Use it to show how to unpack and install a piece of equipment, to show how animals run or fly, or to teach complex gestural inputs. NCR uses digital video to show users how to load tape in cash registers.

- **Show what users cannot see directly**. Use video to show things that are too dangerous, too small, too large, too fast, too slow, too rare, or too expensive to see directly. Use high-speed photography to explicate nearly instantaneous events. Let users advance a video or animation frame by frame to study rapid change in detail [187]. Use time-lapse video to accentuate slow, subtle changes and patterns of movement that ordinarily escape notice: clouds cascading over a mountain ridge, an office building erupting from a vacant lot, cars funneling through a traffic bottleneck, your hair growing, and a computer user's hand bouncing back and forth between mouse and keyboard. Use video to show rare events, those that seldom occur or that few are privileged to observe [187]. Also, use video to remind the viewer of historical events captured on film or video-tape.

- **Motivate users**. Video is universally familiar and accepted by almost everyone. Users unanimously like video sequences of relevant real-world scenes and believe such sequences help them learn [132]. Interactive video especially benefits users with low verbal abilities [15]. Use video segments to provide a context to help users understand how information can be applied. Help people see themselves applying the concepts your online document discusses. Video can make a situation seem real if viewers identify with what they see in the video.

- **Show human behavior and emotions**. Use video to study human behavior and to show the same behavior from different perspectives. Help people recognize their own behavior. For communicating emotion, nothing beats the human face. Harvard Business School is experimenting with multimedia case studies, because they found that movies of people telling their stories were more effective in conveying a true picture of real-life business situations than reading the synopsis of an investigator.

Making video practical

Video is expensive in design time, production effort, storage requirements, and processing power required for playback.* To make it practical for use in online documents, use it only where no less expensive medium works better and use only as much video as you need. Design the video well, because video that fails to communicate is too expensive at any cost.

Size the window appropriately

The smaller the image, the less storage it requires and the smoother it plays. Simple objects may need only a small image. Test with prospective viewers. Dr. Alan Shelton, a Los Angeles ophthalmologist, used small-window video to explain surgical techniques to his patients. He soon realized, however, that many of them had trouble understanding the 160x120-pixel images. He made the display segments larger [10].

Shorten the segment

The longer the video segment, the more storage it requires. Here are some tricks to reduce the length without reducing content:

- **Show only key events**. Identify, record, and show the key moments of a procedure or process. Show where something unexpected happens, where decisions are made, where events change direction.

- **Loop**. For repetitive movements, do not show 15 separate cycles of movement. Select the best and loop it so that it will repeat automatically.

- **Use a static shot to establish the scene**. Do not waste frames of video on a static scene, such as the establishing shot used at the beginning of a segment. If it takes viewers 5 to 10 seconds to understand the scene, start with the video paused on an establishing shot. Let the viewer trigger play after examining the static shot.

---

*In this section, we are talking about video that is stored and displayed on the computer. We are not talking about computer-controlled replay of images from videotape or videodisc. These cases are best handled by traditional video production techniques.

Balance the needs of audio and video

Sound takes storage and processing power, and high-quality sound can make video skip. If your user is going to listen to the sound on a single, low-quality speaker, recording high-fidelity, stereophonic sound can actually reduce the quality of the results. Stereo sound can be a problem for small-window video when the distance between speakers is 10 or 20 times the width of the video window.

Making video easy to understand

Users expect high production values for video segments that look like TV programs. However, the success of shows like *America's Funniest Home Videos, I Witness,* and *Cops* shows that TV viewers do not demand broadcast-quality images—provided the images contain interesting information [10]. Using small-window video may actually lower a user's expectations for high production values and improve the credibility of the material at the same time [162]. To gauge whether a scene will work in small-window video, squint one eye, close the other, and watch the scene through gauze. Then design it to work under these difficult conditions.

Simplify camerawork

Eliminate the visual noise that results from illogical or unnecessary camera movements. Move the camera only with good reason. Good reasons include following action, gradually discovering a scene, or revealing a landscape.

- Move the camera to simulate movement of the viewer's eye or a change in the viewer's attention. Mimic the way our eyes and heads move as we follow a moving object to search for an object of interest.

- If the object of interest is moving, consider keeping the camera still and letting the natural movement of the object carry it through the field of view.

- Avoid jump cuts or elaborate transitions in small-window video. For smoother cuts, maintain consistency in the direction and speed of motion vectors, location, lighting, color, and so forth [295].

- Avoid sudden shifts in focal length. When moving in, do so in gradual steps so that the viewer can see that each shot is the same scene from a closer viewpoint. Likewise, when zooming out, do not move back so quickly or drastically that the viewer loses track of the subject of the scene.

- Complete a pan or tilt entirely in one shot. If you must cut within a camera movement, continue the same direction of movement in the next shot.

Clarify movements

Quick, uneven, unpredictable movements are hard to follow. Make movements distinct and easy to recognize.

- **Move steadily**. Make movements slow and predictable. Accelerate and decelerate gradually. Give the viewer time to notice the object moving and then to follow its path of movement.

- **Move only one object at a time**. The human eye can attend to only one moving object at a time.

- **Use histrionic (stage acting) style**. Have actors use broad, clear gestures in the manner of a stage actor whose actions must be clear to those in the fifteenth row of the mezzanine. Ironically, small-window video may penalize good actors and reward hams. Subtle gestures and soulful glances do not show up on the computer screen.

Simplify the scene

In a small, grainy window you cannot show intricacies. Excessive small details become noise that annoy and confuse the user. To simplify the scene:

- **Remove small objects**. In video of any sort, avoid small objects and thin lines. Eliminate objects smaller than 4 pixels in the resulting image. Objects smaller than this carry no recognizable detail and may sparkle annoyingly. Thus, avoid shiny jewelry and reflections from eyeglasses.

- **Eliminate patterns and textures in clothing**. Select clothing colors and patterns to stand out from the background, set, and props. If using a *chromakey* effect (an effect which replaces all of a single color with an image), avoid any colors even near the unique solid color that is keyed to disappear when the images are combined. Avoid tiny patterns: fine checks, stripes, and herringbone patterns can produce a *moiré* pattern of shimmering colors.

- **Use stage makeup**. Use makeup to cover cuts, scratches, freckles, scars, and other minor blemishes. Also remove circles under the eyes, repair wrinkles, and lift drooping jowls. Use makeup positively too. Emphasize eyes, raise cheek bones, accentuate the perfect nose. Apply a foundation to even out skin tones. Take care to match the natural skin color of the actor. Use face powder to tone down shiny spots. Apply makeup under actual lighting conditions—on the set if possible.

- **Use close-ups, not panoramic shots**. With small-window video, you cannot use the traditional panoramic establishing shot to set the context. Instead, start with a medium shot followed by close-ups of significant and familiar details, each clearly recognizable. Also use recognizable sound effects to imply a particular locale. Take care to establish the size of any familiar object.

Do not waste money on invisible details. Before building an elaborate set, consider a photographic enlargement or painted backdrop behind hastily constructed furniture. Because viewers of low-resolution images cannot tell the difference between pine or mahogany or between burlap or silk, costs of sets, costumes, and props are less for small-window video.

Simplify color

Limit the range of colors in the scene. Design the set and select props and costumes from the same family of colors. When digitizing your scenes, carefully select a palette of colors that best matches those of your video segment. By limiting the number of distinct colors, you can get by with a smaller color palette—thus reducing storage size. You also have more freedom to customize the palette to match the colors present in the scene.

Limit contrast in the scene

Reduce contrast in scenes for video. Few details are visible in dark areas and white areas lose texture. Avoid dark suits with white shirts or blouses. Even good video cameras can record only about nine levels of brightness. As a rule, make sure adjacent colors in a video scene differ by at least two brightness levels [295].

Flat lighting better accommodates a medium—such as television—which has a limited contrast range. With flat lighting, the camera can capture colors accurately throughout the scene. Flat lighting lets you shoot from a variety of angles without having to adjust lighting. It suggests cleanliness, truth, efficiency, and happiness. However, flat lighting can also appear mechanical and impersonal [295]. Flat lighting tends to bleach out skin tones, making people look like zombies, and reveals little more than the contour of the object and its most prominent details.

Set up even, flat lighting across the scene so that none of the action gets lost in dark shadows and bright highlights do not bleach out detail. Do not shoot directly into a bright light. Do not pose people staring into a bright light. Keep the main light at least 15 degrees from the camera and from the subject.

MIXING MEDIA

Now that all media are possible, which do we use? How do we combine the strengths of various media? Even though all media may be possible, not all media are practical. How do we make effective compromises?

Which medium or media?

There is no magic formula for deciding which media to use. The decision requires taking into account the preferences and perceptions of users, the costs of various media, and the priorities of the message you must convey. Here are some principles to consider:

- Media preferences vary considerably by age [186]. Younger viewers prefer dynamic visual media; older ones, static textual media.

- Most of the time, the combination of good still images and clear sound work as well as full-motion video [88]. If animation is difficult, consider showing a static image with appropriate sounds.

- Never try to make a point by showing characters talking about a subject. If words are necessary, have an off-camera narrator explain the concept or display the words.

- Start with the pictures. Then add other media. Say as much as you can in images, sound effects, and music before you start adding text [7]. Videotex failed in the late 1970s because users disliked reading long passages of text from TV screens [10].

- Many users trust text more than video. They see it as more truthful and scholarly [162]. As our ability to manipulate visual images increases, photography will cease to be the standard of truth and text will regain the mantle of honesty [3].

- Drawings and animation can ignore distracting details a camera cannot. Use drawings and animation to selectively emphasize and deemphasize items in a scene.

- Use visual media to communicate with hearing-impaired users. Use sonic media to communicate with visually impaired users.

- Users cannot attend to two visuals or two sounds at the same time. They can, however, attend to a sound and a visual simultaneously, especially if they represent the same concept.

When considering moving pictures, you must decide if moving pictures are appropriate and whether to use animation, video, or both. Although both animation and video can perform the same basic functions, neither works in all circumstances. In general, the differences between animation and video resemble those between drawings and photographs.

Use animation	Use video
To show movement and action by generic objects or people	To show movement by particular objects or people
To avoid distracting details	To show rich levels of detail in a scene
To reduce storage and processor requirements	When budgets are adequate
For a light tone	For a serious, documentary tone
To show abstract concepts	For concrete objects only
If the presentation must be revised later	Only if all filming can be done at once

Integrate media smoothly

Select and integrate media so smoothly that users gain information without noticing the media providing the information [207]. Users should not have to stop and think, "Is this a photograph or a still video frame?"

Mix media for powerful messages

Combine media for complex subjects and varied audiences. The Playground Physics portion of *The Visual Almanack*, for example, contains a table, a graph, and a movie all recording the speed of a spinning merry-go-round as children move in and out. As users watch the movie, they see the graph develop. They can then select any point on the graph or any line in the table or any frame in the movie to access the corresponding items in the other media [133].

Combine text and dynamic graphics

Text and dynamic graphics are an especially powerful combination. Provide textual explanations of animations. Let users read the text before or after the animation (not just during!). Or let them listen to the explanation as the animation plays [262]. Combine the still video frame and related text in the same display, much like a picture on the page of a paper document. Let the user study the still, read the text, and play the video all on the same display [159].

Combine pictures and sounds

Do not play sound without something for users to relate the sound to [45]. Show or tell what the sound represents; otherwise, users will find their own associations for the sound.

To intensify and amplify visuals, choose music and sounds congruent with the events being shown. When sound and picture share the same rhythm, the effect is powerful. Take care, however, to vary the rhythm. If the rhythm is too regular for too long, viewers become bored.

To spur thought and get the user to reconsider visual associations, use sounds and music contrary to the visuals [295]. In picture-sound counterpoint, the rhythm and mood of pictures contrasts with that of the sound. A slow sequence of relatively static pictures can be punctuated by fast, upbeat music.

Use media consistently

Ensure that every media element fits the style of the topic and of the document [10].

> The tone, rhythm, and speed of the sound track should complement the weight and motion of the visual elements and underscore the emotional context of the scene [241, p. VC-19].

If media elements appear together, edit them together. The meaning of text depends on the graphic displayed at the same time and vice versa. The words of narration make sense only when seen with the video segment they describe [180].

Give users a choice of media

Make some media elements optional. Let users decide whether they want to see paragraphs of text, hear words spoken, scan tables, review equations, view charts, play animation or video, or combine these media.

Include a separate index or table of contents listing all the media elements. These function like the List of Tables or List of Illustrations common in military manuals.

Consider what media the user can play back. If the user lacks the ability to play sound or video, you can have the installation program omit those elements from the document and remove the buttons that trigger them. Another solution is to have the document analyze the user's hardware and software and deactivate (gray out) buttons for those media the user cannot play. This reminds the user of the presence of these media and provides an incentive to upgrade to a more capable system.

Storage costs of media

The storage space required for various media can exert a triple cost. They require storage both on disk and in memory. And the larger the volume of data, the higher the processing power required to display it. Here are some typical figures for different media:

Medium	Unit	Format	Amount
Displayed words	100 words	Displayed	1K
Spoken words	100 words	Read aloud	1K
		Phonemes	2K
		Allophones	10K
		Recorded voice	500K (see Sound)
Music	1 minute	Recorded	10 MB (see Sound)
	1 minute	MIDI	10 K
Picture	640x480 bit map	1 bit (black and white)	38K
		8 bit (256 colors or shades of gray)	300K
		24 bit (16 million colors)	921K
Sound	1 minute	Top quality, 48kHz, 24 bit, stereo	17.28 MB
		CD Audio, 44kHz, 16 bit, stereo	10.56 MB
		High, 22kHz, 16 bit, stereo	5.28 MB
		Good, 22kHz, 8 bit, stereo	2.64 MB
		Moderate, 22kHz, 8 bit, mono	1.32 MB
		Low, 11kHz, 8 bit, mono	660K
		Voice quality	330K
Video	1 second	Full screen, 30fps, full color	12.5 MB

Compression

Compression techniques can greatly reduce the storage requirements for various media. Selecting a compression method, however, often involves a trade-off: speed of playback or loss of details. There are two kinds of compression: lossless and lossy. *Lossless*, as its name implies, restores the original uncompressed data without any loss of detail or quality. *Lossy* compression can save more space but at some loss of detail or quality. Lossy compression schemes may be adequate for video where users seldom notice minute details, especially in moving objects. In any case, test with typical data.

Here are some typical ranges of compression ratios (compressed divided by uncompressed):

Medium	Lossless	Lossy
Text	0.8 to 0.5	(Do not use)
Graphics	0.8 to 0.4	0.5 to 0.05
Animation	0.7 to 0.2	0.4 to 0.05
Video	0.6 to 0.2	0.4 to 0.05
Sound	0.9 to 0.7	0.8 to 0.1

PUTTING THESE IDEAS TO WORK

Essential ideas of this chapter

➡ Use sound and motion where appropriate.

Use this type of display . . .	For this purpose . . .
Displayed text	For short passages that the user must study critically or for promises the user must trust
Graphics	To establish ideas, to show spatial or logical relationships, or to show what something looks like
Filters	To combine different layers of information in a graphic
Audible signals	To alert the user to a special condition or completion of a lengthy operation
Spoken words	To narrate or instruct, especially while visuals are displayed
Visual transitions	To symbolize the relationship between the old and new topics and to guide the user's eye to the intended area of the display
Builds	To progressively introduce layers of information in a complex display
Animation	To show smooth, continuous change or motion
Video segments	To show moving objects and to teach people to perform manual operations

➡ Let the user start, stop, speed up, slow down, and reverse the action in a dynamic display.

➡ Make the computer's speaking voice distinct from others around the user, but have it speak in a natural rhythm at a normal rate using standard grammar and pronunciation.

➡ Simplify video shown in a small window on the screen.

For more ideas and inspiration

Ambron, Sueann and Kristina Hooper, eds. 1990. *Learning with Interactive Multimedia: Developing and Using Multimedia Tools in Education*. Redmond, WA: Microsoft.

Apple Computer. 1993. *Demystifying Multimedia: A Guide for Developers from Apple Computer, Inc.* San Francisco: Vivid.

Cotton, Bob and Richard Oliver. 1993. *Understanding Hypermedia: From Multimedia to Virtual Reality*. London: Phaidon Press.

Noake, Roger. 1988. *Animation Techniques.* Seacaucus, NJ: Chartwell.

Thomas, Frank and Ollie Johnson. 1981. *Disney Animation: Illusion of Life.* New York: Abbeville Press.

Utz, Peter. 1989. *Video User's Handbook: The Complete Illustrated Guide to Operating and Maintaining Your Video Equipment.* New York: Prentice Hall Press.

Winston, Brian and Julia Keydel. 1986. *Working with Video.* New York: Amphoto.

Zettl, Herbert. 1990. *Sight, Sound, Motion: Applied Media Aesthetics*. Belmont, CA: Wadsworth.

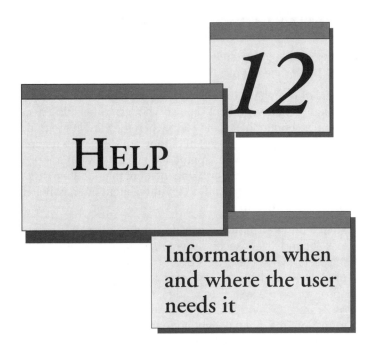

HELP

12

Information when and where the user needs it

Help is one of the most common and most important kinds of online documentation. It has become such an expected feature for personal computer programs that magazine reviews roundly criticize programs that lack adequate Help facilities. Although Help facilities are common, effective ones are still rare. This chapter suggests ways to make sure yours is effective.

WHAT IS HELP?

What, then, is a Help facility (or Help for short)? And how does it differ from other forms of online documentation? Help is online documentation that users request and read in the middle of an online task to aid them in performing that task.

What is different about Help?

The way people use Help is different from the way they use other online documents. These different uses lead to different expectations and perceptions.

- **Users of Help have other things on their minds**. People do not read Help for relaxation or entertainment. They do not give the Help document their full attention. They normally access Help when they are in the middle of a business task, usually only as a last resort after they are stuck. The readers of Help have to integrate information about a particular task, the computer program they were operating to perform that task, the incident that led them to request Help, and operations of the Help facility. Very little attention may be left over for the content of the Help document.

- **Help is an interruption.** Accessing and reading Help takes time away from the task at hand. Every second spent reading Help is one second not spent performing useful work. New users of a system are impatient. They expect to perform productive work on the system almost immediately, and prefer learning by trial and error on the system to reading manuals—online or printed [49]. Experienced users are even more impatient and resent interrupting their work to look up information in a manual. Even though users request Help, they still view it as an interruption of the work they would rather be doing.

- **Help is part of the product**. To users, Help is just another part of the program, not a separate product or system. It is just as much a part of the application as the menus, icons, and forms. Users expect the Help facility to look and work like the application.

- **Help is to help users do something**. Users access Help while they are trying to perform a task. Usually their questions are how to overcome a problem or how to get unstuck. Users are tightly focused on the task at hand and demand information to help them perform that task. They reject other information.

Design for these differences

Although most everything in this book applies to Help facilities, the differences between Help and other forms of online documentation lead us to apply some guidelines more vigorously than others.

- **Help with the user's task**. Design task-oriented Help that focuses on the immediate goals of the user [188]. Help is not to teach users all about the product but to aid the user with small, specific actions. Use computer tutorials or online reference manuals to provide the big picture and to assist the user in developing strategies for using the product. Remember, Help is for reading to do, tutorials are for reading to learn.

- **Keep it simple**. Help facilities can easily overwhelm tired, frustrated, distracted users, especially if they require long, intricate procedures to find information. An overly complex Help facility can decrease learning and productivity by over-whelming already burdened users [188]. Ask yourself, could a bright teenager with a migraine headache operate this thing? If the answer is no, your Help fa-cility is probably too complex.

- **Make it concise**. Busy, impatient users will not read much. Get to the point, cut to the chase, deliver the punch line. Make all nonessential information optional.

- **Make it quick.** Unless users find the answer to their questions immediately, they seek other, perhaps less reliable, sources of information. Help must respond quickly and provide a direct path to answer the user's question.

- **Integrate Help with the application**. Make Help a seamless part of the program it serves. Let users jump back and forth between the application and Help. Make Help and the application consistent, so that users do not have to learn many new rules or remember exceptions.

TYPES OF HELP FACILITIES

Several types of Help are possible. They generally differ in the way the user identi-fies a topic and in how much information they contain. Help facilities range from simple systems with but a single Help display to complex systems that automati-cally reference large online manuals to find helpful information for the user.

Reference summary

Reference summary help is an online version of the quick-reference card that comes with many programs. It is sometimes called *crib-sheet* help. Such Help provides little more than a summary of the commands of the program. For example:

```
ZipComm Batch File Commands

RECEIVE fromfile tofile     receive a file from another workstation
SEND fromfile tofile        send a file to another workstation
DISPLAY file                display file from another workstation
CONNECT workstation         connect to another workstation
LIST directory              display directory on another workstation
DELETE file                 delete file on another workstation
CHDIR directory             change directory on another workstation
DO command                  execute command on another workstation
DOHERE command              execute command on your workstation
SET parameter=value         set SPEED, TERMINAL, or SECURITY
QUIT                        end ZipCom session
```

For a one-window application, reference summary Help may consist of a picture of
the window annotated with the function of various buttons and icons.

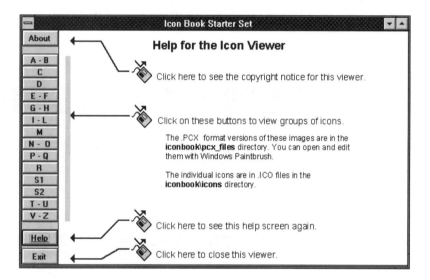

These electronic crib sheets jog the experienced user's memory, but are seldom
enough for learning the system from scratch. Such quick-relief documents do, however, overcome the complaint of many users that it takes too long to find what they
are looking for. By removing irrelevant information, customizing documents for
specific groups of users performing common tasks, and highlighting key points,
quick-relief documents let people find information faster.

Reference topic

Reference-topic Help facilities provide access to a library of separate topics. The user displays a particular topic by letting context sensitivity find the topic or by specifying the name of the topic.

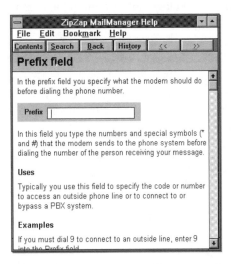

With *context-sensitive* access, the topic displayed depends on where the user is in the program when requesting Help. If the user is executing a particular command, for instance, he or she would get Help on that command. If an error has just occurred, then an explanation of that error will result.

Pop-up Help

With *pop-up* Help, the user points to an item on the screen and up pops a brief explanation. Apple's version of pop-up help is called *Balloon Help* after the way Help messages appear in speech balloons. For example:

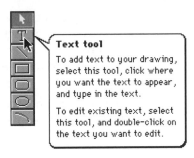

Pop-up Help is good for answering questions such as "What is this?" "What can I do with it?" "What's new in this version?" and "What else can it do?" However, if the messages pop up unbidden, they can startle and annoy users. Most users tolerate the balloon barrage of Apple's balloon help for only 10 minutes before they turn off the facility. I'd suggest having the pop-up message appear only when the user presses a special function key, not just when the cursor passes over the object.

Diagnostic Help

Diagnostic Help facilities identify the user's needs and supply information to meet those needs. To diagnose the user's needs, such systems typically engage the user in a dialog. As a result of the dialog, the facility gives the user information or performs a task for the user.

```
================================================================
Printer configuration                    Diagnostic help
How will the printer be connected to your computer?
a. LPT1          e. COM1          i. over network
b. LPT2          f. COM2
c. LPT3          g. COM3
d. LPT4          h. COM4
Answer ==> b
================================================================
Which operating systems will you use with the printer?
a. DOS      b. Windows      c. OS/2      d. SCO Unix
Enter all that apply?
Answer ==> a, b, d
================================================================
At what resolution do you want files printed?
a. 300 dpi (fastest)      b. 600 dpi (best quality)
Answer ==> b
================================================================
Do you want customized installation instructions …
a. Displayed on the screen
b. Printed on the printer now on LPT1
c. Saved in a file
Answer ==>
```

Prototype systems have used natural-language recognition and synthesis to simulate an experienced colleague. Less ambitious, but more practical, systems have used menus to guide the user to express his or her needs in terms and concepts for which the Help facility can offer information. Several varieties have appeared in commercial products.

- **Wizards**. In Microsoft Excel, Word, Publisher, and Access, wizards lead users through a difficult task by asking them to make simple decisions and then carrying out the work based on the users' decisions.

- **Coaches**. In WordPerfect 6.0 for DOS, coaches walk the user through a task a step at a time. Unlike a traditional tutorial, they give users the option of having the coach explain what to do, or do the work. Coaches work with the user's actual data.

- **Experts**. In Borland's Quattro Pro for Windows 5.0, experts lead users through complex procedures, showing them at each step what the results will look like and giving them the option of continuing, canceling, or making changes.

- **Interactive Tutors**. In Borland's Quattro Pro for Windows 5.0, interactive tutors teach like regular CBT lessons, but let users work with their actual data rather than that provided by the tutor.

- **Advisors**. Harvard Graphics 2.0 for Windows provides Quick Tips on performing common tasks and Design Tips on making better presentations. These advisors can stay on screen while the user works.

Though helpful, such systems are not a panacea. Merely doing things for users or telling them in great detail exactly what buttons to press may leave them with no clear understanding of what they accomplished. Have the diagnostic Help leave a record of what it did and how users could do the same thing on their own. Also, be sure to clean up afterward. Leave the system in the state it was before the users invoked the diagnostic Help.

MAKE IT EASY TO GET HELP

If the user of a program is not aware that Help is available or does not know how to display that Help, all is for naught. If a user's first attempt to use Help yields useful information, he or she will continue to use Help. If the first attempt fails, users seldom try again. Make sure all users know how to get to Help and how to use it. Make getting Help so simple and dependable that it becomes second nature.

Teach users how to use Help

Users prefer to ask people rather than read Help messages, especially if they have never used the Help facility before. To overcome this resistance, teach users how to use Help and other forms of online documentation as part of their training. Teach or tell users about Help at every opportunity, including in:

- Classroom training
- Computer-based training and tutorials

- Other online documents

- Paper manuals and reference summaries

- Installation and getting-started guides

- Customer-support hotlines

- Sales brochures and demonstrations

Prompt at start of the program

When the user starts the computer or runs the program, quickly and succinctly say how to get Help. For instance:

```
If you need Help, press F1 at any point.
```

Do not, however, depend on the user remembering complex instructions 20 minutes later. Keep in mind that displaying the Help-available message every time the program starts up will annoy expert users. Consider dropping the message after the first few times the user has run the program.

Include Help on menus

Include a Help option on all menus. On text menus, label this option *Help*, *Explain*, *Online Document*, or *User's Guide*.

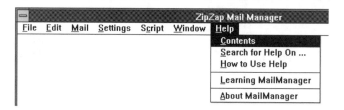

Graphical systems can use a Help icon, for example, with a boxed question mark.

If space permits, include a Help option on all dialog boxes, data-entry forms, and icon bars.

Assign a function key

Designate a key on the keyboard as the Help key. To summon Help, the user merely presses this key.

- **Label the Help key**. If the key is not clearly labeled, novices will not know which key to press and may hesitate to experiment, fearing a scolding beep or worse. If the keyboard does not have a key labeled *Help*, give the user a stick-on label to identify the Help key.

- **Place the key in an obvious location**. Don't hide the Help key, but place it where users will notice it and can find it even without taking their eyes off the screen. Intergraph, for example, puts the Help key at the upper-left corner of the keyboard. Never, however, place the Help key next to keys that perform destructive actions. Don't, for example, place the Help key next to the power switch.

- **Use the same key in all programs**. In all commands, all programs, and all utilities consistently use the same key to select Help. Most programs on the IBM PC, for example, use function key F1 as the Help key, as specified in the IBM's *Common User Access* guidelines. Some of the worst violators of this de facto standard are, alas, programs for authoring online documentation.

Respond to obvious choices

In command or menu systems, allow the user to access Help through a logical and intuitive command. For example:

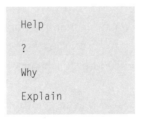

```
Help

?

Why

Explain
```

Do not force the user to press sequences or combinations of keys suited only for a contortionist.

Include multiple commands

Provide several commands to let the user access specific Help topics or other related online documents. Here are the suggested or required entries for the Help pull-down menu in various graphical user interfaces:

IBM CUA [139]   **Apple** [9]   **OSF/Motif, re-designed** [213]   **Microsoft Windows** [183]

Make Help consistent for all programs

Make Help available anytime, anywhere on the system [82].

> The person who uses several programs should be able to get assistance on them consistently. The same types of assistance (examples, definitions, summaries, etc.) should be available across different programs, and they should be accessible in the same way [259, p. 105].

For this to happen, developers of various programs must agree on a standard Help facility, or the operating system must provide a single, integrated facility to manage Help requests from all programs on the system.

Streamline access to the correct topic

Just getting to Help from the application is only half the quest. Provide a simple direct path to the needed topic.

- Use context sensitivity to link each place in the application directly to the topic that explains that context.

- Provide an index of how-to procedures for the most common tasks users perform with the product.

- Cross-reference related topics so users can get from the almost-right topic to the exactly right one. For example, context sensitivity can take the users to the explanation of a particular feature and then a cross-reference link can take them to a how-to procedure that uses that feature.

INCLUDE INFORMATION THE USER NEEDS

To assist users, Help facilities must supply the information users need when they need it. Sadly, many systems do not.

> HELP messages, when not seeming crudely translated from a foreign language, generally repeat some phrase from the manual telling you what you already know (instead of what you want to know) about the specifics of what you're looking at rather than how it relates to anything else, which is usually what you need to know [189].

Provide Help for all users, novice and expert, computer naive and superprogrammer. Provide Help to explain displayed prompts or questions, show examples of correct and incorrect input, define terms, interpret entries on a menu, and show the current status of a process or the system as a whole. Do not omit information because you think it is obvious. Researchers Susan Dumais and Thomas Landauer tell the sad story of one user who knew what database he wanted to access, knew how to search for titles and keywords, and even knew how to construct sophisticated search expressions—but had forgotten the name of the program to use [68].

Parts of the system

In Help include topics for each major part of the system. Include a topic for each:

- Program in the system
- Command
- Menu
- Field on a menu
- Option selectable from a menu
- Error message
- Status message
- Prompt
- Icon
- Special function key

To conserve space you may combine short topics in a single display, but do not ignore any subject the user may ask about.

Common tasks the user may perform

The purpose of Help is not to teach novices everything they will ever need to know to operate the system. Help should provide step-by-step instructions to tell occasional and transfer users how to perform the most common tasks. Find out what most users do with the system and provide instructions for these tasks. Remember that most users do the same few tasks over and over and that they do them in the simplest way possible.

Such task-oriented information is not limited to step-by-step procedures. It can also include guides on deciding what procedure to follow or which option to select. It may even include conceptual information, if that information is necessary for performing a task.

Answers to questions the user may ask

Help exists to answer questions. To decide what to put in Help, anticipate the questions users may ask and provide quick, clear answers. What kinds of questions can we anticipate from users? Just about any kind: How do I . . . ? When do I . . . ? What if I . . . ? What is a . . . ? Is it true that . . . ? What is the difference between . . . and . . . ? What caused . . . ? What did I do wrong? Why won't this work? What else can I do? For more specific questions, we must recall when and why people press the Help button. Here are some questions users often ask while using products:

- Where do I begin? What can I do now? What are my options?

- Where do I enter the information? What screen or menu? What field or slot?

- What do I do next? What information do I enter now?

- Is this input required? What happens if I leave it out? Must I enter the information in a particular format? What is that format?

- What is the computer asking me to do now? Where do I get the information the system is asking for? How do I find it?

- Is the computer waiting for me to do something? Is it still processing my last input? How much longer will it take? Is it stuck? Can I enter more data now or must I wait for a signal from the computer? What is the signal?

- What does that displayed term mean? What does that abbreviation stand for?

- Why did the computer beep at me? What did I do wrong? What is wrong with my input? How can I correct it? Must I correct the problem now or can I continue? How?

- I'm lost! How do I find my way back?

- How do I quit? If I quit now, what happens to the data I have entered?

Ways users can verify their own solutions

Often the best way to solve a problem is to provide resources for users to verify their own attempts at a solution. Users often ask human helpers to verify their understanding of a problem or their proposed solution [50]. Help facilities can provide aids such as these:

- Tests for verifying the success of a procedure

- Criteria for judging success or failure

- Descriptions or pictures of successful results

- Links to run programs that verify the user's data

Where to get more information

Finally, tell the user where to turn for more information. If Help can't answer a question, direct the user to someone or something that can.

- Electronically cross-reference other online documents. If the Help display does not answer the question, the user can search for the answer elsewhere in the online manual.

- Recommend related paper documents, such as repair and maintenance guides, theory of operations, self-study course materials, and catalogs of other programs.

- Give phone numbers of customer-support hotlines.

FIT SMOOTHLY INTO THE USER'S WORK FLOW

Design Help to make users more productive at their work. Provide specific answers in the context of the user's work environment with minimal disruption.

Get the user back to work quickly

Make Help easy to access if needed, but do not let it get in the way of the productive use of the system. The user is in the middle of doing something important and is interested in the task at hand and not the online document [49].

Don't make the user choose between the program and the online document. Let the user view and work with both at the same time. To solve problems, the user often must combine information displayed by the program with information from the online document. Sometimes the user needs information from the document to decide what action to take in the program, yet many online documentation systems fill the screen and lock the user out of the program while viewing the online document. The user must then memorize details or write them down before returning to the program. Good systems do not tax the user's short-term memory or require the user to write down information on slips of paper.

Let users do work while in the document

Some Help facilities let the user enter data while viewing the online document. When the document is dismissed, the data entered are passed back to the original program as if the user had entered the data there. This technique, known as *passthrough*, is especially useful in online documents that explain prompts or items on a menu. Diagnostic Help systems let users enter information while still in Help.

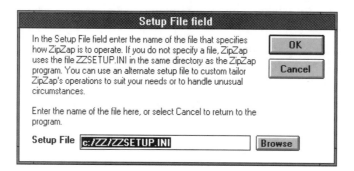

Display document and program together

Multiprocessing, multiwindow applications let the user simultaneously run the program and read documents for that program [19]. The user can see and interact with both at the same time.

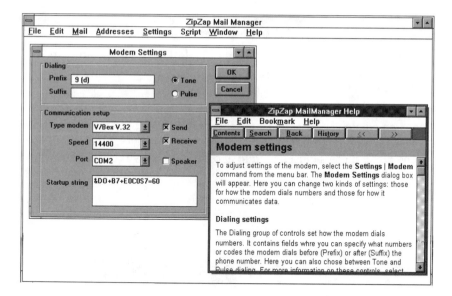

Cover as little as possible of the user's work display. Any time Help covers more than one-fourth or one-third of the application's work area, usage of Help falls off dramatically. Cover the application only if the user requests more detailed Help. If you must cover up part of the application, position the Help window so it covers the least valuable part of the application window.

Make Help displays self-explanatory

Make Help displays obvious and self-contained. Title them with the name of the command, menu item, field, or other object on which information is offered. Make the name on the Help display exactly match the name as it appears in the program. Make it immediately obvious that this is a Help display, either graphically or with the words "Help for . . ." in the title. When you give the user instructions, make sure the user knows not to apply them until back in the program.

Do not forget to provide a Help file and a tutorial for the Help system. Teach the user how to use the Help facility. Never assume it is obvious even to expert users. Explain:

- How to get to Help from anywhere in the system. Users may know only one route. Tell them the easiest and fastest way.

- How to navigate within Help. Explain how to scroll or page through a topic and how to jump to related topics.

- The meaning and function of all parts of the Help display.

Keep Help displays simple and to the point

Users of Help have more than Help on their minds. Do not expect the user to read more than about three Help displays at a time [69] or to remember more than about five points [229].

Put the answer first and the explanation later in the topic. Answer the most likely questions immediately; do not make the user scroll down or flip through displays. Present general rules and principles directly; do not make users infer them [24]. Reduce the amount users must attend to at once. A lengthy procedure in which each step is simple and self-contained may prove less forbidding than a cryptic summary [78].

Keep Help information accurate and up to date. Inaccurate or out-of-date information will destroy the trust of the user.

Make your Help file compact

If users perceive the Help facility is a waste of resources, they reject it. Editorials in computer-user magazines frequently bemoan the space taken up by Help files. If the Help facility is too large or does not obviously add value, users will not install it or will remove it to free up disk space.

While working on the Help facility for one large application, I noticed that the marketing department would object any time the Help file grew larger than half the size of the application. Recently I conducted a survey of the Help facilities for 35 PC and Macintosh applications and found that the average size of the Help file was 50.5 percent the size of the application itself. Help files larger than 50 percent tended to include extensive graphics, animation, and interactivity that clearly added value to the bare-bones Help facility. So, either keep your Help file less than half the size of the application or make its extraordinary value immediately obvious.

INTEGRATE HELP WITH OTHER DOCUMENTS

Do not try to answer every question and satisfy every need with just a Help facility. Combine Help with other online and paper documents to form a comprehensive question-answering system.

Use Help to provide immediate access to just the information users need while performing procedures. Add a tutorial to train novices not knowledgeable enough to take advantage of the succinct expressions preferred in Help by experienced users. For comprehensive reference, include an online reference manual to provide more background theory, deeper details, and broader coverage of the information in Help.

Provide electronic cross-references to weave Help and other online documents into a consistent, unified source of information.

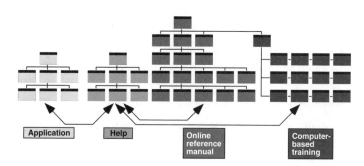

Just as users can jump from the application into Help, they should be able to jump from Help into the online reference manual for more details or to computer-based training for conceptual understanding. If a Help topic uses terms users are unfamiliar with, users can look them up in the online glossary. If users still do not understand, they can jump to the tutorial for a short lesson on the concept behind the term. If a lesson requires users to issue certain commands, users can summon Help to look up the format or icon for those commands. Help, then, is just a gateway to all forms of electronic information.

Users no longer have to decide which document contains the information they need. Links provide the advantages of one-stop shopping and solve a common problem with how users perceive online documentation. I have noticed that users of online documents do not understand the concept of separate, independent documents. To them, the computer is the document and they expect everything to be there in one seamless information cloud with a consistent user interface.

PUTTING THESE IDEAS TO WORK

Essential ideas of this chapter

➡ Make it obvious how to get Help. In training courses teach how to use the Help facility. Include reminders at the start of the program and on menus.

➡ Include a Help key on the keyboard and a Help icon on the screen. Label it *Help* or *Explain*. If possible, put it in an obvious location and have all programs respond to it.

➡ Respond to obvious requests for Help, such as typing "HELP", "EXPLAIN", or "?"

➡ Don't let Help disrupt users' work. Leave users' work visible on the screen, and let users resume work where they left off.

➡ Make Help displays self-explanatory. Include instructions on how to operate the Help facility or at least on how to obtain such instructions.

➡ Include Help topics for all parts of the program or system, for common tasks users may perform, and for questions users are likely to ask.

For more ideas and inspiration

Boggan, Scott, David Farkas, and Joe Welinske. 1993. *Developing Online Help for Windows*. Carmel, IN: Sams.

Elkerton, Jay. 1988. "Online Aiding for Human-Computer Interfaces." In *Handbook of Human-Computer Interaction*. Amsterdam: North-Holland. 345-364.

Kearsley, Greg. 1988. *Online Help Systems: Design and Implementation*. Norwood, NJ: Ablex.

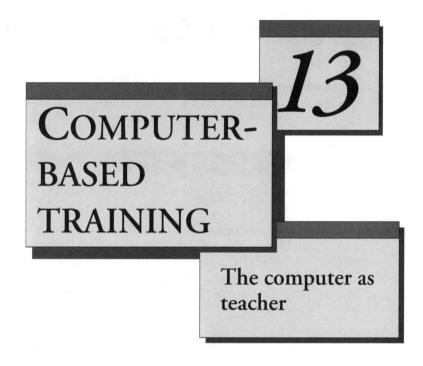

COMPUTER-BASED TRAINING

13

The computer as teacher

Computer-based training (CBT) is broadly defined as "all forms of the use of computers in the support of learning" [246, p. 314] and as "anytime a person and a computer come together and one of them learns something" [221]. A more precise definition may be "an interactive learning experience between a learner and a computer in which the computer provides the majority of the stimulus, the learner must respond, and the computer analyzes the response and provides feedback to the learner" [109, p. 6].

Computer-based training is a type of online documentation. It uses the same media and applies the same design principles of access, organization, and dialog design as other types. Computer-based training is often a part of a complete information package that includes paper documents and other forms of online documentation.

WHERE TO USE COMPUTER-BASED TRAINING

The user has much to learn: the user interface of both the product and the online documentation software, the organization of the document, and the content of the document—all at the same time. Can computer-based training help?

CBT can train and educate

Dozens of studies show that CBT can improve learning, attitudes, and job performance [73, 74, 153, 191, 208].

- Andersen Consulting used interactive multimedia for training its 60,000 employees in 300 locations throughout 67 countries. By reducing the time required to take the Business Practices Course from 40 hours of classroom instruction and 60 hours of self-study to 38 to 45 hours of computer-based training, Andersen saved $2 million a year. As a result, Andersen plans to convert about 35 percent of its training to interactive multimedia [51].

- By one estimate, a CBT with interactive video can provide in 45 minutes a learning experience that would take four hours in the classroom [143].

- Over 30 studies have found interactive multimedia increases learning, according to Rodney L. Miller, editor of *The Multimedia and Videodisc Monitor* [3].

- Students tutored with an electronic COBOL tutor performed 10 percent better than other students, even though they needed less instructor help [211].

- Trainers at IBM's Washington System Center used NetView to replace three days of classroom training, resulting in a savings of $1.9 million [87].

What does computer-based training offer?

But where does computer-based training fit in an integrated communication program? In general, computer-based training works well when you have specific objectives for teaching factual matter, and not so well when the subject matter is subtle, abstract, or implicit [74]. Computer-based training is ideal for teaching routine details and facts. Such subjects include spelling, grammar, vocabulary, simple math, foreign language mechanics, programming languages, electronics, typing, and statistics. It is not as well suited to more creative pursuits such as philosophy or creative writing. Use computer-based training for:

- **Training where and when the user needs it**. CBT can provide training at remote sites and at varying schedules. CBT is ideal for students who, because of location or work schedule, cannot attend traditional classroom instruction. Neither instructor or student have to travel. Newly hired employees can get training immediately from CBT without waiting for a class to form [3]. With CBT, students receive immediate and continual feedback. Papers are graded instantly. CBT is *just-in-time training*.

- **Consistently high-quality training**. CBT can provide high-quality instruction for the masses. Standardized training can ensure a minimum level of mastery for all students. CBT can incorporate the strategies of the best instructors and protect learners from incompetent teachers. In studies, test scores were higher from the online than from the paper version of tutorials [232]. An experimental online tutor on the LISP programming language increased test scores 43 percent although students spent 30 percent less time doing exercises [75].

- **Reducing training costs**. CBT can lower administrative and support costs for providing training. About 90 percent of the cost of training is the salaries and benefits of the students and instructors [244]. Students can complete CBT instruction quicker than classroom instruction. In the classroom, instruction is paced by the slowest learners. With CBT, the pace is set by the individual learner. One study found that CBT reduced training time by 14 to 67 percent [73].

- **Training for difficult systems**. CBT lets users learn to operate expensive or dangerous equipment without the risk or cost of learning with the actual equipment. CBT can offer more practice trials for systems that respond slowly. A space shuttle simulator, for example, can show the results of an orbital maneuver immediately, jumping ahead several orbits without the expense or danger of an actual launch.

- **Fitting the training to the user**. CBT systems adapt to the learner's needs. They proceed at the user's pace and provide instruction in a form that matches the learning style of the user (concrete or general, visual or verbal, conceptual or example based) [286]. The self-pacing of CBT is ideal for those with learning or sensory disabilities. They can proceed at their own rate and can review material as much as necessary.

- **Making training fun**. Students learn in private, so failures are not embarrassing. Because the computer can be strict without seeming judgmental, students feel free to guess, play, imitate, invent, and take risks—all activities inhibited or suppressed in the classroom [34]. Failures are easily corrected. People gladly take criticism from a computer that would hurt if coming from a human. One student described a computer-based training program as "the mother of discipline" [3].

CBT is not always the answer

Computer-based training is not without drawbacks.

- **CBT is expensive to develop**. Lessons are difficult and time consuming to create. Although estimates for the amount of time required to prepare an hour of instruction vary widely (from 2,286 hours to 6 hours in one study [73]), a common estimate is that it takes 200 hours to produce one hour of CBT in contrast to 60 hours for an hour of instructor-led training [54, 184]. Generally, each hour of CBT accomplishes three to eight simple learning objectives and consists of about 100 screens [244]. Designers must also master sometimes complex authoring systems. In France, some teachers are given a year off to learn a CBT authoring language [74].

- **Learners often dislike traditional CBT**. Most people prefer to learn by asking another person. Most avoid online tutorials, feeling they take too long [66] and that they are boring and frustrating [109]. CBT is often lonely. The learner feels isolated and misses interaction with other learners. It may not be ideal for teaching activities performed by a team [234]. Often learners worry that the computer is keeping a record of their mistakes and that they will be held accountable later.

- **CBT cannot evaluate performance well**. Systems are limited in their ability to evaluate students' responses. The lesson writer must anticipate all the ways a student can answer a question. CBT systems cannot tell if the student got the right idea unless the student uses the words the instructor anticipated. Communication is restricted to the media provided by the computer. Natural language systems are rare and imperfect.

- **Training is not always needed**. We can do many tasks without having to learn to do them. Users find little reason to study and learn how to perform a task they will perform only once or rarely. You can dial a phone number without learning it. For many tasks, the user just wants to do the task and forget it [289]. CBT is for learning, Help is for doing.

- **CBT demands careful design**. Two hundred hours of design does not guarantee an hour of effective instruction. One study found that online tutorials were limited to training in simple operations [63]. One study with 40 MIT students found that the choice of paper or computer as an educational medium did not affect test scores [3]. A review of 54 studies on CBT and CAI found that although students liked it, it generally improved performance only slightly [73]. A review of CAI used from 1965 to 1985 found that effectiveness varied widely, depending on design and implementation [228].

Most of the objections to CBT can be overcome, but only with careful design and patient development.

TYPES OF COMPUTER-BASED TRAINING

Computer-presented training draws on a rich heritage of experimentation and research stretching back to the programmed instruction of the 1940s, teaching machines of the 1950s, and early computer-aided instruction of the 1960s [74]. From that heritage have sprung several varieties of computer-based training.

Computer tutorial

Computer tutorials are instructions and lessons about the computer presented by the computer. They teach users how to perform common tasks while letting users interact with the computer.

Keep in mind, though, that online tutorials are not electronic equivalents of paper training manuals. Almost no one reads a training manual. Training manuals are used for reference 95 percent of the time [265]. Online tutorials, however, are poor reference sources. No user reruns a tutorial to look up a single fact. It takes too long.

Guided tour

A *guided tour* combines features of the computer tutorial and the demonstration program to lead the user through the breadth and depth of the system. Guided tours are more interactive than demonstration programs, but generally lack the question-and-answer format of many tutorials. Tours are effective in answering questions such as "What can I do with this product?" or "What's new in this version?" Such a bottom-up learning of structure prepares users to find their own way and improves their ability to recover from errors [256].

Embedded training

Embedded training is "online instruction which is an integral part of a system" [153, p. 279]. Students learn on the same equipment that they are learning about. Embedded training differs from other forms of computer-based training in that it "is problem-solving in nature and tries to assist or advise the user rather than lecture or teach . . ." [153, p. 280]. In a broader sense, embedded training may include menus, messages, the Help facility, and other instructional aids found at the user's worksite. An advantage of embedded training is that:

> . . . learning does not stand alone as an isolated activity: with embedded training it is an ongoing aspect of using a system or product [153, p. 280].

Drill and practice

In *drill and practice,* a concept is presented and the user is repeatedly questioned on it. If the user misses the question, an explanation or hint is given and another question presented. This cycle is repeated until the learner has clearly memorized the concept. It is sometimes called *tell-and-test* training.

Drill and practice has come under heavy criticism because it is often boring and is seldom effective in teaching abstract concepts. These criticisms are better aimed at designers who blindly use a single technique for all forms of instruction. Do not lose sight of the value of drill and practice for helping people master specific knowledge and skills.

Use drill and practice to help learners automate low-level knowledge and skills so they are free to concentrate on learning higher-level skills. Drill and practice is also effective in helping learners memorize specific facts.

Simulations

The goal of training is not just to present information but to engage the learner's thought and curiosity. One of the best ways to do this is through an interactive simulation.

> If a picture is worth a thousand words, hands-on examples are worth a thousand pages [185, p. 62].

Simulations range from simple textual interfaces that tell how the system would respond to inputs all the way to full-immersion virtual reality systems that try to create an all-encompassing sensory environment that replicates the system being simulated. One of the best simulations is the product itself, with the tutorial instructions displayed alongside on the screen.

As an example, consider this simulated control panel for an audio recording system.

This training is more effective than any read-and-type exercises [181]. By experimenting with the actual system and seeing the outcomes of their actions, learners form a more accurate mental model than by merely observing the system in operation or reading about it [157].

An effective simulation mimics real tools from the learner's work environment. All elements (sights and sounds) of the simulation should reflect aspects of the system being simulated, but the lesson need discuss only the aspects relevant to the task at hand. For example, to teach electronics technicians to isolate faults in circuit boards, give them a simulated workbench, complete with clamps for holding the board, grounding strap, and a logic probe hooked to a simulated oscilloscope. Such interactive simulations give users *soft laboratories* or *microworlds* in which they can experiment without danger, expense, or mess [169].

Educational games

Educational games let users learn while competing with one another or with their earlier efforts in solving problems. Games usually involve the simulation of a relevant, real-world problem for the user to solve. Users are scored on how quickly and effectively they solve the problem.

Games can take some of the tedium out of mastering a subject. Games also encourage learners to infer rules and principles, set goals, develop strategies, and test hypotheses.

If the game is not related to the learning objective, it is a motivational sham. In educational games, the reward should be solving the problem. Do not use playing a game as a reward for successfully completing a boring drill-and-practice segment.

Intelligent computer-aided instruction

Intelligent computer-aided instruction (ICAI) systems add elements of artificial intelligence and expert systems to computer-based training. ICAI infers from the student's actions his or her goals, characteristics, and current knowledge. It then tailors instruction and feedback to fit these plans and to correct the student's misconceptions [227]. For example, the tutor for IBM's TIRS (The Integrated Reasoning Shell) tracks errors by the user. If the user's error rate exceeds a threshold, the tutor informs the user. If errors continue, the tutor offers different kinds of advice [53].

ICAI requires recognizing patterns of behavior and inferring the user's state of mind. As you may guess, ICAI systems are difficult to develop. Scattered successes [73], however, show its potential. The contribution of ICAI may not come from full-scale ICAI systems but from modest applications of ICAI techniques in conventional systems. One way to apply ICAI is to infer what the user knows and then display only the information the student does not know. To determine what the user knows, the system can observe and analyze which topics the user has read or lessons the user has taken, what procedures the user has accomplished successfully and unsuccessfully, and what strategy the user appears to be following.

LEARN FROM LEARNING THEORY

People have been teaching people ever since there were people. Thousands of years of experience and study have taught us much about how human beings learn—and left much unknown. No designer of CBT should ignore the lessons of the past, and no good designer slavishly follows any narrow doctrine or theory.

What works

What do we know about how adults learn? Although much disagreement remains, there seems a consensus on some points [49, 73, 110, 160, 208, 289, 293].

Learning is best when learners . . .	What this implies for designers of CBT
Are active	Have users apply information for themselves, rather than just read about it.
Have specific goals	Help users form and refine goals. Suggest goals by showing what users can do with a product.
Value the information	Make information available the moment the user wants it (on-demand training). Show users why information is important. Relate it to real-world problems.
Take responsibility for learning	Let learners initiate training. Tell them they are responsible. Avoid design that puts the user in a passive role.
Feel in control	Let users control what and when they learn. Let users select among short lessons.
Continually learn	Design learning as a process and not an event. Make training continuously available.
Think long and deeply about the information	Provoke thought about the meaning and implications of concepts, not just surface appearances. Seduce learners into reading and viewing more.

Teach in small steps

Keep lessons short and present information in small chunks. Limit the amount of information in each lesson and display, depending on the audience and the difficulty of the material. Use smaller steps to make the lesson go more smoothly. Users do not learn more with smaller units, but they do make fewer errors [232]. Keep lessons short and include more frequent practices [66].

Because computer tutorials demand more participation from the user than paper tutorials, you can make lessons a bit longer [245]. Recommended lengths of lessons range from no more than ten minutes each [185] to about 20 to 30 minutes [36, 290] and up to 30 to 45 minutes [245]. My own experience is that shorter is better. Users are more likely to select and complete a ten-minute lesson than a 20-minute one. And finding 45 uninterrupted minutes may be impossible for many busy users.

Keep users actively thinking. Do not require learners to read or view more than 15 to 20 seconds of material before they begin to think about how they will respond [32].

More show, less tell

Examples and illustrations are more potent in communicating complex concepts than abstract descriptions. Almost everyone would rather be shown how to do something than be told. Examples, case studies, and illustrations are a staple of good trainers. And for good reason. Users can often infer and apply principles from just a single example [168].

Use examples to show how

Use examples to show how to do something, not just to illustrate an abstract concept. In one study using carefully explained examples, the performance of less successful programmers improved, almost to that of better programmers [217].

Help users see relationships between input and output. In examples of operating instructions, show what the user's input should be and what the system's output will look like. If there is a delay between input and output, shorten it in training simulations so that the cause-effect relationship is clear.

Use examples to define concepts

To communicate a concept, present concrete examples that establish the concept and near examples to limit it. Start with typical examples that clearly epitomize the concept. Continue with a range of examples that show the extent of the concept. Finally, introduce near examples to show the boundaries of a concept and help the user successfully discriminate borderline cases. Thus, for each concept, include at least a typical example, an example that barely illustrates the concept, and a near example that is almost an example of the concept.

Help users see the general concept illustrated in an example and understand where else they can apply that concept. If users can form good mental models from examples, they can apply the principles shown in the examples to related situations [217].

Include case-study templates

Include realistic, typical examples that demonstrate the details of operating the system and that the user can use as templates for performing his or her own tasks. Show responses as they actually appear on the screen. Do not limit yourself to if-everything-goes-right cases. Show what happens if the user makes a common error.

Complete, realistic sessions help the user form a full picture of the system and how it operates.

Keep users mentally active

Learning requires an active mind. It requires more than making multiple-choice selections or repeatedly pressing a Continue button. Mental interactivity requires that the user observe and understand information displayed by the computer, form a goal, decide how to pursue the goal, and give an input to begin. What leads to such mental interactivity?

Anything that makes the user think deeply about an idea encourages understanding and learning. One way to do this is with questions or *eliciting statements* that compel the learner to respond mentally [208]. Here are some techniques for using questions and eliciting statements [45, 180]:

- **Use pauses creatively**. Pause when it is time for the user to examine something closely or to think about what he or she has just experienced.

- **Tell the user to imagine or consider something**. Explicitly instruct the user to think about some fact or concept. "Consider what would happen if the format of the two report templates is not compatible."

- **Make the user wonder "Why?"** Include a statement that will cause users to stop and say, "Why?" and then seek the answer. Suggest that the learner guess the reason for something. Make an unsupported statement that invites the user to explain why it is true. Do this casually without implying any penalty for not guessing or guessing wrong. "You've probably noticed that the PassThru command is more efficient than the PassRelay command."

- **Challenge the user to explain**. Ask the user why some fact is true or why an example had certain results. "Can you explain why the bar is now green and not yellow?"

Motivate users

CBT should challenge, but never frustrate. CBT must take special steps to ensure that users, especially anxious novice users, do not become frustrated and give up. To ensure the success of users and to keep them enthusiastically involved with the lesson, borrow standard motivational techniques from creative writing, video games, and instructional design.

- **Make progress quickly**. Show users an immediate return on their invested efforts. You have about seven minutes to get the user doing something useful. After that, the user will lose interest [193]. Get results right away.

- **Make it fun**. Make the first screen of each lesson visually attractive, like the cover of a magazine or the preview of a movie. Introduce just enough variety to keep the lesson from becoming monotonous.

- **Help users set goals and monitor progress**. Help the user set a clear goal with intermediate milestones to monitor progress. Provide immediate and specific feedback about progress toward that goal.

- **Give encouragement**. Help users build confidence. The harder we think the task is, the less motivated we are to try. We are less likely to try a task if we expect to fail. Provide an undaunting series of small steps and periodically remind users of their progress.

- **Challenge but do not thwart**. Vary the level of difficulty to ensure that users are challenged but not frustrated. As users get better at an activity, make it harder. Adjust the level of difficulty so that an expert can perform the test perfectly without any training and an absolute novice will fail without training.

Beware one-theory designs

Unfortunately, research on learning is not unanimous on many issues. Educational theorists do battle with the zeal of religious partisans. Sects include behaviorism, neobehaviorism, cognitivism, neurolinguisticism, humanism, constructivism, deconstructivism, nondirectionism, facilitation, and explorationism. Hundreds of conflicting studies, however, prove only that no particular medium or strategy of instruction is clearly superior to others [55].

Theories tend to divide learners into categories by their *cognitive style*, that is, their predilection for a particular way of learning and problem-solving. Learners are classified as visual vs. verbal, field-dependent vs. field-independent, introverted vs. extroverted, sequential vs. conceptual. Such classifications seldom translate into a particular strategy for a real situation. Other factors such as familiarity, pressure for results, anxiety, work environment, and presentation of the material may have a larger effect [260].

Theories likewise tend to fragment information: declarative vs. procedural, descriptive vs. prescriptive, conceptual vs. instance, fact vs. emotion vs. skill. In any real-world situation, especially one involving learning to use a product or solve a problem, many different kinds of information are required.

Furthermore, human beings are more complex than narrow categories allow. Harvard cognitive psychologist Howard Gardner enumerates several forms of intelligence: linguistic, logical-mathematical, musical, spatial, bodily kinetic, intrapersonal (self-knowledge and self-sensitivity), interpersonal (knowledge and sensitivity to others) [102]. Practical activities require us to use several such forms of intelligence.

Different people learn different subjects different ways in different circumstances. Any system designed around a narrow theory will work extremely well for a few people part of the time. Understand what theory tells us, but do not design your entire system on the tenets of one theory or dogma.

DESIGN COMPLETE LEARNING PROGRAMS

Computer-based training should let users start without prior instructions, proceed without outside help, and achieve mastery without having to memorize instructions or procedures. Designing such effective computer-based training requires clear goals, a well-defined strategy, and systematic design.

Define instructional strategy and goals clearly

Successful training starts with a clear idea of what and whom you are teaching and how you will go about teaching them. In designing teaching systems, task analysis and a clear instructional strategy matter more than a precise simulation or clever metaphor [227]. Write a clear, concise objective stating who will be able to do what under what circumstances and to what degree of success. Make the objective simple to understand and easy to verify, for example:

> After taking this computer tutorial, new users, without referring to written instructions and relying entirely on menus and online documentation, will be able to create a new job-tracking database within 30 minutes.

Once you have established your overall objective, spell out more specific objectives and goals for each lesson and display. To organize a tutorial,

> . . . list all of the tasks you would like the learner to be able to perform when he completes the tutorial. Then organize the tasks into three to five lessons, each of which can be completed in 20–30 minutes [290, p. ATA-101].

Title each lesson with a phrase that summarizes the tasks the user will be able to do after taking the lesson. For example:

```
Log onto a public database
Send electronic mail
Type a memo
Analyze a statistical distribution
Write a backtracking algorithm
```

Teach what users want and need to know

Teaching the wrong information can be as bad as teaching nothing. What do users need and want to learn? Most users want to do something right away [49]. So, make lessons task oriented [217].

For teaching and guiding people in performing procedures, help them avoid, recognize, and recover from common errors. Teach users how to gauge their own success and failure. Point out the sights and sounds that result from errors and successes.

Students can become frustrated when information is presented at the wrong level. The document may discuss step-by-step procedures while the user wants to know how to decide which procedure to perform. Teach users how to do useful work, not how to select menus and type in values. Teach general procedures and principles that they can apply broadly for whatever task they want to perform.

Finally, teach learners how to learn and to do on their own. Do not teach just the answers to specific questions. Instead, teach users to answer their own questions.

The next step on the way from objectives and strategy to finished course is to divide the material into lessons and to organize lessons in a coherent pattern and sequence. A course consists of lessons (*topic clusters*), which are usually divided into individual displays (*topics*), sometimes called *frames* or *panels*.

Turn novices into experts

Much training aims at getting novices started with a product. Often equally significant gains are available by guiding novices through stages of competence, proficiency, and even mastery. Experts are highly productive workers. In one case, experts were about four times faster than novices in solving problems. Studies of experts reveal how they differ from novices. Such studies also suggest how CBT can reduce the time and effort required for a user to become an expert [79, 178].

Expert-novice difference	What to do in CBT to raise novices to expert level
Experts are better at abstracting the essential principles that apply in a situation, but novices are easily distracted by surface characteristics and idiosyncrasies.	In examples and case studies, explicitly point out the important concepts at work.

Experts have broader knowledge of the tools at their disposal. Novices tend to learn a few tools and stick with them.	As a hint, tell novices what commands experts use. Showing novices a list of commands in order of frequency of use by experts helped them learn sophisticated search mechanisms [80].
	Use a "Did you know" interface to point out uses of commands suggested by experienced users [202].
Experts tend to solve problems top down; novices bottom up.	Give novices access to high-level plans and strategies corresponding to those applied by experts. Also provide rules for selecting among these plans. To help users learn strategies, provide flow diagrams showing the decision-making process of expert users [78].
Experts classify situations into more precisely defined categories than novices, and experts tend to organize these categories more logically.	Organize information by expert categories. Make these classifications explicit.
Experts have a coherent conceptual model of how the system works. They consult this mental model to solve problems and plan strategies.	Give novices explicit mental models. Base these models on those of experts in the field.
Experts work with larger chunks of information. Expert programmers think in terms of whole subroutines, while novices struggle with one command at a time.	Provide task-oriented procedures for accomplishing large pieces of work rather than just individual steps.
Experts have memorized many low-level details and can use them without conscious thought.	Use drill and practice to help novices quickly automate low-level details.

Teach ill-structured knowledge

Much knowledge is ill structured. No general rules apply without exception to all cases. Categories overlap and no simple hierarchical classification scheme is possible. There are no pure cases or perfect prototypes. Factors critical in one case are unimportant in others. Each case appears singular and defies simple analysis [147].

To teach ill-structured knowledge, provide access paths that simulate the real-world information-gathering activities of experts practicing in the field. Define case studies where the student must decide what information is needed, access the information, analyze it, and apply it to solve a problem. Provide access to standard reference works, test results, simulated advisors, and other case studies. Simulate the actual work environment. To teach safety inspectors, for example, show a scene and have them pick out the hazards and recommend ways of fixing them. You can present situations in displayed textual descriptions and dialog, in spoken dialog, or in video segments with actors.

One especially effective technique uses trigger video. *Trigger video* presents video segments to trigger thought by a viewer or discussion among a group of viewers [234]. Show the user a video segment presenting a situation that the user is likely to encounter. Then ask the user how he or she would respond. For each response, show the user what would result from that response. Give the user the opportunity to repeat the scenario and make another choice. Base the responses on the experiences of knowledgeable users.

For training in team activities, let users simulate conversations with video images of people from the real-world situation. Show a brief video clip to which the user must respond.

PROVIDE HELPFUL FEEDBACK

How am I doing? Is that right? Do I understand correctly? Do I know enough to stop learning and start doing? These are all questions that a learner might ask a human tutor. We learn largely by forming and testing hypotheses. How, then, can a computer tutor evaluate the user's understanding and skill, and how can it correct misconceptions and get the user back on track?

Evaluate user's answers

How does the online trainer evaluate the performance of the user? Typically you pose a question for the user to answer or a problem for the user to solve, and then evaluate the user's response. But how does the system get that response? Several methods exist, each with advantages and disadvantages.

True/false questions

True/false questions ask users to make a binary decision: Is a statement right or wrong? Will a procedure work or not? Is an action safe or unsafe?

True/false questions are easy to construct, but they require little thought by the learner and encourage guessing. They can be effective, however, when the learner's job requires making just such decisions, for instance, a quality-control inspector accepting or rejecting parts or a loan officer approving or rejecting loans.

To correctly gauge the user's knowledge, you must ask several true/false questions. For each concept, ask the question in different ways so that sometimes the correct answer is true and other times it is false. Phrase the questions in an absolutely neutral tone so as not to imply the answer. Provide clear response for incorrect answers.

Multiple-choice questions

Multiple-choice questions are the most common form of user input in online training. These questions have two problems, though. Multiple-choice questions encourage users to guess, and they also force users to think about incorrect answers, which they may later recall instead of the correct answers.

Some authorities counsel against ever using multiple-choice questions [238]. Considering the difficulty and expense of alternatives, though, you may want to improve how you do use multiple-choice questions before abandoning them altogether. For better multiple-choice responses:

- **Make clear what the user is to do**. Write a prompt or stem introducing the alternatives and prompting the user to act.

- **Vary the action**. Pick the correct answer. Pick the incorrect answer. Pick the best answer. Pick all correct answers.

- **Anticipate misconceptions**. Make each choice equally plausible. Phrase choices so they are consistent in grammar and tone with each other and with the question. Keep choices about the same length or size (if visual).

- **Vary the position of the correct answer**. If you detect that users are guessing (selecting each answer in turn), switch the order of answers each time they are displayed.

- **Make each choice reveal a different common misconception**. Let the lesson provide feedback appropriate for each.

- **Increase the number of choices**. Include choices of "none of the above" and "all of the above" where appropriate.

- **Ask "Why?"** Don't ask just "What?" or "How?"

- **Present choices visually**. Have the learner select the picture or icon that best answers the question. Presenting choices visually is especially effective if it is how users will do real work. "Which icon would you select on this menu to copy the results without reformatting?"

Matching items

Another easily evaluated response is to let users *match* items from separate lists, for example, terms and definitions or features and applications of them.

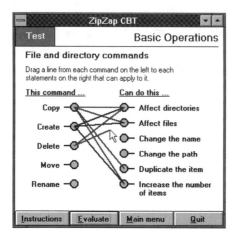

To avoid process-of-elimination guessing, make one list longer than the other or allow multiple matches to some items.

Short-answer questions

Short-answer questions test the user's recall of specific words or phrases. They are effective when the user must learn and type in the names of things, for example, in learning a programming language.

Short-answer questions work well where the number of correct responses is small and the rules for distinguishing right from wrong responses are simple. Phrase prompts for short-answer questions to elicit specific words or their synonyms.

Essay questions

Essay questions invite the user to write a paragraph or two in answer to a question. Essays can ask open-ended conceptual questions. Unfortunately, evaluating the answers is not so easy. Despite progress in natural-language recognition and semantic analysis, few systems can evaluate answers to anything but the most specific questions. Furthermore, essay questions may require too much typing for many users, who would rather press a key or point to an answer on the screen.

If you do use essay questions, phrase them so that they naturally constrain the format and vocabulary of the answer. You may then be able to discriminate right from wrong answers by the presence or absence of specific words or phrases. For a question like:

> How is OS/2 like other operating systems?

you might scan the answer to see if it contains the names of other operating systems (DOS, UNIX, CP/M, VMS) and of features contained in OS/2 and other operating systems (virtual memory, interprocess communication, multitasking).

Another way to evaluate essay answers is to collect the responses and have them evaluated (offline!) by a human teacher. Yet another is to ask the students to verify their solution by finding the points of their answer in the online documentation. Have users tag the topics that prove their answer is right. This is not wasteful if it gets users to review the lesson or teaches users how to navigate a reference document that they will use later.

Perform procedure and evaluate results

In user-led dialogs, there may be several equally effective ways to accomplish an objective. For such systems, you can give users a task to perform on the real system and then defer evaluation until the user requests it. Then evaluate the results accomplished by the user, not his or her action. Some systems include *computer-based critics,* which are routines that examine work done by the user and offer suggestions for improvement [84].

Allow small mistakes

Let users make small mistakes but do not let them clobber the system. Give feedback before learners get so far off track that they become frustrated and lost.

Some authorities recommend giving feedback immediately, within two seconds if possible [73]. Immediate feedback, however, may prevent users from thinking deeply about their task and may lead them to adopt a guessing strategy. Asking questions immediately after presenting information tends to test only short-term memory. In one test, telling learners exactly what keys to press (giving them a keystroke line) reduced comprehension and annoyed some learners [44]. Provide keystroke-level instructions only as a hint after mistakes or only on demand.

Let users turn off the tutorial's monitoring of their inputs. That way they can take off the training wheels and explore on their own. If you do let users depart from the tutorial's path, provide a Back-to-lesson button.

Provide progressively less feedback

Provide more extensive prompts and hints earlier in the learning sequence. Give progressively less feedback as learners demonstrate mastery. Early in the lesson, supplement positive feedback messages with a short explanation of why the answer was correct. After the first few correct responses, users do not need explicit feedback on correct responses. Usually a simple *Right* or *Correct* and movement to the next screen is sufficient. Skip the effusive praise and trumpet fanfares.

Respond clearly to incorrect answers

Make responses to incorrect answers simple, polite, and clear. Begin both remedial and subsequence loops by telling users what they did wrong. Write such you-made-a-mistake displays with special care and sensitivity. Do not call the user by name. Many adults are offended, especially if the message is negative. "Hey, Juan, you just reformatted your hard disk!"

Don't patronize the user or dwell on the mistake. Set it right simply and directly. Deliver a polite message pointing out the error and explaining in detail what do to next.

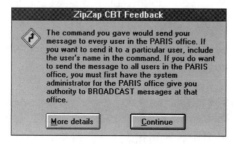

Evaluate user's performance intelligently

Let users try various answers and evaluate and respond to each. For responses, accept more than a single correct answer. Accept synonyms, extra words, different orderings, and misspellings. Anticipate and respond to common incorrect and partially correct responses by learners. Test the document and observe the responses that are common.

If the user does this	Have the system respond by . . .
Input is not obviously wrong.	Give the user a message such as: "Answer was not recognized. Please check spelling and try again." If the user repeats the same input, provide a hint and then the correct answer.
Makes the same incorrect response again and again.	Point out this behavior to break the user out of this pattern. Suggest he or she adopt another strategy or rethink the problem.
Fails to answer a question answered correctly earlier in a different form.	Remind the user of the earlier response and the concept common to both cases.
Cannot demonstrate understanding of the concept.	Offer an opportunity to try again or to seek help. If the student asks for help, remind the him or her of the principles, rules, and concepts taught in the lesson. If the student still cannot solve the problem, lead the student through the solution of the problem one step at a time. If the student still cannot solve the problem, have the student retake the lesson [132].
Repeatedly fails to perform a complex task.	Break it into subtasks and teach them one at a time.
Makes a small error.	Accept input the first time the user makes this error. Point out the error. Reject the input the next time.
Performs a step early.	Point out that the step is not needed yet.
Performs an unexpected and irrelevant action.	Point out that the action is not needed for this procedure.
Repeats steps unnecessarily.	Point out that the step has already been done.
Performs a series of irrelevant and seemingly unconnected actions.	Remind the user of the task at hand. Offer help getting back on track.
Misses the point of a video or animation segment.	Replay the segment at a slower speed. If the user still does not notice the key point, pause the segment on the crucial frame. Or replay the segment with a different commentary.

Keep users on track

How do we correct users' misconceptions? Users who do not demonstrate a clear understanding are typically shunted through a loop that corrects the misconception before returning them to the main sequence.

In a *remedial* loop, the error is explained, and the user is allowed to reattempt the action that caused the error. Use a remedial loop when the error is simple and easily corrected.

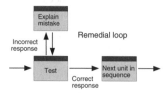

In a *subsequence* loop, the user branches to a supplementary lesson, complete with additional material and a test of this material. Upon completing this lesson, the user advances to the next unit in the main sequence. Use a subsequence loop when the error is caused by a fundamental misconception or lack of prerequisite knowledge.

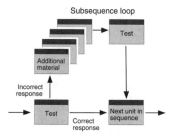

Provide a separate remedial or subsequence loop for each common misconception users are likely to have. This is better than merely repeating the same information for each incorrect response.

SHARE CONTROL WITH THE LEARNER

One of the most contentious issues in the CBT field is whether to let learners control their own sequence of experiences. The answer is yes, within reason.

Allow but do not force learner control

Forcing users through a stultifying series of activities against their will usually teaches them nothing except to hate CBT. Users become frustrated when forced to perform activities they already know how to do, or others they will never have to do in a real situation. Exploration, on the other hand, can be fun, and it leads users to form mental models of the system. Merely following prescribed procedures does not [49, 217].

Learning by exploring, however, can also be inefficient and cruel. Exploration can force a user ". . . to suffer through a lengthy trial-and-error process to solve a trivial problem that a teacher (or manual) could explain in a few moments" [289, p. 42].

Learner-controlled learning can be inconsistent. Some will study forever while others do the absolute minimum. With discovery learning, you cannot ensure that the user will discover the right principles and concepts [289]. Without guidance, users tend to select familiar items and paths and tend to learn less than users who select items in an order provided by the author [254].

Learners often do not know enough to control their own learning activities. As a method, learner-controlled learning is efficient only if learners know what they know, what they do not know, what they need to know, and how to learn what they need to know. Most learners need some degree of direction to efficiently structure their learning activities.

Let users control their own learning, but do not force them to. They should decide how much control to take. At any point, let the user ask for hints as to what to study next, or return control to the CBT system. Let the user resume control at any time too.

Let users select lessons

If learners must master a broad area of knowledge, you should control subjects they must learn. They should decide in what order and at what pace to learn them. In a menu, list the lessons in the order you feel most users should complete them. This order becomes the default path through the course, but the user can still override it to take lessons in another order.

Lessons may be arranged in a recommended sequence and at the same time available individually through a hierarchy of menus.

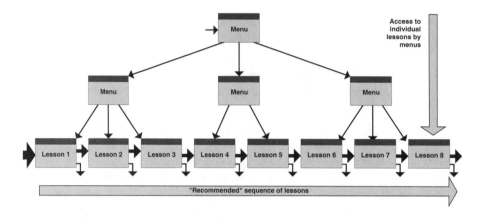

Letting users select tasks allows them to skip tasks they never perform and others they have already mastered. It also lets users return for focused refresher courses on specific topics without taking the entire course [290].

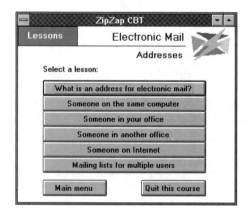

Because users learn best when solving realistic, relevant problems, let them select from a library of sample problems.

Let users skip ahead and repeat

Let nonsequential learners jump about, taking lessons out of sequence, skipping over lessons not important to them, and returning to earlier lessons for a refresher.

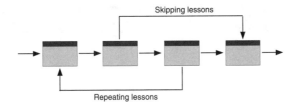

Provide diagnostic tests so users can identify the topics or lessons to skip. An *advanced placement* test selected from the introductory topic can be provided. Users who demonstrate the required knowledge can skip the lesson; those who do not can continue in the lesson.

Provide learner-lead paths too

One way to resolve the learner-control vs. author-control issue is simply to provide for both. Create author-led paths and supplement them with learner-exploration links and branches. For exploratory learning, give users a compass (a way of knowing when they are off track), a map (so they can plot a new route), and a rescue signal (to have the system show them the solution). Provide explanations to help exploratory learners correct and refine the mental models and concepts they have formed on their own. At any time, let learners select a *Show Me* button to have the system demonstrate how to perform a step or a *Back-to-lesson* button to resume an author-led sequence.

For users who can't decide what to do next, provide a Suggest or Chef's Choice button that takes them to a plausible next topic.

Link to related information

Motivated users learn by exploring related pieces of information. When information is made accessible, users learn by guided or unguided exploration. When users use links to explore related information, they learn more from online documents than from paper ones [218].

Provide cross-reference links to related lessons and reference materials. Let users easily find related facts, alternative procedures, and background theory. Make the surface layer or default path concise but provide a safety net of details at a deeper layer.

DESIGN STANDARD LESSON SEQUENCES

The craft of CBT has evolved common techniques and structures. Though not ideal in all cases, these techniques provide a starting point for better designs.

Begin by introducing the lesson

The introduction of a lesson sequence must gain the user's interest and prepare him or her to take the lesson.

Start each lesson by telling the student what he or she will learn by taking the lesson. This concise learning objective lets the student decide whether or not to proceed with the lesson and prepares the student to begin study. Make the objective clear, but do not state it in long-winded, educational gobbledygook. Provide a link to a more detailed rationale. Explain what each lesson teaches and how this information fits in with information in other lessons, especially those the user has taken recently.

Also, make prerequisites explicit. One way to present prerequisites is to provide a problem or question that requires the user to apply the prerequisite knowledge.

Proceed in a logical order

Arrange learning segments in a logical order so that sequential learners can proceed steadily through the material, acquiring and applying new skills. For teaching procedures, start users with elementary procedures. When they have learned (*internalized*) these procedures, broaden and refine their knowledge with conceptual information. Then let them tackle more complex tasks. Do, understand, then do more [217].

In general, proceed from:

- Known to unknown
- General to specific
- Whole to parts

Within a lesson sequence, develop ideas by reminding the user of previously learned knowledge, presenting new information, and then showing how this information relates to other ideas.

Make instructions progressively shorter as the user gains more experience. Explain in detail only the first time the user confronts a new task.

Include a summary

At the end of each lesson, provide a concise summary. Format the summary as a checklist or table. Make sure it includes the same tasks as the introductory menu, in the same order. In the summary, recap the essential ideas the user should remember from the lesson.

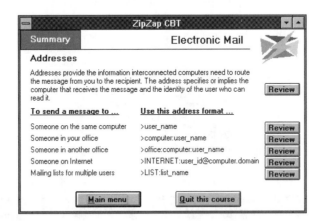

Let users test their knowledge

End the lesson by giving the user a way to try out what they have learned. To test the user's knowledge of a concept, have the user:

- Define the term

- Name the concept

- Recognize an example or near example

- Separate examples and near examples

- Supply an example

- Compare and contrast it with related concepts

To test procedural information, give the user a task to perform on the system or a hands-on exercise. Test the user's knowledge with a short quiz or a series of review questions.

> What command would you use to send a
> message to AKKI in the TOKYO office if you
> do not know the name of the computer AKKI
> uses?
>
> Answer   SEND >TOKYO:*:AKKI

Or, pose typical problems in the way that they might appear in a real work situation. Such scenarios direct users to apply abstract concepts and generalizations to specific cases with which they are familiar.

> The report on the XYZ project is due in Paris
> tomorrow, but it missed the last shipment to
> the Paris office. The report is in the file
> XYZ.RPT on PROPOSALS1 in your office.
>
> Use electronic mail to send the report and
> instructions on how to print it out to RENE in
> the PARIS office.

Make learning permanent

To ensure that users retain information from a lesson, remind them of the information and encourage them to relate it to outside knowledge and personal interests.

- Show realistic examples of where the concepts apply. Video clips of case studies work well, especially if learners can identify with the people in the video.

- Provide additional practice problems. Make them optional, but challenge users to further test their knowledge. Make these examples as realistic as you can.

- Suggest additional resources for in-depth reading and study. Provide links to lessons on advanced features.

Build templates for lessons

Create standard sequences of introductions, objectives, menus, descriptions, exercises, and tests for the course. Use these standard sequences as templates for producing lesson modules. Here is such a template, based on the suggestions in this chapter:

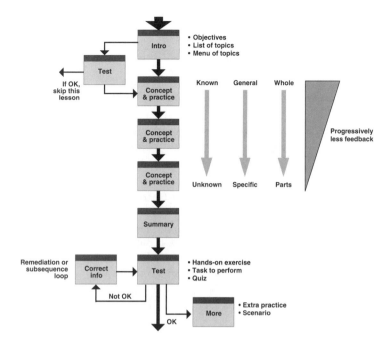

PUTTING THESE IDEAS TO WORK

Essential ideas of this chapter

➡ In general, computer-based training works well when you have specific objectives for teaching factual matter, but not so well when the subject matter is subtle, abstract, or implicit.

➡ CBT can provide consistently high-quality training where and when the user needs it—but only if it is designed well.

➡ Creating effective CBT is difficult, typically requiring 200 hours of preparation for each hour of instruction.

➡ Training is most effective when users have specific goals and actively pursue them, when they take responsibility for learning and feel in control of the learning process, and when they think deeply about what they learn.

➥ Allow, but do not force, users to control the sequence and pace of learning. Give users a choice of when and in what order to take lessons. Make it easy for them to skip over material they already know or do not need to know.

➥ Provide ways for users (and you) to gauge their understanding. The best test is practical application of the concepts taught in the lesson.

For more ideas and inspiration

Dean, Christopher. 1992. *Handbook of Computer-Based Training.* New York: Gulf Publishing.

Eberts, Ray. 1988. "Computer-Based Instruction." In *Handbook of Human-Computer Interaction.* Amsterdam: North-Holland. 599-627.

Gery, Gloria J. 1987. *Making CBT Happen: Prescriptions for Successful Implementation of Computer-Based Training in Your Organization.* Boston: Weingarten Publications.

Price, Robert V. 1991. *Computer-Aided Instruction: A Guide for Authors.* Pacific Grove, CA: Brooks/Cole.

Walter, Dick. 1985. *The Systematic Design of Instruction.* New York: Scott-Foresman.

THE FUTURE

14

Technologies, trends, and unresolved issues

Pushed by the information deluge and pulled by the lure of more efficient storage and retrieval, the trend is irreversibly toward online documentation. Technological advances are making possible communications systems unimaginable a few years ago. This chapter examines some of the advances we are likely to see in the coming years and proposes ways to take advantage of these advances.

BARRIERS REMAIN

The ultimate success of online documentation is far from assured. Several technological and social obstacles must be overcome.

Technology gaps

Despite enormous advances, technology for storing, transmitting, and displaying documents still has far to go. Advances that will unlock the potential of online documentation include these:

- **High-legibility displays**. Improved monitors and display circuitry promise computer screens with the resolution and crispness of paper. Sophisticated antialiasing techniques will smooth curves and improve legibility to the point where the screen is as easy to read as paper.

- **High-capacity storage**. Online documents containing color pictures, animations, and digitized sound have a voracious appetite for storage. Today optical disks provide 550 megabytes of readable information on a medium the size of a floppy disk. Optical disk jukeboxes put dozens of gigabytes online. Small-town libraries will soon fit in a match box, and by the end of the century, a shoebox may hold the Library of Congress with room left over for the digitized pictures of the Louvre and the Metropolitan Museum.

- **High-speed communication networks**. High-speed fiber optic data communications networks will allow users to access documents across the globe with the same speed they read documents on their local disk. When that happens, we will not need to store thousands of copies of documents. A few copies in accessible locations on the network will suffice.

Awkward and inefficient authoring tools

Many of the tools for authoring online documents are as awkward as word processors from the 1970s. Authors must insert cryptic codes into text, must memorize and type in names of related files, and must manually format topics. They must run separate programs to convert from file format to file format. One writer put it this way, "When I went from writing paper documents to writing online documents, I felt I'd gone back to the Dark Ages of publishing." Authoring tools are improving, though. Here are some of the advances now or soon to be available:

- **Multiple-format previews**. Users can rapidly see how the document will look in different sizes of windows, in monochrome and color, and on paper.

- **Structural editing**. Authors can sort and arrange topics as easily as they type in words.

- **Multimedia**. Authors can work with all media through a single tool. File formats are converted automatically as needed.

- **Automated consistency**. New tools provide templates, style sheets, and rules to perform routine formatting tasks.

- **Software engineering support**. Tools assist in tracking components, verifying consistency, and automating testing.

Inconsistent and incompatible products

Solving large, complex problems requires composing solutions from simpler parts. Complex online documentation systems may combine parts from many different manufacturers and organizations. For the pieces to fit together, standard interfaces or protocols must define how modules swap and exchange information. Standards are evolving in many related fields. Standards of special interest to online documentation designers include:

- **Z39.4**. American National Standards Guidelines for Indexes for Information Retrieval. Prescribes organization, format, and content of indexes used to retrieve documents.

- **ISO 8879**. Standard Generalized Markup Language (SGML). Meta-language for defining markup languages for encoding the structure of a document, independent of format.

- **Z39.50**. Standard Z39.50 covers retrieval of bibliographic records based on the MARC format (Z39.2).

- **ISO 10744**. Hypermedia/Time-based structuring language. Extension to SGML that accommodates dynamic media such as video and music.

- **ISO DIS 10180**. Standard Page Description Language (SPDL). Page-description language based on PostScript Level 2.

- **ISO 8613**. Office Document Architecture (ODA). Comprehensive standard for interchangeable electronic documents. Covers structure and layout of the document.

- **Dexter Hypertext reference model**. A generic description of hypertext systems independent of a particular implementation. May serve as the basis for interchange standards [121, 123].

- **Amsterdam Hypermedia model**. A generic description of hypertexts that include dynamic media [126].

A bad standard, however, may be worse than none. Usability tests showed that the standard OSF/Motif Help menu confused users and misled them about the kind of information provided by each option. The standard was changed to incorporate lessons learned by testing with users [213].

Lack of necessary skills

Creating a successful online document requires skills and experience few now possess. We have thousands of years of experience learning to communicate with pen and ink, but lack similar experience with hypertext. In fact, many of the prescriptions of traditional rhetoric (flowing passages, variety in word choice and sentence structure, figurative language) make online documents less accessible and less understandable.

We must move quickly to develop a new rhetoric based not on literary tradition, but on human factors—how people see, understand, and remember. It must embody principles that apply to documents people use as part of their work, not just documents read for pleasure or amusement.

Readers must learn the conventions of online documentation (or we must teach them). Just as users learned to operate scroll bars and to arrange windows on the screen, they must learn effective search strategies to overcome the lost-in-hyperspace and information-overload problems. Educational institutions must consider information access as a fundamental learning skill.

Legal uncertainty

Our legal system is based on paper and by and large has not anticipated the movement to electronic media. Many issues are not covered by legislation or tested in the courts:

- Is a printed version of a web-structured hypertext a valid copy? Is the author liable for misinterpretations resulting from such a printout? What if users have modified the document?

- What is the liability of suppliers for the accuracy and timeliness of their information? Is online documentation held to the standards of print media or of software? What happens if an online medical handbook crashes in the middle of a surgical procedure? On the other hand, can effective online documentation make products more reliable in the hands of customers? Will this increased reliability reduce legal claims?

- Who is responsible for a user's patterns of accessing information? Many online services and computer bulletin boards contain so-called adult material. How is access limited to those above a certain age? Who is responsible if minors access such information? Is knowledge about users' reading habits confidential?

- With limited space and fonts available for display, how are legally required warnings and cautions provided with adequate prominence and clarity?

- How much can one quote from a multimedia work? What is the distinction between quotation, satire, and robbery? To what degree is the look and feel of an online document covered by copyright?

Information overload

As more and more information goes online, the problem of finding a single item grows more difficult. Systems seem better at inundating us with useless information than at answering our questions. We search and the computer responds, "863 items found. Do you want to read the first one?"

Researchers are working on special *search engines*, combinations of special circuits and programs that can search for the proverbial needle in a haystack—at the rate of 3 million words per second. Other specialized search procedures and combinations of techniques will give users access to the global library. These include *filters* that follow rules set by the user to weed out irrelevant information and *agents* that actively seek out information the user may need.

Horseless-carriage thinking

Perhaps the biggest barrier is the way in which we think about information. The first automobiles were called horseless carriages, steered with rudders, and came with buggy-whip holders as standard equipment. Why? They were manufactured by the same people who made horse-drawn carriages. Every new medium is born nearsighted. The first movies were made by a positioning the camera in the fourth-row center seat of a stage play. Decades went by until innovators such as Sergi Eisenstein and D.W. Griffith showed what could be done by moving the camera to follow the action, to zoom in on important details, to show panoramic views, and to make actors recognizable. Radio was originally called *wireless telegraphy*. Early TV news programs were nothing more than a television picture of a radio announcer reading the news. The announcer did not even make eye contact with the viewer. Today most online documentation systems offer the user nothing more than television pictures of paper pages. The term *electronic book* is as shortsighted as *horseless carriage* or *wireless telegraphy*. We need better models, perhaps a cross between the Delphic oracle and a video game.

MORE STUDY IS NEEDED

About the only thing researchers in online documentation seem willing to state with certainty is that "more research is needed." We need not just more research but better research as well. We need research based on:

- **Scientific methods**. Studies must apply the same rigorous scientific methods as those used in medicine. Tests must include control groups, and the statistical validity of results must be reported. Researchers must describe test procedures clearly enough that other researchers can replicate the results.

- **Variety of test subjects**. Too many studies use only undergraduate students as test subjects. Undergraduates are atypical in visual acuity, reaction time, psychological motivation, and other characteristics shown to affect real-world results. Research studies should test with people of different ages, genders, cultural backgrounds, and levels of computer experience.

- **Full-scale systems**. Many techniques proven in studies on small systems fail when scaled up for production-sized systems.

- **In-depth study**. Studies must measure the long-term results, not just first impressions. More studies should follow users from novice through expert stages of use.

- **Up-to-date technology**. By the time much research is published and understood, technology has evolved to the point where it is irrelevant. Researchers must be given access to current systems. They must make educated guesses as to which technologies will move into the mainstream.

AUTHORING WILL NEVER BE THE SAME

I have spent much of the last five years working with writing groups making the transition from paper to electronic media. For many writers, it is not just a change of technique but of professional and personal identity as they must learn new skills, take on new roles, and redefine careers.

New literacy

Creating online documents, especially those incorporating new media, demands new knowledge and skills. Literacy now means the ability to effectively communicate using:

- **More visual media**. Online documentation is primarily a visual medium and communicators must rely more on drawings, diagrams, photographs, charts, tables, and lists.

- **Multiple media**. Authors must be fluent in displayed words, not just printed words. They may also need to write for the spoken word. But words are only the beginning. Complete literacy includes understanding and communicating in animation, video, sound, and music.

- **Dynamic media**. In documents that include moving pictures and sound, authors must deal with issues of pace, tempo, and synchronization.

- **Mixes of media**. Not only must authors master individual media, they must learn to combine them to communicate more powerfully and reliably while compensating for the weaknesses of individual media.

- **Nonlinear media**. Documents are not limited to simple sequences or hierarchies. Authors must design ad-hoc and web structures.

New roles for writers

Online documentation requires considerable compromise and adjustment from a traditional business or technical writer. For some it means a shift from working alone to working in a group. Decisions the writer could make alone must be discussed and considered by the team. For others it may seem like a demotion. For paper documents, the writer is typically in charge. For online documents, the writer may be just one member of a team of other media specialists. Online documentation is more like making a movie than writing a novel. Skill with words is important but not by itself a sufficient qualification to head the team. The writer who was on top is now on tap. The solo performer is a member of the band.

Paper documentation

Online documentation

For still other writers, online documentation requires a change of self-image. If you see yourself as primarily a writer and define writing as what novelists and journalists do, then moving toward online documentation takes you further and further from your ideal self. Going online means changing from a private writer in charge of the project to a collaborative communicator working on a team.

New careers

Electronic publishing and online documentation are redefining jobs and duties. Unions are folding and entire departments are being eliminated. At the same time, new skills are vital for managing and using advanced technologies. In the future, the jobs of technical writer and illustrator may be replaced by titles such as these from the electronic want ads of 1999:

Topic writer   Creates entries in a document database. Creates small, independent modules of specific information that can be combined in various configurations for specific purposes.

Media creator   Writer, illustrator, musician, animator, video producer, or other media specialist who creates the media elements included in topics.

Document weaver   Creates document organizations. Selects document modules, organizes them in an appropriate structure, and supplies appropriate transitions. Creates meaningful reading sequences that serve as default trails, from which readers are encouraged to make side trips.

Document stylist   Creates document formats. Defines the presentation format for a class of documents. Coordinates decisions about typography, color, sound, and animation.

WILL ONLINE DOCUMENTS REPLACE PAPER?

Will all documents go online? Yes. Will online documents replace paper? No. Gradually our reliance on online documents will grow and our reliance on paper will decline. Some years hence, a pollster on the evening news will report that recent surveys reveal that we get more information from online documents than from printed ones. That, however, is no great milestone, as the same pundits have informed us for years that most people get more information from TV than from newspapers and books. In other words, we already get more information from the video screen than from the printed page. The real test of online documentation may be whether it can surpass television as a source of information.

The transition from paper to online documents will be gradual and require consid-erable overlap. Documents will exist in both forms for a generation. Perhaps for-ever. The reason is simply that people prefer to use both. Users of the online *Oxford English Dictionary* frequently use it to find words or phrases of interest and then switch to the paper version for lengthy reading [215].

> The complementary features of paper and computer-based documentation systems suggest to us that even the most technologically-advanced online documentation system will be surrounded by paper documents of its own creation. Every prophecy of a "paperless office" or "paperless society" seems countered by more conservative forecasts in which paper remains in an important, albeit changed role [113, p. 1316].

Each new competing medium changes more than replaces the current media. Photography did not replace painting any more than movies replaced theater or TV replaced movies. Each of these new media did force its predecessors to take on a new identity and to serve new purposes. It will be interesting to see what new role paper documents assume as online documents advance.

OUT OF THE OLD INVENT THE NEW

The development of online documentation is a part of a vastly larger change in the way our species communicates. As James Burke pointed out in his TV series and book, *Connections*, the greatest social changes result not from monumental scien-tific discoveries, but from the coincidence of small discoveries that interact in unexpected ways. In the field of communication, we are seeing coincident advances in data storage, wireless communication, data formats, and other fields that will completely change the way people get information, at least as much as the perfection of printing with movable type and perhaps as much as the invention of the alphabet. We must make this change productive, not traumatic.

No mere collection of rules and guidelines can guide us through that change. As Joseph Itten has wisely pointed out:

> Doctrines and theories are best for weaker moments. In moments of strength, problems are solved intuitively, as if of themselves [142, p. 7].

Use this book in those weaker moments until you can design intuitively. Use it as a ladder to climb, and when you reach the last rung, fly.

REFERENCES

1   3M Meeting Management Institute. Use of Electronic Media in Presentation and Training Applications Austin, TX: 3M Meeting Management Institute, 1992.

2   Acosta, Teresa. "CBT Opening Doors." *CBT Directions*, November 1991. 31–33.

3   Adams, John A. "Applications, Implications." *IEEE Spectrum*, March 1993. 24–31.

4   Ahlberg, Christopher, Christopher Williamson, and Ben Shneiderman. "Dynamic Queries for Information Exploration: An Implementation and Evaluation." In *CHI '92 Proceedings*. New York: Association for Computing Machinery, 1992. 619–626.

5   Akscyn, Robert M., Donald L. McCracken, and Elsie A. Yoder. "KMS: A Distributed Hypermedia System for Maintaining Knowledge in Organizations." *Communications of the ACM,* 31 (7) July 1988. 820–835.

6   Alschuler, Liora. "Hand-crafted Hypertext—Lessons from the ACM Experiment." In *The Society of Text.* Cambridge, MA: The MIT Press, 1989.

7   Ambron, Sueann. "Multimedia Composition: Is It Similar to Writing, Painting, and Composing Music? Or Is It Something Else Altogether?" In *Learning with Interactive Multimedia.* Redmond, WA: Microsoft Press, 1990. 69–84.

8   ANSI. *Safety Color Code for Marking Physical Hazards.* (ANSI Z53.1). New York: American National Standards Institute, 1979.

9   Apple Computer. *Macintosh Human Interface Guidelines.* Reading, MA: Addison-Wesley, 1992.

10 Apple Computer. *Demystifying Multimedia: A Guide for Developers from Apple Computer, Inc.* San Francisco: Vivid, 1993.

11 Arnheim, Rudolf. *Art and Visual Perception: A Psychology of the Creative Eye.* Berkeley, CA: University of California Press, 1974.

12 Baecker, Ronald and Ian Small. "Animation at the Interface." In *The Art of Human-Computer Interface Design.* Reading, MA: Addison-Wesley, 1990. 251–267.

13 Bailey, Robert W. *Human Performance Engineering: Using Human Factors/Erogonomics to Achieve Computer System Usability.* Englewood Cliffs, NJ: Prentice-Hall, 1989.

14 Bannon, Cynthia J. "The Perseus Project." In *Hypertext/Hypermedia Handbook.* New York: Intertext Publications/McGraw-Hill Publishing Co., Inc., 1991. 480–487.

15 Barba, Roberta H. and Barbara E. Armstrong. "The Effect of *HyperCard* and Interactive Video Instruction on Earth and Space Science Students' Achievement." *Journal of Educational Multimedia and Hypermedia,* 1 (3) 1992. 323–330.

16 Barker, Philip. "Hypermedia Interaction for the Disabled." *Journal of Educational Multimedia and Hypermedia,* 1 (2) 1992. 187–208.

17 Barratt, Krome. *Logic and Design in Art, Science, and Mathematics.* New York: Design Press, 1980.

18   Barrett, Edward. "Introduction: A New Paradigm for Writing *with* and *for* the Computer." In *Text, ConText, and HyperText: Writing with and for the Computer.* Cambridge, MA: The MIT Press, 1988. xiii–xxv.

19   Barstow, Thomas R. and Joseph T. Jaynes. "Integrating Online Documentation Into the Technical Publishing Process." *IEEE Transactions on Professional Communication,* PC–29 (4) December 1986. 37–41.

20   Basara, Diane, Darrell Burgin, Gabrielle Ryan, et al. "A Case Study of Online Information: Second Generation Systems Design." *IEEE Transactions on Professional Communication,* PC-29 (4) December 1986. 81–86.

21   Beasley, Robert E. and Joaquin A. Vila. "The Identification of Navigation Patterns in a Multimedia Environment: A Case Study." *Journal of Educational Multimedia and Hypermedia,* 1 (2) 1992. 209–222.

22   Begeman, Michael L. and Jeff Conklin. "The Right Tool for the Job: Even the Systems Design Process Falls Within the Realm of Hypertext." *Byte,* October 1988. 255–266.

23   Bernstein, Mark. "Deeply Intertwingled Hypertext." *Technical Communication,* 38 (1) First Quarter 1991. 41–47.

24   Black, J. B. and Thomas P. Moran. "Learning and Remembering Command Names." In *Proceedings of Human Factors in Computer Systems Conference.* Gaithersburg, MD: Institute for Computer Sciences and Technology, National Bureau of Standards, 1982. 8–11.

25   Blair, D. C. and M. E. Maron. "An Evaluation of Retrieval Effectiveness for a Full-Text Document-Retrieval System." *Communications of the ACM,* 28 (3) March 1985. 289–299.

26   Blattner, Meera, Denise Sumikawa, and Robert Greenberg. "Earcons and Icons: Their Structure and Common Design Principles." *Human-Computer Interaction,* 4 (1) 1989. 101–118.

27   Bolter, Jay David and Michael Joyce. "Hypertext and Creative Writing." In *Hypertext'87 Papers.* Chapel Hill, NC: University of North Carolina, 1987. 41–50.

28   Bonura, Larry. *The Art of Indexing.* New York: John Wiley, 1994.

29   Borenstein, Nathaniel S. "Help Texts vs. Help Mechanisms: A New Mandate for Documentation Writers." In *Proceedings of SIGDOC'85* . New York: Association for Computing Machinery, 1985. 8–10.

30   Borgman, Christine, Jason Resenberg, and AndreaGallagher. "Children's Use of a Direct Manipulation Library Catalog." *SIGCHI Bulletin,* 23 (4) October 1991. 69–70.

31   Bork, Alfred. "Information Display and Screen Design." In *American Education Research Association Conference.* New York: American Education Research Association, 1982.

32   Bork, Alfred. "Interaction: Lessons from Computer-Based Learning." In *Interactive Media: Working Methods and Practical Applications.* Chichester, England: Ellis Horwood Limited, 1987. 28–43.

33   Boyle, Craig. "To Link or Not to Link: An Empirical Comparison of Hypertext Linking Strategies." In *SIGDOC'92: The 10th Annual International Conference on Systems Documentation.* New York: Association for Computing Machinery, 1992. 221–231.

34   Brand, Stewart. *The Media Lab: Inventing the Future at MIT.* New York: Viking, 1987.

35   Bresko, Laura L., Christopher Gray, and Jon Grubb. "Hyper-Help: Uniting Humans and Machines." In *Proceedings of the 38th International Technical Communication Conference.* Arlington, VA: Society for Technical Communication, 1991. VC 41–43.

36   Brockmann, R. John. *Writing Better Computer User Documentation: From Paper to Online.* New York: John Wiley & Sons, 1986.

37   Brockmann, R. John, William Horton, and Kevin Brock. "From Database to Hypertext: An Information Odyssey." In *The Society of Text: Hypertext, Hypermedia, and the Social Construction of Information.* Cambridge, MA: The MIT Press, 1989.

38   Brown, Marc. "Exploring Algorithms Using Balsa II." *Computer* May 1988. 14–36.

39   Brown, P. J. "Turning Ideas into Products." In *Hypertext'87 Papers*. Chapel Hill, NC: University of North Carolina, 1987. 33–40.

40   Brown, P. J. "Hypertext: Dreams and Reality." In *Proceedings of the Hypermedia/Hypertext and Object Oriented Databases Seminar*. London: Brunel University, 1989.

41   Buck, J. R. "Visual Displays." In *Human Factors: Understanding People-System Relationships.* New York: John Wiley, 1983. 99–136.

42   Burchard, Gina and Sam Dragga. "Computer-Based Instruction and the Humanizing Impulse." *Technical Communication,* 36 (1) First Quarter, February 1989. 13–18.

43   Campagnoni, F.R. and Kate Ehrlich. "Getting There When You Don't Know Where 'There' Is: Navigational Strategies in a Hypertext Help System." *SIGCHI Bulletin,* 21 (3) January 1990. 17–18.

44   Campbell, Gwendolyn. "The Effectiveness of a Keystroke Line in Interactive Tutorials." *SIGCHI Bulletin,* 20 (2) October 1988. 27–29.

45   Campbell, Robert and Patricia Hanlon. "HyperCard: A New Deal in the Classroom." In *Learning with Interactive Multimedia.* Redmond, WA: Microsoft Press, 1990. 257–286.

46   Carbonell, J. R., J. I. Elkind, and R. S. Nickerson. "On the Psychological Importance of Time in a Time-Sharing System." *Human Factors,* 10 1969.1 135–142.

47   Carey, Tom, Blair Nonnecke, and John Mitterer. "Prospects for Active Help in Online Documentation." In *SIGDOC'92: The 10th Annual International Conference on Systems Documentation*. New York: Association for Computing Machinery, 1992. 289–296.

48   Carlson, Patricia Ann. "Hypertext: A Way of Incorporating User Feedback into Online Documentation." In *Text, ConText, and HyperText: Writing with and for the Computer.* Cambridge, MA: The MIT Press, 1988. 93–106.

49   Carroll, John. *The Nurnberg Funnel: Designing Minimalist Instructions for Practical Computer Skill.* Cambridge, MA: The MIT Press, 1990.

50   Carroll, John and Amy Aaronson. "Learning by Doing with Simulated Intelligent Help." *Communications of the ACM,* 31 (9) September 1988. 1064–1079.

51   CBT Directions. "A Global Commitment to Multimedia-Based Training." *CBT Directions,* November/December 1992. 30–31.

52   Chadwick, John. "The Development of a Museum Multimedia Program and the Effect of Audio on User Completion Rate." *Journal of Educational Multimedia and Hypermedia,* 1 (3) 331–340.

53   Chiang, Alice and Kevin McBride. "Online Tutorial Design for a Hero's Journey." In *Proceedings of the 39th Annual Conference*. Arlington, VA: Society for Technical Communication, 1992. 323–326.

54   Clark, R. "Getting Out of the Classroom." *Data Training,* 10 (2) January 1991. 26–34.

55   Clark, R. E. and G. Salomon. "Media in Teaching." In *Handbook of Research on Teaching.* New York: Macmillan, 1986. 122–158.

56   Cleverdon, C. W. "Optimizing Convenient On-Line Access to Bibliographic Databases." *Information Service Use,* 4 37–47.

57   Collier, George H. "Thoth-II: Hypertext with Explicit Semantics." In *Hypertext'87 Papers*. Chapel Hill, NC: University of North Carolina, 1987. 269–289.

58   Colquhoun, W. P. "Evaluation of Auditory, Visual, and Dual-Mode Displays for Prolonged Signal-Monitoring in Repeated Sessions." *Human Factors,* 17 425–437.

59   Conklin, Jeff. *A Survey of Hypertext* (STP-356-86, Rev. 2). Microelectronics and Computer Technology Corporation, 1987.

60   Cotton, Bob and Richard Oliver. *Understanding Hypermedia: From Multimedia to Virtual Reality.* London: Phaidon Press, 1993.

61 Crane, Gregory. "From the Old to the New: Integrating Hypertext into Traditional Scholarship." In *Hypertext'87 Papers*. Chapel Hill, NC: University of North Carolina, 1987. 51–55.

62 Cringely, Robert X. "OS/2's Clumsiness Can Be Seen in the Stars." *InfoWorld*, 9 May 1988. 110.

63 Czaja, S.J., K. Hammond, J.J. Blascovich, et al. "Learning to Use a Word-Processing System as a Function of Training Strategy." *Behavior and Information Technology*, 5 (1) 1986. 203–216.

64 DePompa, Barbara. "CD-ROM-Based Documentation: IBM's InfoExplorer." *CD-ROM Professional*, September 1991. 104–105.

65 Diaz, Lily and Halsey Minor. "ML INFO—An On-Line Multimedia Information Center." In *Hypertext/Hypermedia Handbook.* New York: Intertext Publications/McGraw-Hill Publishing Co., Inc., 1991. 475–479.

66 Dionne, Daniel L. and Robert Krull. "The Effects of Module Size and User Practice in Online Tutorials." In *Proceedings of the 39th Annual Conference*. Arlington, VA: Society for Technical Communication, 1992. 669–672.

67 Dumais, Susan T. "Textual Information Retrieval." In *Handbook of Human-Computer Interaction.* Amsterdam: North-Holland, 1988. 673–700.

68 Dumais, Susan T. and Thomas K. Landauer. "Psychological Investigations of Natural Terminology for Command and Query Languages." In *Directions in Human/Computer Interaction.* Norwood, NJ: Ablex Publishing, 1986. 95–109.

69 Dumas, Joseph S. *Designing User Interfaces for Software.* Englewood Cliffs, NJ: Prentice-Hall, 1988.

70 Dunsmore, H. E. "Designing an Interactive Facility for Non-Programmers." In *Association for Computing Machinery*. New York: Association for Computing Machinery, 1980. 475–483.

71 Dunsmore, H. E. "Data Entry." In *Human Factors: Understanding People-System Relationships.* New York: John Wiley, 1983. 335–366.

72 Durrett, H. John and D. Theron Stimmel. "Color and Instructional Use of the Computer." In *Color and the Computer.* Boston: Academic Press, 1987. 241–253.

73 Eberts, Ray. "Computer-Based Instruction." In *Handbook of Human-Computer Interaction.* Amsterdam: North-Holland, 1988. 599–627.

74 Eberts, Ray and John F. Brock. "Computer Applications to Instruction." In *Human Factors Review.* Santa Monica, CA: The Human Factors Society, 1984. 239–284.

75 Egan, Dennis. "Individual Differences in Human-Computer Interaction." In *Handbook of Human-Computer Interaction.* Amsterdam: North-Holland, 1988. 543–568.

76 Egan, D. E., J. R. Remde, T. K. Landauer, et al. "Acquiring Information in Books and SuperBooks." In *Proceedings of the Annual Meeting of the American Educational Research Association.* 1989.

77 Egan, D. E., J. R. Remde, T. K. Landauer, et al. "Behavioral Evaluation and Analysis of a Hypertext Browser." In *Proceedings of CHI'89: Human Factors in Computing Systems*. New York: Association for Computing Machinery, 1989. 205–110.

78 Elkerton, Jay. "Online Aiding for Human-Computer Interfaces." In *Handbook of Human-Computer Interaction.* Amsterdam: North-Holland, 1988. 345–364.

79 Elkerton, J. and R. Williges. "Information Retrieval Strategies in a File-Search Environment." *Human Factors*, 26 (2) 1984. 171–184.

80 Elkerton, Jay and R. C. Williges. "The Effectiveness of a Performance-Based Assistant in an Information Retrieval Environment." In *Proceedings of the Human Factors Society 28th Annual Meeting.* Santa Monica, CA: Human Factors Society, 1984. 634–638.

81 Emdad, Ali. "The Relationships Between Online Help Systems and Print Documentation: An Empirical Investigation." In *Proceedings of SIGDOC'89*. New York: Association for Computing Machinery, 1989. 45–48.

82   Fenchel, R. "An Integrated Approach to User Assistance." *ACM SIGSOC Bulletin,* 13 (2) 1981. 98–104.

83   Fischer, Gerhard, Andreas Lemke, and Thomas Schwab. "Knowledge-Based Help Systems." In *CHI'85 Proceedings*. New York: Association for Computing Machinery, 1985. 161–167.

84   Fischer, Gerhard, Kumiyo Nakakoji, Jonathan Ostwald, et al. "Embedding Computer-Based Critics in the Contexts of Design." In *Proceedings of InterCHI'93* . New York: Association for Computing Machinery, 1993. 67–73.

85   Florin, Fabrice. "Information Landscapes." In *Learning with Interactive Multimedia.* Redmond, WA: Microsoft Press, 1990. 27–49.

86   Fox, Edward A., Qi Fan Chen, and Robert K. France. "Integrating Search and Retrieval with Hypertext." In *Hypertext/Hypermedia Handbook.* New York: Intertext Publications/McGraw-Hill Publishing Co., Inc., 1991. 329–355.

87   Francis, Larry. "W(h)ither Go Tutorials?" In *Proceedings of the 39th Annual Conference*. Arlington, VA: Society for Technical Communication, 1992. 412–415.

88   Frankel, Karen A. "The Next Generation of Interactive Technologies." *Communications of the ACM*, 32 (7) July 1989. 872–881.

89   Frisse, Mark. "Searching for Information in a Hypertext Medical Handbook." In *Hypertext'87 Papers*. Chapel Hill, NC: University of North Carolina, 1987. 57–66.

90   Frisse, Mark. "From Text to Hypertext." *Byte* October 1988. 247–253.

91   Frisse, Mark E. and Steve B. Cousins. "Information Retrieval From Hypertext: Update on the Dynamic Medical Handbook Project." In *Hypertext'89 Proceedings*. New York: Association for Computing Machinery, 1989. 199–212.

92   Fujihara, Hiroko, James R. Snell, and Craig D. Boyle. "Intelligent Search in an Environmental Hypertext Environment." *Journal of Educational Multimedia and Hypermedia,* 1 (4) 401–415.

93   Fuller, Robert. "Setting Up an Interactive Videodisc Project." In *Interactive Media: Working Methods and Practical Applications.* Chichester, England: Ellis Horwood Limited, 1987. 15–27.

94   Furnas, G. W. "Generalized Fisheye Views." In *CHI'86*. New York: Association for Computing Machinery, 1986. 16–23.

95   Furnas, G. W., T. K. Landauer, L. M. Gomez, et al. "Statistical Semantics: Analysis of the Potential Performance of Keyword Information Systems." In *Human Factors in Computer Systems.* Norwood, NJ: Ablex Publishing, 1986. 187–242.

96   Furnas, G. W., T. K. Landauer, L. M. Gomez, et al. "The Vocabulary Problem in Human System Communication." *Communications of the ACM,* 30 (11) 1987. 964–971.

97   Gable, Gene. "Just What the Doctor Ordered." *Publish* October 1993. 23–28.

98   Gait, J. "An Aspect of Aesthetics in Human-Computer Communications: Pretty Windows." *IEEE Transactions on Software Engineering,* SE-11 (8) 714–717.

99   Galitz, Wilbert O. *Handbook of Screen Format Design.* Wellesley, MA: QED Information Sciences, 1985.

100   Galitz, Wilbert O. *Handbook of Screen Format Design.* Wellesley, MA: QED Information Sciences, 1989.

101   Garb, Rachel and Claudia M. Hunter. "Clarifying Abstract Concepts Through Multimedia: Principles for Technical Communicators." In *1993 Proceedings of the 40th Annual Conference*. Arlington, VA: Society for Technical Communication, 1993. 567–569.

102   Gardner, Howard. *Frames of Mind: The Theory of Multiple Intelligences.* New York: Basic Books, 1983.

103   Garzotto, Frank, Paolo Paolini, Daniel Schwabe, et al. "Tools for Designing Hyperdocuments." In *Hypertext/Hypermedia Handbook.* New York: Intertext Publications/McGraw-Hill Publishing Co., Inc., 1991. 179–207.

104 Gaver, William W. "The SonicFinder: An Interface that Uses Auditory Icons." *Human-Computer Interaction,* 4 (1) 71–84.

105 Gaver, William W. "Synthesizing Auditory Icons." In *InterCHI'93.* New York: Association for Computing Machinery, 1993. 228–235.

106 Gaver, William W., Randal B. Smith, and Tim O'Shea. "Effective Sounds in Complex Systems: The Arkola Simulation." In *Proceedings of CHI'91.* New York: Association for Computing Machinery, 1991. 85–90.

107 Gay, Geri and Joan Mazur. "Navigating in Hypermedia." In *Hypertext/Hypermedia Handbook.* New York: Intertext Publications/McGraw-Hill Publishing Co., Inc., 1991. 271–283.

108 Gaylin, K. "How Are Windows Used? Some Notes on Creating an Empirically-Based Windowing Benchmark Test." In *CHI'86 Proceedings.* New York: Association for Computing Machinery, 1986. 96–100.

109 Gery, Gloria J. *Making CBT Happen: Prescriptions for Successful Implementation of Computer-Based Training in Your Organization.* Boston: Weingarten Publications, 1987.

110 Gery, Gloria J. *Electronic Performance Support Systems.* Boston: Weingarten Publications, 1991.

111 Girill, T. R. and Clement H. Luk. "Document: An Interactive, Online Solution to Four Documentation Problems." *Communications of the ACM,* 26 (5) May 1983. 328–337.

112 Girill, T. R., Clement H. Luk, and Sally Norton. "Reading Patterns in Online Documentation: How Transcript Analysis Reflects Text Design, Software Constraints, and User Preferences." In *Proceedings of the 34th International Technical Communication Conference.* Arlington, VA: Society for Technical Communication, 1987. RET 111–114.

113 Glushko, R. J. and M. H. Bianchi. "On-Line Documentation: Mechanizing Development, Delivery, and Use." *The Bell System Technical Journal,* 61 (6) July-August 1982. 1313–1323.

114 Golovchinsky, Gene and Mark Chingell. "Queries-R-Links: Graphical Markup for Text Navigation." In *Interchi '93.* New York: Association for Computing Machinery, 1993. 454–460.

115 Goodman, Danny. "Verbatim." *MacWorld*, 5 (9) September 1988. 101–112.

116 Gordon, Michael. "Probabalistic and Genetic Algorithms for Document Retrieval." *Communications of the ACM,* 31 (10) October 1988. 1208–1218.

117 Gould, J. "Why Is Reading Slower from CRT Displays than From Paper." In *Proceedings of the 30th Annual Meeting of the Human Factors Society.* Santa Monica, CA: Human Factors Society, 1986. 834–835.

118 Gould, J., L. Alfaro, R. Finn, et al. "Reading from CRT Displays Can Be as Fast as Reading from Paper." *Human Factors,* 29 (5) 497–517.

119 Grantham, Dennis G. "Addressing the Needs of a Larger User Community in the Andrew Help System." In *Proceedings of the 35th International Technical Communication Conference.* Arlington, VA: Society for Technical Communication, 1988. ATA 51–55.

120 Gray, Shirley and Terence Craig. "Math Matching Ideas—A Generic HyperCard-HyperTalk Program." *Journal of Educational Multimedia and Hypermedia,* 1 (2) 1992. 235–250.

121 Grønbaek, Kaj and Randall Trigg. "Design Issues for a Dexter-Based Hypermedia System." *Communications of the ACM,* 37 (2) February 1994. 40–49.

122 Gross, Mark. "The Myth that Software Will Save the World." In *1993 Proceedings STC 40th Annual Conference.* Arlington, VA: Society for Technical Communication, 1993. 377.

123 Halasz, Frank and Mayer Schwartz. "The Dexter Hypertext Reference Model." *Communications of the ACM,* 37 (2) February 1994. 30–39.

124 Halasz, Frank G. "Reflections on NoteCards: Seven Issues for the Next Generation of Hypermedia Systems." *Communications of the ACM,* 31 (7) July 1988. 836–852.

125   Hansen, Wilfred and Christina Haas. "Reading and Writing with Computers: A Framework for Explaining Differences in Performance." *Communications of the ACM,* 31 (9) September 1988. 1080–1089.

126   Hardman, Lynda, Dick Bulterman, and Guido van Rossum. "The Amsterdam Hypermedia Model: Adding Time and Context to the Dexter Model." *Communications of the ACM,* 37 (2) February 1994. 50–62.

127   Harman, Donna and Gerald Candela. "Bringing Natural Language Information Retrieval Out of the Closet." *SIGCHI Bulletin,* 22 (1) July 1990. 42–48.

128   Hasslein, Vaughn. "Marketing Survey on User Requests for Online Documentation." In *Proceedings of the 33rd International Technical Communication Conference*. Arlington, VA: Society for Technical Communication, 1986. 434–438.

129   Hawkes, Lory. "The Shrinking Manuscript Page." In *Proceedings of the 34th International Technical Communication Conference*. Washington, DC: Arlington, VA, 1987. RET 130–133.

130   Heeter, Carrie and Pericles Gomes. "It's Time for Hypermedia to Move to 'Talking Pictures'." *Journal of Educational Multimedia and Hypermedia,* 1 (2) 1992. 255–261.

131   Helander, Martin G., Patricia A. Billingsley, and Jayne M. Schurick. "An Evaluation of Human Factors Research on Visual Display Terminals in the Workplace." In *Human Factors Review*. Santa Monica, CA: Human Factors Society, 1984. 55–129.

132   Henderson, Ronald W. and Edward M. Landesman. "Technology-Based Developmental Instruction in Precalculus." *Journal of Educational Multimedia and Hypermedia,* 1 (1) 1992. 65–76.

133   Hooper, Kristina. "HyperCard: A Key to Educational Computing." In *Learning with Interactive Multimedia.* Redmond, WA: Microsoft Press, 1990. 5–25.

134   Horn, Robert. *Mapping Hypertext: Analysis, Linkage, and Display of Knowledge for the Next Generation of On-Line Text and Graphics.* Lexington, MA: Lexington Institute, 1989.

135   Horton, William. "Toward the Four-Dimensional Page." In *Proceedings of the 30th International Technical Communication Conference*. Arlington, VA: Society for Technical Communication, 1983. RET 83–86.

136   Horton, William. "Templates of Thought." In *Proceedings of the 33rd International Technical Communication Conference*. Washington, DC: Society for Technical Communication, 1986. 302–305.

137   Horton, William. *Illustrating Computer Documentation: The Art of Presenting Information Graphically on Paper and Online.* New York: John Wiley, 1991.

138   Human Factors Society. *American National Standard for Human Factors Engineering of Visual Display Terminal Workstations* (ANSI/HFS 100-1988). Human Factors Society, 1988.

139   IBM. *Common User Access Advanced Interface Design Reference.* Cary, NC: IBM Corporation, 1991.

140   Ingebretsen, Dorothy and Steven Tice. "Searching Los Angeles Times DIALOG OnDisc." *CD-ROM Professional*, September 1991. 86–90.

141   Instone, Keith, Barbee Teasley, and Laura Leventhal. "Empirically-based Re-design of a Hypertext Encyclopedia." In *InterCHI'93*. New York: Association for Computing Machinery, 1993. 500–506.

142   Itten, Joseph. *The Elements of Color.* New York: Van Nostrand Reinhold, 1970.

143   Izzarelli, Kathy and Stanley Malcolm. "Whole-Job Simulation." *CBT Directions*, July 1991. 27–30.

144   James, Geoffrey. *Document Databases: The New Publications Methodology.* New York: Van Nostrand Reinhold, 1985.

145   Janda, Kenneth. "Multimedia in Political Science: Sobering Lessons from a Teaching Experiment." *Journal of Educational Multimedia and Hypermedia,* 1 (3) 1992. 341–354.

146 Johnson, Brian. "TreeViz: Treemap Visualization of Hierarchically Structured Information." In *CHI '92 Proceedings*. New York: Association for Computing Machinery, 1992. 369–370.

147 Jonassen, David H., Daniel R. Ambrusci, and Julie Olesen. "Designing a Hypertext on Transfusion Medicine Using Cognitive Flexibility Theory." *Journal of Educational Multimedia and Hypermedia,* 1 (3) 1992. 309–322.

148 Jong, Steven. "Approaching Hyperspeed." In *Proceedings of the 37th International Technical Communication Conference.* Arlington, VA: Society for Technical Communication, 1990. RT 126–128.

149 Joseph, B., E. R. Steinberg, and A. R. Jones. "User Perceptions and Expectations of an Information Retrieval System." *Behavior and Information Technology,* 8 (2) March-April 1989. 77–88.

150 Kaindl, Hermann and Holger Ziegeler. "HIS — An Information System About Hypertext on Hypertext." *SIGLINK Newsletter,* 1 (1) March 1992. 1–6.

151 Kalstrom, Dave. "Archive Project Preserves Columbus Documents Optically." *CD-ROM Professional*, July 1993. 135–141.

152 Kantowitz, Barry H. *Human Factors: Understanding People-System Relationships.* New York: John Wiley, 1983.

153 Kearsley, Greg. "Embedded Training: The New Look of Computer-Based Instruction." *Machine Mediated Learning,* 1 (3) 1985. 279–285.

154 Kearsley, Greg. "Substance or Flash?" *Journal of Educational Multimedia and Hypermedia,* 1 (2) 1992. 251–253.

155 Kendall, Robert. "The Paperless Book." *PC Magazine*, 21 December 1993. 29.

156 Kerr, S. T. "Efficiency and Satisfaction in Videotex Database Production." *Behavior and Information Technology,* 8 (1) January-February 1989. 57–63.

157 Kessel, C. J. and C. D. Wickens. "The Transfer of Failure-Detection Skills Between Monitoring and Controlling Dynamic Systems." *Human Factors,* 24 1982. 46–60.

158 Kiger, J. L. "The Depth/Breadth Trade-Off in the Design of Menu-Driven User Interfaces." *International Journal of Man-Machine Studies,* 20 1984. 201–213.

159 Koons, W. Randall, Anne M. O'Dell, Nancy J. Frishberg, et al. "The Computer Sciences Electronic Magazine: Translating from Paper to Multimedia." In *CHI '92 Proceedings*. New York: Association for Computing Machinery, 1992. 11–18.

160 Kosslyn, Stephen M. and Olivier Koenig. *Wet Mind: The New Cognitive Neuroscience.* New York: Free Press, 1992.

161 Langston, M. Diane. "Background and Initial Problems for the Andrew Help System." In *Proceedings of the 35th International Technical Communication Conference*. Arlington, VA: Society for Technical Communication, 1988. ATA 47–50.

162 Laurel, Brenda, Tim Oren, and Abbe Don. "Issues in Multimedia Interface Design: Media Integration and Interface Agents." In *CHI'90 Proceedings* . New York: Association for Computing Machinery, 1990. 133–139.

163 Leathersich, Jane. "Document Data Bases — Helping to Solve the Information Crisis." In *Proceedings of the 37th International Technical Communication Conference*. Arlington, VA: Society for Technical Communication, 1990. RT 29–32.

164 Lee, Eric and Thom Whalen. "Computer Image Retrieval by Features: Suspect Identification." In *InterCHI'93.* New York: Association for Computing Machinery, 1993. 494–499.

165 Leggett, John. "Automatic Conversion of Linear Paper-Based Documents into Hypermedia." In *Hypermedia'88*. Houston, TX: University of Houston—Clear Lake and NASA/Johnson Space Center, 1988. 47–74.

166 Lesk, Michael. "What to Do When there's Too Much Information." In *Hypertext'89 Proceedings* . New York: Association for Computing Machinery, 1989. 305–318.

167   Leventhal, L.M., B.M. Teasley, K. Instone, et al. "Sleuthing in HyperHolmes: An Evaluation of Using Hypertext vs. a Book to Answer Questions." *Behaviour and Information Technology,* 12 (3) May–June 1993. 149–164.

168   Lewis, C. "Why and How to Learn Why: Analysis-Based Generalization of Procedures." *Cognitive Science,* 12 (2) 1988. 211–256.

169   Liebhold, Michael. "Hypermedia and Visual Literacy." In *Learning with Interactive Multimedia.* Redmond, WA: Microsoft Press, 1990. 99–110.

170   Littleford, Alan. "Artificial Intelligence and Hypermedia." In *Hypertext/Hypermedia Handbook.* New York: Intertext Publications/McGraw-Hill Publishing Co., Inc., 1991. 357–378.

171   Mackay, Wendy, Thomas Malone, Kevin Crowston, et al. "How Do Experienced Information Lens Users Use Rules?" In *CHI'89 Proceedings*. New York: Association of Computing Machinery, 1989. 211–216.

172   Mackinlay, Jock, George Robertson, and Stuart Card. "The Perspective Wall: Detail and Context Smoothly Integrated." In *CHI'91 Conference Proceedings*. New York: Association for Computing Machinery, 1991. 173–179.

173   Mahler, William J. "Interactive Touch Screen Design." In *Proceedings of 34th International Technical Communication Conference*. Arlington, VA: Society for Technical Communication, 1987. VC 72–77.

174   Mander, Richard, Gitta Salomon, and Yin Yin Wong. "A 'Pile' Metaphor for Supporting Casual Organization of Information." In *CHI'92 Proceedings*. New York: Association for Computing Machinery, 1992. 627–634.

175   Marchionini, Gary and Ben Shneiderman. "Finding Facts vs. Browsing Knowledge in Hypertext Systems." *IEEE Computer,* 21 (1) January 1989. 70–79.

176   Marquez, Mark E. and James D. Lehman. "Hypermedia User-Interface Design: The Role of Individual Differences in Placement of Icon Buttons." *Journal of Educational Multimedia and Hypermedia,* 1 (4) 1992. 417–429.

177   Mascelli, Joseph V. *The Five C's of Cinematography.* Hollywood: Cine/Grafic Publications, 1965.

178   Mayer, Richard. "From Novice to Expert." In *Handbook of Human-Computer Interaction.* Amsterdam: North-Holland, 1988. 569–580.

179   Mayhew, Deborah. *Principles and Guidelines in Software User Interface Design.* Englewood Cliffs, NJ: Prentice-Hall, 1992.

180   Mazur, F. E. "Writing Motivationally Supportive Text for Hypermedia Programs: Strengthening a Weak Link." *Journal of Educational Multimedia and Hypermedia,* 1 (3) 1992. 301–308.

181   McKee, John B. "Computer User Manuals in Print: Do They Have a Future?" In *Proceedings of SIGDOC'85*. New York: Association for Computing Machinery, 1985. 11–16.

182   McKnight, Cliff, Andrew Dillon, and John Richardson, eds. *Hypertext in Context.* Cambridge, England: Cambridge University Press, 1991.

183   Microsoft. *The Windows Interface: An Application Design Guide.* Redmond, WA: Microsoft Press, 1992.

184   Miles, Kurt and Edwin Griffith. "Developing an Hour of CBT: The Quick and Dirty Estimate." *CBT Directions*, April/May 1993. 28–33.

185   Miller, Wendy. "The Technical Writer's Role in On-Line Documentation." In *Proceedings of 33rd International Technical Communication Conference*. Arlington, VA: Society for Technical Communication, 1986. 61–64.

186   Mucciolo, Tom and Rich Mucciolo. *Performance Results of Visual Business Presentations 1985-1990.* Austin, TX: 3M Meeting Management Institute, 1990.

187   Nanny, Margo. "Interactive Images for Education." In *Learning with Interactive Multimedia.* Redmond, WA: Microsoft Press, 1990. 85–98.

188 Neerinex, Mark and Paul de Greef. "How to Aid Non-Experts." In *InterCHI'93*. New York: Association for Computing Machinery, 1993. 165–171.

189 Nelson, Ted. *Dream Machines.* Redmond, WA: Tempus Books, 1987.

190 Nelson, Theodor Holm. *Literary Machines.* South Bend, IN: The Distributors, 1987.

191 Nelson, Wayne A. and David B. Palumbo. "Learning, Instruction, and Hypermedia." *Journal of Educational Multimedia and Hypermedia,* 1 (3) 1992. 287–299.

192 Nickerson, R. S. "Man-Computer Interaction: A Challenge for Human Factors Research." *IEEE Transactions of Man-Machine Systems,* MMS-10 (4) 1969. 12–19.

193 Nickerson, R. S. "Short-Term Retention of Visually Presented Stimuli: Some Evidence of Visual Encoding." *Acta Psychologica,* 40 (2) April 1976. 153–162.

194 Nicol, Ann. "Children Using HyperCard." In *Learning with Interactive Multimedia.* Redmond, WA: Microsoft Press, 1990. 141–154.

195 Nielsen, Jakob. *Hypertext and HyperMedia.* San Diego: Academic Press, 1990.

196 Norman, Kent L., Linda J. Weldon, and Ben Shneiderman. "Cognitive Layout of Windows and Multiple Screens for User Interfaces." *International Journal of Man-Machine Studies,* 25 1986. 229–248.

197 Novitski, B. J. "Constructive Communication." *Computer Graphics World,* June 1993. 35–38.

198 O'Malley, Claire E. "Helping Users Help Themselves." In *User-Centered System Design.* Hillsdale, NJ: Lawrence Erlbaum Associates, 1986. 377–398.

199 Odescalchi, Esther Kando. "Productivity Gain Attained by Task Oriented Information." In *Proceedings of the 33rd International Technical Communication Conference.* Arlington, VA: Society for Technical Communication, 1986. 359–362.

200 Oren, Tim. "The Architecture of Static Hypertexts." In *Hypertext'87 Papers.* Chapel Hill, NC: University of North Carolina, 1987. 291–306.

201 Osborne, D. and D. Holton. "Reading from Screen Versus Paper: There Is No Difference." *International Journal of Man-Machine Studies,* 28 (1) 1988. 1–9.

202 Owen, D. "Answers First, Then Questions." In *User-Centered System Design.* Hillsdale, NJ: Lawrence Erlbaum, 1986. 361–376.

203 Papert, Seymour. *Mindstorms: Children, Computers, and Powerful Ideas.* New York: Basic Books, 1980.

204 Parunak, H. Van Dyke. "Ordering the Information Graph." In *Hypertext/Hypermedia Handbook.* New York: Intertext Publications/McGraw-Hill Publishing Co., Inc., 1991. 299–325.

205 Peterson, Tammy J. and Ed W. Rosencrants. "Creating Accessible Online Information." In *Proceedings of the 33rd International Technical Communication Conference.* Arlington, VA: Society for Technical Communication, 1986. 58–60.

206 Petrauskas, Bruno F. "Online Documentation: Putting Research into Practice." In *Proceedings of 34th International Technical Communication Conference.* Arlington, VA: Society for Technical Communication, 1987. ATA 54–57.

207 Picher, Oliver, Emily Berk, Joseph Devlin, et al. "Hypermedia." In *Hypertext/Hypermedia Handbook.* New York: Intertext Publications/McGraw-Hill Publishing Co., Inc., 1991. 23–52.

208 Price, Robert V. *Computer-Aided Instruction: A Guide for Authors.* Pacific Grove, CA: Brooks/Cole, 1991.

209 Radding, Paul, Mike Farrell, and Jean Pendell. "Multimedia Publishing: Business Impacts and Opportunities." In *Conference Record IPCC 92 — Santa Fe.* New York: Institute for Electrical and Electronics Engineers, 1992. 1.1/237–1.1/240.

210 Radl, R. W. "Experimental Investigations for Optimal Presentation-Mode and Colours of Symbols on the CRT-Screen." In *Ergonomic Aspects of Visual Display Terminals.* London: Taylor & Francis, 1980. 137–142.

211 Radlinski, Bob and Jean McKendree. "Grace Meets the 'Real World': Tutoring COBOL as a Second Language." In *CHI'92 Proceedings*. New York: Association for Computing Machinery, 1992. 343–350.

212 Raven, Mary E. "Comparative Read-and-Locate Tests: Online and Hardcopy." In *Proceedings of the 39th Annual Conference*. Arlington, VA: Society for Technical Communication, 1992. 341–344.

213 Raven, Mary E. and Minette A. Beabes. "Redesigning a Help Menu Based on Usability Testing." In *Proceedings of the 39th Annual Conference*. Arlington, VA: Society for Technical Communication, 1992. 159–162.

214 Raymond, Darrell and Heather J. Fawcett. "Playing Detective with Full Text Searching Software." In *Proceedings of SIGDOC'90*. New York: Association for Computing Machinery, 1990. 157–165.

215 Raymond, Darrell R. and Frank William Tompa. "Hypertext and the Oxford English Dictionary." *Communications of the ACM,* 31 (7) July 1988. 871–879.

216 Rearick, Thomas C. "Automating the Conversion of Text Into Hypertext." In *Hypertext/Hypermedia Handbook.* New York: Intertext Publications/McGraw-Hill Publishing Co., Inc., 1991. 113–140.

217 Redmiles, David F. "Reducing the Variability of Programmer's Performance Through Explained Examples." In *Proceedings of InterCHI'93* . New York: ACM, 1993. 67–73.

218 Reinking, David. "Differences Between Electronic and Printed Texts: An Agenda for Research." *Journal of Educational Multimedia and Hypermedia,* 1 (1) 1992. 11–24.

219 Reisner, P. N. "Use of Psychological Experimentation as an Aid to Development of a Query Language." *IEEE Transactions on Software Engineering,* SE-3 (3) 1977. 218–229.

220 Relles, Nathan. "A User Interface for Online Assistance." In *Proceedings of 5th International Conference on Software Engineering*. New York: Institute for Electrical and Electronics Engineers, 1981. 400–408.

221 Reynolds, Angus. "A Computer-Based Learning Glossary for Human Resource Development Professionals." In *Computer-Based Training Today: A Guide to Research, Specialized Terms, and Publications in the Field.* Alexandria, VA: American Society for Testing and Development, 1987. 12–40.

222 Riner, Rob. "Automated Conversion." In *Hypertext/Hypermedia Handbook.* New York: Intertext Publications/McGraw-Hill Publishing Co., Inc., 1991. 95–111.

223 Ripley, G. David. "DVI—A Digital Multimedia Technology." *Communications of the ACM,* 32 (7) July 1989. 811–822.

224 Rivlin, Ehud, Rodrigo Botafogo, and Ben Shneiderman. "Navigating in Hyperspace: Designing a Structure-Based Toolbox." *Communications of the ACM,* 37 (2) February 1994. 87–96.

225 Robertson, George, Jock Mackinlay, and Stuart Card. "Cone Trees: Animated 3D Visualizations of Hierarchical Information." In *CHI'91 Conference Proceedings* . New York: Association for Computing Machinery, 1991. 189–194.

226 Robertson, G., D. McCracken, and A. Newell. "The ZOG Approach to Man-Machine Communication." *International Journal of Man-Machine Studies,* 14 1981 461–488.

227 Robinson, Eleanor R. N. and Frederick G. Knirk. "Interfacing Learning Strategies and Instructional Strategies in Computer Training Programs." In *Human Factors Review.* Santa Monica: The Human Factors Society, 1984. 209–238.

228 Roblyer, M. D. "Alternative Designs for Evaluating Computer-Based Instruction." *Journal of Instructional Development,* 7 (3) 1984. 23–29.

229 Rockley, Ann. "Online Documentation: From Proposal to Finished Product." In *Proceedings of the 34th International Technical Communication Conference*. Arlington, VA: Society for Technical Communication, 1987. ATA 58–61.

230 Roemer, J. M. and A. Champanis. "Learning Performance and Attitudes as a Function of the Reading Grade Level of a Computer-Presented Tutorial." In *Proceedings of Human Factors in Computer Systems Conference*. Gaithersburg, MD: Institute for Computer Sciences and Technology, National Bureau of Standards, 1982. 239–244.

231 Rollins, Lynn and Lisa M. Braz. "Innovative Software Tutorials." In *Proceedings of the 34th International Technical Communication Conference*. Arlington, VA: Society for Technical Communication, 1987. ATA 80–83.

232 Rubens, Brenda Knowles and Reginald Hendricks. "The Psychological Advantage of Online Information." In *Proceedings of the 34th International Technical Communication Conference*. Arlington, VA: Society for Technical Communication, 1987. RET 107–110.

233 Rubens, Philip. "Reading and Employing Technical Information in Hypertext." *Technical Communication,* 38 (1) First Quarter 1991. 36–40.

234 Rushby, Nick. "From Trigger Video to Videodisc: A Case Study in Interpersonal Skills." In *Interactive Media: Working Methods and Practical Applications.* Chichester, England: Ellis Horwood Limited, 1987. 116–131.

235 Sakar, Manojit and Marc H. Brown. "Graphical Fisheye Views of Graphs." In *Proceedings of CHI'92*. New York: Association for Computing Machinery, 1992. 83–91.

236 Salomon, Gitta. "Designing Casual-Use Hypertext: The CHI'89 InfoBooth." In *CHI'90 Conference Proceedings*. New York, NY: Association for Computing Machinery, 1990. 451–458.

237 Salton, Gerard. *Automatic Text Processing: The Transformation, Analysis, and Retrieval of Information by Computer.* Reading, MA: Addison-Wesley, 1989.

238 Schank, Roger. "Learning via Multimedia Computers." *Communications of the ACM,* 36 (5) May 1993. 54–56.

239 Schlesinger, Denny. "The Visiting Developer: Help Documentation System Review." *MacTutor,* November 1987. 79–83.

240 Schwartz, Evan. "CD-ROM: A Mass Medium at Last." *Business Week*, 19 July 1993. 82–83.

241 Search, Patricia. "Structural Design: Movement in Art." In *Proceedings of the 37th International Technical Communication Conference*. Arlington, VA: Society for Technical Communication, 1990. VC 18–20.

242 See, Edward. "Linking to Hypertext: A Comparative Study." In *Proceedings of the 37th International Technical Communication Conference*. Arlington, VA: Society for Technical Communication, 1990. RT 60–63.

243 Semple, Marlene C. "The Electronic Blue Pencil: Editing Online Information." In *Proceedings of the 34th International Technical Communication Conference*. Arlington, VA: Society for Technical Communication, 1987. ATA 140–142.

244 Senbetta, Ghenno. "The Myth of One Hour of CBT." *CBT Directions*, 18 October 1991. 18–22.

245 Shapiro, Linda and Steve Rubin. "The Audiovisual Capabilities of Computers." *Technical Communication,* 35 (1) First Quarter 1988. 16–22.

246 Shirk, Henrietta Nickels. "Technical Writers as Computer Scientists: The Challenges of Online Documentation." In *Text, ConText, and HyperText: Writing with and for the Computer.* Cambridge, MA: The MIT Press, 1988. 311–327.

247 Shneiderman, Ben. *Designing the User Interface: Strategies for Effective Human Computer Interaction.* Reading, MA: Addison-Wesley, 1987.

248 Shneiderman, Ben. "User Interface Design and Evaluation for an Electronic Encyclopedia." In *Cognitive Engineering in the Design of Human-Computer Interaction and Expert Systems.* Amsterdam: Elsevier Science Publishers, 1987. 207–223.

249 Shneiderman, Ben. "User Interface Design for the Hyperties Electronic Encyclopedia." In *Hypertext'87 Papers*. Chapel Hill, NC: University of North Carolina, 1987. 189–194.

250 Shneiderman, Ben and Greg Kearsley. *Hypertext Hands On!: An Introduction to a New Way of Organizing and Accessing Information.* Reading, MA: Addison-Wesley, 1989.

251 Shneiderman, Ben, Charles Kreitzberg, and Emily Berk. "Editing to Structure a Reader's Experience." In *Hypertext/Hypermedia Handbook.* New York: Intertext Publications/McGraw-Hill Publishing Co., Inc., 1991. 143–164.

252 Silverstein, Louis D. "Human Factors for Color Display Systems: Concepts, Methods, and Research." In *Color and the Computer.* Boston: Academic Press, 1987. 27–61.

253 Simpson, C. A. and D. H. Williams. "Response Time Effects of Altering Tone and Semantic Context for Synthesized Voice Cockpit Warnings." *Human Factors,* 22 1980. 319–330.

254 Small, Ruth V. and Barbara L. Grabowski. "An Exploratory Study of Information-Seeking Behaviors and Learning with Hypermedia Information Systems." *Journal of Educational Multimedia and Hypermedia,* 1 (4) 1992. 445–464.

255 Smith, Wanda. "Ergonomic Vision." In *Color and the Computer.* Boston: Academic Press, 1987. 101–113.

256 Soderston, Candace. "An Experimental Study of Structure for Online Information." In *Proceedings of the 34th International Technical Communication Conference.* Arlington, VA: Society for Technical Communication, 1987. ATA 71–74.

257 Soderston, Candace. "Designing a Conversational System to Provide Online Help." In *Proceedings of the 37th International Technical Communication Conference.* Arlington, VA: Society for Technical Communication, 1990. RT 178–182.

258 Soderston, Candace. "An Experimental Study of Structure for Online Information." In *Proceedings of the 37th International Technical Communication Conference.* Arlington, VA: Society for Technical Communication, 1990. CC 12–15.

259 Sondheimer, Norman K. and Nathan Relles. "Human Factors and User Assistance in Interactive Computing Systems: An Introduction." *IEEE Transactions on Systems, Man, and Cybernetics,* SMC-12 (2) March/April 1982. 102–107.

260 Stanton, Neville and Chris Baber. "An Investigation of Styles and Strategies in Self-Directed Learning." *Journal of Educational Multimedia and Hypermedia,* 1 (2) 1992. 147–167.

261 Stanton, N. A., R. G. Taylor, and L. A. Tweedie. "Maps as Navigational Aids in Hypertext Environments: An Empirical Evaluation." *Journal of Educational Multimedia and Hypermedia,* 1 (4) 1992. 431–444.

262 Stasko, John, Albert Badre, and Clayton Lewis. "Do Algorithm Animations Assist Learning? An Empirical Study and Analysis." In *InterCHI'93.* New York: ACM, 1993. 61–66.

263 Stiegler, Marc. "Hypermedia and the Singularity." *Analog Science Fact/Science Fiction,* 109 (1) January 1989. 52–71.

264 Storment, Kim S. "How to 'Dump' Procedures Online Successfully." In *Proceedings of 34th International Technical Communication Conference.* Arlington, VA: Society for Technical Communication, 1987. ATA 114–116.

265 Streit, L. "Structuring Text: Creating Cost-Effective Training Manuals." *Educational Technology,* 26 (9) September 1986. 29–31.

266 Taylor, Joann M. and Gerald M. Murch. "The Effective Use of Color in Computer Graphics Applications." 1986. 515–521.

267 Tenopir, C. "Searching Harvard Business Review Online . . . Lessons in Searching a Full Text Database." *Online,* March 1985. 71–78.

268 Thiel, Thomas J. "The Navy's Paperless Ship." *CD-ROM Professional,* May 1992. 17–26.

269 Thomas, Frank and Ollie Johnson. *Disney Animation: Illusion of Life.* New York: Abbeville Press, 1981.

270 Thorell, Lisa G. and Wanda J. Smith. *Using Computer Color Effectively: An Illustrated Reference.* Englewood Cliffs, NJ: Prentice-Hall, 1990.

271   Thorsen, Linda J. and Mark Bernstein. "Developing Dynamic Documents: Special Challenges for Technical Communicators." In *Proceedings of the 34th International Technical Communication Conference*. Arlington, VA: Society for Technical Communication, 1987. ATA 68–70.

272   Tombaugh, J., A. Lickorish, and P. Wright. "Multi-Window Displays for Readers of Lengthy Texts." *International Journal of Man-Machine Studies,* 26 (5) May 1987. 597–615.

273   Tombaugh, J. W. and Scott A. McEwen. "Comparison of Two Information Retrieval Methods on Videotex: Tree-Structure Versus Alphabetical Directory." In *Proceedings of Human Factors in Computer Systems Conference*. Gaithersburg, MD: Institute for Computer Sciences and Technology, National Bureau of Standards, 1982.

274   Tullis, Thomas S. "Designing a Menu-Based Interface to an Operating System." In *CHI'85 Proceedings*. New York: Association for Computing Machinery, 1985. 79–84.

275   Tullis, Thomas S. "Screen Design." In *Handbook of Human-Computer Interaction.* Amsterdam: Elsevier Science Publishers B.V. (North-Holland), 1988. 377–411.

276   Van Dam, Andries. "Hypertext'87 Keynote Address." *Communications of the ACM,* 31 (7) July 1988. 887–895.

277   Vassiliou, Yannis and Matthias Jarke. "Query Languages—A Taxonomy." In *Human Factors in Computer Systems.* Norwood, NJ: Ablex Publishing, 1986. 187–242.

278   Ventura, C. A. "Why Switch from Paper to Electronic Manuals?" In *Proceedings of the ACM Conference on Document Processing Systems*. New York: Association for Computing Machinery, 1988. 111–116.

279   Vogel, Douglas R., Gary W. Dickson, John A. Lehman, et al. *Persuasion and the Role of Visual Presentation Support: The UM/3M Study.* Austin, TX: 3M Meeting Management Institute, 1986.

280   Vogt, Carlton. "Smarter Cars Need Smarter Tools." *Design News*, 3 October 1988. 154–156.

281   Voss, Daniel W. "STOP! Don't Start Without It." In *Proceedings of the 39th Annual Conference*. Arlington, VA: Society for Technical Communication, 1992. 765–768.

282   Walker, Janet H. "Issues and Strategies for Online Documentation." *IEEE Transactions on Professional Communication,* PC-30 (4) December 1987. 235–248.

283   Wallace, Janet E. "What Is On-Screen Documentation Anyway?" In *Proceedings of 32nd International Technical Communication Conference*. Arlington, VA: Society for Technical Communication, 1985. ATA 39–42.

284   Weiss, Edmond H. *How to Write Usable User Documentation.* Phoenix, AZ: Oryx, 1991.

285   Wertz, Richard K. "CD-ROM: A New Advance in Medical Information Retrieval." *Journal of the American Medical Association,* 256 (24) 26 December 1986. 3376–3378.

286   Weyer, Stephen A. "The Design of a Dynamic Book for Information Search." *International Journal of Man-Machine Studies,* 17 1982. 87–107.

287   Whalen, Thomas and Andrew Patrick. "Conversational Hypertext: Information Access Through Natural Language Dialogues with Computers." In *CHI'89 Proceedings*. New York: ACM, 1989. 289–292.

288   Wilkinson, R. and H. Robinshaw. "Proofreading: VDU and Paper Text Compared for Speed, Accuracy, and Fatigue." *Behaviour and Information Technology,* 6 (2) 1987. 125–133.

289   Williams, Thomas R. and David K. Farkas. "Minimalism Reconsidered: Should We Design Documentation for Exploratory Learning?" *SIGCHI Bulletin,* 24 (2) April 1992. 41–50.

290   Winsberg, Freya Y. "Online Documentation: Tutorials That Are Easy to Take." In *Proceedings of 34th International Technical Communication Conference*. Arlington, VA: Society for Technical Communication, 1987. ATA 101–104.

291   Winters, Bruce I., Neil Larson, and Anthony Philips. "DaTa Knowledgebase Systems™ (Deloitte & Touche Accounting & Auditing Knowledgebase Systems)." In *Hypertext/Hypermedia Handbook*. New York: Intertext Publications/McGraw-Hill Publishing Co., Inc., 1991. 468–474.

292   Woodson, Wesley E. *Human Factors Design Handbook: Information and Guidelines for the Design of Systems, Facilities, Equipment, and Products for Human Use.* New York: McGraw-Hill, Inc., 1992.

293   Wright, Patricia. "Issues of Content and Presentation in Document Design." In *Handbook of Human-Computer Interaction.* Amsterdam: North-Holland, 1988. 629–652.

294   Younggren, Geri. "Using an Object-Oriented Programming Language to Create Audience-Driven Hypermedia Environments." In *Text, ConText, and HyperText: Writing with and for the Computer.* Cambridge, MA: The MIT Press, 1988. 77–92.

295   Zettl, Herbert. *Sight, Sound, Motion: Applied Media Aesthetics.* Belmont, CA: Wadsworth, 1990.

INDEX